India-Sri Lanka Relations
Strengthening SAARC

India-Sri Lanka Relations
Strengthening SAARC

Editors

Prof. R. Sidda Goud
Manisha Mookherjee

ALLIED PUBLISHERS PVT. LTD.

New Delhi • Mumbai • Kolkata • Lucknow • Chennai
Nagpur • Bangalore • Hyderabad • Ahmedabad

ALLIED PUBLISHERS PRIVATE LIMITED

1/13-14 Asaf Ali Road, **New Delhi**–110002
Ph.: 011-23239001 • E-mail: delhi.books@alliedpublishers.com

47/9 Prag Narain Road, Near Kalyan Bhawan, **Lucknow**–226001
Ph.: 0522-2209942 • E-mail: lko.books@alliedpublishers.com

17 Chittaranjan Avenue, **Kolkata**–700072
Ph.: 033-22129618 • E-mail: cal.books@alliedpublishers.com

15 J.N. Heredia Marg, Ballard Estate, **Mumbai**–400001
Ph.: 022-42126969 • E-mail: mumbai.books@alliedpublishers.com

60 Shiv Sunder Apartments (Ground Floor), Central Bazar Road,
Bajaj Nagar, **Nagpur**–440010
Ph.: 0712-2234210 • E-mail: ngp.books@alliedpublishers.com

F-1 Sun House (First Floor), C.G. Road, Navrangpura,
Ellisbridge P.O., **Ahmedabad**–380006
Ph.: 079-26465916 • E-mail: ahmbd.books@alliedpublishers.com

751 Anna Salai, **Chennai**–600002
Ph.: 044-28523938 • E-mail: chennai.books@alliedpublishers.com

5th Main Road, Gandhinagar, **Bangalore**–560009
Ph.: 080-22262081 • E-mail: bngl.books@alliedpublishers.com

3-2-844/6 & 7 Kachiguda Station Road, **Hyderabad**–500027
Ph.: 040-24619079 • E-mail: hyd.books@alliedpublishers.com

Website: www.alliedpublishers.com

© 2013, Centre for Indian Ocean Studies, Osmania University, Hyderabad

ISBN: 978-81-8424-844-9

Published by Sunil Sachdev and printed by Ravi Sachdev at Allied Publishers Pvt. Ltd. (Printing Division), A-104 Mayapuri Phase II, New Delhi-110064

Prof. S. SATYANARAYANA
Vice-Chancellor

[Re-Accredited by NAAC with 'A' Grade]

OSMANIA UNIVERSITY
Hyderabad - 500 007.
Tel   +91-40-27098048 / 088
       +91-40-27682364 / 221
Fax   +91-40-27098003 / 704
email vc@osmania.ac.in

Foreword

With the dawn of the 21st Century, South Asian region has undergone radical transformation. It has witnessed strong democratic sweeps and most of the countries have progressively liberalized their economies in recent years with an effort to integrate with the world economy. They have taken steps to enhance multilateral and regional integration by the formation of regional organizations.

Looking back, regionalism has been a significant phenomenon in the post Second World War international relations in 1950s and 1960s which witnessed the rise of many regional groupings in different parts of the world. Of later international integration schemes have been one of the most important developments in world politics. South Asia, a late and reluctant starter in regionalization is no exception to this trend.

The concept of regional cooperation in South Asia is epitomized in the establishment of SAARC which is based on the principles of sovereignty, equality, territorial integrity, political independence and non-interference in internal affairs of other member states, cooperations for mutual benefit etc.

It is observed that SAARC originally conceived as an engine of regional integration, like European Union (EU) and the Association of South East Asian Nations (ASEAN) over the year has become little more than a forum for annual talks among regional leaders.

The growing emphasis on economics development and bilateral trade in foreign policy is changing the priorities of South Asian states Economic growth and development will be central to the future of SAARC and well to counter SAARC's ineffectiveness, individual states have used bilateral agreements to advance their economic interests. In doing so they are playing a lead role in forestering greater regional cooperation through SAAARC.

In this context Indo-Sri Lankan initiatives in bi-lateral cooperation assume significance. In particular India and Sri Lanka have embarked on measures to build an enduring relationship through the successful economic co-operation with the operationalization of SAFTA in 2006 and with the objective of further enhancing the current economic relations a Comprehensive Economic Partnership Agreement (CEPA) was agreed upon which aims at greater trade, investment flows and enhancing mutual co-operations in overall economic relation.

India and Sri Lanka's bilateral relations have been further strengthened in the recent past with the visit of President Rajapaksa and the top level delegates from Colombo, indicating that India has entered a new and more comprehensive phase of liberal relations with Sri Lanka.

There are a number of challenges with seek the intervention of SAARC and India and Sri Lanka should play a pro-active role to strengthen SAARC.

Against this back drop, the present book is a welcome addition to the scholarly works on the subject. It is a compendium of papers presented at the International Seminar on "Indo-Sri Lankan Relations" held at Osmania University in November, 2012.

The papers in this book lay out and analyze the concept of regionalism and security concerns focusing on India and Sri Lanka on commonalities and diluting differences. It is interesting to note that most of the SAARC objectives like economic, social, cultural and environmental issues have been presented in this book. Majority of the papers deals with trade relations and economics cooperation between India and Sri Lanka. Myriad issues such as micro-finance, health insurance, ethnicity, plurality, governance, human rights media and information technology and communication in e-Governance and urban development and regional planning have been dealt with in this volume.

I complement the Director, Faculty, Scholars and Staff of a the Centre for Indian Ocean Studies, Osmania University for their initiative and pains taking effort in bring out this volume.

(Prof. S. Satyanarayana)

Preface

India and Sri Lanka share common culture and traditions as well as a common commitment to democratic governance. Their relations are based on a sustained and abiding friendship on shared historical experience and common civilizational ties. Both countries have had similar colonial background, gained independence successively in 1947 and 1948. The specific geo-strategic location of Sri Lanka in the *Indian Ocean Region* has been the most important factor in their relations.

Since then, the two independent nations of India and Sri Lanka have proceeded to renew and reinvigorate age old cultural, commercial and strategic links for the mutual benefits of the two nations and their peoples. India-Sri Lanka relations are multifaceted and interconnected. Today, India and Sri Lanka have established a stronger bilateral network of institutions and mechanisms so as to ensure sustained cooperation irrespective of domestic politics and changes in the external environment of the two countries. India is concerned at the long drawn civil war in Sri Lanka which has taken its toll on civilian casualties and resulted in the exodus of refugees to India and abroad and she is of the view that the only way out is a negotiated political settlement which meets the legitimate aspirations of all communities while respecting the unity, sovereignty and territorial integrity of Sri Lanka.

Economic relations between India and Sri Lanka, dating back to pre-colonial times, began to pick up in the 1990s with liberalization of Indian economy. In the post 1990 period, consistent efforts have been made by India and Sri Lanka to upgrade bilateral economic relations. There has been progress in the negotiations between India and Sri Lanka on a Comprehensive Economic Partnership Agreement (CEPA) which would build on the success of the Free Trade Agreement (FTA).

Change in the external environment of the two countries, has led to a new and more comprehensive phase of bilateral relations leading to top level Indian delegations visiting Colombo and reciprocity of Sri Lanka high level political delegations visits to India.

Further geo-strategic location of Sri Lanka in the Indian Ocean compliments India's geo-strategic location. The growing maritime Trade and governance of sea lanes and energy security makes imperative that both the colonies play an important role in the region.

India respecting the Unity, Sovereignty and territorial integrity of Sri Lanka wants to establish a stronger bilateral network of institutions and mechanisms to ensure sustained cooperation irrespective of domestic politics. Post Civil War, island state is strategically harmonizing its ties with its neighbors and with the region.

Interdependence is being accepted as an essential part of modern economic life all over the world. There is a growing realization among the community of nations that economic system represents an integral whole. Thereby, regional integration demonstrates an unified force working towards common interests through mutual cooperation, so as to solve their socio-economic and politico-ethnic problems for achieving collective self-reliance. There are various regional grouping all over the world serving diversified interests like the ASEAN, European Union, EEC etc., which have proved that economic gains will be more if there is proper cooperation among the countries joining the regional organization. Cooperation offers available strategy for accelerated economic development and structural transformation among the developing countries. It would not only lead to rapid economic development but also strengthen this mutual relations. Thus regional cooperation as an instrument for rapid growth has emerged as a new feature of development strategies adopted in different parts of the world.

This dramatic urge in international regional integration schemes has been one of the most important developments in world polities. Now most of the countries are member of at least one regional grouping and South Asia is no exception to this travel, although a late and reluctant starter in regionalization.

The first South Asian summit held at Dhaka, in Bangladesh in December 1985, culminated in the formation of the South Asia Association of Regional Cooperation (SAARC) initially comprising of seven member nations: India, Pakistan, Bangladesh, Nepal, Bhutan, Sri Lanka and Maldives and subsequently Afghanistan joined the grouping in April 2007. The aims and objectives of SAARC was to promote the welfare of the people of South Asian region by improving the quality of life, to accelerate growth, social progress, cultural development in the region and collective self-reliance among the countries of the region. Thus the basic aim was to accelerate the process of economic and social development in member countries through joint action in the agreed areas of cooperation.

SAARC is a project that India needs to nature. India should be able to use SAARC as a regional instrument to consolidate cooperation and peace. Through SAARC India could venture to provide benevolent leadership in the region and make the neighbouring countries in the region comfortable with India's dominating geographical volume and power, by pursuing accommodative diplomacy more vigorously to inspire confidence in her neighbours. SAARC successes is likely to bring enormous economic and security benefits to the smaller South Asian nations.

Within the SAARC forum, Sri Lanka has played a leading role in urging greater momentum particularly in enhancing economic cooperation with operationalization of SAFTA in 2006 and the Indo-Sri Lanka Comprehensive Economic Partnership Agreement (CEPA) which aims at enhancing further mutual cooperation in overall economic relations between the two countries. Thus, Sri Lanka attaches great importance to strengthening relations with her neighbours and is playing a lead role in fostering greater regional cooperation through SAARC. In particular India and Sri Lanka have embarked on measures to build an enduring relationship and are exploring every possibility to forge closer ties for a shared prosperity within the region.

Realizing the importance of India-Sri Lanka Relations and the Strengthening SAARC, the Centre for Indian Ocean Studies (CIOS), Osmania University, Hyderabad, organized an International Conference on **India-Sri Lanka Relations: Strengthening SAARC**, in November 2012 at Osmania University, Hyderabad. The conference had 5 technical sessions covering different areas on the following themes:

- SAARC: Regionalism Focusing on Commonalities and Diluting differences
- Security Concern's : India-Sri Lanka
- Ethnicity, Plurality, and Diaspora
- Economic Cooperation and Trade Relations
- Governance, Human Rights, Media and Urban Development.

Hope this conference volume would provide an opportunity for interaction and exchange of ideas at a time when India and Sri Lanka are adjusting their bilateral relations to the post-civil was situation in the island nation. This Conference volume will continue to facilitate dialogue and enable the bilateral relations of India-Sri Lanka to grow stronger and propose strategies that would ensure a better understanding of bilateral relations. The papers in this volume address these concerns of India-Sri Lanka's relations during this changing phase can bring about positive outcomes for strengthening SAARC.

We would like to take this opportunity to thank all the contributors for their cooperation in bringing out this volume successfully. This book discusses on regionalism, bilateral relations and trade, SAARC as a regional organization, maritime security concerns in Indian Ocean Region, ethnicity and human rights, media and urban development. All scholars, academicians, researchers and general readers alike should find this book useful and interesting.

Hyderabad   *Editors*

Contributors

SAARC: Regionalism and Security Concern—India and Sri Lanka Focusing on Commonalities and Diluting Differences

1. Dr. Y. Yagama Reddy, Professor (Retd.), Centre for Southeast Asian and Pacific Studies, Sri Venkateshwara University, Tirupati–517 502. He was involved in multidisciplinary teaching and research for about 3 decades at the Area Studies Centre for Southeast Asian and Pacific Studies, Sri Venkateshwara University, Tirupati. Prof. Reddy has authored 6 books; 4 edited books, published to his credit 60 papers and 70 research papers presented at various national and international Conferences/Seminars.

2. Prof. P.V. Rao, (Retd.) former Director, Centre for Indian Ocean Studies, Osmania University, Hyderabad–500 007.

3. N. Sathiya Moorthy, is Director and Senior Research Fellow at the Chennai Chapter, of the Observer Research Foundation (ORF), the multi-disciplinary Indian public polity think-tank headquartered in New Delhi. A journalist before taking to full-time policy research, SathyaMoorthy has been focusing on the study of Sri Lanka and Maldives, India's southern neighbours. As a policy researcher, he keeps travelling to these countries frequently, and interacts with political, bureaucratic and academic communities in these counties constantly. He has authored a few books on Sri Lanka and is working one on Maldives.

4. Col. R. Hariharan (Retd.), Military intelligence Officer, Indian Army. specialist on South Asia served with the Indian Peace Keeping Force in Sri Lanka as Head of Intelligence.

5. Dr. Mohammed Khalid, Associate professor in Political Science, Department of Evening Studies, Panjab Univrsity, Chandigarh, India. His primary interest is geopolitics of Indian Ocean. He has worked as Senior Research Fellow in a project funded by Department of Ocean Development, Government of India. He has been a member of Panjab University Senate, Syndicate, Academic Council and Board of Finance.

6. Ali Yasir, Journalist Associated with the Hindustan Times, New Delhi. Yasir has covered, written and edited several news pieces and stories that have been on the subject of national and international governance.

7. Tarun Mathur, PhD Scholar in International Studies, MMAJ Academy of International Studies, Jamia Millia Islamia, New Delhi–110025.

8. Dr. V. Srilatha, Assistant Professor of Political Science, Centre for Indian Ocean Studies, Osmania University, Hyderabad–500 007.

Ethnicity, Plurality, Diaspora, Economic Cooperation and Trade Relations

1. Prof. Rajiva Wijesinha, Coordinator, Regional Affairs Programme (South Asia Chapter), Bandaranaike Centre for International Studies, BMICH, Baudhaloka Mawatha, Colombo 07, Sri Lanka. Former Senior Professor of Languages, Sabaragamuwa University and Leader of the Liberal Party of Sri Lanka. He coordinated the Pre-University English Language Traning Programme for the University Grants Commission from 1993 to 1998 and as Adviser to Ministry of Education was responsible for the reintroduction of the option of English Medium in 2001.

2. Tulika Gaur, is a Ph.D. scholar in Political Science, South Asian Studies, Jawaharlal Nehru University, New Delhi. Her Specilization is an international Relations. She is awarded the Junior Research Fellowship in the Department of Political Science, South Asian Studies.

3. Shreya Upadhyay, Research Scholar, Jawaharlal Nehru University. In the US Area Studies, her topic of research is 'US Stake Holders Responses to Environmental Disasters.

4. Dr. Chalamalla Venkateshwarlu, Post-Doctoral Fellow (ICSSR, New Delhi) Department of Political Science, Osmania University, Hyderabad–500 007. He obtained Ph.D (Political Science) degree in the Department of Political Science, from Osmania University, Hyderabad. He has presented research papers in the National and international Conferences. He has also published several papers/articles in the national and international journals.

5. Samarth Trigunayat and Venkat Siddarth, Chanakya National Law University, BA, LLB (hons) 1st Semester.

6. Dr. Feroz Ikbal, Faculty member, Deccan school of Hospital management, Cellar, Owaisi Hospital and Research Centre, Kanchanbagh P.O., Hyderabad–500058. He is currently working as a Faculty Member at Deccan School of Hospital Management which is affiliated to Osmania University and approved by AICTE. He has over one decade of teaching and research experience. He holds a Ph.D in Management from Osmania University and Masters in Hospital

Administration from Mahatma Gandhi University Kottayam, Kerala.

7. Antaryami Beriha, Research Scholar, Jawaharlal Nehru University, New Delhi. Pursuing Ph.D from Centre for South, Central, South East Asian and South West Pacific Studies/South Asian Studies Division/ School of International Studies, Jawaharlal Nehru University, New Delhi.

8. Ferana Fatima, Associate Professor, Hyderabad Presidency College, Hyderabad, Mohammad Abdul Samad, Associate Professor and Head DBM, VIFCET, Hyderabad and Syed Moizuddin, Sr. Assistant Professor, DBM, VIFCET, Hyderabad.

9. Prof. R. Sidda Goud, Professor of Economics at Centre for Indian Ocean Studies and Director, Centre for Indian Ocean Studies, Osmania University, Hyderabad–500 007.

Governance, Human Rights, Media and Urban Development

1. Dr. Prathiba Mahanamahewa, Attorney-at-Law, LL.B (Hons) (Colombo), LL.M (Hons) (Melb), Ph.D in Law (Queensland), Dean Law Kotelawala Defence University/Senior Lecturer, University of Colombo, Commissioner, Human Rights Commission of Sri Lanka, Visiting Faculty Member BCIS.

2. Dr. V. Suresh, Assistant Professor, Department of Public Administration, Valluvar College of Science and Management, Karur, Tamilnadu– 639 003, India.

3. Eswari Vadlamudi, presently working as H.O.D (P.R.O Department) in Tulasi hospitals, ECIL, Hyderabad (since December 1ˢᵗ 2011). She completed her Master of Social Work in Roda Mistry College of Social Work, Gachibowli, Hyderabad. *Srujana J.* is currently working Research Assistant (RA) at the Centre for Indian Ocean Studies (CIOS), Osmania University, Hyderabad. She did her Master of Social Work (MSW) in Rodamistry College of Social work, Gachibouli, Hyderabad.

Acknowledgements

The Centre for Indian Ocean Studies (CIOS), Osmania University, Hyderabad, organized an International Conference on India-Sri Lanka Relations: Strengthening SAARC, on 8th and 9th November, 2012 at the Osmania University Centre for International Programmes (OUCIP), Hyderabad.

We deeply appreciate the contribution of those who participated and presented papers in the International Conference. We are grateful to Prof. S. Satyanarayana, Honourable Vice Chancellor of Osmania University Hyderabad, for Inaugurating the International Conference.

We also express our thanks to Prof. P.V. Rao Visiting Professor of NALSAR Law University, Hyderabad and former Director of CIOS, who has graciously accepted our invitation to deliver the Keynote Address of the Conference. And we also express gratitude to Col. Hariharan, Retired Military Intelligence officer of the Indian Army, has deliver valedictory address. We express our thanks to Prof. V. Kishan Rao, Registrar of the Osmania University, for Chief Guest of the valedictory function of the International Conference and Major U. Perera, as Guest of Honour for Valedictory Session.

We express sincere thanks to Sri N. Sathiyamoorthy, Director, Observer Research Foundation, Chennai Chapter, New Delhi, for accepting as Guest of Honour for Inaugural Session and distinguished delegates from home and abroad; The Sri Lankan delegation comprising of Major General U. Perera, Prof. Rajiva Wijesinha, Member of Parliament and Advisor to the Ministry of Education, Prof. H.D. Karunaratne, Dean Faculty of Management and Finance, University of Colombo, Prof. Prathiba Mahanamahewa, Dean Faculty of Law, Defense University. We also express our acknowledgments to the State Council for Higher Education, Government of Andhra Pradesh; ICSSR, Southern Regional Centre, Osmania University and Dean, Development & UGC Affairs, Osmania University, faculty members of teaching and non-teaching of C.I.O.S., Osmania University, Hyderabad.

Prof. R. Sidda Goud

Acronyms

ADB	:	Asian Development Bank
ADPC	:	Asian Disaster Preparedness Centre
AIADMK	:	All-India Anna Dravida Munnetra Kashagam
ARC	:	Association for Regional Cooperation
ASEAN	:	Association of Southeast Asian Nations
AUDMP	:	Asian Urban Disaster Mitigation Programme
BIMSTEC	:	Bay of Bengal Initiative for Multi Sectoral Technical and Economic. Cooperation
BMICH	:	Bandaranaike Memorial International Conference Hall
BOI	:	Board of Investment
BTF	:	British Tamil Forum
CAGR	:	Compounded Annual Growth Rate
CEB	:	Ceylon Electricity Board
CEPA	:	Comprehensive Economic Partnership Agreement
CFA	:	Cease Fire Agreement
CoM	:	Council of Ministers
CRBs	:	Co-operative Rural Banks
CSR	:	Corporate Social Responsibility
CTC	:	Canadian Tamil Congress
DDCs	:	District Development Council
DHF	:	Dengue Hemorrhagic Fever
DIMMs	:	Dual Inline Memory Modules
DMC	:	Disaster Management Centre
EDB	:	Exports Development Board of Sri Lanka
EEZ	:	Exclusive Economic Zone
EU	:	European Union
FDI	:	foreign direct investment
FICCI	:	Federation of Indian Chamber of Commerce and Industry
FTA	:	Free Trade Agreement
GATS	:	General Agreement on Trade in Services
GNH	:	Gross National Happiness

GOSL	:	Government of Sri Lanka
GTF	:	Global Tamil Forum
ICETT	:	Joint Commission for Economics, Trade and Technical Cooperation
IDPs	:	Internally Displaced Persons
IDPs	:	Internally Displaced Persons],
ILICEC	:	Indo-Lanka Joint Committee on Economic Cooperation
ILO	:	International Labour Organization
INCG	:	Oil and Natural Gas Corporation
IOMAC	:	Indian Ocean Maritime Affairs Cooperation
IOR	:	Indian Ocean Region
IOZP	:	Indian Ocean as a Zone of Peace
IPKF	:	Indian Peace-Keeping Force
ISFTA	:	Indo-Sri Lanka free trade agreement
ITEC	:	Indian Technical and Economic Cooperation
IUUF	:	Illegal, Unreported and Unregulated fishing
JMCs	:	Joint Maritime Centers
LLRC	:	Lessons Learnt and Reconciliation Commission
LTTE	:	Liberation Tigers of Tamil Eelam
MCs	:	Municipal Council
MDMK	:	Marumalarchi Dravida Munnetra Kazagham
MF	:	Micro Finance
MOU	:	Memorandum of Understanding
MPCSs	:	Multi-Purpose Co-operative Societies
NAM	:	Non-Aligned Movement
NCDM	:	National Council for Disaster Management
NIEO	:	New International Economic Order
NPCGF	:	North Pacific Coast Guard Agencies Forum
OECD	:	Organization for Economic Co-operation and Development
PLOTE	:	People's Liberation Organization for Tamil Eelam
P-TOMS	:	Post-Tsunami Operational Management Structure
RAW	:	Research and Analysis Wing
RBI	:	Reserve Bank of India
RDB	:	Regulated Development Banks

RRDBs	:	Regional Rural Development Banks
RTA	:	Regional Preferential Agreement
SAARC	:	South Asian Association for Regional Cooperation
SAC	:	SAARC Agricultural Centre
SACEP	:	Asia Co-operative Environment Programme
SAEU	:	South Asian Economic Union
SAFTA	:	South Asian Free Trade Area
SAPTA	:	South Asian Preferential Trade Agreement
SARSO	:	Agreement on the Establishment of South Asian Regional Standards Organization
SBSs	:	Samurdhi Bank Societies
SCC	:	SAARC Cultural Centre
SCZMC	:	SAARC Coastal Zone Management Centre
SDC	:	SAARC Documentation Centre
SDF	:	South Asian Development Fund
SDMC	:	SAARC Disaster Management Centre
SEC	:	SAARC Energy Centre
SERP	:	Society for Elimination of Rural Poverty
SFC	:	SAARC Forestry Centre
SHRDC	:	SAARC Human Resources Development Centre
SIC	:	SAARC Information Centre
SLFP	:	Sri Lankan Freedom Party
SLOCs	:	Sea Lines of Communications
SMRC	:	SAARC Meteorological Research Centre
SSCP	:	Sethusamudran Ship Canal Project
STC	:	SAARC Tuberculosis Centre
TCCSs	:	Thrift and Credit Co-operative Societies
TCHR	:	Tamil Centre for Human Rights
TCIF	:	Tamil United Front
TCs	:	Town Councils
TELO	:	Tamil Eelam Liberation Organization
TGTE	:	Transnational Government of Tamil Eelam
TNA	:	Tamil National Alliance
TULF	:	Tamil United Liberation Front
UCs	:	Urban Council

UDHR	:	Universal Declaration of Human Rights
UK	:	United Kingdom
UN	:	United Nations
UNCLOS	:	United Nation Convention on the Law of the Seas
UNF	:	United National Front
UNP	:	United National Party
UPA	:	United Progressive Alliance
USA	:	United States of America
USAID	:	United States Agency for International Development
VCs	:	Village Councils
WHO	:	World Health Organization
WTO	:	World Trade Organization

Contents

Foreword .... *v*

Preface .... *vii*

Contributors .... *xi*

Acknowledgment .... *xv*

Acronyms .... *xvii*

Section–I

**SAARC: Regionalism and Security Concern—
India and Sri Lanka Focusing on Commonalities
and Diluting Differences**

---

1. Endangered Regionalism and Shattered Prospects of Cooperation 3
   in SAARC: Need for Reciprocity for Harnessing the
   Potentials of Commonalities
   Y. Yagama Reddy

2. Indo-Sri Lanka Relations: The Multilateral Context 18
   P. V. Rao

3. India, Sri Lanka and the SAARC 27
   N. Sathiya Moorthy

4. Adding Substance to SAARC: India-Sri Lanka 36
   Experience
   Col R. Hariharan

5. SAARC: Emerging Security Challenges and Need 48
   for Strategic Initiatives in the Indian Ocean
   Mohammed Khalid

6. Bilateral Ties between India and Sri Lanka: 60
   Strategic and Security Implications
   Ali Yasir

7. India-Sri Lanka Relations: Failure of Conflict Management 78
   Mechanism in South Asia
   Tarun Mathur

8. India-Sri Lanka Maritime Cooperation 102
   in Indian Ocean—Prospects
   V. Srilatha

Section–II

Ethnicity, Plurality, Diaspora and Economic Cooperation and Trade Relations

---

9. Plurality and Diaspora 123
   Rajiva Wijesinha
10. Impact of Sri Lankan Tamil Diaspora's Activism 133
    on India-Sri Lanka Relations
    Tulika Gaur
11. Tamil Diaspora Nationalism in Post-Conflict Era 153
    Shreya Upadhyay
12. Ethnic Conflict in Sri Lanka and is Impact on India-Sri Lanka 173
    Relations: The Intervention of SAARC
    Chalamalla Venkateshwarlu
13. India-Sri Lanka Relations: A Dark Past, But a Bright Future 207
    Samarth Trigunayat and Venkat Siddarth
14. Health Care Performance of Sri Lanka and 222
    Indian State of Kerala: Lessons for SAARC Nations
    Feroz Ikbal
15. India-Sri Lanka Economic Cooperation and Trade Relations 230
    Antaryami Beriha
16. Micro Finance: Lessons for India and Sri Lanka 249
    Ferhana Fatima, Mohammad Abdul Samad and Syed Moizuddin
17. An Assessment of India-Sri Lanka Economic and 266
    Trade Relations: An Overview
    R. Sidda Goud

Section–III

Governance, Human Rights, Media and Urban Development

---

18. Computer Monitoring and Right to Privacy: 291
    A Comparative Analysis of Sri Lanka and India
    Prathiba Mahanamahewa
19. India-Sri Lanka Relations with Special Reference 304
    to Urban Regional Planning
    V. Suresh
20. Natural Disaster Magagement in India and Sri Lanka with 321
    Special Reference to Disaster Prevention and Mitigation
    Eswari Vadlamudi and J. Srujana

Author Index 334

SAARC: Regionalism and Security Concern—India and Sri Lanka Focusing on Commonalities and Dilutin   Differences

Endangered Regionalism and Shattered Prospects of Cooperation in SAARC: Need for Reciprocity for Harnessing the Potentials of Commonalities

Y. Yagama Reddy

SOUTH ASIA THROUGH THE PRISM OF HISTORICAL GEOGRAPHY

If the toponym "South Asia" has its etymological significance conforming to the logic of compass, the region's magnificence testifies to geographical causation of history. The region, although endured political fragmentation manifesting in a raft of sub-regions, got itself insulated from the European influence for over millennia until 15th century AD, save the invasion of Alexander in 3rd century BC. South Asia has for long been characterized by diversity in its human population with a mixture of indigenous peoples; and hence the region had sustained the acculturation process. Thus, South Asia was constituted into small and large kingdoms, enjoying various degrees of power and prominence. The plethora of kingdoms and the experience of warfare and internecine conflict in South Asia led to the adoption of inter-state norms on statehood, diplomatic relations, treaties, religious tolerance, neutrality and humanitarian law.

Even as South Asia was politically fragmented into countless native states of various sizes and power potentials often manifesting in inter-state conflicts, never did South Asia resort to political aggrandizement and economic exploitation with respect to its extra-regional powers, except the stray incident of invasion of Sri Vijaya empire by Rajendra Cholan in 1025 AD. The commercial and cultural contacts, for about two millennia from the beginning of Christian era, across the Arabian Sea (between India and Arabian Peninsula and North African coast) and the Bay of Bengal (between India and Southeast Asia) were sustained on the principle of equal footing.

The chain of mountains and expansive desert, forming something like a roof over the Indian Ocean, have got the South Asia region physically separated from the hinterland of African continent, Europe and the Asia interior until the discovery of sea route circumscribing the African continent by Vasco de Gama in 1498 AD. Certainly, the discovery of sea routes to different parts of the Indian subcontinent and Southeast Asia and the British colonization of Australia transformed the Indian Ocean into an arena of conflict and confrontation for the European powers. Eventually, Great Britain that gained almost an effective control over the sea lanes across the Indian Ocean turned the latter into the "British Lake", with virtual exclusion of other colonial masters, like the Dutch, the Portuguese and the French.

It was then a logical corollary for the British to have its colonial empire established over the entire Indian sub-continent (including Sri Lanka). The geo-strategic significance to the littoral part of the Indian Ocean was also well attested in all the geopolitical theories postulated from the beginning of the 20th century. Mackinder's Heartland theory included the Indian Ocean littoral zone as part of the Inner (Marginal) Crescent and the Insular (Outer) Crescent, while Spykman's 'Rimland' theory portended the possibility of Asiatic littoral zone exercising control over the Eurasian Heartland. In fact, the British colonial power accorded top priority to the pursuit of ensuring security to the British India, despite the Great Britain was then enjoying unquestionable naval supremacy befitting its distinction as the 'mistress of the sea lanes'.

The post-War period, though witnessed the sprouting of several in-dependent states, hardly found any power capable of establishing an effective control over the Indian Ocean region. To make the matters worse, the region's strategic significance interlaced with the Indian Ocean turned to become a bane, inasmuch as the Cold War geopolitical nuances and regional conflicts have had their roots in political fragmentation consequent upon decolonization. Indian sub-continent has thus a long history of various phases of transformation—from glorious chapter of cultural and trade relations on equal-footing (good neighbourhood), through European incursions and exploitations (imperialism) manifesting in intrusion into the indigenous societies, to a zone of power contest by super-powers during the Cold War period, which afflicted the South Asia in numerous ways like fomenting the border disputes, mistrust and tensions. Conclusively, the multiple facets of Indian sub-continent testify to the premise of geographical determinism and historical momentum that made this region an arena of geopolitical contest as well as a realm of regional cooperation not merely among the littorals but among the extra-regional powers also.

BASIC LINKAGES PORTRAYING REGIONAL IDENTITY

Of much significance to the South Asian context is the vision of Meinig that "geography, like history, is an age-old and essential strategy for thinking about large and complex matters" and that "geography is not just a physical stage for the historical drama" (Meinig 1987, p. xv). Undeniably, the historical geography of South Asia amply explains that the spatial dimension has always subscribed to the formal relationship between geography and history. The complementary and interdependent relationship of geography and history (McInerney 2011) is signified by "fundamentally inseparable" common terms such as space and time, area and era, and places and events (Meinig 1987, p. xv). The flow of peoples and ideas shattered the South Asia's regional identity and consciousness; yet, geography had its impact on the course of events, to the extent of South Asia getting itself identified as an entity within the Asian realm, typified by a set of commonalities discernible in geography, geology, climate, economy, culture and polity. Significantly, South Asia has its identity based on the geographical features that fetched a semblance of a unity sustaining the cultural, political and economic processes of integration. Throughout history, South Asia has seen the movement of peoples, trade and ideas that have integrated the region both economically and culturally (Inayat 2007).

Further, the network of land and riverine communications, especially between India and the smaller states (with the exception of Pakistan), and the climatic correspondence in South Asia from the Himalayas to the Indian Ocean have led to the evolution of a unique eco-subsystem and a composite culture, which was a blend of Buddhism, Hinduism and Islam, providing a common basis for the norms and lifestyle of all segments of civil society (Singh 2007). Typifying as an integrated ecosystem, South Asia portrays the region's geographical cohesion which is conducive to promoting cooperation over this territory; and SAARC is a logical response to the much awaited need and effort.

SOUTH ASIA'S POTENTIALITIES FOR REGIONAL INTEGRATION

The South Asia region has immeasurable and diversified potentialities, as evident from the following accounts: (1) Landforms and climatic regimes ranging from sea level to the highest mountains and deep gorges; hottest plains to snow clad mountains; wettest to driest places; dissected green valleys to coral islands; (2) Thousands of rivers with immense hydroelectric potential; (3) Mineral resources such as coal, iron and natural gas; and (4) Wide-ranging diversities of forest resources including exclusive varieties of animals, herbs and timber. Yet, the individual countries in South Asia are closer to each other than might be suspected in the light of the political developments of recent years. That South Asia has a long and closely-interwoven history is noticeable in certain cross-border similarities in traditions, languages and customs based on culture, ethnicity and religion. Besides geographical contiguity of the South Asian countries being the cornerstone for the formation of a regional bloc, the historical and cultural ties are connecting people across national borders, so much as to consider South Asia a 'single civilizational whole'. Given the trade complementarities in such areas as textile, cotton, cereals, apparels, cane sugar, plastic and chemical goods (IPCS Panel Discussion 2007), the region is perceived as a 'geo-economic unit' becoming conducive to promoting regional cooperation and thereby regional economic integration. Even on the flipside, South Asia has certain distinct common features, as evident from extreme poverty, mega-urbanization, immense disparities between rich and poor, and fundamental problems in the areas of infrastructure, energy and the environment, besides high levels of internal conflicts and political instability within the region (Delinic 2011).

REGION-BUILDING A GLOBAL PHENOMENON

Regions, regionalism and regionalization are contested and often nebulous concepts. The term 'region', simply a geographical reality, denotes a cluster of states, usually a small group of contiguous states, linked together by both a geographical relationship and a degree of mutual interdependence (Nye 1968). Regions, like states, are of varying compositions, capabilities and aspirations. Regionalism that merits promotion by regional and international communities has many positive qualities as well as negative and worrying aspects. Regionalism, as state-led initiative to foster cooperation, implies a policy whereby states and non-state actors cooperate and coordinate strategy within a given region, with an aim to pursue and promote common goals in one or more issue areas. Regionalism was often analyzed in terms of geographical proximity, social cohesiveness (ethnicity, race, language, religion, culture, history, consciousness of a common heritage), economic cohesiveness (trade patterns and economic comple-mentarity), political cohesiveness (regime type, ideology), and organizational cohesiveness (existence of formal regional institutions). If regionalism is a policy or project, regionalization, a process of cooperation led by markets, is both project and process; but both regionalism and regionalization are clearly global phenomena (Fawcett 2004). The relationship between globalization and regionalization offers distinction between *de facto* economic integration and *de jure* political institutionalization (Higgott 1999). Obviously, region-building has been central to many of the debates and a salient feature of the international system; and the regional organizations are thus regarded as a natural outgrowth of international co-operation.

EARLY ATTEMPTS AT REGIONALISM

The idea of building cooperation in South Asia had its historical roots. India's preponderance in terms of geographical area, population and gross domestic product has always been at the base of its search for a larger Asian identity, as discernible in its integral role in pursuit of freedom for all the colonies; and it was logical for India to view the "concept of neighbourhood as one of concentric circles around the central point of historical and cultural commonalities" (Singh 2007). Efforts for regional cooperation in South Asia can also be traced back to 1945, when Jawaharlal Nehru made a plea for 'a South Asian Federation'. He convened the 1947 Asian Relations Conference even before India's independence. This conference led to the formation of a non-governmental Asian Relations Organization with the objective of creating a pan-Asian framework to build technical cooperation among the countries concerned. Later in January 1950, the Colombo Plan, a product of the Commonwealth Foreign Ministers' Conference, was held in Colombo towards promoting technical cooperation among the South and Southeast Asian countries (Haas 1989). Subsequently, in May 1950, the Baguio Conference in the Philippines also dealt with regional cooperation in Asia. These efforts were culminated in the Afro-Asian Nations Conference at Bandung in 1955.

These attempts made by India to develop regionalism beyond and outside the bipolar framework of the Cold War were, however, frustrated. Meanwhile, the Non-Aligned Movement (NAM), which was launched at Belgrade in 1961, soon absorbed most of India's multilateral diplomatic attention. Contradictory foreign policy alignments of India and Pakistan in the context of the Cold War had also thwarted the efforts towards the establishment of South Asian regionalism. The nonchalant attitude towards regionalism was also due to the absence of any perceived common security threat to South Asia which was fortunately not polarized along East-West lines, save Pakistan's membership in Southeast Asia Treaty Organization. Though Hinduism, Islam, Buddhism, Sikhism and

Christianity are shared by all the countries of the region, the overlapping of religious and linguistic groups across national boundaries becomes a trigger for conflicts (Paul 2012). The geographical contiguity on account of common land borders among the countries of peninsular South Asia has become of no significance for the development of transit facilities and transport network. The weak trade linkages owing to commodity-competitiveness vis-à-vis complementarity in the trade structure manifest in precarious interdependence among the South Asian nations. Further, South Asian countries behave as if they 'do not belong to one civilization, nor do the peoples of South Asia have 'the feeling of belonging to one region', as evident from high levels of internal conflicts and political instability within the region. Differential power-potentials coupled with divergence and apathy has eventually led to the perpetuation of trust-deficit to the extent of inhibiting the spirit of regional cooperation in South Asia.

FORMATION OF SAARC

Partition of British India into India and Pakistan affected not merely their bilateral relations, but the efforts of regionalism in South Asia. Even as the formation of Association of Southeast Asian Nations (ASEAN) in 1967 whipped the idea of forming a regional body in South Asia, a host of factors served as stimulants towards the end of forming a regional organization: the Indo-Pak war (1971) that established the preponderance of India in the region, the Soviet intervention in Afghanistan (1979) and the US interest in building regionalism in South Asia as a bulwark against further Soviet advance. It was during 1979–1981 that the idea of regional cooperation in South Asia was deliberated at various levels. Having given credence to a host of region's commonalities marked by geography, experiences, aspirations, challenges, civilization and so forth, the Indian Prime Minister Indira Gandhi, in her inaugural address to the South Asian Foreign Ministers' meeting held in New Delhi in 1983, favoured a regional grouping:

Our policy is not to interfere in the affairs of others. But ours is a troubled region, most of our countries are multi-racial and multi-religious. It would be idle to pretend that we are not affected by what happens elsewhere. . . . The regional grouping that brings us together is not aimed against anyone else. Nor are we moved by any ideological or military considerations. . . . We are all equals. We are against exploitation and domination. We want to be friends with all on a footing of equality. We should be ever vigilant against the attempts of external powers to influence our functioning (Indira Gandhi 1983).

Having failed in their attempts to find membership in their preferred extra-regional organizations, some of the South Asian Countries tardily turned their attention to the need for forming a regional body in their own geographical area. Despite the lukewarm response from India, the pivotal power of the region, the persistent effort of smaller states of the region, especially Bangladesh, led to the formation of South Asian Association for Regional Cooperation in December 1985. That the SAARC as "a medium for enhancing national prosperity and stability, rather than merely forum for inter-state cooperation" was evident at the First Inaugural Session of the SAARC Summit in 1985, when the King of Nepal, Birendra Bir Bikram Shah Dev, anticipated that "regional cooperation can strengthen the building of a lasting edifice of peaceful co-existence through initiatives and interactions in the fields like the cultural, scientific, technological and economic spheres" (Madhavibhasin 2010). For all its sufferance at various stages of its evolution in the past twenty-five years, the paradigm of regional cooperation has been clearly accepted and even promoted through 16 Summits; and through numerous Ministerial meetings and a whole range of activities sponsored by civil society organizations in diverse fields (Sharma 2010). In his candid speech at the 16th Summit (28–29 April 2010) in the Bhutan capital (Thimpu), the Indian Prime Minister Manmohan Singh shared the "vision of inclusive growth in South Asia both within our countries and for the region of South Asia as a whole" (Manmohan Singh 2010).

SAARC'S RECORD OF ITS OWN ACHIEVEMENT

SAARC activity is a rather modest and more extensive record of achievement. Dr. Christopher Snedden, of Deakin University, states that, 'the fact that SAARC has existed since 1985 is an achievement in itself.' Over the last 25 years, despite extremely difficult political circumstances, SAARC has managed to create situations, institutions and Forums. SAARC has tackled important topics for the region such as a social charter, development agreements and even the sensitive subject of fighting terrorism and has achieved some good results. The food and development banks are important steps in the right direction. Exchanges in the areas of civil society and science have become one of the pillars of South Asian integration efforts. Given the historical legacy and contemporary reality of endemic conflicts and mistrust in the region, the fact that the formal cooperation process in the region has survived recurrent setbacks is testimony of resilience of the organization. SAARC Charter provisions, though led to delays and postponement of Ministerial and Summit meetings, are not necessarily viewed as "obstacles but as safeguards to protect the young organization from entanglement in issues extraneous to regional cooperation".

INHERENT AND INDUCED PROBLEMS FOR SAARC

SAARC is a constellation portraying a host of complexities well discernible in, for instance, population, territory, military power, technological development, infrastructure and political influence (Delinic 2011). SAARC has its inherent limitations that inhibit the expectations: India's multi-faceted enormity coupled with assertive tendencies are contrary to the tenets of multilateralism in regional Cooperation; absence of any perceived external threat hinders the internal cohesion; SAARC was the outcome of concerted efforts of smaller states vis-à-vis leading countries of the region; SAARC's progress has been impeded by the provisions of its Chart, viz., unanimity as the basis for decisions, and the exclusion of contentious and bilateral issues; and SAARC's existence owes little to the patronage of external powers (Singh 2007). In reality, SAARC identity or South Asian solidarity becomes, for the most part, a political rhetoric rather a myth. South Asian countries behave as if they 'do not belong to one civilization, nor do the peoples of South Asia have 'the feeling of belonging to one region', as evident from high levels of internal conflicts and political instability within the region.

Its failure to evolve as a powerful regional body is largely attributed to national interest, rather inward looking, of each member-state. The wavering functional character of SAARC observably manifesting in lack of success points out lack of trust, solidarity, peace and stability among South Asian neighbours. Though external threat perception is lacking in South Asia, the smaller states perceive threat emanating from within the region itself and seek the help of extra-regional powers much to the chagrin of India. These 'xenophobic considerations' render SAARC to languish. The Premier of Bhutan and the Chair of the 16th Summit held in Thimphu (28–29 April 2010) was also critical of the SAARC performance that 'some 200 meetings take place every year among SAARC countries but these meetings are not matched by results' (Muni 2011). The lackadaisical attitude of SAARC was also discernible in the words of Bishwa Pradhan, former Foreign Secretary of Nepal that 'many of the decisions are just in papers in the form of protocols, conventions, reports and studies' (Pradhan 2011).

South Asia has been an area of tremendous political complexities that resulted from colonial legacy of state formation. Issues of political and ideological character, coupled with the issues of strategic conflict and military balance, have perpetuated the inter-state conflicts in South Asia which probably are the highest compared to any other regional blocs. Each of the states in South Asia is found in a state of quagmire: Pakistan has been confronted by frequent political instability, military dictatorship and terrorism, so much so Afghanistan (transitional democracy, Taliban problem), Nepal (Maoist and ethnic problems), Sri Lanka (Tamil separatist movement), Bangladesh (political instability, fundamentalist violence, ethnic violence), India (cross-border terrorism) and Bhutan (problem of Nepali illegal immigrants) (Bhatt nod.). Preoccupation with the intra-state conflicts and inter-state crises has almost restrained the South Asian states to achieve adequate degree of complementarity of interests and pre-empt regional economic cooperation and thereby regional cohesion. South Asian countries hold widely divergent views on many important issues and lack a common political culture; and hence SAARC existence could not blunt the raw edges of historical irritants between members.

That SAARC is an important option, but not the only option for India gives credence to the fact that India is scarcely interested in South Asia vis-à-vis Southeast Asia. Instead, India which was disenchanted with SAARC has been pursuing trans-regional, super-regional, sub-regional, inter-regional and bilateral cooperative arrangements with so much of enthusiasm as to win the appreciation of the members of the multilateral institutions concerned. In fact, even some smaller states have in the recent times entertained fanciful notions rather insatiable thirst for joining the extra-regional institutions. Negative perceptions and misapprehensions about the consequences of increased regional cooperation, as logical corollary of pride and prejudice, manifest in fears of greater domination of India, often borne out of lack of information. The basic apprehension has stemmed from India's geographical size, demographic and economic potential and political weight. That India stands out for dominance in South Asian region is testified by its preponderance in population size (accounting for 75 per cent of the region's population), in area (72 per cent of region's total area) and gross domestic product (78 per cent of the region's GDP). This glaring discrepancy between India and other smaller states of South Asia leads to natural concerns about the potential interference in their affairs. Smaller states in South Asia view India as both a saviour and as part of the problem and are reluctant to work with India, fearing that such cooperation will admit Indian dominance in SAARC (Noreen 2011); on the other hand, India has its own fears of its neighbours in terms of their possible union to oppose the country's interests. Intra-regional political tensions, seldom India at the centre-stage, have resulted in uneven progress of SAARC; and hence SAARC is identified with stigma of being a non-performing entity. Disgracefully, SAARC has become a tool to manage the structural dynamics of the region, instead of offering a mechanism to address regional concerns. In the absence of a specific mandate, SAARC stands out of the coordination activities for intensifying political, economic or strategic processes of cooperation among states.

The difference between SAARC and ASEAN is distinct in that the former typifies a 'system of States', as opposed to the distinction of having evolved as a 'society of states'. SAARC's presence has not prevented violent conflicts, much less settled or resolved them. Regional cooperation is at a very rudimentary stage in South Asia. Conflict management of even a minimalist sort is non-existent at present (Kripa Sridharan 2008). It is the inability of SAARC member-states to subsume the regional peculiarities that tends to inhibit the much expected regional integration and constrain the efforts towards advanced types of regional economic cooperation. Despite sharing certain common civilisational links the member states cannot agree on a common future and there is no consensus on fundamental norms or values; and hence the rhetoric, South Asia was a 'region without regionalism', has its relevance even after the 25 years of SAARC's existence. That the SAARC's journey has not been remarkably success ever since it was created is testified by the statement the Indian Prime Minister Manmohan Singh at the16th Summit in the Bhutan capital (28th April 2010) that SAARC had indeed failed in meeting its aspirations.

Lack of Physical Connectivity

The geographical contiguity on account of common land borders among the countries of peninsular South Asia has become of no significance for the development of transit facilities and transport network. The infrastructure constraints made South Asia as "one of the least connected regions in the world constituting a major structural impediment" and the cost of intra-SAARC trade is the highest in the world (Secretary General 2010). With the exception of Maldives, India has land or sea borders with every other SAARC country, while the other SAARC states do not have common borders among themselves and thereby direct physical access to other SAARC member-states, except the solitary instance of common border between Afghanistan and Pakistan. Similarly, Nepal, Bhutan and Bangladesh are also deprived of direct access among them, on account of their borders being separated from each other by just a few kilometers of Indian corridor. The key impediment to strengthening regional cooperation, as pointed out by the Secretary-General Sheel Kant Sharma in his speech on prospects and challenges of South Asian regionalism at the Indian Council for World Affairs, is "lack of physical and soft connectivity in SAARC" (Secretary General 2010).

Weak Trade Linkages

Commodity-competitiveness vis-à-vis complementarity in the trade structure manifests in precarious interdependence among the South Asian nations. Weak trade linkages in South Asia are thus obligated by an almost identical pattern of comparative advantage in a relatively narrow range of products, little or lack of complementarities in the trade structure, and absence of comparative advantage in capital intensive and high value-added products which act as structural constraints on expanding intra-regional trade. Restrictive trade policies also cause the low level of intra-regional trade. In fact, low volume of intra-regional trade is generally attributed to similarity in trade composition, what is called as commodity-bias. Despite the framework of liberalization through South Asian Preferential Trade Agreement (1995), the trade regimes of South Asia were still quite restrictive; and even the South Asian Free Trade Area Agreement (2006) could not offer the relief from the vestiges of the non-tariff barriers to trade in South Asia. That the SAARC countries have extra-regional powers as trading partners is a great paradox, given the diversified trade basket of India. Trade among the majority of SAARC nations is still negligible; and the smaller economies have a predictable trade deficit with India. Gruesomely, the SAARC accounts for less than one percent of the world trade; and intra-regional trade has also been an insignificant four percent of its total trade. The South Asia's trade basket largely consisting of raw materials and traditional products including basic foods and agricultural products has obviously resulted in unmerited competition among some regional countries. In all the South Asian countries, high tariff structures and import control arrangements have been in vogue mainly to insulate domestic industries from stiff foreign competition and to restrict international trade in the region. Trade-led transformation has become one of the main drivers of interstate and cross-regional ties. India, Pakistan and Bangladesh, which were once part of a single political entity,

British India, should utilize their historical links and shared interests in buttressing economic integration which, in the first instance, calls for a considerable flow of goods and services between them; and their historical links and resulting shared interests should underpin modern-style economic integration. Thus, SAARC requires structural revival for enhancing its intra-regional trade.

IN PURSUIT OF EMPOWERING SAARC

The potentially positive factors unique to SAARC include: member-states have recognized their common problems and collective ambitions for economic development, especially in the field of poverty alleviation (Singh 2007). Agriculture accounts for 19 per cent in South Asia's GDP with industry accounting for 27 per cent and services 54 per cent. The share of industry in GDP of South Asia is the lowest among the Low and Medium Income (LMI) country groupings. SAARC activities cover a wide range of areas, including agriculture and rural development; health and population; women, youth and children; environment and forestry; science and technology and meteorology; human resources development; transport; information and communications technology; biotechnology; intellectual property rights; tourism; and energy. South Asian countries also share a certain commonality of (national) interests, encompassing a whole gamut of social, economic, political, cultural, historical, and other factors. SAARC, on the pessimistic note, has an apparent commonality in its being increasingly vulnerable to geopolitical conflict having its roots in the population-related themes. South Asia with a population of 1.4 billion ranks high in rate of poverty, transnational ethnic groups, sectarian disputes, terrorist groups, massive migration and refugee problems, narcotics trafficking, disputed borders, resource disputes, and rampant political corruption. The countries of South Asia are caught up with extreme poverty, illiteracy, corruption, underdevelopment, mega-urbanization, immense disparities between rich and poor and fundamental problems in the areas of infrastructure, energy and the environment.

As SAARC fails to address the subject of water rights for making best use of international river waters (Singh 2011), Geoffrey Pyatt, the Career Foreign Service Officer of the US Department of State who was posted as Principal Deputy Secretary for South and Central Asian affairs felt the need for 'hydro-diplomacy' for promoting cooperation among the South Asian countries to find solutions on water-sharing of the Himalayan-origin rivers (Pyatt 2011). In the context of mismatch between the demand and supply in the energy consumption, SAARC needs to accrue benefits from the excess energy available in the region through regional cooperation in establishing regional gas and power grids and of importing energy from the neighbouring regions through establishing gas and power grid connected to Central Asia and Southeast Asia. Regional trade in electricity and natural gas should be the logical and important option befitting the win-win opportunities for both the energy resource-surplus countries and those with energy import needs, toeing the line of Regional Power Grid Integration projects as in the case of Europe and Africa (Chaturvedi and Hossain 2011).

There has been a clear shift in South Asian diplomacy; and South Asia's regionalism today is being shaped by new policy tools like summit meetings, special emissaries, public diplomacy and the use of 'track II' (unofficial) channels, and new issues such as human rights, energy resources (potentially nuclear energy) and security concerns. This bears testimony to the SAARC's recognition of the need for forming a strong common identity for their common future and evolving a functional integration process towards strengthening the regional identity. As the heavily formal, procedural, and complex Track I initiatives hardly generated enthusiasm and interest among the people and their leaders in the region, Track II initiatives, or 'beyond the state' diplomacy has of late been recognized as a better mechanism for confidence building towards the reconstruction of South Asia as a community (Madhavibhasin 2010). SAARC, as the representative of South Asia, needs to be looked upon as a "single development unit" for accelerating the movement people, goods and ideas as well as for sharing the capital technology and natural resources (Mohapatra 2008, p. 193). Need to bear in mind is the pertinent call made by the Indian Prime Minister Manmohan Singh at the 16th Summit in last April (2010): "The 21st century cannot be an Asian century unless South Asia marches together. We have created institutions for regional cooperation, but we have not yet empowered them adequately to enable them to be more proactive" (Manmohan Singh 2010).

Even as SAARC was carrying the label of an inert and inept organization owing to its inherent limitations and certain induced problems, SAARC has been captivating the attention of many a scholar and statesman all over the world. Its identity is not necessarily a fascination of a few, but it owes much to region's potentialities and shared qualities. Deserving much appreciation is the People's SAARC Declaration adopted in March 2007:

We, the people of South Asia, not only share a contiguous geographical space but also a social and cultural history that shapes our life styles, belief systems, cultural particularities, material practices and social relationships. Our natural environments are related, interdependent, and form elements of a common eco-system. There is a similarity in our life practices. There have been similarities in our histories as a result of our constant interactions for thousands of years. Our belief systems and cultural practices have been influenced by each other and exhibit some distinct similarities. On the other hand, the unique diversity of our region in all aspects has enriched the common heritage, and we celebrate a sustained history of mutual respect for one another (People's SAARC Declaration 2007).

REFERENCES

[1] Bhatta, C.D., n.d., "Regional integration and peace in South Asia—An Analysis", *Peace Studies Journal*, at www.peacestudiesjournal. org.uk/dl/RegionalIntegration.PDF.

[2] Chaturvedi, Pradeep and Hossain, A.N.H. Akhtar (2011). "Regional Cooperation for Energy Security", *South Asia Journal*, Issue 1, July 2011, pp. 47–65.

[3] Delinic Tomislav (2011). *SAARC–25 Years of Regional Integration in South Asia*, KAS International Reports 2|2011, at SAARC_http.www.kas.dewfdockas_21870-544-2-30.pdf110209123437

[4] Fawcett, Louise (2004). "Exploring regional domains: a comparative history of regionalism", *International Affairs*, vol. 80, No. 3, pp. 429–446.

[5] Haas, M. (1989). The Asian Way to Peace: A Story of Regional Cooperation, (Praeger: New York), pp. 275–76.

[6] Higgottt, Richard, (1999). "The Political Economy of globalization in East Asia: The Salience of 'region building'" in Olds, Kris, in Olds, Kris, Dicken, p. , Kelly, Philip F., Kong, Lily and Yeung, Henry Wai-chung (eds.), *Globalization and the Asia-Pacific*, (Routledge: London), p. 91.

[7] Inayat, Mavara (2007). "The South Asian Association for Regional Cooperation" (Chapter-2), in

[8] Alyson, J.K. Bailes, John Gooneratne, Mavara Inayat, Jamshed Ayaz Khan and Swaran Singh, Regionalism in South Asian Diplomacy, SIPRI Policy Paper No. 15, Stockholm International Peace Research Institute, Bromma (Sweden), February 2007.

[9] Indira Gandhi, "Inaugural Address to the Meeting of South Asian Foreign Ministers", (New Delhi, August 1983), reprinted in India Quarterly, vol. 11, nos. 3 and 4 (January–March 1984), pp. 255–59.

[10] IPCS Panel Discussion (2007). "The 14th SAARC Summit: an Assessment," Institute of Peace and Conflict Studies, 13 April 2007, at South Asia Articles#2270, 20 April 2007).

[11] Kripa Sridharan, 'Regional Organizations and Conflict Management: Comparing ASEAN and SAARC', *Crisis States Research Centre (Destin Development Studies Institute)*, Working Paper Series No. 2, No. 33, London: March 2008.

[12] Madhavibhasin (2010). *SAARC-III Challenges and Prospects*, May 12th 2010, at http://india.foreignpolicyblogs.com/2010/05/12/saarc-iii-challenges-and-prospects/Also see http://india.foreignpolicyblogs. com/tag/saarc/

[13] Manmohan Singh (2010). *SAARC is glass half empty, region needs empowerment:* Address at the 16th SAARC Summit, 28 April 2010, at http://way2online.com/? p=51137

[14] McInerney, Malcolm (2011). "Entwining history and geography", *Spatialworlds,* April 27, 2011, at http://spatialworlds.blogspot.com/2011/04/entwining-history-and-geography. html (Accessed 24 July 2012).

[15] Meinig, Donald (1987). The Shaping of America: A Geographical Perspective on 500 Years of American History, New Haven: Yale University Press, 1987.

[16] Mohapatra, Anil Kumar (2008). *Small States in South Asia: A Security Perspective of the Himalayan States*, (Panchashila: Bhubaneswar), 223p.

[17] Muni, S.D., 'SAARC at Twenty Five', *Institute of South Asian Studies (National University of Singapore)*, Brief No. 160, 04 May 2010, p. 2, retrieved 02 May 2011, at http://www.isas.nus. edu.sg

[18] Attachments/PublisherAttachment/ISAS_ Brief_160_-_Email_-SAARC_ at Twenty_ Five_04052010182800.pdf.

[19] Noreen, Asima (2011). "Challenges for SAARC", Pakistan Times, 17 February.

[20] Nye, Joseph (1968). *International Regionalism*, (Little, Brown: Boston), p. vii.

[21] Paul, Aditi (2012). "What Impedes Regionalism in South Asia?" Counter Currents, 24 March 2012, at http://www. countercurrents. org/paul240312. htm

[22] *People's SAARC Declaration: Justice, Peace and Democracy*, 2007, Kathmandu, Nepal, 25th March 2007, at http://peoplesaarc.blogspot.in/

[23] Pradhan, Bishwa, 'Regional Cooperation: Prospect for Energy Development', *Institute of Foreign Affairs, Nepal,* p. 9, retrieved 20 March 2011, www.ifa.org.np/document/ saarcpapers/bishwa.pdf)

[24] Pyatt, Geoffrey R., "Hydro-diplomacy for Regional cooperation over Himalayan Watersheds", *South Asia Journal,* Issue 1, July 2011, pp. 24–27.

[25] Secretary General (2010). Trade is key to SAARC's Success, Indian Council of World Affairs, 14 September 2010, at http://www.thaindian. com/newsportal/business/ trade-is-key-to-saarcs-success-secretary-general_100428441.html

[26] Sharma, Sheel Kant (2010). "SAARC Secretary General's Address", South Asian Regionalism: Prospects and Challenges, Indian Council of World Affairs, Sapru House, New Delhi, 14 September 2010.

[27] Singh, Prabin Man (2011). "Sharing Rivers for Peace, Security and Development of South Asia", *South Asia Journal,* Issue 1, July 2011, pp. 32–34.

[28] Singh, Swaran (2007). "India and regionalism" (Chapter-3), in Alyson J.K. Bailes, John Gooneratne, Mavara Inayat, Jamshed Ayaz Khan and Swaran Singh, Regionalism in South Asian Diplomacy, SIPRI Policy Paper No. 15, Stockholm International Peace Research Institute, Bromma (Sweden), February 2007.

Indo-Sri Lanka Relations: The Multilateral Context

P.V. Rao

Broadly speaking there are two ways of examining the relations between peninsular India and the island republic of Sri Lanka. While bilateral relations of these two countries are rooted in their ancient histories and cultural past and evolved in varying degrees through the various historical phases, their colonial past provided some kind of multilateral framework for the first time. Commonwealth was the major multilateral group headed by the imperial British empire in which both India and Sri Lanka as the subjects of the Raj shared their experiences and cooperated mutually in certain Commonwealth-administered programmes like education, security, trade, sports and so on. Post-independence, the Commonwealth connection continued to bring these two democratic systems periodically on a common intergovernmental platform.

Next to the Commonwealth partnership, India and Sri Lanka were to engage with each other closely in the Colombo Plan. The Colombo Plan was the first ever attempt at planning Asian economies on a regional basis, a Commonwealth idea which aimed at putting an economic substance into its functioning in order to strengthen the developing and poorer countries of the Asian region, most of them still in the process of rebuilding post-colonial societies. Indian role was significant in directing the Commonwealth's attention in favour of regional economic development.

The Colombo Plan, however, was not very successful in forging the Asian economies into a permanent organisational form. It was neither a plan nor a programme nor a regional organisation. Its members were content to leave it as a loose intergovernmental arrangement guided by periodic ministerial consultative committee which rather preferred bilateral plans than multilateral programmes of coordinated regional economic plans. Nevertheless, the Colombo Plan gained during its first decade impressive results by way of attracting external assistance, offering technical expertise and even higher production levels in certain commodities.

Indian contribution to the members of the Colombo Plan including Sri Lanka had been considerable. She ranked fifth out of the thirteen countries which included the USA, UK, Australia and Japan in providing technical skills and training. India also ranked as the second largest provider of technical experts next to the United States of America. The latter of course had her own cold-war oriented objectives in extending to the Asian partners of the Colombo Plan what today is frequently termed as soft power, a term associated with the well known American political scientist, Joseph Nye. In addition New Delhi also provided capital and technical assistance to the countries willing to be aided by the economic and human resource outlays under the Colombo Plan.1 (P.V. Rao).

While not forming exclusive economic clubs for the purpose India took demonstrated keen interest in fostering Asian economic cooperation within the existing organisations like the Commonwealth of which of course Sri Lanka was actively associated with. Similarly, New Delhi strongly backed the Asia-related regional economic development schemes introduced by multilateral development agencies like the Asian Development Bank (ADB). Under Nehru and later, India vigorously supported economic programmes in various multilateral fora including the Non-Alignment Movement (NAM), NAM-inspired new International Economic Order (NIEO), the North-South Dialogue and South-South Cooperation debates.

It should be underlined here, in order not to loose the main context of this paper, that Sri Lanka was, along with India took active part in all these multilateral debates and negotiations. Not to be ignored is also the fact that the two South Asian republics were in close consultation with each other on key issues of global economic issues and the third world groups or forum mentioned above. In otherwords, both the democracies had shared values and programmes of shaping long-term development visions and plans for the developing countries of the South.

The foundations for such multilateral context in which India and Sri Lanka could interact together with other Asian neighbours was due to Prime Minister's declared philosophy of mutual-interdependence, self-reliance and resistance to neo-colonialism. Nehru's India thus channelized such co-operative spirit through the Colombo Plan, Commonwealth Fund for Technical Cooperation, ADB, ESCAP, and the principle beneficiaries were India's immediate neighbours as also countries in eastern and southern Africa and in the Indian and Pacific oceans. Sri Lanka invariably was one such immediate South Asian neighbours which possibly could not be ignored by Nehru's visionary roadmap. India also played active role in instituting the Asian Council of Ministers for Economic Cooperation and the Bangkok Agreements of 1975.

INDO-SRI LANKAN INDIAN OCEAN PERSPECTIVES

Cold war politics provided for a possible multilateral opportunity for the foreign policies of India and Sri Lanka, both Indian Ocean littoral countries, to work intimately on some of the major issues of foreign policy on which both the countries adopted common positions. As already discussed above, India-sponsored Asian Relations Conference, Nonalignment, New International Economic Order (NIEO), Indian Ocean as a Zone of Peace IOZP), Group of 77 are the major third world multilateral forums or groups which served as the frequent arenas of mutual exchange of views, coordinated policies and partnerships between New Delhi and Colombo.

However, it should not be construed that both India and Sri Lanka always held similar and consensual views on several issues of major importance to both of them. There were therefore certain issues on which both the republics for whatever the individual reasons adopted different approaches in holding their positions. Or if both held similar positions in a broader context, each differed in either diplomatic approach or prioritization or strategy. Given their democratic systems and independent foreign policy styles, it is not unnatural to expect certain divergent areas or issues of mutual interest. Such differing view points on the details of a major international initiative like the NAM are but common to any participating sovereign in any multilateral framework.

On the IOZP for instance, Colombo and New Delhi disagreed on several aspects through the long and protracted deliberations among the Indian Ocean countries on this controversial subject. Colombo which played key role in the formulation and introduction of the IOZP proposal in the United Nations in 1971, was scheduled to host its conference in 1981. However, the decade of eighties had ushered in a new and alarming strategic climate in the Indian Ocean Region (IOR). The new super power competition in the IOR had raised serious doubts about the prospects for the IOZP. Whatever be its theoretical postulates and regional the IOZP concept had begun to loose its initial verve as the regional powers like India, and particular its vocal advocates like Sri Lanka were altering their onetime full support to the cause of the doctrine.2 (Selig Harrisson).

Colombo which was to host in 1981 the scheduled international conference on IOZP had postponed the meeting, rather indefinitely. Moreover, the regime change in Sri Lanka, now led president by Jayawardene who entertained more pro-western leanings, as against his predecessors, was perceived of undermining the cause of IOZP. Indian and Sri Lankan diplomatic positions on the IOZP therefore were seen moving on different wavelengths, if not in opposite directions. In otherwords, the Indian Ocean as a Zone of Peace concept brought to the fore the divergent interpretations, approaches and often the major differences between the Indian Ocean coastal countries, and India and Sri Lanka were no exception to such differing perspectives on the IOZP.

Another Indian Ocean related multilateral issue on which India and Sri Lanka found themselves on opposite poles were the Indian Ocean Maritime Affairs Cooperation (IOMAC). This small body comprising seven littoral states of the Indian Ocean region is an intergovernmental forum in which Sri Lanka played an active role through its formations and administration. IOMAC is headquartered in Colombo with a common agenda mutual cooperation in certain maritime issues of common concern like fisheries, oceanography, marine resource and ecological conservation. India refused to join the IOMAC despite Sri Lanka's keen interest and persuasion, apparently unwilling to co-partner with Pakistan which joined IOMAC. Commenting on the imperative of Indian membership of IOMAC and the possible adverse impact on it if Indian keeps out, a maritime scholar stated:

> "Its (India's) non-participation in IOMAC may also affect the willingness of foreign donors to provide the assistances needed by other Indian ocean states, since such donors might be concerned not to impair their political relations with India."3 (Barbara Kwiatkowska, in, PACEM Proceeding, Madras, 1995, p. 106).

A more recent Indian Ocean forum in which India and Sri Lanka are actively involved are the Indian Ocean Region-Association for Regional Cooperation (IOR-ARC). IOR-ARC was founded in 1995 by fourteen rim states of the Indian Ocean region and its charter was formalised in 1997. India and Sri Lanka are the founder members of the IOR-ARC. Both took keener interest right from the beginning which was widely debated in the formative conclaves at Mauritius which was represented by five IOR littorals including India and Sri Lanka, the so-called P-5, as well as in Australia at Perth, called the P-28. In both these debates on the future IOR-ARC, New Delhi and Colombo were the pioneering members whose efforts, along with littorals, led to conclusive resolutions on the establishment of the IOR-ARC. 4 (Dennis Rrumley).

IOR-ARC was originally conceived as a forum to promote and facilitate intra-regional trade and investment. It is a unique association premised on the concept of open regionalism as against closed regionalism whose replicas are the SAARC, SADC, ASEAN and GCC representing the various subregions of the IOR. Open regionalism, first tried by the APEC during the eighties, is an inclusive regional arrangement which encourages economic cooperation among the likeminded countries on consensual basis and it has an open ended approach to membership which enables any country to join the forum with the unanimous approval of the members.

IOR-ARC today has nineteen countries drawn from every subregion of the IOR- Africa, west Asia, south Asia and southeast Asia. The Association's ability to promote a more freer trade and investment interaction between the members was severely hampered as Australia, India and South Africa who pioneered the forum lost interest as each was diverted by its immediate regional pulls and priorities. However, Sri Lanka and other members like Iran and Oman continue to take active part in the IOR-ARC affairs.

Recently, IOR-ARC, now chaired by India, held its meeting in Bengalure in the second week of November 2011, followed by another in October 2012. This author who represented India at the above two meetings could perceive very keen and active role played by the Sri Lankan delegation. In fact, the Lankan delegation's proposal to establish an Indian Research Centre with financial assistance by the IOR-ARC was fully supported by the Indian delegation. What needs to underscored is that mutual participation by India and Sri Lanka in the IOR-ARC as well as other multilateral forums gives an ample opportunity for these two immediate maritime neighbours, located just less than 30 nautical miles across the Palk Strait in the bay of Bengal, gives them enough scope and opportunity to cooperate on regional issues of common concern.

THE SAARC CONTEXT

The South Asian Association for Regional Cooperation (SAARC), though well recognized as the first truly 'regional' group participated by all the regional countries, going by the above discussion, it could be observed that the participation of most of south Asian countries, if not all of them in several other forums that preceded the SAARC, had rather laid the initial foundations of a multilateral cooperative engagement between them. SAARC is devised to promote multiple levels of cooperation which include political, economic, social, trade, transport and so on. Despite its expressed prohibition on deliberating bilateral issues of the member countries SAARC in fact encouraged such debates. Member countries, in other words, laboured a political space for their mutual concern on the margins of the annual summits, thereby establishing a healthy tradition. It is a different matter whether such exercise resulted in conflict management but the logic of bilateral interactions vested the regional association with added prestige even India with the known opposition to placing bilateral issues before regional forum adopted a tolerant view on the subject.

The Indian prime minister Rajiv Gandhi admitted that that SAARC presented the opportunity for informal discussions both among all seven member states and bilaterally. Thus at the very first summit of the SAARC Rajiv Ganddhi and Zia-ul-huq of Pakistan agreed on allowing Khan Abdul Gaffer Khan, the frontier Gandhi, to attend the centenary celebration of the Indian National Congress in Bombay. At the second summit of the SAARC in Bangalore, Rajiv Gandhi and Jayewardene met separately to find a solution to the boiling Lankan ethnic crisis. India had brought the Tamilnadu chief minister M.G. Ramachandran and the LTTE leader V.Prabharakan to explore the possibilities of a political solution to the Tamil problem. The talks of course failed but it was the first attempt on the summit side-lines to resolve a purely internal dispute in which India took the leader role. This is to emphasise the point that India and Sri Lanka could explore finding solution to an otherwise strictly bilateral issue of serious concern at the regional multilateral forum.

In the economic arena India and Sri Lanka, both as partners in the South Asian Free Trade Area (SAFTA) agreed to exchange trade benefits. SAFTA, after prolonged negotiations, was signed in 2005, and became operative from 2006. Though a laudable regional economic arrangement, SAFTA in reality had little to offer to the member countries. Its trade concessions are very limited, goods covered are mostly less or least traded ones and above all it does not cover investment. Moreover, SAFTA just covers a bare minimum of 4–5 per cent of South Asia's total external trade. It is under the bilateral India Sri Lanka Free Trade Agreement that Colombo gains comparably more in terms of coverage of tradable goods and tariff reductions percentages compared to the SAFTA. Thus under SAPTA concessions offered by India are only 30 items of actual trade interest to Sri Lanka. By contrast, the total number of traded goods on which immediate zero tariff reduction and 50 per cent concessional reductions offered to Sri Lanka under the ILFTA amount to over 280 items. A comparative analysis of Sri Lankan gains under both has been undertaken by a Sri Lankan economist, as illustrated below.

Table 1: Concession on Traded Products to Sri Lanka
by India under SAPTA and ILFTA

HS Code Chapters		Composition of SL Exports to India	No. of Concessions Granted under SAPTA	No. of Concessions Granted under ILFTA[a]
01–05	Live animals, animal products	2.2		2
06–14	Vegetable Products	38.8	6	20
15	Animal or Vegetable fats and oils	7.3		3
16–24	Prepared Foodstuffs	0.8	4	28
25–27	Mineral Products	0.2	2	3
28–38	Chemical products	1.0	6	36
39–40	Plastics and rubber	11.3	4	10
41–43	Leather Products	0.2		4
44–46	Wood Products	0.1	3	7
47–49	Paper Products	9.6	2	21
50–63	Textile articles	10.9		
64–67	Footwear	0.2	1	4
68–70	Stone, Plaster, Cement	1.0		11
71	Pearls	0.3		
72–83	Base metal	14.0	1	37
84–85	Machinery and mechanical goods	1.7		58
86–89	Transport equipment	0.0	1	9
90–92	Optical, photographic equipment	0.1		10
93	Arms and ammunition	0.0		
94–96	Misc. manufactured articles	0.2		19
97–99	Works of art	0.0		
Total	Total	100.0	30	286

Notes: (a) Concessions on the items offered immediate zero duty and fifty percent tariff reduction only.
Source: A.Subramanyam Raju, Reconstructing South Asia, South Asian Publishers, New Delhi, p. 130.

Given the comparative gains and encouraged by the overall growth in bilateral trade under ILFTA, both countries have agreed to upgrade the FTA to Comprehensive Economic Partnership Agreement (CEPA).

India and Sri Lanka are also engaged as partners in a sub-regional cooperation groups called the BIMST- EC. Formed in 1997, its original fullform stood, in alphabetical order for Bangladesh, India, Myanmar, Sri Lanka and Thailand. This acronym however was subsequently changed to mean Bay of Bengal Multisectoral Economic Cooperation. This group is representative of South and Southeast Asian countries which share the maritime peripheries of the poverty-stricken but resource-rich sub-region of the Bay of Bengal. One of the important agenda of the BIMSTEC sub-regional organization has been the regional cooperation through which its member countries might strengthen their external competitiveness. This cooperation might take the form of joint marketing and coordination in third country trading, regional cooperation for dealing with non-tariff barriers in developed world, coordination for WTO negotiations, technical assistance for compliance with WTO commitments and international standards. 5 (RIS, 2004).

BIMSTEC has a regional cooperative action plan in six identified sectors, viz, trade and investment, technology, energy, tourism, transport and fisheries. Activities under each sector were to be coordinated and monitored by an individual BIMSTEC member state nominated as the lead country for that sector. It was agreed that each country would play a prominent role in planning and implementing programmes in each of the areas for a period of nearly three years. The sectors and prominent countries at the inception were: Trade and Investment, Bangladesh; Technology, India; Transportation and Communication, Thailand; Energy, Myanmar; Tourism and Fisheries, Sri Lanka. 6.

However, BIMSTEC is not credited with major success as countries have not in reality demonstrated seriousness in shaping concrete plans of action on the identified sector under each member country's responsibility. Political differences and even bilateral mistrust marred the sub-regional spirit. India, the major country in the group is often blamed for not taking the BIMSTEC seriously. The point to be highlighted in this context is that India and Sri Lanka also have the potential to engage with each other under the canopy of this sub-regional group, if only there is collective effort to make it effective.

REFERENCES

[1] Rao, P.V., ed. *Regional Cooperation in Indian Ocean,* South Asian Publishers, New Delhi, 2003.

[2] Harrisson, Selig S. and Subramanyam, K., eds. *Super power Rivarly in the Indian Ocean, Indian and American Perspectives,* Oxford, 1989.

[3] Kwiatkowska, Barbara, in, *PASSEM Proceedings,* Madras, 1995 (Barbara Kwiatkowska, in, PACEM Proceeding, Madras, 1995, p. 106).

[4] Rumley, Dennis and Chaturvedi, Sanjay, eds. *Geo-Political Orientations, Regionalism and Security in the Indian Ocean,* South Asian Publishers, New Delhi, 2004.

[5] Raju, A. Subramanyam, ed. *Reconstructing South Asia,* South Asian Publishers, New Delhi, 2006.

[6] Research and Information Systems on Non-aligned Countries (RIS), *Annual Report, 2005,* New Delhi.

[7] Devi, T. Nirmala, ed. *BIMST-EC,* Delta Publishers, New Delhi.

[8] Dash, Kishore C., *Regionalism in South Asia,* Routledge, New York, 2008.

India, Sri Lanka and the SAARC

N. Sathiya Moorthy

Partners in the South Asian Association for Regional Cooperation (SAARC), India and Sri Lanka, the closest of South Asian neighbours linked or distanced by the sea, have a lot in common in terms of their collective contribution, to make any study of SAARC's 25-year history purposeful and meaningful. The ups-and-downs in bilateral relations between these two countries is as varied and vigorous as between any other two South Asian nations, yet it is the commonality that gets greater stress in public and academic discourses on the subject than, say, India-Pakistan linkages, for instance.

In a way, sub-continental India, of which the major chunk now constitutes the Indian Union, can call only Sri Lanka its true and historic neighbour—if at all there has been any. All the land-based members barring Nepal and Bhutan have formed a single political unit at some point in history, near or far. The two Himalayan nations while remaining aloof for many centuries and long decades in political terms, there again, culture and religion have derived from one another. History however is replete with royal weddings between Nepal and princely Indian States. So has Maldives, the other islands-nation with a membership in SAARC, where early settlers were believed to have come from the legendary Sarswati Valley civilisation abutting present-day Indian State of Gujarat—with Buddhism too making common cause, until Islam became the national religion in the 12th century. It is only with Sri Lanka that India has had strong and continuing ties of religion and ethnicity, language(s) and culture, politics and economy, even while remaining separate identities as sovereign nations.

In a way, a better understanding of the sovereignty issues involving India and Sri Lanka to an extent, so also between India and Maldives, or Sri Lanka and Maldives, would help in a better and pragmatic understanding of perceived roles and contributions that each member-nation could make to SAARC as a regional association and institution, to preserve unity in diversity, development with dissimilarities and growth through cooperation. The fact remains even two-plus years of existence 'preservation' of the

SAARC identity itself remains a question, for it to move on to the next stage of progress and stability.

This does not mean that SAARC has not stabilised as a regional institution, *per se*. What has been achieved is the acceptance of the *status quo* after years of hiccups, often involving the two prominent members, namely, India and Pakistan. Their historic differences have often influenced the functioning of the SAARC. So much so, from time to time, India in particular has been made to feel that the smaller neighbours might have planned to use SAARC as a regional forum, to neutralise its natural strengths in the South Asian context.

By consistently refusing to fall into the Pakistani trap of throwing up bilateral problems, more perceived than real, with India at SAARC forums, other member-nations have set healthy precedents. In the overall context, thus, the Indian suspicions have melted away. Yet, bilateral tensions between member-nations, particularly with India at the centre, remain. A closer look would suggest pending and emerging bilateral issues between other member-nations, like between Nepal and Bhutan on refugees too remain. In relative terms, they are insignificant in the larger regional and global contexts.

Pakistan, despite being acknowledged the world over as the fountainhead of international terrorism, targeting India and the rest, has no great issues or problems of the kind with other SAARC nations, barring Afghanistan. Here again, the reasons are too wide and complex for being identified with SAARC one way or the other. There is no comparable South Asian model for mutual hurt and suspicion between India and Pakistan.

The historic baggage that India and Pakistan inherited at Partition is not matched even by the one that should have been there between Pakistan and Bangladesh. Instead, the birth of Bangladesh after the 'Liberation War' of 1971, in which the Indian armed forces were directly involved after a time, meant that Islamabad ended up blaming New Delhi for its travails, rather than acknowledging its mighty and avoidable contribution to the problem. Post-Independence India-Sri Lanka relation has been similarly marked by the Colombo's induction of the Indian Peace-Keeping Force (IPKF), under a bilateral treaty, that went sour after a time.

MORE ADMINISTRATIVE THAN POLITICAL

In this background, the achievements of SAARC since inception could be termed more administrative in nature than political. Where administrative mechanisms have to be put in place, be it in terms of education and health, economic cooperation and trade tariffs, unanimity of views have become possible through a process of mutual give-and-take negotiations. Even on fighting terrorism, a controversial but even more sensitive subject in the South Asian context, protocols are in place for a united South Asian fight against the global scourge.

On specifics, however, there has been little progress on specifics in the bilateral context. In the absence of such an understanding that could be transplanted to the regional-level, providing for variables, SAARC remains just an outline super-structure with an inner hollow. The filling up of the hollow with meaningful and substantive measures cannot be undertaken until individual nations addressed individual issues on which they have specific concerns and issues.

Nothing explains this dichotomy better than the issue of terrorism. Even as the post-9/11 era has driven home the need for united South Asian approach to fight the menace that threatens the region both as the ultimate source of international terrorism and as a victim, bilateral complexities remain. Sri Lanka, for instance, has not forgiven India for 'promoting' Tamil militancy on its soil from around the time SAARC came into being in 1985. Yet, there is a growing acceptance of the emerging realities since. The period witnessed, India's silent support for the Sri Lankan armed forces extinguishing the LTTE in May 2009.

On terrorism, for instance, India has continuing problems, the 26/11 Mumbai attacks being only the latest—but possibly not the last, either. In the past, India had harboured proven concerns about territories of other SAARC nations being used for terrorists to target its people and property. The 'Kathmandu hijack episode' and the repeated apprehension of ISI-trained, anti-India terrorists from inside Bangladesh, are pointers from the past. Pakistan's ISI has been behind those attacks. New Delhi is not alone in this, as Afghanistan also shares Pakistan-centric concerns and suspicions.

Many of India's concerns on this score have been addressed by the respective nations, if only over a period. More than the ground-level mechanisms that may have been put in place, the political will of the host-governments, coupled with the proven realisation that they too may have fallen victim of ISI brand terrorism already—expanding to become *jihadi* terrorism in Bangladesh—made the difference.

Yet, India's concerns on this score have however grown to cover possible ISI/*jihadi* activities in Sri Lanka and Maldives, targeting its territory.

Under SAARC now, India, Maldives and Sri Lanka have since resolved to address maritime security issues, collectively. The bi-annual *'Dhosti'* series of Coast Guard exercises between India and Maldives thus included Sri Lanka in the 11th edition of March 2012. The hope is to be able to expand maritime security cooperation of the kind, to include other SAARC nations over time.

The fact still remains that all security cooperation on the terrorism front are still seen as a bilateral or multilateral effort, not a SAARC scheme, *per se.* For that to happen, member-nations have to resolve various bilateral issues and multilateral concerns at their levels. They include terrorism, yes, border disputes (as between India and Pakistan), refugee problems (Nepal and Bhutan), illegal migration (Bangladesh is the irritant, Maldives is a beneficiary—in between India has a problem, both as a destination and transit-point).

Fishing is another source of irritant, particularly between India and Sri Lanka on the one hand, and between India and Pakistan, on the other. India also has a specific problem pertaining to the 'ethnic issue' in Sri Lanka. The sensitivity and seriousness of the issue in India is not often fully understood in Sri Lanka, where successive Governments have either dismissed, or have sought but failed to do so, as the 'Tamil Nadu factor' and nothing more.

The emergence of China as a regional power and an anticipated global power in the post-Cold War era has all-round concerns for India. With the history of the 1962 war still embedded in memory, India needs to look at the large-scale developmental interests of China in the immediate neighbourhood with anxiety. The Indian concerns in this regard are more to do not only with the unspecified Chinese intention but also about the inherent ability of its immediate neighbours to be sensitive to New Delhi's apprehensions about the future.

More than the Gwadar port in Pakistan, India is concerned about the Hambantota port in Sri Lanka—both funded by China. Beijing has also funded a host of other developmental projects in Sri Lanka and other South Asian neighbours of India. In doing so, China has leveraged its hard-currency surplus and global political insularity, which gives it a certain leeway to back individual Governments (as in Sri Lanka), based not on principles but on issues—and at such international forums like the UN, its agencies and institutions, starting with the Security Council.

As the world's largest democracy, and a revived ambition and scope for playing a more purposeful and decisive role in the international arena,

India feels stymied by the absence of an UNSC seat. As a principled State player given still to the national values enshrined in the Gandhian era and image, India also finds it difficult to deviate frequently and decisively from basic human values, as against tools of Statecraft that may demand otherwise.

Resolving such issues so as to make them a comprehensive contribution to the SAARC scheme demands a very high level of political commitment—and 'national will'. However, such national will has also been displayed, if at all, in fits and starts. On the Indian side, the 'China factor', from time to time, dictates perceptions of cooperation with and concessions to neighbours on a wide variety of subjects and issues. There is truth in the Indian perception—often flagged by the nation's strategic community—that those neighbours may have found in the 'China factor' a convenient tool to work on India, rather than with India.

INDIA, ALL-ROUND PIVOT OF SOUTH ASIA

Independent of SAARC too, the role of India as the pivot in South Asia cannot be overlooked. In the regional context, the size of the nation and that of the population in the post-reforms global context have become complimentary as India had not known—or would have believed, earlier. The military might of the country, inherently required to defend the nation's sovereignty, has only been compulsively complemented by the contribution of historic adversities since Independence—with China and Pakistan, not always in that order.

These factors had existed, and had been understood and acknowledged in differing perceptions by India and the rest of South Asia in the 'Cold War' era. The conclusion of the 'Cold War' and the sudden collapse the Soviet Union, on which India had depended for political support and military supplies also unshackled the nation on a whole range of perceptive policies and programmes with their independent origins in the socialist economic model of the Nehruvian era.

All this have contributed to the South Asian neighbourhood acknowledging the Indian position as a facilitator to and catalyst of their own growth and development in the 21st century. Shared concerns over extra-territorial nations swarming the shared Indian Ocean neighbourhood, based on their perceptions and/or propaganda of the emerging geo-strategic scenario, has made South Asian nations nervous, one way or the other. The region's acknowledged status as the epi-centre of global terrorism calls for greater concern and focussed attention as it threatens South Asia from within as it threatens the rest of the world.

The need and justification for international politico-military interventions in the region draws from this ground reality. History and contemporary realities have drawn counter and/or counter-veiling forces from the extended Asian region to South Asia's gate, where they already belong. For India in particular, and South Asia otherwise, such an approach is strewn with consequences. Those consequences are for the whole of South Asia, whatever the trigger and whoever is/are the player(s). The fact has seldom been appreciated in the regional capitals.

It is not without reason. Just as the nations of South Asia—including Pakistan, though possibly grudgingly—acknowledge India's role as the all-round pivot to and in the region, New Delhi has also begun appreciating the role the neighbours can play, in politico-military terms in particular. Call it the mid-term review or whatever, this belated acceptance of the ground reality, a decade or so after the post-Cold War rearrangement of India's geo-strategic priorities seems to acknowledge the neighbours as the first line of defence against external threats, particularly of organised, visible threats from State players. The reverse is also true, and New Delhi seems to understand this, as well.

In between, India's strategic community seemed to have concluded otherwise. During the long and halting run-up to the India-US strategic cooperation treaty in 2005, punctuated as it was by frequent change of political leadership in New Delhi, the pundits, borrowing ideas from the western counterparts, saw the nation emerging as a global super-power in the undeterminable yet foreseeable future. They relied on projections that were not supported either by facts or emerging ground realities, be it on the global economic and/or military fronts.

Post-War world has had only two models for nations attaining super-power status. One is the failed Soviet way of jack-booting neighbours and losing it. The other is the American way of carrying the neighbours and the neighbourhood with it. For India or any other nation to aspire for global power status, it has to have their neighbours with them, in a successful economic partnership and as dependable political allies on the international front. India seems working on it continually over the past years, but gives the impression of doing so in fits and starts. This owes to the pre-prioritised aspirations and achievements for New Delhi, which makes for a perception of zigzag Indian approach towards the neighbours and the neighbourhood.

LEARNING FROM INDIA-SRI LANKA TIES

For contemporary reasons, India-Pakistan relations are a stand-alone affair in the context of SAARC. Against this, India-Sri Lanka relations can be a prime example of the various ups and downs that is not uncommon involving the SAARC pivot. It is as complex as it is simple. The reverse is equally true. On the political front, 'Eelam War IV' (2006–09) in Sri Lanka marked a new chapter in bilateral relations, which had been upset since the Eighties, for a variety of reasons. Three years down the line, 2012 has marked a new sub-text, when India voted against Sri Lanka, in the company of the US and the rest of the West at the UNHRC, Geneva.

There are issues and issues, including the 'Tamil Nadu factor' in India, as many Sri Lankans see and seek to believe as the corner-stone of bilateral relations in the ethnic context. There are those in the two countries who overlap such concerns with their perceptions of the Indian position on the 'China factor' in bilateral relations. Yet, post-Geneva 2012, there seems to be a perceptible distinction drawn by the two neighbours between their shared security concerns in their shared waters—and the ethnic issue, where the dynamics of domestic politics is also a factor, but not *the* factor in India.

This owes to the un-kept promises of Sri Lanka on finding a political solution to the ethnic impasse, which has since been coloured inevitably by 'accountability issues' flowing from Sri Lanka's conduct of 'Eelam War IV'. The dichotomy on this score too is perceptible, as India is believed to have helped dilute the criticism that the West sought to breathe into the anti-Sri Lanka motion that they all voted together at Geneva in March 2012. While a lot will depend on Sri Lanka standing by the commitments made at Geneva since, bilateral developments since has indicated the possibility of both nations working towards minimising the strains and suspicions, and strengthening commonalities where they can hope to work together for common good, starting with geo-strategic security in the shared Indian Ocean neighbourhood, which is of equal concern to most, if not all SAARC members.

Bilateral and multilateral relations in South Asia owe as much to economic cooperation as to a shared political will to shared issues and concerns. On trade and investments, India and Sri Lanka have come a long way since the former opened up on the economic front. The India-Sri Lanka bilateral Free Trade Agreement (FTA) is still hailed as a model for New Delhi's furtherance of FTAs of the kind with other nations in the region and elsewhere, too. Where there were hiccups, both India and Sri Lanka learnt quickly to sort them out through mutual discussions and understanding.

Issues still remain, of Sri Lankan exports facing non-tariff barriers in particular in India. But such concerns have not stopped investors from India going to Sri Lanka in a big way, or Sri Lankan investors likewise coming to India. China is making forays into Sri Lanka (as in rest of South Asia) in terms of trade and investments. Yet, a realistic assessment of future situations would demand that India's neighbours, starting with China, begin seeing the benefits of strong bilateral and regional economic cooperation in its perspective, much as they may be swayed in the interim, by the immediate benefits accruing to their respective nation, and the political advantages that may accompany the same in the domestic context in the short-term.

The on-going negotiations for a Comprehensive Economic Partnership Agreement (CEPA) between India and Sri Lanka have been held back owing to the 'small nation' concerns of Sri Lanka. A mutual appreciation of the issues involved would be beneficial not only in taking forward CEPA when signed, but will also in the evolution of bilateral understanding of the kind between various SAARC members, and ultimately to a full-fledged SAARC mechanism of the kind for the whole region.

What is thus required is political will on the part of SAARC member-nations, independent of the short and medium-term conclusions that each one of them may have been tempted to draw. At the end of it all may be the creation of a common South Asia currency and monetary policy, as Sri Lanka President Mahinda Rajapaksa mooted some time ago—about which no one in the region is however talking after the unsure nature of euro's fate.

Still, however, three is a need for SAARC nations to consider a common forex policy for the region, to check against avoidable loss for individuals and institutions, caused by the continued adoption of the dollar as the common global currency. Maldives, for instance, had moved India and Sri Lanka in this regard, and none of them can benefit from such an arrangement in any big way, unless India and Sri Lanka agree to the same. With India regaining its prime position as the highest tourist-sender to Sri Lanka, and the latter becoming the single largest tourist destination for Indians, a new dynamics is working between two South Asian nations, which is capable of replication between and among other South Asian nations, particularly through the mechanism of SAARC.

Otherwise, the Sri Lanka-India land-bridge, about which much is being said from time to time, can open up the whole of South Asia and the rest of Eurasia too, to Sri Lanka and Sri Lankans, to travel and trade with. The reverse is even more true, and the think dividing line along the Palk Strait is what needs to be bridged, to make South Asia one big family that it otherwise is! Again, what is needed is political will in India and Sri Lanka, which too is reflective of the inherent constraints in bilateral relations in SAARC but overcoming which again is mostly a mind-game, and nothing more!

Adding Substance to SAARC: India-Sri Lanka Experience

Col R. Hariharan

[This article includes extracts from the valedictory address delivered by the author at the International Conference on "India-Sri Lanka Relations: Strengthening SAARC" organised by the Centre for Indian Ocean Studies, Osmania University Hyderabad on November 8 and 9, 2012.]

INTRODUCTION

There is a widespread feeling of pessimism among South Asians at the halting progress made by the South Asia Association of Regional Co-operation (SAARC) since its inception in 1985. Though SAARC is world's largest regional grouping of 1.47 billion people, it has not been able to assert its collective strength like the Association of South East Asian Nations (ASEAN) or the European Union (EU).

But the comparison is a little unfair as both ASEAN and EU were formed in different historical contexts and environments. They were conceived when the world was in the grip of Cold War.[1] The European grouping came about to minimize the impact of twin threats: post war economic privations of Europe and the fear of Soviet Union destabilizing Europe. For ASEAN, the U.S. penchant for building regional alliances to fight Communist threat in Southeast Asia provided the incentive.

When the Cold War compulsions vanished, both the groupings seamlessly focused on other fronts—energy, resources, economic development, environment protection and counter terrorism—to benefit from collective strengths. Both ASEAN and EU streamlined structural frameworks of their members to take the best advantage of global economic liberalization that came about towards of the end of the last century. They coordinated their policies and practices to reap maximum advantage for the members. And this process is constantly reviewed to remove the functional kinks and minimize damages due to external and internal pressures.

On the other hand, SAARC came about without the trappings of ideology and external pressures. Unlike the more prosperous ASEAN and EU groupings, SAARC has the largest number of people below poverty level in the world. Its members have some of the highest population densities in the world. And the region has been the scene of extremism and insurgency from the 1950s when most of the members became free nations. This scourge later gave birth to both Jihadi terrorism and the Liberation Tigers of Tamil Eelam (LTTE) who accounted for some of the worst acts of terrorism the world had ever seen. So the growth of SAARC has been stunted from birth.

ASEAN took nearly three decades to gather full momentum; the EU took even longer—nearly four decades—to master its act. Compared to this, the progress made by SAARC in two and a half decades of active existence is not too bad. But the sad truth is SAARC has remained a potted plant. It is yet to make a difference in the lives of South Asians, despite pious speeches made by leaders at every SAARC conference.

Both EU and ASEAN have shown that bonding between members was the key to their success as a group. Their members used the strength of bilateral relations to minimise negative influences during group formation and later in their group operations. This was brought to bear upon in shaping collective responses to issues relating to larger issues of strategic security and terrorism, environmental threats, and global trade and commerce.

The reasons attributed to SAARC's slow progress are unequal size and relative strength of member- nations, memories of shared history, bilateral problems of members, political and economic compulsions of nations, and differences in responding to external influences—global power play, terrorism, and competing political and economic interests. But these are neither unique nor special to SAARC; both ASEAN and EU also have been facing the same problems since their inception.

India's domination of South Asia is often cited as the main reason in the way of SAARC's progress. It is true India's influence derived from its huge geographical size and economic, political and military power overwhelms the region. And it forms a major part of the historical experience of most the member-nations. They have also been impacted by India's soft power which has become a part of their religious, social and cultural influences. In this environment, India's success as a democracy and rise as a dominant economic power have given rise to contrarian feelings of love and hate among SAARC members. The fear of being overwhelmed by India is probably a constant in their security calculus, although its impact on their decisions may not always be negative. These feelings also often influence their internal politics as well the world view. Often India is branded as a bully or "hegemon" (if such a word can be coined) by them.

India appears to be aware of the positive and negative vibrations it generates among other SAARC members. Over the years, India has tried to understand this "contrarian chemistry" and temper its policy prescriptions with some success. However, the bitter India-Pakistan relations, bloodied by wars and skirmishes, continue to hobble the full bloom of SAARC. Recently, with a democratic government staging a painful comeback in Pakistan, there are hopeful signs of improved relations between India and Pakistan.

There was increasing realization among SAARC members, including India and Pakistan, that group's progress cannot be hostage to the bilateral relations of these two important members. As a result, SAARC had been able to take halting steps to identify areas of cooperation and tried to build upon them and take a few initiatives. It has made progress in evolving outlines for action in five areas of common interest for cooperation: terrorism, economic growth, social issues, energy and environment management, and development of inter-connectivity. It has managed to evolve conceptual frame works in all these areas.[2]

In particular, the SAARC protocols adopted to combat terrorism in the region are of special relevance as the region has become the epicenter of Jihadi terrorism.[3] Similarly, SAARC initiatives taken to rationalise economic structures of member countries for collective advantage are encouraging.[4] But the initiatives have not been fully translated into action except in a few areas. So, overall rhetoric rather than action still dominates SAARC.

To make SAARC vibrant, a qualitative change is required among SAARC members to improve the form and content of bilateral relations among members. It will help create better understanding among members to appreciate the nuances of collective cooperation. In this context, growth of India-Sri Lanka relations during the last three decades is an interesting example of building win-win relationship. In this period, the bilateral relations of both nations have weathered conflict situations without suffering serious damage.

INDIA-SRI LANKA RELATIONS

India and Sri Lanka have always enjoyed a special relationship not only due to their close geographical proximity but because of their cultural, religious and ethnic affinities and shared history. Sri Lanka President Rajapaksa has aptly described India-Sri Lanka relations as "family." Of course, even such a sibling relationship has had its ups and downs.

There are three national and "notional" concerns that affect India and Sri Lanka relationship: strategic security; grant of citizenship to people of Indian origin in Sri Lanka; and troubled relations between the Sinhala majority and the Tamil minority. All the three issues had tested India-Sri Lanka relations in various times.

Sri Lanka's geo-strategic location as a vanguard of India's peninsular south, dominating the Indian Ocean astride the sea lanes of Indian Ocean is, one of the centre pieces of Indian strategic thinking. This is more so after China's foot print started enlarging in Sri Lanka considered by India as part of its area of influence. On the other hand, Sri Lanka's feeling of geographic vulnerability is enhanced by the Tamil Nadu's strong sympathies for Tamil minority struggle in Sri Lanka. India's growing economic power and strategic strength supported by two-million strong army and a powerful Navy also imposes caution on Sri Lanka's strategic perceptions. However, both nations have tried to remove these fears by adopting close strategic cooperation between the defence forces as well as by regular exchange of their perceptions.

The denial of Sri Lanka citizenship rights to descendents of Tamils, who were inducted into Sri Lanka as plantation labour in the British colonial days after the country attained independence, used to be a matter of India's concern. However, this vexing issue has ceased to be a contentious one, thanks to the far-sightedness of the leaders of both countries. The Shastri-Sirimavo Pact 1964 and the Sirimavo-Gandhi Pact 1974 partially resolved the issue. Subsequently thanks to the initiative of the leader of Indian Tamil community Saumyamurthy Thondaman, after Sri Lanka passed Act No 35 of 2003 granting citizenship status to all stateless persons, the issue ceased to be a cause for Indian concern.[5] Sri Lanka's inability to provide equitable treatment to Tamil minority in its country has a history of five and a half decades and it has rocked India-Sri Lanka relation more than once. Tamils, who form around 12 per cent of Sri Lanka's population, have close links with their brethren across the Palk Straits in Tamil Nadu from times immemorial. And the denial of equitable rights to Tamils in Sri

Lanka which became a major political issue since 1956 had its impact in Tamil Nadu politics as well. Tamil Nadu's concerns came to a head when a politically orchestrated anti-Tamil pogrom took place in July 1983 in Colombo. Marauding Sinhala gangs killed Tamils and pillaged Tamil business and property. This set off a massive exodus of Tamil population from Sri Lanka with Tamil Nadu as the major destination.

Over 100,000 refugees sought shelter and succour in Tamil Nadu. And along with them came Tamil insurgency groups including the LTTE seeking refuge. The suffering of Tamils touched off wide sympathy the world over. It was natural that the fate of Sri Lanka Tamils became a major political issue and humanitarian concern not only in Tamil Nadu but also in India. It was in this period the Tamil quest for autonomy into a full blown insurgent struggle for separatism and received India's support. Thus the narratives of India-Sri Lanka relations as well as the rise and fall of the most powerful Tamil insurgent group—the LTTE—became closely inter-woven with Indian support to Sri Lanka Tamil aspirations to preserve their identity and culture in their traditional "Homeland" in North and East Sri Lanka.

HIGHLIGHTS OF RELATIONSHIP

In spite of their strategic concerns, both India and Sri Lanka have so far never wavered from their long term objective of maintaining a cordial and friendly relationship between them. The journey of India-Sri Lanka relations through its crests and toughs since independence provides interesting insights into their relationship management:

1. *1947 to 1983:* In this period India's passive policy interventions were mostly driven by concerns for people of Indian origin as already discussed. Though the adoption of socialism as national policy brought about ideological cohesion in both countries brought, Colombo's strict neutrality during India's wars with China in 1962 and Pakistan in 1971 was a disappointment to India. However, India did not allow it to affect the larger interests of both India and Sri Lanka. When JVP insurgency threatened to destabilise Sri Lanka in 1971 India readily responded to her request for military help and sent a battalion of troops to help Sri Lanka. The signing of two key agreements to resolve the citizenship issue and the demarcation of India-Sri Lanka maritime boundary were the positive achievements of this period.

2. *1983 to1990:* It was a period of active Indian intervention, triggered by the 1983 pogrom against Tamils in Colombo. Though India had supported the Tamil cause and militancy, it tried out all possibilities to help Sri Lanka and its Tamil minority to amicably settle their differences. These included bringing both the Sri Lanka Government and the Tamils to resolve their differences across the table, and working with Sri Lanka to help evolve a consensus on devolution for Tamils. The signing of the India Sri Lanka Agreement on July 29, 1987 was in a way culmination of these efforts. However, the Agreement also had a strong flavour of India's Cold War considerations due to the ongoing Soviet conflict in Afghanistan and American efforts to gain a foothold in Sri Lanka. Indian Peacekeeping Force (IPKF) was inducted into Sri Lanka at Sri Lanka President's request to help implement the Agreement. However, IPKF involvement in a conflict with LTTE after it refused to lay down arms in terms of the Agreement created a lot of antagonism. At different times during the conflict, India came under severe criticism from the Sri Lankan Government, Sinhala political opposition, and Tamil separatist segments, notably the LTTE. Sri Lanka's new President Premadasa's ultimatum to India to withdraw the IPKF and his assistance to the LTTE even as IPKF was fighting it led to a lot of bitterness in India. IPKF's ignominious pullout in 1990 sent India-Sri Lanka relations to a new low. In the wake of Bofor scandal, India's Sri Lanka policy fiasco became one more tool for the Indian opposition campaigns against Rajiv Gandhi that resulted in his defeat. Though few weaknesses made the Agreement self-defeating and political changes resulted in the IPKF not completing its assignment, India managed to achieve a few things.[6] Constitutional recognition of Tamil autonomy when provincial councils were created following the introduction of 13th Amendment in Sri Lanka Constitution.[7] It was also loud affirmation of India's support for a united Sri Lanka, signalling end of Indian support to Tamil insurgency. It made both nations realise that cooperation rather than confrontation would be the cornerstone in their relations. It was also a demonstration in India's power assertion to defend its interest in its neighbourhood, sending a strong message to the global strategic community.[8]

3. *1991 to 2006:* This period saw sea change in global power equation: dismantling of the Soviet Union ended the Cold War; China increasingly flexed its economic and military power to challenge American influence in Asia Pacific. Rajiv Gandhi's assassination by

LTTE in 1991 further singed Tamil Nadu's enthusiasm for Sri Lanka Tamil problem. After a brief pause, India and Sri Lanka slowly started rebuilding their relations. India kept aloof from Sri Lanka's conflicts with LTTE during this period. India chose to keep out of the International peace process 2002 in Sri Lanka though it led to the legitimate entry for other major powers—the US, Japan, EU and Norway—in India's area of influence changing the security environment.[9] The signing of India's first ever Free Trade Agreement with Sri Lanka was a major milestone in the journey to a win-win relationship.[10] It could mature into a Comprehensive Economic Partnership Agreement (CEPA) proposed by India to benefit both the countries.

4. *2006 to Date:* Despite domestic pressures, India fully supported Sri Lanka during the Eelam War IV. Although it provided only limited supply of arms Sri Lanka wanted during the war, it extended diplomatic, intelligence and other material support to Sri Lanka. Its naval cooperation and intelligence were useful for Sri Lanka in destroying LTTE's supply ships which greatly helped it win the war. At the same time, India constantly reminded Sri Lanka of the need to fully implement the 13th Amendment and devolve powers to Tamil community as part of Sri Lanka's strategy. Unfortunately, Sri Lanka has not even started the process. Sri Lanka's poor handling of international concerns over allegations of human rights violations and war crimes in the post war period has burgeoned into a minor international crisis affecting Sri Lanka's credibility. It has created dilemma for India in extending unflinching support to Sri Lanka in international forums. The elimination of the LTTE removed a major obstacle to India's active engagement with Sri Lanka Tamils. India has given Sri Lanka nearly $ 4 billion in aid and extended credit for Sri Lanka's post war recovery of economy and reconstruction of Tamil areas. However, Sri Lanka has not been able to take advantage of these favourable developments because politically it wants to project a "homemade solution" as the only way for united Sri Lanka.

GRITTY ISSUES IN THE RELATIONSHIP

India and Sri Lanka relations are facing a number of gritty issues generated in the wake of Eelam war. The durability of their good relations would depend upon how they manage these issues in future:

1. *China's Increasing Profile in Sri Lanka:* China became a major source of weapons and political support in UN for Sri Lanka during the Eelam War. After the war, the Chinese has emerged as a major financial

source for construction of a number of infrastructure projects in Sri Lanka. Some of them like the construction of modern port facilities at Hambantota are part of China's non military power projection in India's neighbourhood. China's recent interest in understanding the Tamil ethnic issue indicates its increasing interest in Sri Lanka political affairs as well. Thus China could emerge as a major contender to check Indian influence in Sri Lanka and the Indian Ocean region.

2. *Increasing Militarism and Centralization of Power:* The 200,000-strong Sri Lanka army has emerged as a powerful force with high morale after the success against LTTE. The continued deployment its major strength in Northern Province even after three years of war and their employment in non-military duties even outside the war zone have become matters of concern for civil society. It does not augur well for democracy as Colombo is showing increasing tendency to centralize power in the hands of Rajapaksa clan, use the parliament to reduce executive president's accountability, weaken civil society institutions and curb of opposition and media. Assertion of Sinhala triumphalism has encouraged xenophobia and hardened Sri Lanka's attitudes towards devolution of powers to minorities. It could strengthen anti-Indian lobbies in Sri Lanka leading to a backlash in favour of Eelam separatism and anti-Sri Lankan lobbies in Tamil Nadu.

3. *Delay in Reconciliation Process:* President Rajapaksa failure to keep up his promise to implement the 13th Amendment in full to empower provincial councils has weakened India's position both internally and externally. Sri Lanka's casual attitude to India's and international concerns over allegations against Sri Lankan army's war crimes, human rights abuses, custodial killings and abductions in the post war period, compelled India to vote for a U.S. sponsored resolution seeking Sri Lanka's accountability in the UN Human Rights Council meeting in March 2012. This has soured the relations between the two countries. Sri Lanka's continued indifference to Tamil concerns could affect New Delhi's ruling coalition's fortunes as it depends upon the support of Dravidian parties from Tamil Nadu. If no course correction is applied it could also affect the electoral fortunes of Congress-led coalition in New Delhi in the long run.[11]

4. *Negative Impact on Policy Making:* These issues have provided an incentive for the revival of Tamil separatism among Tamil Diaspora. It has helped pro-LTTE fringe elements in Tamil Nadu to come to the political limelight which could harden the larger Dravidian parties' stance on Sri Lanka and negatively impact policy making in both

India and Sri Lanka affecting their friendly relations. Increased support to Tamil separatist elements has the potential to turn into a security risk to both India and Sri Lanka. If left unchecked it could pose a major challenge for national leaderships in both countries in their relationship strategy.

TAKEWAYS IN SAARC CONTEXT

The progressive growth of relation between India and Sri Lanka provides valuable takeaways in relationship building which are relevant to improving relations among SAARC members:

1. *Transparency in Transactions:* Lack of transparency in transactions in international diplomacy is taken for granted as a matter of routine. However, the public involvement in policy making has increased tremendously through social media and blogging networks. So probably time has come for nations to achieve a level of transparency in their international transactions without jeopardizing national interests. Lack of transparency of transactions was a major reason for the poor public credibility India-Sri Lanka Agreement 1987 enjoyed during implementation. Neither public nor political parties were taken into confidence either during the Rajiv-Jayawardane talks or when the Agreement was signed. In fact it was rushed through in unseemly haste giving rise to misapprehensions. Publication of white papers on policy matters periodically could help improve the situation.

2. *Keeping Open communication Channels:* In this era of real time news and powerful social media, it is essential that communication channels between countries are kept open at various levels to avoid misunderstanding. This was done effectively during the Eelam War by both India and Sri Lanka. In addition to this there were periodic meetings between the policy makers in both makers as well as within the country. Equally important is to create effective public communication channels. It played an important role in LTTE's successful image building exercise during its conflict with IPKF and subsequently in earlier episodes of Eelam War. Understanding this, Sri Lanka used improved public communication through electronic and print media to successfully neutralize LTTE propaganda machinery during Eelam War IV. India's credibility during the Eelam War IV and after was affected due to poor public communication particularly in Tamil Nadu.

3. *Managing Political Compulsions:* Political compulsions affect policy making in bilateral relations. This cannot be wished away in democratic

societies; however, its negative fallout can be minimized by adopting of coordinated political strategies in both countries to manage. India and Sri Lanka maintained excellent communication between decision makers at all levels to handle critical issues with finesse barring a few exceptions.

4. *Policy Commitment and Continuity:* In democracies where leadership change is common, it is essential countries identify, preferably together, their objectives and maintain continuity of policy to build a win-win relationship. The main reason for the successful growth of India-Sri Lanka relations was the policy the commitment and its continuity even during brief setbacks in between. Continued interaction at the leadership level and regular people to people contact managed to erase the negative feelings generated in the aftermath of Indian intervention from 1987 to 1990. The high level of strategic cooperation and the signing of the India-Sri Lanka FTA and striving to improve its value addition is a good example of this strategy.

5. *External Pressures:* Though Cold War is over, global power play is increasingly bringing pressure on nations in their inter-relations with other countries. After the emergence of China as a challenger to the U.S. power in Asia-Pacific, SAARC nations are increasingly being subject to pressures of external power play. Both India and Sri Lanka have adopted consultation, cooperation, and coordination as the strategies to tackle the impact of such external pressures to handle national and regional issues affecting each other, particularly in international forums. This mutually reinforces their relations with each other. On the other hand, such strategies would work if only nations respond in time to international concerns. This was amply demonstrated by Sri Lanka's progressive loss of international credibility when it chose to ignore mounting international concerns in the UN on its human rights accountability. This has the potential to affect bilateral relations.

NOTES

1. ASEAN was formed on August 8, 1967 by Indonesia, Malaysia, Singapore and Thailand. Since then Brunei, Burma (Myanmar), Cambodia, Laos, and Vietnam have been admitted making a total of ten members at present. EU conceived in July 1952 took present form under the Treaty of Maastricht in November 1, 1993.

2. In 1991 the Committee for Economic Cooperation was set up. The framework agreement for the SAARC Preferential Trading Arrangement (SAPTA) was finalized in 1993 and operationalised in December 1995. South Asia Free Trade

Agreement (SAFTA) became operational from January 1, 2006. This Agreement provides for a phased tariff liberalization programme (TLP). The non-LDCs would bring down tariffs to 20 per cent, while LDCs will bring them down to 30 per cent. Non-LDCs will then bring down tariffs from 20 per cent to 0–5 per cent in 5 years (Sri Lanka in 6 years), while LDCs will do so in 8 years. [www.saarc.org]

3. SAARC Convention on Terrorism (1987) is remarkable because it came up before 9/11 terror strikes which prompted global initiatives in countering terror. SAARC updated its terrorism strategies with Additional Protocol on Terrorism (2005).

4. In 1991 the Committee for Economic Cooperation was set up. The framework agreement for the SAARC Preferential Trading Arrangement (SAPTA) was finalized in 1993 and operationalised in December 1995. South Asia Free Trade Agreement (SAFTA) became operational from January 1, 2006. This Agreement provides for a phased tariff liberalization programme (TLP). The non-LDCs would bring down tariffs to 20 per cent, while LDCs will bring them down to 30 per cent. Non-LDCs will then bring down tariffs from 20 per cent to 0–5 per cent in 5 years (Sri Lanka in 6 years), while LDCs will do so in 8 years. [www.saarc.org]

5. On 30 October 1964 Indian Prime Minister Lal Bahadur Shastri and Ceylon Prime Minister Sirimavo Bandaranaike signed the *Sirima-Shastri Pact* (also known as the *Indo-Ceylon Agreement*) under which India agreed to the repatriation of 525,000 Indian Tamils. Another 300,000 would be offered Ceylon citizenship. The fate of the remaining 150,000 Indian Tamils was to be decided later. On 28 June 1974 Indian Prime Minister Indira Gandhi and her Ceylon counterpart Sirimavo Bandaranaike signed the *Sirimavo-Gandhi Pact* under which India and Sri Lanka agreed to grant citizenship to the 150,000 Indian Tamils whose status was left unresolved by the *Sirima-Shastri Pact*. In 1982 India abrogated the *Sirima-Shastri Pact* and *Sirimavo-Gandhi Pact*. At this point 90,000 Indian Tamils who had been granted Indian citizenship were still in Sri Lanka and another 86,000 were in the process of applying for Indian citizenship. In 1988 the Sri Lankan Parliament passed the *Grant of Citizenship to Stateless Persons Act* which granted Sri Lankan citizenship to all Indian Tamils who hadn't applied for Indian citizenship under previous agreements. On 7 October 2003 the Sri Lankan Parliament unanimously passed the *Grant of Citizenship to Persons of Indian Origin Act No.35 of 2003* which granted Sri Lankan citizenship to all Indian Tamils who had been residing in Sri Lanka since October 1964 and their descendents. This amounted to 168,141 persons and included those who had been granted Indian citizenship under previous agreements but were still living in Sri Lanka. All Indian Tamils living in Sri Lanka had finally been granted Sri Lankan citizenship, 55 years after independence. [http://en.wikipedia.org/wiki/Ceylon_Citizenship_Act]

6. See R. Hariharan 'Discarded accord and the unwanted war' The Hindu, August 7, 2007 for an analysis of the India Sri Lanka Agreement 1987.

7. Sri Lanka parliament passed the 13th Amendment to the Constitution on November 14, 1987. It led to the creation of among others North-eastern provincial council which included what Tamils considered as their 'Homeland.'

8. India's first exercise in asserting its power in its neighbourhood in 1971 resulted in the creation of Bangladesh when Indian forces helped by East Bengal freedom fighters to defeat Pakistani forces. Indian action in 1971 kindled expectations among Sri Lankan Tamils and while apprehension among Sinhalas that IPKF was in Sri Lanka to help the creation of Tamil Eelam which was never India's intention.

9. The four nations were known as the co-chairs of the peace process. India did was not actively involved in the process presumably for two reasons. The Oslo agreement had recognised the LTTE as the sole representative of Tamils ignoring a large segment of Tamils represented by other political parties and former militant groups that had supported the India-Sri Lanka Agreement 1987. Moreover, the LTTE remained unrepentant for carrying out the assassination of Rajiv Gandhi in 1991 and remained a proscribed organisation in India. Its attitude to India remained unpredictable, and India did not trust it.

10. A study titled 'Regional Economic Cooperation and Connectivity is South and South-West Asia: Potential and Challenges' edited by Dr. Saman Kelegama, Executive Director, Institute of Policy Studies of Sri Lanka and released by the UN-ESCAP in September 2012 shows that the India-Sri Lanka Free Trade Agreement (ISFTA) has helped narrow the trade gap between the two countries in favour of Sri Lanka while attracting more Indian investments into the country. It said "An FTA in the region that has experienced significant benefits of trade creation for both parties involved is the FTA between India and Sri Lanka, which was an early experiment towards regional economic integration in South Asia...which provides useful lessons for other South Asian economies in terms of the progress in strengthening trade and economic linkages." According to the study over 70 per cent of Sri Lanka's exports have been undertaken within the framework of FTA preferences, compared to around 30 per cent of India's exports. On the other hand, only around 14 per cent of Sri Lanka's imports from India have been under the FTA. Therefore, the FTA has assisted in narrowing the trade gap between the two countries in favour of Sri Lanka and has contributed towards more equitable and balanced growth of bilateral trade. [Oct. 17, 2012 'FTA with India further narrowed the trade gap of Sri Lanka-Study' www.island.lk]

11. Support for Tamil Eelam died down in Tamil Nadu after the LTTE's assassination in 1991 of Rajiv Gandhi, India's former Prime Minister. However, public indignation over the plight of Tamils in Sri Lanka during the Eelam War and allegations of atrocities on them came in handy for Ms Jayalalithaa of AIADMK party to espouse the Tamil Eelam cause during the parliamentary poll in 2009. When she became chief minister of Tamil Nadu, she demanded imposition of trade sanctions against Sri Lanka and UN inquiry into allegations of war crimes. Smarting under the electoral debacle in Tamil Nadu assembly polls in 2010, her bête noir Karunanidhi, leader of DMK, has revived of the defunct Tamil Eelam Supporters Organization (TESO) he had formed in 1986 to pursue the Tamil Eelam agenda. Their support to the separatist cause legitimizes it and provides political space to pro-LTTE fringe parties in Tamil Nadu that deify Prabhakaran. If the DMK seriously activates TESO, its link-up with Transnational Government of Tamil Eelam (TGTE), an organisation of LTTE members and supporters overseas, would become a reality. This increases the risk of Tamil Nadu becoming a hothouse of Tamil extremism, with serious implications for national security. Already, Sri Lanka is seriously concerned at these developments. It would also stoke sentiments inimical to Indian interests in Sri Lanka. [R Hariharan 'While building economic linkages, also bridge ethnic divide' Indian Journal of Foreign Affairs, April–July 2012.]

SAARC: Emerging Security Challenges and Need for Strategic Initiatives in the Indian Ocean

Mohammed Khalid

ABSTRACT: The South Asian Association for Regional Cooperation (SAARC) was founded in 1985 at Dhaka on the basis of respect for sovereignty, territorial integrity, political equality and independence of all member states. Its member states viz., Afghanistan, Bangladesh, Bhutan, India, the Maldives, Nepal, Pakistan and Sri Lanka have committed themselves to 16 areas of cooperation. From Dhaka in 1985 to Thimpu Summit in 2010 SAARC has issued 16 Summit declarations. Its members have signed many agreements and conventions so far. Incidentally these efforts have not made SAARC a strong regional organisation like for example ASEAN. After the end of Cold-War new security challenges have emerged in the Indian Ocean region which threatens trade and commerce of SAARC countries. However, all these years, it has ignored or paid less attention to the rising security challenges which emanate from the Indian Ocean. SAARC countries have not devised any collective mechanism to fight sea piracy, norco-terrorism, drug trafficking, security of Sea Lines of Communications (SLOCS) or surveillance of Ocean around their 11,129 km long coastline. The paper looks at these problems and possible strategic initiatives by sea-facing SAARC countries.

The South Asian Association for Regional Cooperation (SAARC) was founded in December 1985 dedicated to economic, technological, social, and cultural development and emphasising on collective self-reliance of South Asian nations. The Organisation based itself on the respect for sovereignty, territorial integrity, political equality and independence of all members states; non-interference in the internal matters; cooperation for mutual benefit; take all decisions unanimously; keep aside all bilateral issues and discusse multilateral (involving many countries) concerns. Its eight member states *viz.,* Afghanistan, Bangladesh, Bhutan, India, the Maldives, Nepal, Pakistan and Sri Lanka, have committed themselves to 16 areas of cooperation such as agriculture, biotechnology, culture, energy, environment, economy and trade, finance, funding mechanism, human resource development, poverty alleviation, people to people contact, security aspects, social development, science and technology; communications and tourism.[1]

Defined objectives of SAARC include to promote the welfare of the people of South Asia and to improve their quality of life; to accelerate economic growth, social progress and cultural development in the region and to provide all individuals the opportunity to live in dignity and to realize their full potential; to promote and strengthen selective self-reliance among the countries of South Asia; to contribute to mutual trust, understanding and appreciation of one another's problems; to promote active collaboration and mutual assistance in the economic, social, cultural, technical and scientific fields; to strengthen cooperation with other developing countries; to strengthen cooperation among them in international forums on matters of common interest; and to cooperate with international and regional organisations with similar aims and purposes.

In order to promote cooperation SAARC countries have devised a four tier system. At the summit level there are head of states and governments and there have been 17 Summit declarations so far from Dhaka in 1985 to Addu in 2011. The summit declarations project the overall policies of SAARC showing commitment to the need for regional integration and cooperation in different fields included in its Charter.[2]

Its Charter committees include Council of Minsiters (CoM) comprising of the Foreign Ministers of the Member States to formulate the policies of the Association and review progress of cooperation under SAARC. The Standing Committee, comprising of the Foreign Secretaries of the SAARC Member States, has been created to take measures/decisions relating to overall monitoring and coordination of programme under different areas; approve projects and programmes, including modalities of their financing; determine inter-sectoral priorities; mobilise regional and external resources; and identify new areas of cooperation. It has Technical Committees comprising representatives of Member States, to implement, coordinate and monitor the programmes in respective areas of cooperation. Technical Committees work on their respective areas to provide support to SAARC activities include Technical Committee on Agriculture and Rural Development, Technical Committee on Health and Population Activities, Technical Committee on Women, Youth and Children, Technical Committee on Science and Technology, Technical Committee on Transport, and Technical Committee on Environment.[3]

To assist the Standing Committee, a Programming Committee was set up in December 1985 to select regional projects, including their location, cost-sharing modalities among the Member States, and mobilisation of external resources etc. SAARC has also developed other mechanisms for cooperation on Agriculture and Rural Development; Research-Extension–Farmer Linkages; Social Development; Trafficking and Child Welfare; on HIV and AIDS; Energy Renwable Energy; Technology Transfer and Knowledge sharing. SAARC has set up regional centers such as SAARC Agricultural Centre (SAC), Dhaka; SAARC Meteorological Research Centre (SMRC), Dhaka; SAARC Tuberculosis Centre (STC), Kathmandu; SAARC Documentation Centre (SDC), New Delhi; SAARC Human Resources Development Centre (SHRDC), Islamabad; SAARC Coastal Zone Management Centre (SCZMC), Maldives; SAARC Information Centre (SIC), Nepal; SAARC Energy Centre (SEC), Pakistan; SAARC Disaster Management Centre (SDMC), New Delhi; SAARC Forestry Centre (SFC), Thimpu; SAARC Cultural Centre (SCC), Sri Lanka.[4]

Its Ministerial Declarations include Rawalpindi Resolution on Children of South Asia, August 1996; New Delhi Declaration of Environment Ministers, April, 1997; Declaration of Commerce Ministers, May 1998; Common Position on Climate Change, November 1998; Colombo Declaration on a Common Environment Programme; Colombo Statement on Children of South Asia; Islamabad Declaration on Health, 2005; Ministerial Declaration on Global Economic Crisis, and Declaration on Cooperation in Combating Terrorism, February 2009.

SAARC countries have signed agreements to fulfill its Charter obligations. Important agreements they have signed so far include: Agreement on south Asian Free Trade Area (SAFTA); Agreement for establishment of SAARC Arbitration Council; Final Agreement on Avoidance of Double Taxation; Final Agreement on Customs Matters; Agreement on establishing the SAARC food bank; Charter of South Asian Development Fund (SDF); and Agreement on the Establishment of South Asian Regional Standards Organisation (SARSO).

SAARC Conventions held so far include SAARC Regional Convention on Suppression of Terrorism of November 1987; SAARC Convention on Narcotics Drugs of November 1990; Convention on Promotion of Welfare of Children and Convention on Combating and Prevention of Trafficking in Women and Children for Prostitution of January 2002; Additional Protocol on Terrorism, Jan 2004 Convention on Mutual Assistance on Criminal Matters of August 2008.[5]

SAARC Charter, its 17 Summit meetings, declarations, agreements and conventions prima facie give a very glorious picture of emerging cooperation among the member states in different fields. Still many feel that SAARC is not a vibrant regional organisation like for example ASEAN. It is argued that smaller countries in the region feel insecure because India is too large and is clearly the big brother. India-Pakistan relations, or rather tensions are main trouble for SAARC to grow as a strong organization. At Thimpu Summit in 2010 SAARC leaders admitted a collective failure to develop their conflict-ridden region and to forge a united front against the threats of climate change and terrorism.[6]

Prime Minister of Bhutan Jigme Thinley in his address, said, "... Saarc's journey has not been one of outstanding success" and "We are losing focus. He further said that the squabbles and tensions between the bloc's member-states had prevented implementation of its numerous, but ultimately toothless, commitments to change. Concluding his address he warned that "Fractious and quarrelsome neighbours do not make a prosperous community."

Tensions in Indo-Pakistan relations are also cited as the reasons for SAARC's failure along with other geographical, ethnic, historical and political factors that have gridlocked SAARC. Overawing geographical presence of India, differences in political systems, historical differences, pangs of bloody partition of British India, which has left unresolved partition disputes and problems of ethnic Indian minority communities in Sri Lanka, are only some of the problems in the way of integration of SAARC countries.

Apart from the commonly known and discussed failures of SAARC, my contention is that SAARC has not shown the dynamism to live up to the fast changing regional and global situation. The organisation was created in 1985 when the Cold War was on its last legs. After the Cold War, the world in general and South Asia in particular face a new set of security challenges.

South Asia's strategic location in the middle of Southeast, Central and West Asia, and at the centre of the Indian Ocean, leaves it open to face many security challenges. For example, of eight SAARC countries, five *i.e.,* Pakistan, India, Maldives, Sri Lanka and Bangladesh are either on the Indian Ocean littoral or islands. Total estimated coastline of SAARC countries comes to about 11,129 km. This includes 1,050 km coastline of Pakistan, 7517 km of India, (including 6100 km of Indian mainland) 644 km. of Maldives, 1,340 km of Sri Lanka and 580 km of Bangladesh.

Continental shelf of these countries averages 200 km in the Ocean. Apart from the coast they have their respective Exclusive Economic Zone (EEZ), over which each state has special rights of exploration and use of marine resources, including production of energy from water and wind.[7]

The number of pirate attacks worldwide has tripled in the past decade, and sea piracy is becoming a key tactic of terrorist groups. To monitor and protect their territorial waters, Pakistan, India, Maldives, Sri Lanka and Bangladesh have created their respective Coast Guards but have not made any effort to devise a common startegy to protect their coasts or other economic interests in the surrounding waters.

Indian Ocean is life line for the SAARC countries but in it 17 Summit Declarations there is not a single reference to it. There is no agreement there about creation of a common military strategy, or force or common surveillance or sharing information with each other in order to secure their maritime boundaries. Neglecting such an important issue has caused a maritime disorder and incidents like 26/11 in Mumbai. In our neighbourhood, the countries of Pacific Rim initiated The North Pacific Coast Guard Agencies Forum (NPCGF) in 2000 to foster multilateral cooperation through the sharing of information on matters related to combined operations, exchange of information, illegal drug trafficking, maritime security, fisheries enforcement, illegal migration, and maritime domain awareness.[8] SAARC countries need to take initiatives to chalk out common strategies to secure their water fronts.

Around 90 percent of the world's trade is carried out through the oceans. Among the SAARC nations, 96 percent of Pakistan's trade is seaborne. India has very limited trade with its neighbours by land and about ninety percent of its trade is by sea. More than 80 percent of Bangladesh, the entire trade of Maldives and Sri Lanka is dependent on the waves of the Indian Ocean. Substantial amount of Nepalese and Bhutanese trade depends on sea which is carried through the Kolkata, Haldia ports. Despite our overwhelming dependence on sea SAARC has not devised any collective measures to protect our trading ships in our maritime boundaries. This initiative is long overdue and should be redressed at the earliest.

In the post Cold War era many countries liberalised their economies resulting into huge economic growth resulting in increase in trade and commerce. This brought into prominence the importance of Sea Lines of Communications (SLOCs) in the Indian Ocean. SLOCS are important to the countries of South Asia due to dependence of their trade on sea and this would be further increased in the coming years. The security of SLOC is now one of the priorities in the strategic thinking and policy making for the trading nations. Some of the most critical sea lanes connecting the oil rich Middle East, to East Asia have become highways of international trade and they pass through the vicinity of South Asia. Passing through the Gulf of Harmuz and Sea of Oman, Lakshadweep Sea, and the Andaman Sea, these SLOCS have become life lines for the nations. Without ensuring the security of SLOCs no SAARC country can dream of the safety of their trading ships. All the SAARC countries heavily import oil from different countries of Middle East and thus dependent on trouble free supplies. In all its deliberations during the last 26 years since 1985, SAARC has not discussed any collective initiative to protect these SLOCS. This initiative needs an urgent attention especially by India, a burgeoning economy of 21st century.[9]

Piracy in the Indian Ocean has become the greatest threat to the movement of maritime traffic. Threat perception is very high where the ships have to criss-cross through the narrow straits. South Asia has two major choke points—the Strait of Hormuz, and the Strait of Malacca—near its borders. Pakistan's port of Gwadar is just 400 km from the Strait of Hormuz and Malacca Straits lie near India's Andaman Islands. Rising from the lawless coast of Somalia, the pirates prowl the Arabian Sea and have attacked ships more than 1,500 nautical miles (2778 km) from Somali coast. Using increasingly sophisticated weapons, tactics and planning, pirates operate as far east as Maldives in good weather. Piracy threat emerged in the late 1980s and nearly 2700 piracy related incidents have been recorded since 1984 which occurred mostly in territorial waters while ships were at anchor or berthed. Pirates have attacked or hijacked hundred of ships in the Arabian Sea including super tankers for ransom. Rising pirate attacks have led to a 12–15 per cent rise in insurance premiums and a hike from $500 to $20,000 of the special risk insurance for each ship passing through the Gulf of Aden. In the days of growing trade and commerce, this menace needs to be tackled collectively. Of the SAARC countries, India and Maldives are most affected by pirates. India has large presence in the shipping industry in the world. India and Pakistan have deployed their naval ships in the Arabian Sea and Gulf of Aden. SAARC as an organisation has least discussed about the need for a collective initiative in this regard.[10]

Sea Terrorism was not given much importance in the 1980s. The enormity of its threat became clear in the 1990s, as there was a sudden rush in the number of sea attacks. Such attacks are more devastating in the ports when most crews of cargo ships are unarmed and defenseless to an armed attack. In such attacks, the disabling of a ship at port is enough to halt all activity at that port for some time, especially if the disabled ship is blocking the movement for other vessels. Such an attack has disastrous economic impact. In 2000, attack on the American Naval Warship, USS Cole in the Port of Aden stunned the world in which Seventeen American sailors were killed, and 39 were injured.[11] Sri Lankan Tamil mercenaries attacked Maldives in 1988, overpowered the Maldivian Militia and attacked the President's residence. SAARC countries have about 20 major ports which include Karachi, Chennai, Cochin, Kolkata, Mumbai, Port Blair, Visakhapatnam, Chittagong, Mongla, and Colombo. Although there are many government sponsored agencies involved with port security in each country, but a collective protection shield to secure ports can also be considered at the SAARC level.

Surveillance of ocean is another important initiative which needs a serious consideration by SAARC. India being technologically competent can take the lead in this direction. With the support and cooperation of other SAARC countries India can launch intelligence satellite intended to keep an eye on ship movements in the waters around South Asian coast. Data collected from an ocean surveillance system can be immediately relayed to member states if an unusual ships movement is detected. Satellite ocean surveillance can be effectively used to strengthen security of seas around. Setting up monitoring stations around the coastal areas of South Asia is another option to keep watch on ship movement. In fact India has already started this process by setting up high-tech monitoring station in northern Madagascar to tackle piracy and terrorism.[12] For this purpose, Astola Island, which is Pakistan's largest offshore island and the only significant offshore island in the northern Arabian Sea, can be used for surveillance of pirate and terrorist activities in the sea of Oman and Gulf of Harmuz. Similarly Churna Island off the Karachi Harbour, used as a firing range by Pakistan Navy, can be used for this purpose. Indian islands of Diu, Lakshadweep, and Andaman islands can be equipped with monitoring devices to check activities of pirates in the North Bay of Bengal or Malacca Straits. In Sri Lanka Analativu a small island off the coast of Jaffna Peninsula, Talaimannar, the northern tip of Mannar Island and Dondra—southern most tip of the countries can provide strategic surveillance stations. India and Sri Lanka can take the initiative to set up surveillance stations at these places.

Spread of small arms and their illicit trafficking is not a new phenomenon in itself, but has attained a new dimension with the end of the Cold War.

There is strong funding link between terrorist groups and drug trafficking. Waters of the Indian Ocean surrounding South Asian sub-continent have been frequently used for this purpose. SAARC countries are particularly affected because the region is infested with all kind of terrorist groups. There are a number of terrorist groups active in India. Pakistan has many domestic and trans-national terrorist outfits which are a big threat not only for Pakistan but also for the neihbouring India. Bangladesh, Nepal and Sri Lanka also have active terrorist groups in their respective countries. These outfits use sea routes clandestinely to import small arms to carry out their activities.[13] The two largest opium producing countries in the world—Myanmar and Afghanistan—are either part of SAARC or in its vicinity. The main drug of interest to transnational criminal groups in the Indian Ocean Region is heroin, cultivated in two main areas referred to as—the 'Golden Triangle' and the 'Golden Crescent'. Drugs and the money accruing from this illegal trade are often laundered through illegal means. This contraband is sent to other parts of the world using drug mules, fishing boats, container ships etc. SAARC has addressed to this problem in its various summit declarations but has not so far developed any collective mechanism to stem the ocean routes used for drug and arm trafficking. SAARC has not taken any tangible initiative to check this nexus. This initiative is need of the time.

Map 1

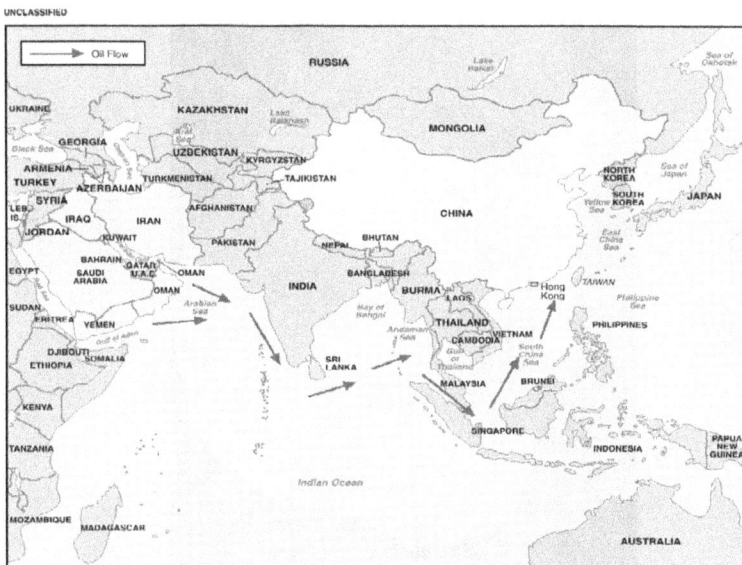

Critical Sea Lines of Communication near South Asia

Map 2

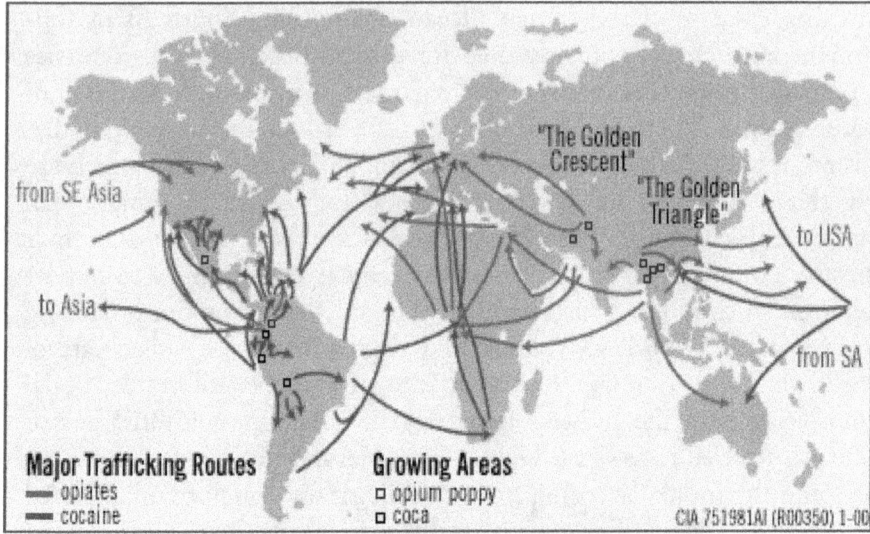

International Drug Trafficking Routes.

Map 3

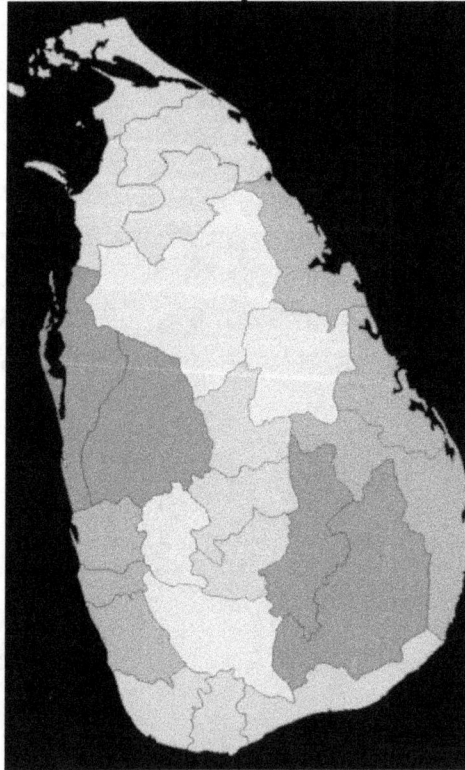

Sri Lanka

Map 4

Map 5

Map 6

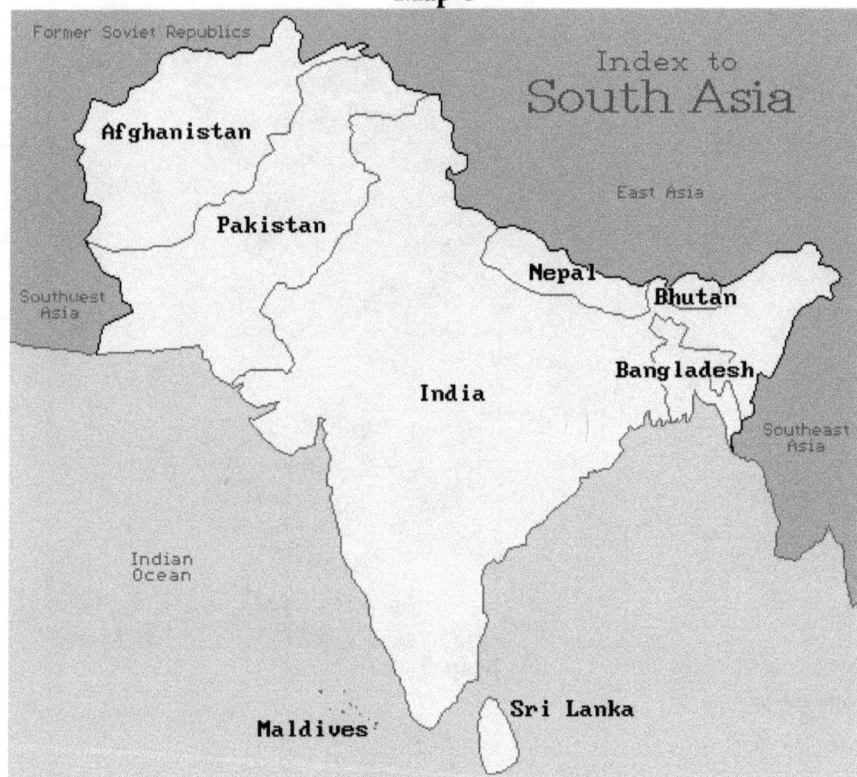

SAARC Countries

CONCLUSION

Indian Ocean, the third largest Ocean in the world is inextricably interwoven with and has huge and growing strategic significance for South Asia. Their history, economies and security is greatly dependent on the Indian Ocean. To develop cooperation among them countries of South Asia formed SAARC with some determined areas of cooperation. They signed many agreements and conventions forging collaboration in different fields. Due to internal contradictions SAARC has failed to become a vibrant organization. It has not lived up to the changing geopolitical environment in the Indian Ocean. With the rising spate of terrorist activities around the Indian Ocean and growing menace of sea piracy a new set of security threats is looming on South Asia. SAARC as an organization has not addressed the issue of these threats. There is need to counter the terrorists and pirates collectively. Security of ports, trading ships and Sea Lines of Communications is equally important for economic development of South

Asian nations. As the region is close to the 'golden triangle' and the 'golden crescent', they need to cooperate to fight against the drug-arms nexus. Sharing strategic information and setting up surveillance posts are some of the initiatives which are highly required by SAARC to secure the waters around South Asia. India and Sri Lanka, two maritime nations can lead to take these initiatives.

REFERENCES

[1] For areas of cooperation, see, official website of SAARC at, http://www.saarc-sec.org/SAARC-Charter/5/#

[2] For Summit declarations, see, http://www.saarc-sec.org/Summit-Declarations/67/

[3] Upreti, Bhuwan Chandra (2000): SAARC: Areas and dimensions of cooperation, Delhi, Kalinga Publications, p. 9; Kashikar, Mohan (2000): SAARC: its genesis, development and prospects, Mumbai, Himalaya Pub. House. p. 5, 56, 64.

[4] Ibid.

[5] See, official website of SAARC, op., cit

[6] "Saarc leaders admit to collective failure", Gulf Times, April 29, 2010; also see, The Nation, April 29, 2010.

[7] For geography of the Indian Ocean see, Ferenc A Váli (1976): Politics of the Indian Ocean region: the balances of power, Free Press, p. 25

[8] "North Pacific Coast Guard Forum NPCGF—What Is It?", see, Canadian Coast Guard, available at, http://www.ccg-gcc.gc.ca/e0007869

[9] Ye Hailin, "Securing SLOCs by Cooperation—China's Perspective of Maritime S Security in the Indian Ocean", International Maritime Conference 3, National Maritime Policy Research Center, Bahria University Karachi, Pakistan, March 2009; Ji Guoxing, "SLOC Security in the Asia Pacific", Center occasional paper Asia-pacific center for security studies, Honolulu, Hawaii, February 2000

[10] Anna Bowden *et al.*, "The Economic Cost of Maritime Piracy", One Earth Future Working Paper, December 2010, available at, http://oceansbeyondpiracy.org/sites/default/files/documents_old/The_Economic_Cost_of_Piracy_Full_Report.pdf

[11] "Terrorist Attack on USS Cole: Background and Issues for Congress", CRS Report for Congress, Congressional Research Service, The Library of Congress, available at, news.findlaw.com/cnn/docs/crs/coleterrattck13001.pdf

[12] "India activates first listening post on foreign soil: radars in Madagascar", The Indian Express, July 17, 2007.

[13] Aparajita Biswas, "Small Arms and Drug Trafficking in the Indian Ocean egion", Working Paper: No. 4, Centre for African Studies, University of Mumbai.

Bilateral Ties between India and Sri Lanka: Strategic and Security Implications

Ali Yasir

India's policy towards the ethnic conflict in Sri Lanka has shifted from a policy of active involvement in the 1980s to a hands-off policy after the assassination of Rajiv Gandhi. In the post LTTE era, the bilateral ties between India and Sri Lanka are suffering from stagnation. The aggressive stance of Tamil leaders against Sri Lanka, attacks on the Sri Lankan citizens irrespective of their background in different parts of Tamil Nadu does not augur well with the bilateral relations between the two countries along with future of Tamils in the island. Moreover, Colombo's overtures vis-à-vis Pakistan and China has Indian security establishment worried.

In the quest of a new paradigm to define the security and bilateral ties with Colombo, India has been trying to balance the aspirations of regional Dravidian parties, keeping up the international pressure on the Sri Lankan government to do justice with the minority Tamil group and devolve power as per the accord with India and maintaining an equitable, balanced relations with its southern neighbour.

The paper seeks to study worry among the Indian establishment as China continues to make significant inroads into Sri Lanka by financing a slew of infrastructure and developmental projects. Sri Lanka is also engaging with China and Pakistan in military participation. There are speculations that China is using its economic and development presence in Sri Lanka to gain intelligence gathering capabilities against India and Pakistan is recruiting Sri Lankan Tamil refugees who have returned to the island nation after the end of the Eelam war to spy on India. Against the background of growing Chinese economic muscle in Sri Lanka, India's economic and trade relations with Sri Lanka are also not picking up as per their potential.

In this paper I propose to highlight that state and Centre views contradict in most of the occasions when it comes to dealing with Sri Lanka. While

India should constantly express its concerns on human rights violations and plight of the Tamil people in Sri Lanka at international forum, it should not allow these issues to affect bilateral engagement.

THE OPENING ARGUMENT

A bus carrying pilgrims, some of them from Sri Lanka, was stoned by local residents in Tamil Nadu. In another incident Tamil Nadu chief minister J Jayalalithaa suspended a civil servant for permitting a soccer team from a Sri Lankan school to play in a match in a government stadium in Chennai. The action against the official came close on the heels of the Chief Minister demanding suspension of joint military exercises with Sri Lanka.

These are some of the recent incidents that warrant our attention when we come across suggestions in the media that bilateral relations between India and Sri Lanka have reached a stage of stagnation. But this is not the aim of this paper. Through the scope of this paper I would like to discuss India's relations with Sri Lanka with the beginning of ethnic conflict in the island state, India's interventions and the factors that led to India, being the regional superpower, adopting a policy of strict non-interventionism.

The paper would then focus how in the present scenario Sri Lanka is vital to India's geo-strategic ambitions and interests and how countries with which New Delhi has long-standing issues—with a special study of China—are harbouring the Island nation as a close ally. I would also discuss the implications of these developments in the course of strategic as well as security implications for India and the domestic political compulsions that have played an important role in shaping both India and Sri Lanka's policy towards each other.

As B. Raman, one of India's best known experts on intelligence, noted that if the Dravidian parties do not conduct themselves with a sense of balance and responsibility and "indulge in competitive exploitation of the discontent in certain sections of the population over Sri Lanka-related issues, they may end up creating passions beyond control in both countries". This becomes even more pertinent with the parliamentary elections approaching in 2014. (Raman 2012)

While Colombo seems least interested in seeking India's advice on devolution of power—financial and administrative—to the provinces, the least India could afford is a backlash against the Sinhala tourists on its land.

The government of India must find a way out to remove these irritants as it cannot intervene directly in such matters as constitutionally, law and order is a state subject. However, it is high time that India should free its foreign policy towards Sri Lanka of its domestic political compulsions since both China and Pakistan have been harbouring Lanka as strong economic, military and political ally. As Raman suggests, India does not have much of a card for coercive diplomacy against Colombo.

There is no denying the seriousness in Indian establishment regarding its policy towards Lanka but then it's time that some out of the box solutions should be manufactured to re-invent and re-invigorate the ties between the two neighbours. New Delhi's ambition to grow politically and capture a seat on the global high table goes through the sinews of its political, economic and diplomatic muscle in its immediate neighbourhood.

THE CONFLICTS IN SRI LANKA: POLITICS OF DOMESTIC COMPULSIONS

The compulsions of domestic politics have played a significant role in deciding the direction of bilateral relations between India and Sri Lanka. It is especially true with India as with the advent of coalition politics the smaller regional parties had been seen to arm-twist the national parties into following and formulating policies on key security issues to suit their electoral interests. It was most evident in the 1980s when Tamil parties used their numbers in parliament as leverage to move the direction of Indian foreign policy on Sri Lankan conflict to suit their interests.

Most recently, this was manifested in the objections raised to the training of Sri Lankan personnel in India and the protests that marked the October 2012 by Sri Lankan president Mahinda Rajapaksa to India.

It was not very different in the case of Sri Lanka where successive governments ignored genuine concerns of the Tamil minority to appease the majority Sinhalese and by inept handling turned into a 'us versus them' debate. Not only the Tamils were not given participation in the power politics but also denied their share in the educational, economic and social development of the country. This majoritarian view of the society by the Lankan political parties helped fuelled mistrust towards India and attempts by Indian governments to broker a peace formula among the warring groups.

The complex bond between India and its neighbour on the southern-most tip has been characterized by the compulsion of one to ensure peace in its immediate neighbour and the other's fear of the perceived hegemonic aspirations of the big brother and its close linkages with the most vocal ethnic minority among its population.

Taking into account available myths and folklore, it has been established by scholars that Sri Lanka's Sinhalese and Tamils are of Indian provenance (Foweracker 1995; Tarrow 1994). It is only natural that Tamils living in southern India have a close affinity to the lot of their brethren across the Palk straits. And this is true for other populations in India living in border regions who share common ethnic bonds with adjacent countries. Just like Tamils in Sri Lanka, Muslims in Kashmir, Punjabis with their cousins in Pakistan, people living in the border region of Terai of Nepal and even Keralites' ties to those living in Gulf countries. The broad territorial division of ethnic groups within India and the strength of regional ethnic identities ensure that Indian policy towards the countries in question is often attentive to the preferences of domestic actors in these regions, as with Sri Lanka, where at one time the Indian government acquiesced in the armed tactics of the Liberation Tigers of Tamil Eelam (LTTE) (Dixit 1998).

These domestic factors are largely responsible for what is believed to be a reactive approach to international issues and related domestic subjects.

1983 RIOTS IN LANKA: EARLY INTERVENTION BY INDIA

Ethnic violence in 1983 in Sri Lanka became one of the turning points in bilateral relations between the two countries. The riots that broke out in July 1983 between the Tamils on the Island and the Sinhala community proved a watershed in the Tamil-Sinhalese relations on the Island. The riots followed the Lankan economy's transition into an open market economy, which vastly helped the entrepreneurial Tamils.

The Indian connection was yet again evident. India connection at again evident the open market reforms allowed a large number of Tamils to utilize their ethnic and business connections with Indians and become upwardly mobile. Thus, if the pre-1977 era saw Sinhalese heavy and small industrialists, shopkeepers and traders utilize their ethnic identity to procure quotas, licenses and general access to scarce resources, the open market reforms allowed the Tamils to become successful traders and industrialists in their own right. The subsequent prosperity catapulted previously lumpen Tamil groups into the middle and upper class strata while their Sinhalese counterparts, unable to compete with the cheap and superior imports inundating the marketplace, became stripped of their status as "captains of the industry (Gunasinghe 1984).

A complete institutional breakdown marked rampant violence against Tamils, which in many cases was allegedly abetted by the government machinery. The meek response by the administration further fuelled speculation of the government being complicit with the rioters, who looted to inflict maximum damage on the Tamil entrepreneurial class. President JR Jayawardene did not impose curfew and addressed the nation until three days after the riots. Back home in India, it was a major diplomatic challenge for the Indira Gandhi government. Not only the government had to reach out to the battered Tamil community in Sri Lanka but it also had to ensure that its efforts were not construed as intervention in its internal affairs by the Jayawardene government.

Another major concern for India was to see to it that the situation does not escalate to a level where it attracts intervention by any other power. It was particularly important in view of media reports that Sri Lanka had sought military assistance from the US, Britain and Pakistan.

Mrs Gandhi sent her foreign minister, PV Narasimha Rao, to Sri Lanka and later told Indian Parliament that New Delhi does not want to interfere in Lanka's internal affairs but would extend its good offices to broker peace between the two warring groups. She also warned that involvement of any third power could further complicate matters for the two countries (Rao 1988). The speech stirred feverish activity and both the Sri Lankan and the Tamil United Liberation Front (TULF) gave enough assurances to Indian government that they were ready to talk peace. Both promised to cede ground on each others' demands. Mrs Gandhi entrusted Gopalaswamy Parathasarthy with preparing a framework for negotiated settlement of the ethnic conflict. Despite, its reservations and the continued mistrust of its neighbour's intentions, the Sri Lankan government agreed to talk to the TULF over the framework provided by India because its plans to rope in international assistance to quell Indian efforts to gain an upper hand in its affairs fell flat on their face. President Jayawardene was frustrated in his efforts to reach out to the US and the UK as New Delhi moved quickly to tell these powers that any attempts to meddle in Sri Lankan affairs would be viewed seriously. However, the All Party Conference in 1984, bilateral relations deteriorated further with Sri Lanka accusing India of harbouring and training Tamil militants.

India's intervention in the post-riot situation was, however, not solely guided by the Congress government's bid to forge an electoral alliance with Tamil Nadu regional parties but also the geopolitical fallout of the crisis. India could not have allowed involvement of a foreign power as it had far reaching security implications for New Delhi.

THE INDIA FACTOR

For long India had been painted black by the Sri Lankan media for being the intruder in its internal affairs and backing insurgency but since 1987 New Delhi has maintained a strict non-interference in the Sri Lankan affairs. The policy became more pronounced after the assassination of former Prime Minister Rajiv Gandhi by the LTTE militants. It did not even discourage Sri Lanka from seeking weapons from even Pakistan and China, *vis-à-vis* which India does have a security concern, leave alone strategic information and intelligence-sharing by security agencies on either side, which did play a role in defeating the LTTE that is acknowledged by Sri Lankan officials in private discussions (Behuria 2012: 742–743).

India invested US\$ 110 million in foreign direct investment in Sri Lanka in 2010—the biggest for the country in order to further deepen and strengthen bilateral ties. But despite its strict non-interference policy and such generous economic overtures, the mistrust did not allow signing of a comprehensive economic partnership agreement (CEPA). There is an unfounded suspicion that such agreements are backed by forces in Sri Lanka who are either funded by India or external agencies, and thus will hurt national interests of Sri Lanka. Close interaction with people associated with the Rajapaksa government reveals that there is an invisible competition for influence going on in Sri Lanka between the so-called anglicised elite—being increasingly dismissed as a relic of the colonial past, having questionable links with foreign forces and guided more by their narrow self interest than national interest and crowding the think tanks and academic institutions—and a more rooted, native and nationalistic counter-elite, which has come to fore with the rise of Rajapaksa, may be actively patronised by him and organically linked to his philosophy, as brought out in the *Mahinda chintana* (Behuria 2012: 742–743).

This political constituency believes that India has a vested interest in Sri Lanka and does not want to let the past bogey disintegrate. As long as the incumbent government handles this segment and realizes that take away for Sri Lanka in the event of non-friendly ties with India is only problems, the building of mutual trust would remain a challenging task to achieve.

THE IPKF EXPERIENCE

The induction of the Indian Peace Keeping Force (IPKF) was made through an agreement between Sri Lanka and India on July 29, 1987. Strangely enough, the deployment started the very next day. It would not be hard to comprehend that long drawn discussions and already been done beforehand and the signing of the agreement provided a mere ratification of the decision to send Indian armed forces into the Lankan conflict zone.

India's policy towards the ethnic crisis in Sri Lanka had been conceived within an operating framework that was delicately poised between denying absolute victory to the Sinhala-dominated Sri Lankan government while, simultaneously, obstructing the establishment of a Tamil Eelam. India's dual purpose was to stop or reverse the ingress of Sri Lankan Tamil refugees into Tamil–Nadu, but also to establish a cordon sanitaire around India's southern security perimeter. Preserving Sri Lanka's unity and integrity was believed to be imperative; otherwise, the emergence of two economically weak, vulnerable states would create the objective conditions wherein external powers that could be inimical to India might establish a presence in Sri Lanka (Chari 1994:2).

To ascribe certain legitimacy to the deployment of India troops in Sri Lanka, Indian officials cited "request by Sri Lanka." However, former national security adviser JN Dixit had explained very clearly that the move was "to counter the Sri Lankan government which had started looking for external support to counter Tamil militancy, which would have had security implications for us" (Dixit 1998).

It was explained by both governments that the role of Indian troops would be to maintain peace and ensure the political transition of the Tamil rebels and help efforts to rehabilitate those who had given up arms as well as the local Tamils. But soon after the LTTE disassociated itself from the agreement on the grounds that the problems of the affected people have not been taken care of in the agreement, the peacekeeping role of Indian soldiers became irrelevant. This led to confrontation and LTTE rebels started hindering the IPKF bid to restore administration in northern and eastern provinces. The October 1987 cyanide incident in which 17 LTTE militants committed suicide after being captured by the IPKF exemplified the complete breach in relations.

Among the many successes of the IPKF in Sri Lanka were creating the ground for political transformation in the Tamil majority areas, it ensured a free and fair presidential and parliamentary elections in Sri Lanka the following year of its deployment in the Island nation and the troops helped immensely in providing relief and rehabilitation to the displace Tamils. The IPKF's military task was to disarm the LTTE. Despite their dispersal from Jaffna, the LTTE was able to continue their armed struggle from its jungle hideouts. The nature of the counter-insurgency operations had perforce to change from proceeding against an urban to a rural and forest-based guerrilla force that used terror tactics as a psychological weapon. The strength of the IPKF was augmented to meet these extended obligations and was estimated to have reached a total of around 1.5-lakh if paramilitary forces were also included (Chari 1994: 11).

Apart from the challenges of hostile terrain, language barrier and a complete lack of local intelligence, the IPKF had also been fighting the perceptory challenge of being recognized among local Tamil population, who considered LTTE as nationalists and freedom fighters, and the IPKF as an external force serving an imperialist purpose. Without local support the counter-insurgency operations soon became stale-mated.

Then there were problems from the command and the general lack of motivation to serve in Lanka. Field Marshal Manekshaw had observed, *"The Fighting Command had too many masters giving different orders and different assessments ..!.!. the insurgents were getting trained in India, were being supplied with large quantities of arms and equipment, money and moral support from Tamil Nadu. Surely, this could not but have a deleterious effect on their [troops] morale ..!.!. [they] had the feeling that the government of India was not certain as to what it wanted the IPKF to achieve."* (Chari 1994: 13)

In fact, the failure of IPKF in achieving the stated objectives of curbing the militancy and ensuring political transition of an ethnic conflict could be placed in the experiences of US in Vietnam and the USSR in Afghanistan. In all these cases, the regional power was drawn militarily into an ethnic conflict in a neighbouring state and that is why experts suggest that an early withdrawal could have averted the misadventure by Indian policymakers. It was evident in the case of Mukti Vahini in Bangladesh in which the failure of early withdrawal by Indian forces could have robbed the Mujib government of its legitimacy. Complaints of harassment, torture, and so on associated with all counter-insurgency operations world-wide became more strident against the IPKF, but this was only to be expected.

Despite the promulgation of skillful apologia, this ineluctable truth asserted itself in the IPKF experience in Sri Lanka. This didactic lesson has permeated into the collective Indian consciousness and seems to be guiding the current foreign policy elite. India's approaches to intraregional, tension-laden situations has become more circumspect, as apparent from Delhi's quiescence towards continuing LTTE intransigence in Sri Lanka, Pakistan's proxy war in Punjab and Kashmir, the unending flow of immigrants from Bangladesh, and the expulsion of settlers of Nepali origin from Bhutan into India. Despite the provocation contained in these situations, India has refrained from military activism, but has restricted its protests to the normal channels of diplomacy and interstate parlance (Chari 1994: 18).

THE OTHER SRI LANKA—INDIA RELATIONS: EARLY DAYS

As discussed earlier in this paper, India's problems were not just political pandering to the domestic players but geopolitical in nature. From the beginning, Indian intervention in the ethnic conflict in Sri Lanka was not only aimed at forging a lasting peace in its neighbourhood but also to deter any other power from intervening in issues that were raging in its backyard. To maintain its security deterrence it was imperative for India to have an iron grip on the Indian Ocean and any other global players would have used it to Indian disadvantage had it got to play a role in Sri Lankan affairs.

But Indian efforts did not deter Sri Lanka from seeking military aid from Western and non-Western nations. President Jayawardene reached out to the US, seeking military assistance to ramp up defence against Tamil insurgents but without any success. But apart from Israel that helped train Sri Lankan forces in counter-insurgency tactics, both Pakistan and China took this opportunity to help Sri Lanka, further strengthening Lanka's perceived Indian hegemony in the region. President Zia-ul Haq openly supported his Lankan counterpart Jayawardene's "war on terror". Apart from training, Pakistan supplied military hardware to Sri Lanka along with Beijing.

Sri Lanka had been talking about "decisive action" against Tamil insurgents as early as 1985. This despite the first ceasefire between the government and insurgents after Rajiv Gandhi took over the reins in India. The first ceasefire between the insurgents and the government was actually used by the Sri Lankan government to ramp up its defences against the rebels and recoup and re-strategise for the "decisive battle". After the failure of the

Thimpu Talks in 1985, the Unites States cut down aid to the Island nation and its insurgency-hit economy was in further doldrums.

CHINA—HAND-IN-GLOVE

"Asians don't go around teaching each other how to behave,' he said. 'There are ways we deal with each other—perhaps a quiet chat, but not wagging the finger."

This quote by Sri Lanka's foreign secretary Palitha Kohona, in an interview, sums up the game between two Asian giants that saw the decimation of Tamil rebels from the Sri Lankan territory. A massive military exercise that was able to root out the LTTE from Sri Lankan soil but often at a huge human cost.

However, this could not have been possible without the continued military, economic and diplomatic support of one neighbour, China, and the strict non-interference policy of India.

Not only China equipped and trained Lankan security forces to take on the Tamil rebels but it also invested in the Island nation without putting any conditionalities. The huge monetary aid to Sri Lanka was not subject to upholding of human rights or containment of alleged atrocities on Tamil rebels during the counter-insurgency operations. The civilians killed in the exercise were dismissed as collateral. Perhaps the account books of Chinese dollars did not have any such columns! The Western aid, to the contrary, had been curtailed various times to push Sri Lanka to find a negotiated settlement with the LTTE but Beijing's generosity did not know any such boundaries.

According to the Stockholm International Peace Research Institute, Chinese exports of conventional military equipment made up 52% of military transfers within the Asia-Pacific region between 2004 and 2008. Pakistan, Sri Lanka, and Bangladesh were the main beneficiaries which cannot be separated from Beijing's geostrategic role in the South Asia. Faced with this international Western pressure, Colombo saw the benefits of regionally aligning with Beijing, whose deep pockets held cash, weapons, a UN Security Council veto, and a common distaste for secessionist movements. The international legal norm of territorial integrity has been a cornerstone of Chinese foreign policy as Xianjiang, Tibet, and Taiwan each pose threats to Beijing. Chinese diplomatic, economic, and military support for Sri Lanka was pivotal in rapidly transforming the military between 2006 and 2009 (Parasram 2012: 13)

At the height of this operation against LTTE—one of the biggest counter-insurgency operations in the world—when the rebels were holed up in the "no-fire zone", it was only Beijing that supported Sri Lankan assertion that if they would cease fire at that moment it would push the battle against the rebels back by at least 30 years.

But diplomatically what China did was even unforeseen by the Sri Lankan government. Not only it embraced the Rajapaksa government, it also paved the way for the same "unconditional" support from its allies such as Pakistan and Iran. While Pakistan, despite its own set of huge militancy problems, supplied arms and trained Lankan soldiers, Iran offered oil at a concession. Apart from oil, Iran extended soft loans and invested over one billion dollars in Sri Lanka.

The effects of the generous largesse bestowed upon the Island nation earned China the epithet of "real superpower of the world which was helping Sri Lanka and its "beloved people's President" Mahinda Rajapakse to fight against the West (Alwis 2010:436). This is in stark contrast to India's image among the Sinhalese majority. Building upon the Rubber-Rice pact between Sri Lanka and China, Beijing and Hong Kong combined make up the second largest importer to Sri Lanka, behind India. Chinese companies have set up garment, leather, telecom and electronic manu-facturing facilities in Sri Lanka, with further investments expected through lucrative tax concessions being offered to Chinese entrepreneurs in the Special Export Processing Zone in Mirigama. All Chinese entrepreneurs who invest a minimum of US$25 million will be provided with a Sri Lankan passport in lieu of what has been termed a 'second home' passport (Naizer 2009).

On the verge of losing its trade preferences from the European Union, Sri Lanka got a huge relief from China which lent US$1.2 billion to the Island nation—this is about half of the amount of total foreign aid, US$2.2 billion received by Lanka in 2009 (Alwis 2010: 437). The money was given towards building railways, power plant, a port and an airport. A major chunk of these investments were made in projects in President Rajapaksa's constituency of Hambantota. For a country suspicious of Indian efforts to bring about lasting peace in the nation, Chinese help was nothing short of a godsend.

The vigorousness with which China had been nursing its relations with Sri Lanka could be gauged from the fact that within a period of five years, Beijing upped its aid to Lanka by five times. India also has to walk a tight rope, as unlike China, it has a large Tamil diaspora which is assertive and has gained enough political clout—especially in an era of coalition politics—to at least influence if not even dictate policy to New Delhi.

China has been long attracted by Sri Lanka's advantageous location in the centre of the Indian Ocean—a crucial international passageway for trade and oil transportation. The billion-dollar port and oil bunkering/storage facility Chinese engineers are now building in Hambantota, on Sri Lanka's southeast coast, is perceived to be the latest 'pearl' in China's strategy to control vital sea-lanes linking the Indian and Pacific oceans by assembling a 'string of pearls' in the form of listening posts, special naval arrangements and access to ports (Chellaney 2009).

China, along with India, has also received the rights to prospect for oil and gas in the Gulf of Mannar, in Sri Lanka's north-west. The 'semi-permanent presence' of the Chinese in Sri Lanka, notes a perturbed former RAW director, B. Raman, 'will bring them within monitoring distance of India's fast-breeder reactor complex at Kalpakam near Chennai, the Russian-aided Kudankulam nuclear power reactor complex in southern Tamil Nadu and India's space establishments in Kerala' (Raman 2008).

Diplomatically, harbouring as strong an ally as China in the United Nations has paid rich dividends to Sri Lanka. It was seen in May 2009 when the minnow on the global high table was able to turn on its head a Swiss resolution in the Security Council, backed by the UK and France, calling for an investigation of human rights violations by the Sri Lankan government, as well as the LTTE, during the war. With the help of China, India and Russia, Sri Lankan negotiators were able to achieve an unlikely victory against the western powers. While India maintains hands off approach on Tibet, Sri Lanka is a great votary of One China policy—endorsing Beijing's policy towards Taiwan and Tibet. When Sri Lanka helped China to get an observer status at SAARC, the move was reciprocated by China by supporting Sri Lankan demand for a similar status at the ASEAN.

For the past 25 years or so of the ethnic conflict in Sri Lanka, India's dominance within the South Asian region has been strong, extensive and unchallenged. But China's entry into the power game and its close liaisons with Sri Lanka has complicated matters for Indian strategicians of foreign policy. India shares a national border with China and has already weathered several disputes with regard to it, so it must tread particularly carefully when dealing with this neighbouring giant.

The US concerns in the region add another dimension to the strategic equation in Sri Lanka. The United States, engaged in a strategic partnership with India, does not only have to counter the rising Chinese influence in the region but is also eying the Trincomalee harbour—the fifth largest, all weather, non-tidal natural harbour in the world, with a 56 km shoreline making it most effective for fuel receipt, storage and supply—as a guarantee in case it could not be able to use the Karachi port. As per the 1987 Indo-Sri Lanka agreement, Trincomalee or any other port in Sri Lanka 'will not be made available for military use by any country in a manner prejudicial to India's interests'. India also ensured that Sri Lanka did not sign an accord with US, which would have allowed the US to use Sri Lankan ports and airspace.

The geo-strategic importance of Sri Lankan island could be gauged from the fact that it has emerged as one of the strongest pawn in the power game in Asia. India, China and the US are engaged in a game of one upmanship by offering a massive booty to the Lankans to gain a controlling stake in the Island nation. The US Pacific Command is currently providing training and equipment worth over US$100,000, to the Sri Lankan Army to support its de-mining efforts in the north (*News Line* 2009). In addition, the Pacific Command is funding the work of the United States Agency for International Development (USAID) to rebuild schools and hospitals in the east (*US Pacific Command Blog* 2009).

As one of the leading international partners for the development of the war-torn north, China has gifted de-mining equipment and heavy machinery, invested in infrastructural support systems such as railway and road networks, and provided humanitarian aid in the form of tents and a cash donation of US$100 million (*Zee News* 2010). Outright gifts from China, such as the Supreme Court Complex, the Central Telecommunication Exchange and the redevelopment of the Lady Ridgeway Children's Hospital are scattered across Colombo, the capital city, but none of them are as impressive or of such symbolic significance as the Bandaranaike Memorial International Conference Hall (BMICH) which was built during the heyday of the Non-Aligned Movement, as a mark of friendship between the peoples of China and Sri Lanka, and is now undergoing a very costly refurbishment courtesy of the Chinese government. The National Performing Arts Theatre, currently being constructed by the Chinese government, promises to be another gigantic symbol of friendship between the two nations, which will be indelibly etched in the memory of future generations of Sri Lankans (Alwis 2010: 437).

India, like China, is also currently involved in revitalising the war-ravaged Northern Province and has been supporting Sri Lanka's de-mining as well as relief and resettlement efforts in that region (*The Hindu* 2010). It had offered a US$108 million aid package that would include the restoration of rail links, upgrading of the Palaly airbase (the only civilian airport for residents in the north) and setting up a consulate in Jaffna (*The Hindu* 2010). Indian companies have been invited to build technology parks and invest in telecommunications in the north (Parasram 2012: 13).

India is also involved in the rehabilitation of the southern coastal railway line from Colombo to Matara by providing credit worth US$167.4 million. In addition to these more recent interventions, India has considerable investments in Sri Lanka in the retail fuel, telecommunication, hotel, cement, banking, tyre, rubber and information technology sectors.

According to the Stockholm International Peace Research Institute, Chinese exports of conventional military equipment made up 52% of military transfers within the Asia-Pacific region between 2004 and 2008. Pakistan, Sri Lanka, and Bangladesh were the main beneficiaries which cannot be separated from Beijing's geostrategic role in the South Asia Sino-Indian war of 1962.85 Faced with this international Western pressure, Colombo saw the benefits of regionally aligning with Beijing, whose deep pockets held cash, weapons, a UN Security Council veto, and a common distaste for secessionist movements. The international legal norm of territorial integrity has been a cornerstone of Chinese foreign policy as Xianjiang, Tibet, and Taiwan each pose threats to Beijing. Chinese diplomatic, economic, and military support for Sri Lanka was pivotal in rapidly transforming the military between 2006 and 2009 (Parasram 2012).

CONCLUSION

The troubles in South Asia, its endemic tensions, mutual distrust, and occasional hostilities are largely considered products of the contradictions of India's security perception with that of the rest of the countries of the area. India's neighbours perceive threats to their security coming primarily from India whereas India considers neighbours as an integral part of its own security system. The pre-eminence of India in the South Asian power configuration given its geography, demography, economics, and ecology is something about which neither India nor its neighbours can do nothing but accept. But the image of India in South Asia is that of a power that demands habitual obedience from its neighbours. According to the strategic doctrine of India drawn from that of British India, the country's defence perimeter is given not by the boundaries of India but by the outer boundaries of its immediate neighbours. Thus, the main theme of this doctrine is that South Asia is to be regarded as an Indian backyard. No wonder then, that there have always been certain psychological misgivings on the part of the smaller states about their all-powerful neighbour India (Malhotra, *South Asia-Political and Economic Region, DU*).

A massive change of heart in Indian establishment post-liberalisation of the Indian economy witnessed India's foreign policy getting out of clutches of ideological doctrines and seeking new grounds for the development of a robust and sustainable relationship with its neighbours, regional superpowers and engaging the world powers in a meaningful and mutually fruitful partnership. It saw the United States replacing the erstwhile USSR and then Russia as the centre of India foreign policy objectives. No doubt, some great successes have been achieved at that front. The Indo-US nuclear deal, which ended the nuclear apartheid against India, is the centerpiece of that endeavour.

India has also been able to gain a massive hike in bilateral trade with Washington and was able to achieve assurances for backing of India's claim to a permanent seat in the United Nations Security Council. Unites States' ambiguous and sometimes selfish interests affecting its ability to intervene transparently in matters relating to Pakistan notwithstanding, bilateral relations between the two countries have been at their best. Apart from the US, India has also been able to improve relations with ASEAN countries and broad base its ties with Israel and European countries. This is particularly important in terms of India's efforts to widen its reach to acquiring military technology and hardware. Gone are the days when Russia was the sole supplier of arms to India. US and Israel have emerged as the biggest suppliers of defence technology to India and the recent Rafael fighter jet deal with France will help it to strengthen its footprints in the European arms consortiums.

But despite such advances real concerns remain closer home. India's relations with its immediate neighbours—Pakistan, China, Sri Lanka and Bangladesh—have not seen the kind of progress that they should have made. It is to some extent responsible for hindering India's rise as a regional superpower and claiming its rightful due on the global high table.

Despite several rounds of composite dialogue with Pakistan, ties have not moved much in the recent past. Islamabad has not been able to stem the infiltration of terrorists into India and after 26/11 Mumbai terror attack relations are at the nadir, mistrust is at its peak. The recent developments in the northeastern state of Assam over the constant influx of refugees from Bangladesh have further underlined the inability of the establishment in the two countries to contain a human tragedy. Apart from this, several issues including a pact on Teesta have remained in the freezer, courtesy Indian government's inability to contain its former ally Trinamool Congress that rules West Bengal.

Similarly, the domestic political players in Tamil Nadu are out again to rock the boat of India's relations with Sri Lanka. Bilateral ties have not made any commendable progress but they are also not in doldrums. It is imperative on Indian government that it should remove these irritants and engage with the Island nation to find a way that the relations between the two countries could be insulated and formulated independently of such issues. These regional foreign policy challenges are more pertinent in the light of China's efforts to throw an "arc of influence" around India. Beijing has been vigorously pursuing both Pakistan and Sri Lanka while India grapples with perennial potential security threats emanating from China. India and China, while cooperating in a variety of multilateral processes ranging from trade negotiations to discussions on climate change, are increasingly competitors in a global race for wealth, energy and influence as emerging (or, in China's case, now emerged) powers.

China's penetration of India's neighbourhood presents a finely calibrated challenge to Indian foreign policy, seen by some as deriving from the following calculus: 'Restricting India to the Asian subcontinent remains Chinese policy. The tactics are simple: keep borders with India tranquil but do not solve the [border] dispute, trade with India but arm Pakistan and wean away Nepal, Bangladesh, and Myanmar.'

India is uniquely positioned to be a driver of interstate cooperation in South Asia, which is a 'predominantly Indo-centric region' because, in terms of religion or culture, or both, 'India has something in common with [each of] its immediate neighbours but the neighbouring states of India do not share similarities of such magnitude or depth among themselves.' Yet India has been unsuccessful in generating such cooperation. Despite the great strides it has made in economic growth, it remains mired in the security dilemmas of its own region.

REFERENCES

[1] Foweracker, Joe (1995). *Theorizing Social Movements*. Boulder: Pluto Press.

[2] Tarrow, Sidney G. (1994). *Power in Movement: Social Movements, Collective Action and Politics*. New York: Cambridge University Press.

[3] Dixit, J.N. (1998). *Across borders: fifty years of India's foreign policy*. New Delhi: Picus Books, pp. 182–93.

[4] Gunasinghe, Newton (1998). *The Open Market and Its Impact on Ethnic Relations in Sri Lanka* in *Sri Lanka: The Ethnic Conflict: Myths, Realities, and Perspectives*. Committee for Rational Development, New Delhi: Navrang, p. 199.

[5] Rao, P. Venkateshwar (1988). *Ethnic Conflict in Sri Lanka: India's Role and Perception*. Asian Survey, Vol. 28, No. 4. Apr.

[6] De Votta, Neil (2000). *Control Democracy, Institutional Decay, and the Quest for Eelam: Explaining Ethnic Conflict in Sri Lanka*. Pacific Affairs, Vol. 73, No. 1, pp. 55–76.

[7] Ganguly, Rajat (2004). *Sri Lanka's Ethnic Conflict: At a Crossroad between Peace and War*. Reviewed work(s): Source: Third World Quarterly, Vol. 25, No. 5, pp. 903–917.

[8] Behuria, Ashok K. (2011). *Rajapaksa's Sri Lanka: Time to Move Beyond Complacency*. Strategic Analysis, 35:5, 739–744.

[9] Clarke, Ryan (2011). *Conventionally Defeated but Not Eradicated: Asian Arms Networks and the Potential for the Return of Tamil Militancy in Sri Lanka*. Civil Wars, 13:2, 157–188.

[10] De Alwis, Malathi (2010). *The 'China Factor' in post - war Sri Lanka*. Inter-Asia Cultural Studies, 11:3, 434–446.

[11] Parasram Ajay (2012). *Erasing Tamil Eelam: De/Re Territorialisation in the Global War on Terror*. Geopolitics, DOI:10.1080/14650045.2012.654531.

[12] Marshall, Larry (2010). *Introduction: Sri Lanka after the war, Global Change*. Peace and Security: formerly Pacifica Review: Peace, Security and Global Change, 22:3, 327–330.

[13] Arambewela, Nadeeka and Arambewela, Rodney (2010). *Post-war opportunities for peace in Sri Lanka: an ongoing challenge?* Global Change, Peace and Security: formerly Pacifica Review: Peace, Security and Global Change, 22:3, 365–375.

[14] Raja Mohan, C. (Jul.–Aug., 2006). *India and the Balance of Power*. Reviewed work(s), Foreign Affairs, Vol. 85, No. 4, pp. 17–32.

[15] Crossette, Barbara (2002). *Sri Lanka: In the Shadow of the Indian Elephant*. Reviewed work(s): World Policy Journal, Vol. 19, No. 1, pp. 25–35.

[16] Uyangoda, Jayadeva (Feb. 23–29, 2008). *The Discreet Charm of India*. Reviewed work(s): Economic and Political Weekly, Vol. 43, No. 8, pp. 8–9.

[17] Crenshaw, Martha (2000). *Democracy, commitment problems and managing ethnic violence: The case of India and Sri Lanka*. Terrorism and Political Violence, 12:3–4, 135–159.

[18] Chari, P.R. (1995). *The IPKF Experience in Sri Lanka*. Arms Control, Disarmament, and International Security Occasional Paper.

[19] Mukherjee, Rohan and M. Malone, David (2011). *Indian foreign policy and contemporary security challenges http://www.chathamhouse.org/sites/default/files/public/International%20Affairs/2011/87_1mukherjee_malone.pdf*

[20] Malhotra, Nitasha. *South Asia-Political and Economic Region.* The Association for Geographical

[21] Studies. http://ags.geography.du.ac.in/Study%20Materials_files/Nitasha%20Malhotra 2_KNC.pdf

India-Sri Lanka Relations: Failure of Conflict Management Mechanism in South Asia

Tarun Mathur

ABSTRACT: The conflict management failed as a mechanism in South Asia and especially in Sri Lanka. The conflict has transformed in Sri Lanka from ethnic movement to terrorist movement. The case of Sri Lanka is an appropriate example of conflict transformation when, in the late 1970s Tamil youth rose up, demanding their due share and protesting against the Sinhalese discrimination against the Tamils in Sri Lanka, leading to acts of violence. The Tamil—Sinhalese problem could have been controlled had it been dealt with properly but not formulating policies that were very blatantly pro-Sinhalese at the expense of the Tamil minority. The issue got aggravated when the issue of injustice or discrimination was handled by force instead of appropriate political reforms in the administrative structure. India being a regional power has a role to play in the process of conflict management in Sri Lanka. India failed in fulfilling its responsibility as a conflict manager in its own region. India took a turn in its approach to the conflict, when in 2007; New Delhi began to rather explicitly support the Sri Lankan government in disregard of its traditional preference for a peaceful solution and its sensitivity for the fate of Sri Lankan Tamils. While domestic and historical pressures led to India's decisive approach during the years 2003–2007, starting from 2007 regional and international factors—most notably the skillful diplomacy of the Sri Lankan government and the growing Chinese presence there, induced New Delhi to support the government side in order to keep some leverage on Sri Lankan affairs. It is ethnic diversity which is a cause of armed conflict, but rather ethnic politics. It is the injection of ethnic differences into political loyalties and the politicization of identities that is so dangerous. India's long term interests in Sri Lanka will be a political solution which guarantees the safety and security of all minority groups in the unified country and the removal of extra-regional forces which pose a threat to India's security environment. Sometimes Indian attempts to reconcile differences with Sri Lanka are restricted due to Tamil Nadu's attitude over the issue of Tamil—Sinhalese rivalry. The SAARC has a role to play in the conflict management between India and Sri Lanka. SAARC, as a regional organization needs to focus more on the bilateral relations between India—Sri Lanka, so that the region could get benefit out of their mutual cooperation. India, being a major player of SAARC can play an active role in promoting bilateral relations and peace between India and Sri Lanka.

In the contemporary world, we feel happy when we look around and see all round development. A world characterised by increase in economic, political and societal/cultural accomplishments headed by globalisation and the most importantly increase in democratic regimes. But, if we turn the coin upside down, the picture is not the same on both the sides. Instead, today every state is fighting over each other on one or the other issue which includes territory, economic resources, cultural and political rights etc.

Amongst such issues, ethnic issue is one of the most alarming problems, faced by many countries, particularly in South Asia such as Pakistan, Sri Lanka, Nepal etc. The basic concern with regard to ethnic issues is the question of relationship between diverse groups of people often characterised by distinct races, culture and religions living within the political boundaries of States. The notion of distinction apart from being evident in some of the objective and tangible facts is strongly present in the perceptions of the groups about themselves or in the opinion of others who hold them to be different. Thus, the relationship ranges from a relatively harmonious form to one of antagonism and open hostility of conflictual type.

Therefore the relationship between different countries in South Asia and their Foreign Policies keep changing with conditions and situations. In this regard, the current India-Sri Lanka relations are harmonious yet hostile. Despite India's insistence upon a political solution to the Tamil issue, Sri Lanka maintains friendly relations with India. Sri Lanka does not allow contentious issues such as, illegal fishing and poaching in each others' water, supply of poor quality medicine, diesel power unit for railways and other issues to affect the friendly relations between the two countries. Both countries are attempting to solve these and other issues through bilateral dialogue. The current Sri Lankan Government officially considers India as a 'relative' and China as a 'good friend'. Sri Lanka has also attached importance to strengthening relations with other South Asian countries and is playing a leading role in promoting greater regional cooperation through the South Asian Association for Regional Cooperation (SAARC). Sri Lanka's relations with Pakistan and Bangladesh are further strengthened by Pakistani President Asif Ali Zardari's visit to Sri Lanka in November 2010 and by President Mahinda Rajapaksa's visit to

Bangladesh in April 2011. However, it is said, "Grass always looks green from the other side", as such when questions comes to issues like identity politics or refugee problems eyebrows are always high. In this sense, India feared that a successful liberation movement in Sri Lanka could inspire radical nationalistic groups in Tamil Nadu and leading to separation or instability within its own boundaries. Thus, India has formulated much of its foreign policy and peace initiatives in Sri Lanka keeping domestic issues and interests in mind. India's decision to limit its involvement after the 1990s reflects the impact of the death of over 1,000 Indian Peace Keeping Force (IPKF) troops and the assassination of its Prime Minister by a Liberation Tigers of Tamil Eelam (LTTE) member.

BACKGROUND OF THE SRI LANKAN CONFLICT

Sri Lanka's conflict has been characterized by a puzzle. The main parties to the conflict have repeatedly abandoned opportunities to work out a peace settlement through negotiations.[1]

Jayadeva Uyangoda argues that at least part of the explanation of the puzzle lies in the fact that Sri Lanka's ethnic conflict and the difficulties in its termination are embedded in the non-negotiability of the vital question of state power. The protracted war has redefined the core issue of state power as one without negotiable options. Similarly, the fact that the government of Sri Lanka and LTTE continue to approach the possible negotiated solutions in minimalist (minimum "devolution") and maximalist ("Confederal" autonomy) perspectives has made the war the main strategic path through which the dynamics of the conflict continue to be defined.[2]

Jayadeva Uyangoda's study on Sri Lanka offers three conclusions. The first is that the circumstances of political engagement—and the political engagement itself—have not been adequate to move Sri Lanka's main parties to the conflict in the direction of a credible compromise. Mediation, facilitation, and negotiations have been necessary but inadequate instruments for effectively altering the conflict. This is because at the heart of this conflict-sustaining trajectory has been the non-negotiability of the central issue of contestation—namely the state power. The second conclusion is that, to understand the changing and reproductive dynamics of Sri Lanka's conflict, it is necessary to distinguish its ethnic conflict character from the ethnic war process. Although the "ethnic conflict" may presuppose the possibility of bargain able compromises, Sri Lanka's "ethnic war" is fought on non-negotiable preferences and options because it is propelled forward by two contradictory and mutually exclusive state-formation agendas. The third conclusion is that negotiations between the government of Sri Lanka and the LTTE can be effective in deescalating the war only if such negotiations aim at, and lead to, reconstituting state power along ethnic lines in an advanced framework of regional autonomy.[3]

In 1986, reports about massacres in the North against the Tamil population by the Sri Lankan government caused the Indian government to send relief supplies into Jaffna by air after a flotilla carrying food supplies was blocked. The Hindu Tamil population of Sri Lanka received much sympathy from its Hindu counterpart in India, who believed that the Buddhist Sinhalese majority on the island was oppressing the Tamil group.

Finally, in July 1987, the Indo-Lanka Accord was signed between Indian PM Rajiv Gandhi and Sri Lankan President Jayawardene. The Sri Lankan government conceded many of the Tamil demands, allowed for devolution of powers in the Northern and Eastern provinces and provided official status to the Tamil language. In return, India sent the Indian Peace Keeping Force (IPKF) in order to establish order in the North and East and disarm the Tamil militant groups. By November 1987, there were 20,000 IPKF in north Sri Lanka.

While most of the militant groups turned in their weapons to the IPKF, the LTTE refused and the IPKF engaged the LTTE in a series of conflicts for two years. The Sinhalese Peoples Liberation Front or Janatha Vimukthi Peramuna (JVP) also resisted the IPKF in the south since these Sri Lankans did not agree with President Jayawardene's collaboration with India or the concessions he had agreed to for the Tamils. Thus, in 1988–1989, the IPKF engaged in battles with the Tamil rebels in the north and the Sri Lankan security forces and JVP in the south. With more than 1,000 soldiers dead in these confrontations, the Indian engagement was heavily criticized at home.

In 1989, a new government under President Premadasa took power in Colombo, and asked the Indian troops to withdraw and leave the conflict. The result was a negotiated scheduled departure, an embarrassing act for the world's fourth largest army—and all IPKF troops left by 1990. The behaviour of Premadasa's government had challenged India's hegemonic power in the region. After the withdrawal, India established a 'hands-off policy' in Sri Lanka. However, in 1991, Indian PM Rajiv Gandhi was assassinated during an elections campaign while in Tamil Nadu while in Tamil Nadu by a suicide bomber believed to be a member of the LTTE.

After the assassination, India labelled the LTTE as a terrorist organization, preventing any official interactions with them. Thereafter, the role of India was limited as an active player in conflict resolution and peacekeeping in Sri Lanka. India was nevertheless always involved in the process, as it faced waves of Sri Lankan refugees, many settling in the state of Tamil Nadu. Beginning with the first wave in 1983–1987, 134,053 Sri Lankan Tamils arrived in India, of which 25,585 returned after the Indo-Sri Lankan Accord. The second wave was after 1989 with the state of Eelam War II when 122,000 Tamils came. Eelam War III in 1995 prompted another 23,356 refugees into India, which stopped with the 2002 ceasefire agreement. Having to meet the needs of an influx of thousands, India was constantly drawn into the Sri Lankan-Tamil conflict.

In the 2000s when other nations, such as Norway, the US, etc. (as discussed later) were taking part in promoting peace in Sri Lanka, India chose to keep a minimal profile. In 2006, the Indian Defence Minister Pranab Mukherjee stated that "India fully supports the peace process in Sri Lanka but will not play an active role because it may complicate the situation."

Although after 1991, India kept a minimal profile as an active part in the peace process, it was still an important player due to its regional dominance. Due to the hostile relations that developed between India and the LTTE, many of the Sinhalese believed that India was "interested in keeping Sri Lanka united and preventing the establishment of an independent Tamil Eelam."

Throughout the peace process, India has continued to reiterate its belief in the need for a united Sri Lanka. As mentioned earlier, cautious of the separatist movements within its own state, India's policy has always been to safeguard the sovereignty and territorial integrity of Sri Lanka. Further, although India chose to separate itself from the peace processes, the international community and the Sri Lankan government both understood that India could undermine the entire process if overlooked.

Thus, during the talks leading to the Cease Fire Agreement (CFA), the Norwegian envoy kept India involved by consulting it at all stages. India, although supportive throughout the peace process, maintained its role at verbal communications without any intention to formally engage with the conflict. It should be noted that India also maintained a very strict position against the LTTE throughout the peace processes, seeking to bring the LTTE leadership to trial in India. Further, as stated by a high-ranking official in the Indian High Commission in 2004, India was willing to conduct business with all groups in Sri Lanka but the LTTE.

STRUCTURAL DIMENSIONS OF CONFLICT IN SRI LANKA

Security

Though sometimes caricatured as an "introverted" civil war, the international and regional dimensions of the Sri Lankan conflict have become more evident and arguably more influential. Here three inter-related areas of change in the external context can be identified.

First, the launch of a global war on terror after September 11, 2001 has had important ramifications in Sri Lanka as elsewhere. In global terms, it is a bad time to be a non-state military actor. Instability in the global south is seen to endanger the domestic or "homeland security' concerns of core northern powers. This is reflected in a range of inter-connected measures including U.S. military support for front line states fighting "terrorism', the proscription of "terrorist" organizations, and efforts to "strangle" the trans-national networks that fund non-state military groups.

Second, since the early 1990s there has been growing and increasingly robust international intervention in zones of instability in the global south. Arguably, this has marked a shift in the center of gravity in international relations from states toward individuals—manifest for example in the U.N. Agenda for Peace of 1992 and, more recently, the 'responsibility to Protect" agenda. The erosion of sovereignty is linked to a lowering of western inhibitions to intervene in other people's wars. Third, there has arguably been a trend toward regionalization as well as internationalization. India's hegemony in the region is a point of continuity. However, Sri Lanka is also located in a dynamic, confident, and increasingly assertive wider Asian region.[4]

Political

The conflict in Sri Lanka is recognized as a crisis of the state rather than an "ethnic conflict". This is not to deny the ethnically patterned nature of conflict in Sri Lanka and the processes through which governance, development, and social relations have become increasingly ethnicized. But a focus on the nature of the state and the quality of governance in Sri Lanka generates insights about the inter-relations between different forms of militarized violence in the North-East and the South. Societal discontents are seldom sufficient to trigger widespread conflict until they penetrate the state itself. Violent conflict is therefore rooted in its failure to institutionalize democratic politics.

First, the state remains exceedingly centralized and clientalistic. Second, democracy and intolerant nationalism have been organically linked. Third, violent challenges to the state have emerged from the periphery, driven by a sense of exclusion and alienation. Fourth, though the state is centralized, it is also fragmented and it has become more so during the course of the conflict. A form of partial or layered sovereignties has emerged and the tensions around these competing systems of governance have been exposed during the course of the peace process. Fifth, there are pressures on the state from above as well as from below. Globalization and the growing involvement of international actors in Sri Lanka have contributed to shifts in the distribution of sovereignty. Transnational engagement, therefore, interacts with and plays a role in shaping the nature of domestic governance.[5]

Social

War is the result of and creates a particular kind of political economy. It is also sustained by an emotional economy. Like the war economy, this emotional economy is likely to persist well after the signing of a ceasefire agreement, and if persistently mobilized by political entrepreneurs, may endanger the transition to peace. Evidently, the discourse of victimhood, ethnic scapegoating, and competing nationalisms cannot be turned on and off like a tap. The "binary moral frameworks" of extreme nationalism have permeated the body politic and the wider society.[6]

Sri Lanka suffers from a "politics of anxiety" and possibly these anxieties have been sharperned by the peace process. The recent period of the conflict (2000–2005) can be divided into four phases: (1.) Run up to the ceasefire: in a context of an enduring military stalemate and declining economic conditions, the United National Front (UNF) wins elections in December 2001, (2.) Ceasefire and peace talks: a ceasefire agreement (CFA) is signed within a month and the United National Front (UNF) government and the LTTE embark on six rounds of talks, (3.) The breakdown of talks and political instability: Talks become deadlocked; the LTTE suspends its participation and subsequently submits a proposal for an Interim Self Governing Authority (ISGA), and (4.) The post-tsunami response: Negotiations between the government and LTTE about a post-tsunami response mirror the political dynamics of the peace process. It takes almost half a year to reach an agreement on a Post-Tsunami Operational Management Structure (P-TOMS), thus boosting the hopes for peace, despite the lack of legal clarity and the turmoil generated among both Sinhalese and Muslim constituencies.[7]

CONFLICT DYNAMICS

The UNF-LTTE peace negotiations followed a phased approach that involved ending the violence, creating a peace-dividend, and dealing with the core political issues. International actors were central to this strategy by providing security guarantees and reconstruction assistance, and facilitating peace negotiations.

This strategy failed to deliver a lasting or even interim settlement. First, the CFA froze rather than transformed security dynamics. Both parties continued to re-arm and strengthen their military capabilities. Although "no-war, no-peace" has meant an end to large scale militarized conflict, there have been high levels of political violence, including over three thousand ceasefire violations. Insecurity has grown in the East since the emergence of the Karuna break-away faction of the LTTE.

Second, although there was a peace-dividend of sorts, it has been unevenly distributed and its impacts attenuated. Reconstruction funding was caught up in the politics of the peace process, thus limiting the peace dividend in the North-East. In South, macro economic reforms introduced by the UNF undermined the economic dividend and led to the perception that the government was unconcerned with the plight of the poor. The lack of a clear communication strategy about either the peace process or the reform agenda accentuated this view.

Third, the step-by-step approach was based on the assumption that a limited peace could ultimately led to a transformative peace. With hindsight, however, there could never be complete "normalization" until the core political issues were addressed. It proved impossible to circumnavigate or deal indirectly with the pivotal core of the conflict, this being the question of power sharing and the LTTE hegemony in the North East. Without a clear road map for peace talks, the nature of the end goal was always unclear, which created anxieties among external and internal stakeholders. The peace process acted as a "lightening rod" for wider political and social tensions, exposing the multi-polar and multi-dimensional nature of conflict in Sri Lanka. The bilateral government-LTTE relationship could not be addressed in isolation from other key inter and intra group relationships.[8]

INTERNATIONAL STAKEHOLDERS IN THE PEACE PROCESS

Norway

Norway has been involved as a facilitator since 1999 and is committed to this role so long as both sides request it. Norway has two comparative advantages as a facilitator of the peace process. First, it is acceptable to both sides and, importantly, also to India. It is viewed as a non-threatening and neutral intermediary. Second, Norway has a track record as a peacemaker.

India

As the dominant power in the region, India has played numerous roles in the past, from power mediator to protagonist and even spoiler. It is commonly assumed that India will not tolerate a model of devolution or federalism that is more far-reaching than the Union of India itself. India will not involve itself directly in mediation, but expects to have a significant influence on the final outcome of the peace process. India proscribed the LTTE following the assassination of Rajiv Gandhi and does not deal with them directly. There has been growing cooperation between India and the Government of Sri Lanka (GoSL) on security, intelligence, trade, and aid. The interest and involvement of Tamil Nadu has declined, though the LTTE continues to have connections with groups such as the MDMK and the Tamil Nationalist Movement.

USA

The U.S. is one of the four co-chairs of the peace process. Sri Lanka is not viewed by the U.S. as a priority in South Asia compared to India and Pakistan. Its primary concern in Sri Lanka has been counter terrorism, and the LTTE was proscribed in 1999. However, the peace process and the interest of Richard Armitage, former Deputy Secretary of State, brought Sri Lanka to unusual prominence on the U.S. agenda. The extension of United States Agency for International Development (USAID) funding and the choice of Sri Lanka for the Millennium Challenge Account, suggest an ongoing, though moderate level of engagement. The U.S. tends to align itself closely to the position of the Indians and GoSL. In relation to LTTE it plays the role of "bad cop", by applying pressure on issues such as terrorism, political killings of Tamil dissidents, child recruitments, and human rights, while providing security assistance to the Sri Lankan government.[9]

Role of India

As a dominant power in South Asia and a neighbour of Sri Lanka, India is a powerful player in regards to the conflict. India's involvement in the Sri Lankan conflict is motivated by a number of factors. First, as Sri Lanka's giant neighbour,' India believed that the conflict would not be resolved without its active participation. Due to its geographical location, India has viewed itself as the 'security manager' and closely watched the developments of the conflict in Sri Lanka.

Furthermore, there is a linkage in ethnicity between the 55 million Tamils in the southern Indian state of Tamil Nadu with the Tamil people in north and east Sri Lanka. The two populations of Tamils may be physically separated by the Palk Strait but they share common cultural, linguistic and religious ties.

The Indian view is that whatever solution is found has to be within the framework of constitutional arrangements which preserves Sri Lanka's territorial unity and integrity, a logic which India applies to its own violent separatist movements in different parts of the country. India feared that a successful liberation movement in Sri Lanka could inspire radical nationalistic groups in Tamil Nadu and lead to separation or instability within its own boundaries. Thus, India has formulated much of its foreign policy and peace initiatives in Sri Lanka keeping domestic issues and interests in mind.

India has long been the country with the greatest influence over Sri Lanka, but its policies to encourage the government there towards a sustainable peace are not working. Despite India's active engagement and unprecedented financial assistance, the Sri Lankan government has failed to make progress on pressing post-war challenges.[10]

India's approach has so far paid only limited dividends. Deepening militaryzation and Sinhalization in the Northern Province have increased the insecurity and political marginalization of Tamils and are undermining prospects for inter-ethnic reconciliation. The government continues to resist any investigation on accounting for mass atrocities in the final months of the war.

India's reluctance to put serious pressure on the Sri Lankan government is also due to strategic considerations, in particular its desire to counter the growing influence of China, whose financial and political support the Rajpaksa government has been cultivating. India's own growing economic interests in Sri Lanka have also tempered its political activism. New Delhi's traditional reluctance to work through multilateral bodies or in close coordination with other governments—due in part to its fear of international scrutiny of its own conflicts, particularly in Kashmir—has also significantly weakened its ability to influence Sri Lanka.[11]

India nonetheless, has strong reasons to work for fundamental changes in Sri Lanka's post war policies. It has a clear interest in preventing either a return to violent militancy or the consolidation on its borders of another authoritarian government with an overly powerful military.

India's support for the negotiations between the Sri Lankan government and the Tamil National Alliance, which belatedly began in January 2011, has been useful and should be maintained.[12]

India will need to coordinate more closely with Japan, Western donors and international development banks. Together they have the political and financial leverage to influence the Rajpaksa administration should they choose to use it. India should broaden its political agenda from focusing solely on devolution and ensuring the rights of Tamils. Without a reversal of the Sri Lankan government's growing authoritarianism, centralization of power and continued repression of dissent, any devolution will be meaningless and the risks of renewed conflict will increase. India's longstanding interest in a peaceful and politically stable Sri Lanka is best served by strong messages to Colombo to end impunity and reverse the democratic decay that undermines the rights of all Sri Lankans. By raising political concerns that affect all of Sri Lanka's communities, India can also counter suspicions among Sinhalese and eventually strengthen its hand with the government.[13]

The civil war in Sri Lanka, which came to an end with the military defeat of the separatist LTTE in May 2009, has been internationalized since a few years after its inception in the 1980s.[14]

The years 2006–2009 were marked by the collapse of the ceasefire brokered by the Norway in 2002 and by a gradual escalation of the war up until the military defeat of the LTTE. These events were accompanied by massive war crimes and human rights violations, the displacement of thousands of people—mainly Tamils, and huge losses among the civilian population.

In particular, India should have adopted conflict-management mechanism in order to prevent the escalation of violence in its immediate vicinity. In the case of Sri Lanka this could be done by India's tradition of involvement in Sri Lankan affairs, and since India has repeatedly emphasized its preference for a peaceful solution and a political settlement of the ethnic conflict. However, India didn't, in fact, act as a conflict manager and didn't actively engage to stop the violence in Sri Lanka. Moreover, from 2007 on, the Indian government quietly supported the military offensive of the Sri Lankan government and even took a clear position against the investigation of war crimes by the United Nations Human Rights Council after the end of the hostilities in May 2009.[15]

MANAGING REGIONAL SECURITY

Since the 1990s a trend towards the regionalization of conflict management initiatives has been observed.[16] This was related, among other factors, to the "overstretch" of the UN and the reluctance of the US to get involved in conflict management initiatives, especially in remote regions.[17] As a consequence, the UN started promoting forms of "regional task sharing"— delegating competences to regional organizations.[18] However in the case of South Asia, which lacks any kind of multilateral security arrangement because the South Asian Association for Regional Cooperation (SAARC) explicitly excludes contentious and political issues from its areas of activity. According to Kanti Bajpai, "conflict management is essentially a bilateral possibility."[19]

India as the predominant country—the regional power—in South Asia and as a state directly affected by spill-over effects from the civil war in Sri Lanka should have played a prominent and active role in managing the Sri Lankan conflict according to its preferences. India's unequivocal preponderance of material capabilities at the regional level, further strengthened by its geopolitical position as the centre of a hub-and-spokes regional setting, would reinforce India's ability to influence its region according to its wishes. In the vital policy area of conflict management, this should hold true even more, especially with a decade long bloody civil war at stake.[20]

THE CIVIL WAR IN SRI LANKA

The ethnic conflict in Sri Lanka, rooted in the discrimination against the Tamil minority by the Sinhalese majority after the end of British colonial domination, turned into a full-fledged civil war in 1983. The LTTE, formed in 1976 under the leadership of Velupillai Prabhakaran, had by the early 1980s emerged as the main rebel organization fighting for the establishment of an independent state for Sri Lanka's Tamils in the Island's northeast.

Their fight against the Sri Lankan state led to an armed conflict that lasted for 26 years. The war was marked by phases of high intensity interrupted by different efforts to find a negotiated solution, which failed altogether.

INDIA'S APPROACH TO SRI LANKA DURING EELAM WAR IV

After the assassination of Rajiv Gandhi India followed a strict policy of non-interference in Sri Lankan affairs and she refused to act altogether as a conflict manager in the Sri Lankan war. However, India was not indifferent to the happenings of Sri Lanka. Besides keeping an eye on the events unfolding in Sri Lanka, India also had some clear preferences for the resolution of the civil war. Since the 1980s when it had tried to mediate a compromise in Thimpu, New Delhi had been interested in a political solution of the ethnic conflict.[21] Despite the failures of the agreement of 1987 and of the IPKF deployment, those two undertakings had also aimed to achieve a peaceful settlement. Similarly, during the years of Norwegian mediation the goal of "lasting peace" became a standard formulation in India's declarations, confirmed by India's quiet support for the peace process. And from 2003 to 2009 India repeatedly expressed the goal of a "negotiated political settlement" encompassing forms of power devolution meeting "the aspirations of all communities." More specifically India had a clear preference for the "unity, sovereignty and integrity" of Sri Lanka, which was related to New Delhi's fear of secessionist spill-over effects on single Indian states, most notably in Tamil Nadu. In the statements issued between April 2003 and May 2009, a more concrete reference to the kind of arrangement favoured by India emerged only once.[22]

Things changed slightly in the period 2007–2009, when the escalation of violence in Sri Lanka and the growing pressure from Tamil Nadu induced New Delhi to put some degree of pressure on the Sri Lankan government concerning its approach to civilians in the war. On October 6, 2008, Indian National Security Advisor Narayanan summoned the Sri Lankan deputy high commissioner to protest Sri Lanka's conduct of the war, and ten days later, India actually made an explicit (though unspecified) threat, when the external affairs minister stated that India would "do all in its power" in order to improve the humanitarian situation in Sri Lanka. Despite this hardening of political rhetoric, however, New Delhi refrained from making its threat more compelling, let alone enforcing it. India's half-hearted attitude was met by the Sri Lankan government with an appeasement policy characterized by reassurances about the safety and well being of the Tamil community and by minor concessions, while the military campaign against the Tigers continued unabated, without concern for civilian losses.[23]

India at the diplomatic level continued to prefer for a peaceful resolution of the civil war and a political settlement of the underlying conflict management initiatives. Instead of proactive engagement India resorted to an ad hoc response to the course of events by radically changing its policies: In 2007, India began to abandon its rigorous non involvement approach and started to take an indirect but highly significant role in the military conflict. This new approach was manifested, on one hand, in the crackdown on LTTE networks in Tamil Nadu, which helped the Sri Lankan government in its fight against the Tigers, and, on the other hand, in the provision of military hardware, mainly in the form of "defensive" equipment, and in other forms of military cooperation with the Sri Lankan government.[24]

After the end of the war, India also diplomatically supported Sri Lanka in international forums. On May 28, 2009, a special session of the United Nations Human Rights Council was held to investigate the reported war crimes and atrocities committed by both the LTTE and the Sri Lankan armed forces. Two motions were discussed: one requesting an international investigation and the other one elaborated by the Sri Lankan government, which urged the international community to support Sri Lanka's reconstruction efforts. The latter motion, which "welcomed" the liberation of Sri Lankan Tamil civilians from the clutches of the LTTE but did not mention the shelling of civilians and the need to provide international organizations with access to IDP camps, was ultimately approved. Not only China, Russia, Pakistan, and several Arab and African countries supported this motion, but also India voted for it. While this voting behaviour corresponds to India's traditional preference for non-involvement in other countries' internal affairs, it again calls into question India's concern about the fate of Tamil civilians and further highlights to what extent New Delhi came to follow the Sri Lankan government's position.[25]

PAKISTAN AND CHINA

Pakistan's involvement in the Sri Lanka conflict is not clearly historically recorded, and most records are only speculations. However it is clear that Pakistan has played a significant role in the conflict, mainly for regional interests. While India may have involved itself with the conflict because it holds a large Tamil population in its own country, India also wanted to assert its political might over the South Asian region. Pakistan, a rival of India, most likely became involved with the Sri Lanka conflict as a means to upsetting India and asserting its own power over the region.

In the late 1990's it had been speculated by the LTTE that Pakistan was involved with the aid and support of the Sri Lankan military offensives. At this time both Sri Lanka and Pakistan denied these accusations, as Pakistan asserted that the conflict was an internal matter that was of no concern for them. However Pakistan has long considered Sri Lanka to be an ally. In 1997 it became an open secret that Sri Lanka military officers were being trained in Pakistan. The U.S. and the U.K., aware of this connection, advised Pakistan not to use the LTTE to destabilize India. However it had been reported that in 1993 the LTTE accepted a consignment of arms from Pakistan. The specific details of Pakistan's direct involvement with the LTTE is unclear, although it has been highly speculated that the LTTE did buy arms from Pakistan, as the senior LTTE leader Sathasivam Krishnakumar (aka Kittu) had been seen going in and out of the country buying arms. Whether these arms were directly bought from the government or from the illegal black market it is unsure. Pakistan does hold the largest illegal arms market in the subcontinent.

It is impossible to determine whether or not Pakistan may have perpetuated the conflict by providing weapons to the LTTE. However it has been observed that Pakistan's aid and support for the Sri Lankan government has served as clinching factor in the government's victory over the LTTE in 2009. Any Pakistani involvement in the conflict before 2000 has been difficult to research. It may be likely that any involvement was kept a secret so as not to threaten India. After Pakistan acquired nuclear weapons by the end of the 1990's, Pakistan became more open with their involvement in the conflict. This may also have happened due to China's encouragement towards Pakistan to increase military aid towards Sri Lanka (which will be discussed in the following section). It is difficult to define Pakistan's foreign policy and strategy, as it is particularly in the case of the Sri Lanka conflict, however it is clear that the nation-state supported the Sri Lankan government which contributed to its victory over the LTTE. Pakistan's policy towards Sri Lanka changed under the rule of President Pervez Musharraf. From 1999–2008 Pakistan emerged as the second largest (after China) military aid supplier to Sri Lanka. The exact weaponry sold is had not been recorded, however certain deals have been made public, such as the sale of 22 Al-Khalid tanks worth $110 million to Sri Lanka in 2006. The Sri Lankan government had also ordered a list of weapons worth millions more from Pakistan. August 14, 2006 a suicide bomber went off aiming to kill Colonel Bashir Wali Muhammed, the former senior officer of Pakistan's Inter-Services Intelligence (ISI) and the foreign ambassador to Sri Lanka. While Bashir survived, 8 Sri Lankan commanders were killed in the blast. The Sri Lankan government issued a statement claiming that the Pakistani envoy was targeted by the LTTE. Bashir however alleged that India's external Intelligence Agency was behind the blast. India dismissed the allegation as preposterous and absurd.

It is more than likely that the LTTE was behind the blast, probably threatened and angered by Pakistani's support for the Sri Lankan government. Bashir's accusations towards India, improbable as they may be, do imply that Pakistan's involvement may have been a result of trying to shake up India. India was concerned about Pakistan's involvement in the Sri Lanka conflict. In 2006 it was reported that members of the Pakistani Armed Forces had been stationed in Colombo to guide Sri Lankan forces. Numbers of civilian deaths continued to increase on both sides. In a report by the former counter-terrorism chief of India's external intelligence, B. Raman concluded that, "Under the influence of the Pakistani advisors, the Sri Lankan government's counter-insurgency operations are becoming increasingly ruthless."

By 2008 Pakistan had boosted its armed military assistance loans to Sri Lanka to nearly $100 million. There has also been some less-documented speculation that at a time Pakistani's ISI may have provided arms for the LTTE. Kayalapattinam is a village in the Indian Tamil Nadu state that is commonly "The specific details of Pakistan's direct involvement with the LTTE is unclear, although it has been highly speculated that the LTTE did buy arms from Pakistan"

Subsequently in the following year China gave six F-7 jets to Sri Lanka as 'a gift'. In the same years as China was increasing its military aid to Sri Lanka, it also encouraged Pakistan to contribute its own military aid to Sri Lanka. Such military aid blatantly tilted the balance in favor of Sri Lankan government forces. It appears that some of China's domestic policies may have spilled over to Sri Lanka. Lanka Newspapers reported that Chinese aid helped weaken and scare civil society, emboldened by the unstinted Chinese support the government set in motion, the militarization of society, and the employed control of information as an instrument of war.

Indeed in the final months of the war the number of Tamil civilian killings dramatically increased. It has been estimated that more than 7,000 Tamil civilians were killed, however the Sri Lankan government claims that these casualties occurred because the LTTE's leaders were making hostages of their own people using them as human shields as their army advanced on their final stronghold. There may have been many more civilian casualties. A U.N. humanitarian coordinator in Sri Lanka has suggested that the government numbers do not add up: General Fonseka (who led the Sri Lankan Army) claimed that 22,000 Tigers were killed in the final two years of the war, and yet in 2006 he claimed that the LTTE had only 10,000 cadres. Numbers of casualties however are uncertain, as an unrecorded amount of civilians from both sides have been killed.

It is certain that China's military aid for the Sri Lankan government helped secure a victory over the LTTE. After the U.S. stopped its own military aid due to human rights abuses, China stepped in, implying that matters of human rights did not concern the country and that rather it supported a government's right to defend itself from internal threats, even at the cost of human lives. China's political clout over the region also encouraged Pakistan to increase military aid for the Sri Lankan government, which combined gave the government the eventual.

Since it first began to emerge as a global leader China has consistently provided aid for Sri Lanka. Support for Sri Lanka drastically increased in the last decade of the conflict, support that most likely was the biggest contributing factor to the Sri Lankan government's victory over the LTTE in 2009. China asserted that the conflict in Sri Lanka was an internal affair, but openly supported the government's right to defend itself from internal threats. Supplying Sri Lanka with military aid is argued by some as being part of China's strategy to gain Sri Lanka as an ally and to add it to China's "String of Pearls".

After the IPKF stepped out of Sri Lanka in 1991 Sri Lanka formed an alliance with China, and as a result several naval craft and aircraft were delivered to the government.

Small measures of aid continued throughout the years, but it wasn't until 2007 when Chinese military aid boosted fivefold. This came as a direct result of the U.S. ending direct military aid to Sri Lanka after concluding that its human rights record was deteriorating. China then became Sri Lanka's largest military donor, giving almost $1billion in aid. Weapons supplied, such as Chinese Jian-7 fighter jets, anti-aircraft guns, JY-11 3D air surveillance radars and others were concluded to have all played a central role in the Sri Lankan military successes against the LTTE. In April 2007 the Sri Lankan government signed a $38 million pact to purchase ammunition from China.

China's involvement may likely have been part of their strategic foreign policy to slowly assert dominance over the region, especially over India. It also has been alleged to have been part of its "String of Pearls" strategy, as China is now building a $1 billon port in Hambantota.

Although Sri Lanka may just be a teardrop nation to other regions, for India, Pakistan, and China, it is an important factor to regional security and power balances. All three have played a role in the Sri Lanka conflict as way to assert power over the region. Although India attempted to resolve the conflict through more-or-less peaceful means, from this analysis it appears that China and Pakistan were more successful in 'ending' the conflict by giving more leverage to the Sri Lankan government with military aid.

ROLE OF REGIONAL ORGANIZATION—SAARC

The framework of SAARC provides its member states with a regional space for policy making and implementation at the South Asian level. Globalization has unleashed both opportunities and challenges. It has been proceeding at such a pace that unless South Asian states act together there is every possibility that they will be left behind. South Asia has been unable to act together, even in terms of articulating common ills like poverty, while dealing with global leaders setting the tunes of future trade, environmental protection, and poverty reduction strategies throughout the world.[26]

The international community needs a peaceful South Asia; it is therefore kin their interests to make some productive efforts in resolving conflicts and for ensuring cooperation in South Asia. The SAARC as a body needs some reforms too, so to efficiently deal with any issue of regional or global concern; and greater seriousness is demanded in terms of moving this regional framework over any deadlocks. Zahangir Kabir from the SAARC Human Resource Development Centre concludes his analysis on SAARC with these powerful words, "In its third decade, SAARC should substantially be brought out of five star hotels and be placed to the closer if the teeming millions of the region for their welfare. The Association must get rid of the accusation that the organization has become for 'talk shops' and only organizing the numerous meetings without generating any meaningful result."[27] The SAARC has to get deeply rooted into the lives of people in all of its member states; and this can be achieved by permitting civil society's presence in the SAARC platform.[28]

CHALLENGES TO PEACE NEGOTIATIONS: THE SRI LANKAN EXPERIENCE

According to Sukanya Podder, the ethnic conflict in Sri Lanka is a good example of how peace negotiations in civil war situations can be elusive. From the experience of negotiating peace in Sri Lanka three prominent and recurrent variables come to the fore. These are: first, the competing nationalisms in the state-building project of Sri Lanka; second, the political outbidding practiced by the two major Sinhalese parties; and third, the authoritarian character of the LTTE which thrives on a rationale of war and terror. These variables have informed spoiler behavior and foiled attempts at a decisive settlement of the ethnic conflict.[29]

> Ethno-political conflicts are fought not just about resources or power, but about protecting group status, culture and identity. Identity and belief are non-negotiable, yet the means by which they are protected can be and have been the subject of creative compromises.[30]

In the field of conflict resolution the idea of negotiation has gained currency given a number of successful instances where conflicts have been settled or terminated through talks or discussions among parties involved.[31] In common parlance, negotiations often imply a set of communicative processes through which individuals or groups try to resolve mutual disagreements. In the context of conflict termination, however, negotiations primarily aim at changing the behavior of conflicting parties so as to engender a conflict settlement, which in turn can pave the way for conflict resolution.

Ethnic conflicts exhibit a measure of intractability that makes the exercise of negotiating a peace settlement quite challenging. Establishing the conditions for effective inter-group peacemaking is a formidable task in severe ethnic conflicts. In this context the Sri Lankan case is both instructive and interesting for grasping the complexities involved in conflict negotiations.[32]

Kripa Sridharan argues that ASEAN- despite its weak formal mandate to resolve conflicts-has been more effective in enhancing regional security and order, albeit in an indirect way. SAARC, on the other hand, has yet to take off and contribute towards the creation of a predictable and orderly regional environment.[33]

> Conflict management combines three elements: prevention, containment and termination.[34] The first relates to avoiding conflict

situations or at least ensuring that no violent conflict occurs. It dampens disputes to a point where no use of force is contemplated. This may even mean shoving under the carpet with a view to dealing with it at an unspecified time in the future.[35] Conflict containment refers to restraint in the use of force with the aim to deny victory to the aggressor and to prevent the spread of conflict, which could enmesh other actors and result in escalation of violence. Termination of conflict is a two stage process involving both settlement and resolution.[36] Settlement implies bringing violent hostilities to an end while resolution goes much further than that. It aims to eliminate or eradicate the very sources of conflict, and transform the attitude and behaviour of the conflicting parties. Obviously this last stage is extremely difficult, but if a regional organization can help achieve even the first, *i.e.* prevention of violent conflict—then it can be considered reasonably effective. In Southeast Asia renouncing the threat or use of force to settle disputes and relying instead on peaceful processes have conducted towards this end.[37]

Indo-Sri Lankan relations have been no less acrimonious, ranging from India's intervention in the island's ethnic conflict because of its sympathies towards the Tamils, to competing maritime claims. Indian troops were deployed in Sri Lanka in 1987 to bring the civil war to an end but the effort proved a failure. Indian forces were despised by both the government and the militant rebel group, the LTTE. Indian intervention bred suspicion and ill will and the 1989 SAARC summit was cancelled because of Colombo's objections to the presence of Indian troops in the country.[38]

The role of a region's pre-eminent power in ensuring regionalism's effectiveness is important in at least two respects: the contribution of the pivotal power in the formation of the regional organization and the equations between the region's big and small powers.

The odd thing about SAARC was that it became possible due to the initiative of the smaller states of the region. Bangladesh is credited with taking the lead. At the formative stage of the process India fretted that the forum would be used by the other members to exert their combined pressure on issues that bedevilled their relations with New Delhi.[39] There was also a feeling that behind the regional initiative lurked an unseen external hand which could prove injurious to Indian interests.[40] Hence India was lukewarm in its support of SAARC.[41]

SAARC encompasses a region where the use of force is still an instrument of foreign policy. SAARC's presence has not prevented violent conflicts, much less settled or resolved them. Regional cooperation is at a very rudimentary stage in South Asia. Conflict management of even a minimalist sort is non-existent at present. South Asia is yet to cross the Rubicon and make regionalism effective enough to build trust among its members and use it as a collective forum to manage inter-state conflicts.[42]

CAUSES OF THE FAILURE OF CONFLICT MANAGEMENT

Historical and Domestic Factors

The dismal failure of the IPKF operation and the assassination of Rajiv Gandhi forced India to assume a "hands-off" approach and to remain on the sidelines. Any kind of conflict management function became impossible for India to adopt; the military blunder of the IPKF precluded a renewed military intervention, while the ban on the LTTE prevented India from acting India as a facilitator to achieve a negotiated solution. Therefore, historical factors contribute largely to explaining India's inability to act as a conflict manager during Eelam War IV. At the same time, however, domestic political factors constantly dragged India into Sri Lankan affairs. In particular, the pro LTTE attitude of some political parties in Tamil Nadu was further intensifies by the composition of governing coalitions in India. During the years 2004–2009, the Dravid Munnetra Kazhagam (DMK), some of whose representatives had clear sympathy for the LTTE, was the third largest member of the Congress-led United Progressive Alliance (UPA) central government.[43]

Regional Factors: Sri Lanka's Skilful Diplomacy

The Sri Lankan government had a strong interest in gaining India's support against the Tigers. The strengthening of economic ties and a policy of balancing with India's rivals China and Pakistan were the main tools employed by President Rajpaksa.

International Factors: Indo-Chinese Competition

The Sri Lankan government greatly strengthened its ties with Beijing. This occurred by means of economic cooperation, the construction of huge infrastructure projects in Sri Lanka, and China's provision of weapons for the Sri Lankan government's fight against the LTTE. This gradual increase in Chinese influence in Sri Lanka clearly clashed with India's unstated goals of "having its say" in the South Asian region, and "preventing a hostile power gaining a foothold in Sri Lanka". As a consequence, the factor that has most strongly impacted India's reactive policy shift on Sri Lankan affairs is arguably Indo-Chinese competition for influence on the island.

CONCLUSION

> Three years after the war, reconciliation remains a distant dream as the government and the Tamil National Alliance engage in political posturing. Meanwhile, ordinary Tamils struggle to rebuild their lives, culture and identity, battling the fatigue of 30 years of conflict and neglect.[44]

Soon after the Eelam War IV ended, the Sri Lankan government began moving into Northern Province with its infrastructure development programme. There was generous help from the international community as well, initially for relief and demining and later for rehabilitation and infrastructure development. According to the Indian High Commission, apart from the construction of 50,000 houses in Northern and Eastern Provinces launched on October 2, 2012, India is heavily involved in developing activities in the North. They include restoration of the Northern Railway, Kankesanthurai harbour and Palaly airport; the construction of five vocational training centres; the renovation of the Duraiappa Stadium in Jaffna, the construction of a new cultural centre in Jaffna, and the setting up of a 500 MW coal-fired power plant at Sampur. India also announced a soft line credit of $800 million.

G.L. Peiris (Sri Lanka's External Affairs Minister), in an interview with Nirupama Subramanian and R.K. Radhakrishnan remarked that there is no denying the fact that there was deep disappointment over the Indian vote in the UNHRC on March 22, 2012. He also said that in the relationship between countries, there are ups and downs. And Sri Lanka and India relationship is a crucial one. Both the countries are bound to each other by a variety of ties. So it is necessary for both the countries to look to the future rather than be obsessed by one episode, however significant it may have been.[45]

REFERENCES

[1] Uyangoda, Jayadeva, "Ethnic Conflict in Sri Lanka: Changing Dynamics", *East-West Center* (Washington, D.C.), Policy Studies 32, 2007, p. VII.

[2] Ibid.

[3] Ibid, pp. VIII-IX.

[4] A Report by Jonathan Goodhand, Bart Klem, Dilruksi Fonseka, S.I. and Shonali Sardesai, "Aid, Conflict and Peacebuilding in Sri Lanka, 2000–2005", 2005, *The Asia Foundation*, pp. 23–27.

[5] Ibid, pp. 23–27.

[6] Ibid, pp. 23–27.

[7] Ibid, p. 7.

[8] Ibid, p. 8.

[9] Ibid, pp. 23–27.

[10] Author Anonymous, "India and Sri Lanka after the LTTE", No.206, 23 June 2011, *Asia Report, International Crisis Group*, p. I.

[11] Ibid.

[12] Ibid, pp. I–II.

[13] Ibid, p. II.

[14] Oberst, Robert C., "The Impact of International Diffusion on the Escalation of the Sri Lankan Conflict" in Stephen E. Lobell and Philip Mauceri (eds.), *Ethnic Conflict and International Politics: Explaining Diffusion and Escalation* (New York: Palgrave Macmillan, 2004), pp. 165–79.

[15] Destradi, Sandra, "India and the Civil War in Sri Lanka: On the Failures of Regional Conflict Management in South Asia", *German Institute of Global and Area Studies* (Hamburg), Working Paper No.154, December 2010, p. 6.

[16] Algappa, Mutiah, "Regionalism and Conflict Management: A Framework for Analysis", in *Review of International Studies* (Ceredigion), Vol. 21, No. 4, 1995, pp. 359–87.

[17] Bercovitch, Jacob and Jackson, Robert, *Conflict Resolution in the Twenty-First Century* (Ann Arbor: University of Michigan Press, 2009), p. 122.

[18] Bercovitch, Jacob and Jackson, Robert, *Conflict Resolution in the Twenty-First Century* (Ann Arbor: University of Michigan Press, 2009), pp. 119–36.

[19] Bajpai, Kanti, "Managing Conflict in South Asia" in Paul F. Diehl and Joseph Lepgold (eds.), *Regional Conflict Management* (New York: Rowman and Littlefield, 2003), p. 212.

[20] Destradi, "India and the Civil War in Sri Lanka: On the Failures of Regional Conflict Management in South Asia", p. 7.

[21] Bouffard, Sonia and Carment, David, "The Sri Lanka Peace Process: A Critical Review", *Journal of South Asian Development* (Murdoch, Australia), Vol.1, No.2, 1996, p. 168.

[22] Destradi, "India and the Civil War in Sri Lanka: On the Failures of Regional Conflict Management in South Asia", p. 12.

[23] Ibid, pp. 12–13.

[24] Ibid, p. 13.

[25] Ibid, p. 16.

[26] Shahab, Zahid Ahmed and Bhatnagar, Stuti, "Interstate Conflicts and Regionalism in South Asia: Prospects and Challenges", *Center for Strategic Research* (Ankara), Spring-Summer 2008, p. 16.

[27] Kabir, Zahangir, *Challenges of SAARC in its Third Decade* (Islamabad: SAARC Human Resource Development Centre, 2005), p. 11.

[28] Shahab and Bhatnagar, "Interstate Conflicts and Regionalism in South Asia: Prospects and Challenges", p. 19.

[29] Podder, Sukanya, "Challenges to Peace Negotiations: The Sri Lankan Experience", *Strategic Analysis* (New Delhi), Vol. 30, No. 3, July–September 2006, p. 576.

[30] Gurr, Ted Robert, "Peoples against States: Ethno-Political Conflict and the Changing World System", *International Studies Quarterly* (Bloomington), Vol. 38, No. 3, 1994, p. 365.

[31] Among the most celebrated negotiated settlements in civil wars are the pacts that ended fighting in Namibia, Cambodia, El Salvador, Nicaragua, Mozambique and South Africa.

[32] Podder, "Challenges to Peace Negotiations: The Sri Lankan Experience", pp. 576–577.

[33] Sridharan, Kripa, "Regional Organizations and Conflict Management: Comparing ASEAN and SAARC", *Crisis States Research Centre* (London), Working Paper 2, No.3, 2008, p. 1.

[34] Algappa, "Regionalism and Conflict Management: A Framework for Analysis", p. 369.

[35] Zakaria, Ahmad Haji, "The Structure of Decision Making" in Sharon Siddique and Sree Kumar (eds.), *The Second ASEAN Reader* (Singapore: ISEAS, 2003), p. 31.

[36] Mitchell, C.R., *The Structure of International Conflict* (New York: St. Martin's Press, 1989), pp. 275–77.

[37] Sridharan, "Regional Organizations and Conflict Management: Comparing ASEAN and SAARC", pp. 3–4.

[38] Ibid, p. 9.

[39] Dixit, J.N., *My South Bloc Years* (New Delhi: UBS Publishers, 1996), pp. 383–84.

[40] Muni, S.D., "Post Cold-War Regionalism in Asia: With Special Reference to the SAARC Region", *Institute of Developing Economies* (Tokyo), VRF Series 258, 1996, p. 54.

[41] Sridharan, "Regional Organizations and Conflict Management: Comparing ASEAN and SAARC", p. 14.

[42] Ibid, pp. 22–23.

[43] Destradi, "India and the Civil War in Sri Lanka: On the Failures of Regional Conflict Management in South Asia", pp. 16–17.

[44] Subramanian, Nirupama and Radhakrishnan, R.K., "Rising from the Ruins", *Frontline* (Chennai), Vol.29, No.22, 3–16 November 2012, p. 4.

[45] Ibid, pp. 18–19.

India-Sri Lanka Maritime Cooperation in Indian Ocean—Prospects

V. Srilatha

The Indian Ocean is the third largest ocean in the world, and borders over thirty nations. A special feature of the Indian Ocean is that it is virtually surrounded by land on three sides [three continents Africa, Asia and Antarctica]. It is only the southern part of the ocean which easily links up with both the Atlantic and the Pacific Oceans. It is a resource rich ocean, with enormous reserves of oil, natural gas, minerals and a wealth of biological resources. In view of the vast distances of these sea routes for the countries of Asia and Africa, the importance sea lines of communications increases considerably has twenty per cent of the cargo transported through the Indian Ocean is traded within the region; the remaining eighty per cent is extra regional. It must be noted that the stability and maritime security of the Indian Ocean is vulnerable to external threat.[1]

The new legal regime of the sea United Nation Convention on the Law of the Seas [UNCLOS] formalized in November 1994 legitimized the claim of a number of countries of the Indian Ocean to an extended maritime zone. This includes an exclusive economic zone of 200 nautical miles for the mainland and island territories as well as a legal continental self of 200. As a result 30% of the Indian ocean is presently under the EEZ[i] of coastal states.[2] The EEZ of these countries could increase further to 350 nm based on the scientific data submitted to the UN. Sri Lanka's geo strategic location, highlights the fact that it is virtually in the centre of Asia and the sea lanes between the Far East the African and the Arab world. The island nation occupies an important place in the critical sea lanes of communication and much of the World trade and naval activity in the Indian Ocean.

Because of the geostrategic position of India and Sri Lanka, both the countries can play an important role in the Asian resurgence, has the centre of gravity of the global economy moves towards the Indian Ocean and the Pacific. By some statistics over fifty (50) percent of the world's container traffic and seventy (70) percent of global energy trade transits through the Indian Ocean.[3] These numbers are only expected to grow over the next decade, fuelled by the Asian economic expansion and the growing need for raw materials and energy resources from Africa and the Middle East. U.S. defines this Greater Indian Ocean area as encompassing the Red Sea, Arabian Sea, Bay of Bengal, and Java and South China seas. Referring to the U.S. Marine Corps "Vision and Strategy" statement covering the years to 2025, Kaplan observes that "Along with its continued dominance in the Pacific, the U.S. clearly seeks to be the preeminent South Asian power. This signals a momentous historical shift away from the North Atlantic and Europe."[4] The US strategy in Asia is influenced by a combination of balance of power and containment to prevent being "pushed out of Asia" by a China that sees itself as "consolidating Asia into an exclusionary bloc deferring to Chinese economic and foreign policy interests"[5] China to meet its increasing demand for oil and other raw materials, as well as to secure its maritime trade routes through the Indian Ocean, has either built or reportedly planned to construct vital facilities in Bangladesh, Cambodia, Burma (Myanmar), Pakistan, Sri Lanka, and Thailand.[6]

The construction of the massive seaport at Hambantota, a small fishing village of 21,000 people on the southeastern coast of Sri Lanka, is cause for serious concern in India and US. In May 2009, *China National News* reported that Sri Lanka resorted to generous financial, military, and diplomatic support from China after India and the United States declined to assist Sri Lanka in defeating the Tamil Tigers.[7] In exchange, China has now begun to reap the benefits of its strategic investment on the island by using the seaport as a re-fuelling and docking station for the Chinese PLA Navy.

Sri Lanka's only international border is its maritime boundary with India (see Map-1). In the northwestern quadrant of Sri Lanka the EEZ and other areas of maritime jurisdiction adjoin those of India[ii] and as a result are restricted to narrower zones than around the rest of the island. Sri Lanka's Exclusive Economic Zone (EEZ) [reportedly as 517,000 sq. km.] is 7.8 times the total land area of the country. Under the United Nations Convention on Law of the Sea, the country can also claim an extensive additional extent of seabed area. The total area including the EEZ is suspected to be 23 times larger than the total land area and can be used for exploration and exploitation of minerals and hydrocarbon resource.[8] Thus making its position in the Indian ocean region all the more important. With US and China vying for more strategic position in Sri Lanka, India has to protect its interests which are strategic and proximate. As one of the two largest countries in Asia and geographically strategically located as it is, India has responsibilities in ensuring security of the commons, as well as legitimate concerns, as China expands its economic and maritime networks in the South China Sea and the Indian Ocean.

Map 1: Maritime Zones of Sri Lanka

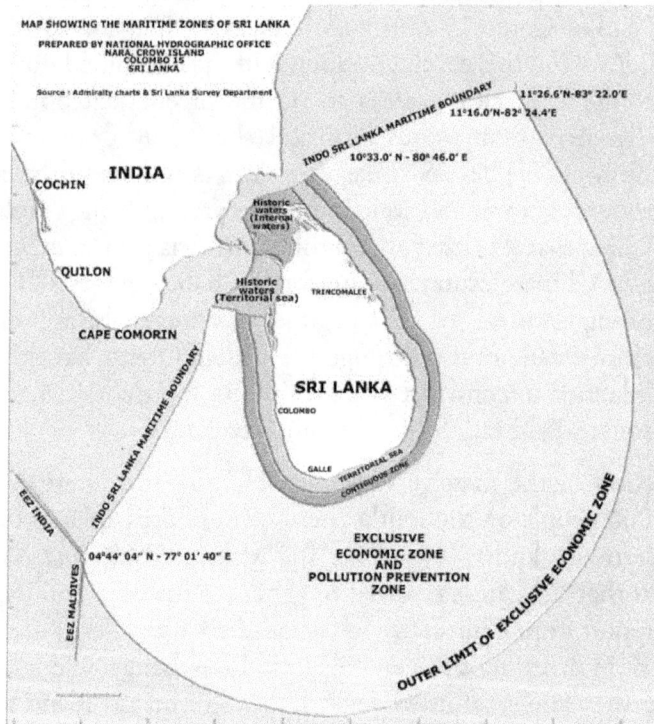

Source: http://www.seaarounds.org/eez/144.aspx

Maritime security not only affects oceangoing vessels, but also the national security of coastal nations. Cooperation among countries with interests in the Indian Ocean is essential to effectively fight state and non-state actors. It is in India's long-term interest to see maritime cooperation play a crucial role in promoting a strong and stable neighbourhood in the Indian Ocean Region.

IRRITANTS IN MARITIME COOPERATION

Though

India had settled maritime boundary issues with all its neighbours except Pakistan and Bangladesh, in reality, India has still issues to be settled with Sri Lanka. Despite the existence of two maritime agreements of 1974 and 1976 there are certain irritants between the two neighbours.

The main issue is the status of Katchchativu, a small barren island in the Palk Bay area (see Map-2). India agreed to Sri Lanka's sovereignty over Katchchativu but with some safeguards to its Indian fishermen through Article 5^{iii} of 1974 agreement. But, a fishing war is straining relations between India and Sri Lanka as Indian fishermen, often poor and desperate, regularly cross into Sri Lankan waters and run a-foul of the Sri Lankan Navy. Figures differ, but according to one report at least 100 Indian fishermen have been killed and 350 seriously injured in recent years. The dispute is rooted in a complicated blend of local factors: the steady depletion of fish stocks, partly because of overfishing by Indian trawlers; the aftermath of the 2004 tsunami, which saw relief funds partly used to expand the Indian fishing fleet even as fish populations declined; and the end of the long Sri Lankan civil war in 2009, which has meant the return of the nation's fishing boats to waters once plied almost exclusively by Indians. In February 2011, Sri Lankan fishermen formed a flotilla and captured 18 Indian trawlers and 112 fishermen before releasing the boats under government pressure.[9]

Map-2: Katchchativu Island

Source: www.newyorktimes

The dispute is intensified by history and proximity though Central Government of India laid to rest the issue of sovereignty over the tiny rock of an island, Kachchativu. Passions are still very much alive on either side of the Palk Strait over territorial waters and the rights of either side to exploit resources.[10] At the closest point, the two countries are separated by barely 10 nautical miles, even as both sides are bound by ethnicity. Tamils dominate India's southern state of Tamil Nadu and have close cultural ties to Tamils in Sri Lanka, even providing support to Tamil rebels or accepting refugees during the fighting that ended with a government victory. The postwar tensions remain in Tamil Nadu. The state's chief minister, Jayalalitha, was against India's joint exercises with the Sri Lankan military, suspended a bureaucrat who allowed a Sri Lankan school to play a soccer match in the state and confronted pilgrims from Sri Lanka who had come to Tamil Nadu for a religious event.

The question of maritime boundaries has become a touchy one. In Tamil Nadu, the lingering notion has been, that this small island, barely over one square kilometer in landmass, was ceded to Sri Lanka by the central government without the consent of the periphery. Today, many fishermen in Tamil Nadu, as well as the state's elected leaders, want to reclaim the island and the fishing rights as part of what they consider their heritage. According to Sri Lanka at the time of negotiations, India was never able to establish it had sovereign rights over the island in order to cede it. Its most ardent argument was that the Rajah of Ramnad (Rameshvaram) had authority over the islands and collected revenue from it. The Sri Lankan side argued that the Rajah was appointed by British as a part of the Zamindari system in which the Rajah was a mere tax collector and therefore did not represent a sovereign. Also, maps dating back to the Dutch period proved that Kachchativu was part of the Jaffna administrative region. When faced with such overwhelming evidence the Indian side withdrew its claim to Kachchativu. Thus the Sri Lankans argue that while India was amicable and cooperative in resolving the Kachchativu issue it at no point ceded or 'gifted' the island to Sri Lanka since it could not establish sovereignty over it to begin with.[11] Hence the fishing rights belong to Sri Lankan.

During the Sri Lankan civil war, the Sri Lankan Navy distracted by the war, allowed Indian boats to operate freely. Post War with Sri Lankan fishermen returning to the sea have problems of poaching and overfishing by Indians—especially the extensive Indian use of bottom trawlers and monofilament nylon nets, which have been banned in Sri Lanka. The fisheries issue was always a cause of friction between the two countries that a Bilateral Joint Working Group on Fisheries has been long established. But, being defunct during the civil war, it has been revived recently. Delegations to the working group meetings are led by senior officials of the Ministries of Foreign Affairs in India and Sri Lanka. The delegations include officials from the Ministry of Fisheries, Ministry of Defense, the Attorney General's Department, Immigration and Emigration Authority, and the Navy and related agencies in the two countries, representing the government. Prior to the formal meetings, it was also decided to enhance and promote contacts of informal discussions between the fishers' associations and governmental officials.[12] As the issues related to a string of attacks on Indian fishermen by the Sri Lankan navy have heightened tensions recently both country's coast guards held four-day discussions on maritime issues so has to mitigate the problem.

SETHUSAMUDRAM SHIPPING CANAL PROJECT

Another maritime issue exists in the form of Sethusamudram Shipping Canal Project (see Map-3). India does not enjoy a continuous navigable sea route in its territorial waters, Indian vessels must circumnavigate Sri Lanka to travel from India's western to its eastern coast. The government of India established the Sethusamudran Ship Canal Project (SSCP) on July 2, 2005, in order to dredge the Palk Strait and facilitate direct transportation. The SSCP will substantially reduce the distance between ports in India. Apart from cutting short distances for Indian ships navigating between eastern and western coasts of India, the Canal is expected to boost the underdeveloped coastal regions of Tamil Nadu.[13] There has been considerable objection from political parties and groups in Tamil Nadu, Civil society organizations, environmentalists, and independent experts who expressed concern about the adverse impact the SSCP would have on economic and environmental interests.

Map-3: Sethusamudram Ship Canal Project

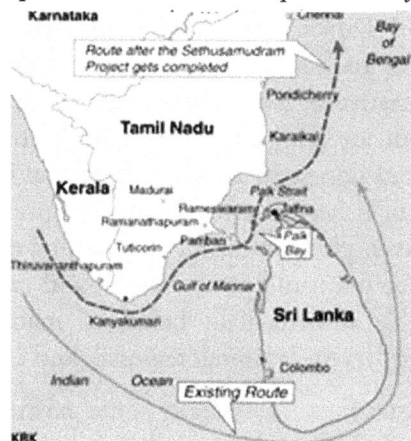

www.tamilnation.org

The SSCP has implications for Sri Lanka, including concern over environmental and livelihood issues. These concerns include the impact on the marine ecosystem and water quality; the implications of dredging and dumping over 80 million cubic meters of ocean floor material; the possibility of blasting, resulting in destruction of marine life and disturbance of marine ecology; damage to the coral reef; and depletion of fish stocks and ensuing loss of local livelihoods. Commercially, Sri Lanka is more concerned about the loss of container traffic at its Colombo and Galle ports. The government of Sri Lanka conveyed these concerns to the government of India through official political channels. India agreed to cooperate and offered to facilitate the continuation of Indo–Sri Lanka consultations, including at the expert and technical levels, "with a view to reaching a common understanding".[14] The bottom line is that environmental concerns must be addressed jointly, and that close economic cooperation in the Palk Strait area must be established. The complementary areas generated could be exploited by the Sri Lankan shipping industry. The commercial implications of opening and expanding ports in South India were also evaluated, and it was generally agreed that the port in Colombo would continue to attract international shipping business. Both countries are looking into yet another area of cooperation between the two countries could be in the form of a land bridge between Rameshwaram in Tamil Nadu and Talaimannar in Northwestern Sri Lanka which is still in the proposal stage. India and Sri Lanka agreed to resume the ferry services between Colombo and Tuticorin and between Talaimannar and Rameswaram.[15]

COOPERATION BETWEEN INDIA AND SRI LANKA

For both India and Sri Lanka, the surrounding maritime environment continues to contribute to national interest. In order to counter the challenges created by maritime issues, cooperative mechanisms could be developed that focus on an array of areas: security challenges, maritime threats posed by state and non-state actors, navigational issues, the political and social dimensions of fisheries concerns, marine pollution and coastal degradation; the impacts of global warming and natural disasters, increasing joint management of the maritime environment, and exploiting maritime resources in a sustainable and mutually beneficial manner. These mechanisms function on many levels: bilateral, regional, and eventually global.[16]

In the case of South Asia, there are already some existing mechanisms so Cooperation "may include measures such as joint naval patrolling, controlling of smuggling and piratical activities, and the strengthening of communication networks." From an Indian perspective it is obvious that the various maritime challenges must be addressed on a multi-layered basis. Tracking of smugglers and gunrunners would lead to greater military involvement and possibly interdiction and arrest as well. Of the various transnational security threats, maritime piracy and terrorism would most directly and extensively involve nations' naval forces. But the Indian Ocean and the Southern Asian region lack "channelized" efforts towards addressing maritime challenges.[17] As part of combating these problems bilateral and at best, trilateral arrangements can lead to a multilateral approach to combat maritime disorder. India-Sri Lanka maritime co-operation can be multifolded, keeping aside the irritants same of the possible areas of cooperation are Oil and Gas Exploration.

Map-4: India's grabens contain significant accumulations of oil and coal. Nearly all were formed during the breakup of the giant Gondwana continent

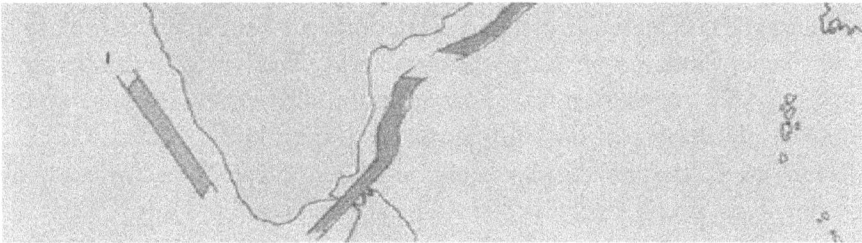

Source: www.slaas.lkhydrocarbondepositsin Indian Ocean around Sri Lanka

Map-5

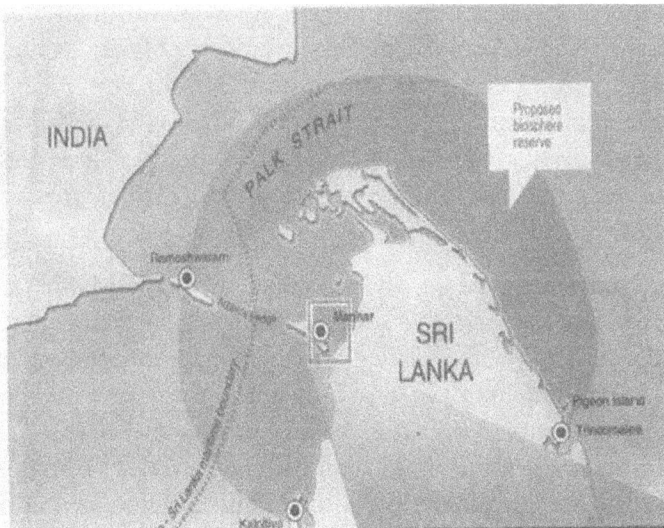

To the northwest of Sri Lanka are the Mannar and Cauvery Basins and the Palk Basin lies between Sri Lanka and India in a possible rifted basin system coast of India (Andhra-Orissa region) graben, where several deltas are forming (e.g. Krishna-Godawari and Mahanadi) with producing oil and gas fields today. The Palk-Cauvery-Mannar graben system, which probably formed when the original Gondwana continent fragmented and drifted forming the potentially rich oil basins in this area (see Map-4). These three basins are within the offshore economic zones of both India and Sri Lanka with the India-Sri Lanka marine boundary "clearly" demarcated under the Law of the Sea jurisdictions (see Map-5).[18] However, with oil basins shared between jurisdictions, some legal problems could arise if and when hydrocarbons are discovered and produced in the future. Further, the Mannar-Cauvery-Palk region is also a proposed Marine biosphere conservation area which will come into conflict with offshore petroleum activities. The Mannar Basin has had a long history over 40 years of hydrocarbon exploration, It is only recently serious attempts at exploration started and with the new Petroleum Exploration Act. Four offshore exploration blocks were offered for bids and one Block (Block-1) was awarded to Cairn (India) for exploration. The Mannar Basin discoveries represent what is undoubtedly the first promising petroleum system in Sri Lanka. Indian companies are serving Sri Lanka's energy market and exploring the Island's off-shore oil resources. Lanka Indian Oil Corporation (Lanka IOC) has a 30 per cent market share in Sri Lanka's retail petrol market, operating 151 retail outlets on the island. Lanka IOC is building and operating storage facilities at the Trincomalee Tank farm, which as stated earlier, is of critical importance in the maritime strategic environment. India also has a significant stake in exploration of oil resources off Sri Lanka's coast. India's Oil and Natural Gas Corporation (ONCG) has been promised one of the five drilling blocks in the Mannar basin.[19] The Mannar basin, thought to contain the equivalent of one billion barrels of oil, has three remaining blocks up for auction (besides the one promised to India, the second of the five has been granted to China).

Recently, Sri Lanka allocated an exploration block in the Mannar Basin to China for petroleum exploration. This allocation would connote a Chinese presence just a few miles from India's southern tip, thus causing strategic discomfort. In economic terms, it could also mean the end of the monopoly held by Indian oil companies in this realm, putting them into direct and stiff competition from Chinese oil companies. At Hambantota, on the southern coast of Sri Lanka where Beijing is building bunkering facilities and an oil tank farm. This infrastructure will help service hundreds of ships that traverse the sea lanes of commerce off Sri Lanka. The Chinese presence in Hambantota would be another vital element in its strategic circle including, Myanmar and Bangladesh.[20]

Marine Pollution and Oil Spill Management

Another area of great concern is the *marine pollution* caused by various methods, including the dumping of industrial and other waste into the sea from shore and the discharge of waste from oceangoing vessels. Monitoring marine pollution is a difficult undertaking, but all the more disturbing, is that is not often even addressed by coastal nations. Given the nature of the common security and environmental threats facing the oceans, it is clear that individual nations acting in isolation will not be able to effect comprehensive or long lasting solutions.

With both India and Sri Lanka on the path of maritme trade and shipping Oil Spills management becomes an important issue. Oil spills are an ever-increasing problem with serious consequences for marine ecological systems and have economic impact on the countries. The environmental effects are of long-term or short-term duration, with many effects of disasters involving LPG tankers have yet to be understood. Shipping industry is very much concerned with major oil spills or wrecks of oil tankers in the coastal waters and high seas has they can seriously affect the flow of merchant shipping traffic. The spillage can include difficulties of jetties, storage capacity, and longer routing leading to compounding of economic losses, foreign currency and higher insurances. Hence, both the countries can contribute to the structuring of "spill response centers" with mandatory power to inspect oil tankers.[21]

Piracy

Somalian piracy, starting as a fairly localised activity in the Gulf of Aden, has grown to become a threat to ships plying routes far beyond the Somali coast into the Arabian sea. Somali piracy has become a complex issue, not only as organised crime but also suspected to be linked in other endeavours, namely the smuggling of people, arms and drugs.[22] Recently more than thirty Somali pirates were apprehended in Maldivian waters. The Indian Navy has been playing an important role in survelliance and escorting the ships plying in the region, there has been instances where the somalian pirates came close to Indian waters. The Sri Lanka Navy has also arrested some of the Somalians who were suspected of piracy and drifted towards Sri Lanka. The total economic cost of piracy, when considering the costs of insurance, naval support, re-routing of ocean traffic and all other steps taken to protect vessels from this threat, has been estimated at close to 10 billion US Dollars per annum and existing international maritime laws and practices have proven ineffective in combating the activities of the pirates. Some countries such as the United States have adjusted their maritime laws to enable private security personnel to travel on board merchant vessels. A few countries have even expressed an interest in sending personnel from their national militaries on board merchant vessels to provide protection for those ships, and have requested Sri Lanka's assistance during transit. Sri Lanka has been a hub for private-security firms in the region providing such services. Sri Lanka has been allowing to carry weapons in and out of the country. But Sri Lanka wants to close these arms warehouses has the fear lingers that the weapons might fall into the hands of local militants and thus hinder its security. Though the steps taken by ship owners are largely ineffective, Sri Lankan government is unlikely to back down on this decision even though the international shipping community objects to these proposed changes.[iv, 23]

Map-6: LTTE Controlled and Active Areas before November 117, 2005

Source: Frontline, 27 February 2009, p. 7.

The lasting solution to threats of this nature cannot be undertaken by individual nations in isolation, but only through greater international cooperation. The lack of a coordinated international effort to uphold maritime security not only affects oceangoing vessels, but also the national security of coastal nations, has experienced by Sri Lanka in combating the Liberation Tigers of Tamil Eelam [LTTE]. The LTTE through its maritime wing Sea Tigers has not only controlled the northern and eastern coast of Sri Lanka (see Map-6) but also smuggled in a formidable arsenal of weapons that included mortar, artillery, anti-aircraft guns, surface to air missiles, armoured vehicles and even light aircraft. Using over twenty large vessels and a considerable number of trawlers registered under different flags, the LTTE shipped this equipment to Sri Lanka through international waters.[24] While large vessels lay anchored in international waters more than a thousand nautical miles away from Sri Lanka, Smaller vessels were dispatched to smuggle the items they carried to the coast. During the Humanitarian Operation to defeat LTTE terrorism, which took place between 2006 and 2009, the Sri Lanka Navy went into deep seas on five occasions to destroy eight of these floating warehouses. All coastal nations are vulnerable to threats from the sea, and terrorists will exploit the weak points in defences to their advantage. To combat this threat, it is vital that the maritime big powers like India cooperate by sharing intelligence, and enhance maritime domain awareness through joint and coordinated patrols as well as exercises to enhance interoperability. Thus providing assistance to improve the resources and capabilities of less advanced naval powers will also enhance overall maritime security in the region.[25]

Human Trafficking

South Asian sea routes are also used for human smuggling and drug trafficking. Further, the movement of refugees has had an impact on the domestic political developments in the affected countries and causes friction among many countries of the region. After the military defeat of the LTTE in Sri Lanka, the remaining ships that operated in that group's international supply network began engaging in this illegal enterprise both in India and Sri Lanka. Charging many thousands of dollars per illegal immigrant, these vessels have been transporting hundreds of people through international waters to western countries such as Canada and Australia. As human trafficking benefits from a legal framework that has no proper mechanisms to deal with such vessels in international waters, it is cooperation and coordination among nations that can minimize the threat Effective bilateral and multilateral coastal surveillance, patrols and effective intelligence network can mitigate the problem particularly in the South Asian region.

Drug Trafficking

Both the countries could cooperate in tackling drug trafficking has it is the major issue effecting South Asian region. Drug smuggling, has become a lucrative source of income for terrorists, insurgents and large criminal networks. The defeat and the death of LTTE chief Velupillai Prabhakaran has changed the dynamics of drug trade in the subcontinent.[v] The LTTE also generated enormous sums of money through other illegal drugs network that operated in Europe, South Asia and South East Asia. The drug infested Golden Crescent used the same modus operandi used by arms smugglers, using fishing boats and specially modified craft to conceal the cargo. The Indian and Sri Lanka Navy have come across many fishing boats transporting drugs across border through legal containerised cargo that is processed through the ports. In the present era, the increasing sophistication of criminal networks and non-state actors makes it difficult for individual nations to withstand the threats posed by them alone.[26] Both the countries can combate this problem by greater information sharing, better screening practices and better coordination among the navies and the coastguard. With growing maritime trade the other venues of cooperation would also increase.

Illegal, Unreported and Unregulated Fishing [IUUF]

Apart from these threats to nations, IUUF poses major risk to oceanic resources. Fishing is an important and only livelihood for many people in both the countries and IUUF threatens livelihood of many people in the regions. It has been estimated that the total economic cost of pirate fishing runs into billions of dollars per annum and has become a major contributor in devastating the fishing environment. As the EEZ of both the countries tend to increase, monitoring the problem of Illegal, Unreported and Unregulated fishing, becomes all the more difficult and acting against it is even more so. Thus the countries can protect their interest through a concerted regional effort.[27]

Other Areas of Cooperation

The Indian Register of Shipping[vi] is helping to develop Sri Lanka's shipping and maritime industry. A new IT applications "Ship Mate" is being used for Sri Lankan owned vessels has a goodwill to support the local shipping industry. As the international interest in Sri Lanka is increasing due to its strategic location, Sri Lanka is upgrading resources that are ideal for maritime technology, ship building and repairs. Many major international shipping lanes pass the south of Sri Lanka, only a few nautical miles away from the newly developed Hamban\tota Port. Has maritime and shipping industry is shifting from West to East, India and Sri Lanka should cooperate multifold to harness its industry to attract more vessels and to own more ships. The new software, the first of its kind in the world is aimed at providing the ship's crew with the information they need to manage the safety of their ships. *Ship Mate* gives the crew information about the stability of the ship, in both floating and grounded conditions. If the ship is grounded or damaged, *Ship Mate* informs the crew about the likely problems caused by the water flowing in and what effect any proposed remedial action may have' Ship Mate is useful in normal conditions too as it provides information on corrosion levels in tanks and holds, and identifies any structural components that need to be renewed."[28]

Naval Cooperation

Transnational threats, have spawned a multitude of additional "out of area" operational roles for navies, and thus dramatically increased the maritime security challenges of the South Asian region. Countering these threats and challenges requires consistent cooperation between the states affected and the associated maritime agencies. As the largest naval power in South Asia, India plays a major role in upholding the maritime security of this region.

The establishment of *Joint Maritime Centers (JMCs)* and *"Oil Spill Response Centers.",* comprising *navies and coastguards of India other countries* could enable rapid and coordinated responses to smuggling, piracy, humanitarian disasters, illegal migration, environmental incidents, and search-and-rescue operations, has these are crucial areas that require cooperation. The centers may also provide a venue for intelligence sharing and combat the hazards of oil spills due to various reasons. These response centers could be amalgamated with the JMCs for better coordination and management. Regional states could also develop marine technology and a joint strategy to ensure the safety of ports and harbors.

Towards this end, Sri Lanka has recently revamped and expanded its Coast Guard Department whilst further strengthening its vastly experienced Navy Despite relations between the two countries not being at its best in recent times following the Indian vote for a resolution against Sri Lanka at the United Nations Human Rights Council in March 2012, defence and security cooperation between the two countries are firmly looking up. On the Sri Lankan side, the post-war availability of ships to participate in an exercise allowed the resumption of the five-day SLINEX exercise between the Indian and Sri Lankan navies in September 2011—their first joint naval exercise since 2005.[29] In January 2012, India and Sri Lanka launched their annual defense dialogue in New Delhi, with maritime security among the top issues discussed by their defense secretaries. A few months later, the Sri Lanka Coast Guard was invited to participate in the two decades-old bilateral DOSTI exercise between the Indian and Maldivian coast guards in April 2012.[30] India is also in the process of building two off Shore Patrol vessels for Sri Lanka.

CONCLUSION

It is imperative that Indian Ocean issues are addressed both regionally and globally, has their complex nature involves security and strategic concerns that affect the region. The South Asian Association for Regional Cooperation (SAARC) is an appropriate mechanism to play an active role in bringing about the necessary cooperation on maritime issues in the region. As South Asia occupies a central position in the Indian Ocean, it is important for the region to spearhead the response to maritime issues, collaborating with organizations in other regions, particularly those in Southeast Asia, West Asia, and the Horn of Africa. As the maritime domain becoming the main stake holder in emerging geo strategic changes unfolded by emerging economy of China, the medium can mutually benefit collaboration between the two neighbouring countries. It not only promotes better understanding and cooperation between India and Sri Lanka on maritime issues such as the settlement of the maritime dispute, enhancing and institutionalizing economic cooperation in the exploration and exploitation of sea resources in the Indian Ocean and bilateral under-standing on respective fishermen's problems but also provides prospects for greater potential for ship-building, weather forecasting, prevention of pollution, and to combating in maritime terrorism. The prospects of maritime cooperation are far reaching, provided the countries are not carried away by the passions of the people in resolving the irritants in the relations.

REFERENCES

[1] See Sergei De silva Ranasinghe, "Why the Indian Ocean Matters", *The Diplomat* March 2, 2011, www.thediplomat.com

[2] Schofield, C., 'A Complex Mosaic: Maritime Jurisdictional Claims in the Indian Ocean', Indian Ocean Survey, Vol. 3, s. 1 and 2, 2007, p. 3, Endnotes 3–4. The

UK'sBritish Indian Ocean Territory (BIOT) consists of the Chagos Archipelago, which includes the atoll of Diego Garcia. France's Indian Ocean territorial possessions includeRéunion Island, Tromelin Island, Mayotte Island, Bassas da India, Europa Island, Glorioso Islands, and Juan de Nova Island.

[3] Robert D. Kaplan's "Monsoon: The Indian Ocean and the Future of American Power", Random House 2010; *Neville Ladduwahetty* US-India-China and the Indian ocean: impact on Sri Lanka, Posted on July 14th, 2012, *The Island* http://www. lankaweb.com/news/items/2012/07/14/us-india-china-and-the-indian-ocean-impact-on-sri-lanka.

[4] Robert D. Kaplan's, "Monsoon: The Indian Ocean and the Future of American Power" Random House, 2010.

[5] Henry, A. Kissinger, The Future of US–Chinese Relations, Foreign Affairs, March/April 2012; Urmila Venugopalan, "Harbouring Ambitions: China Invests in Indian Ocean Ports," *Jane's Intelligence Review*, Oct. 15, 2009, 20.

[6] Michael Richardson, "Full Steam Ahead for Naval Might," *The Straits Times*, January 15, 2009. See the eprinthttp://app.mfa.gov.sg/pr/read_content.asp? View,11921. Also see K. Alan Kronstadt and Bruce Vaughn, *Sri Lanka: Background and U.S. Relations*, U.S. Congressional Research Service, Washington, D.C., June 4, 2009 and Peter Lee, "Beijing Broods Over Its Arc of Anxiety," *Asia Times*, December 4, 2009; also see1514 Christopher Pehrson, *String of Pearls: Meeting the Challenge of China's Rising Power across the Asian Littoral* (Carlisle, PA: United States Army War College, 2006), v.

[7] Gamini Weerakoon, "Hambantota in the Great Game of the Indian Ocean," *The Sunday Leader*, February 7, 2010. http://www.thesundayleader.lk/?p=7211. Urmila Venugopalan, "Harbouring Ambitions: China Invests in Indian Ocean Ports," *Jane's Intelligence Review*, Oct. 15, 2009, 20; 1 See "Chinese Billions Helping Lanka Ward Off Western Peace Efforts, Fight LTTE," *China National News*, May 2, 2009 (see above).

[8] Leslie Joseph National Report of Sri Lanka, on Theformulation of a Transboundary Diagnostic Analysis and Strategic Action Plan For The Bay Of Bengal Large Marine Ecosystem Programme, 2002.

[9] Dr. N. Manoharan "Fishermen Issue and India-Sri Lanka Relations http://www. vifindia.org/article/2012/june/29/fishermen-issue-and-india-sri-lanka-relations.

[10] W.T. Jayasinghe, *Kachchativu and the Maritime Boundary of Sri Lanka*, A Standard Lake publications, 2003.

[11] "Time to assert Sri Lanka's Territorial Rights", *Ceylon Today*, Jan. 8, 2012; T S Subramanian, "Straits of Tension," Frontline, Vol. 24, Issue 6, 24 March–6 April 2007.

[12] Geethangani de Silva "Indian Ocean Resource and Governance Challenges" in Ellen Laipson, Amit Pandya ed; Maritime Issues in South Asia, The Henry L. Stimson Center, 2009.

[13] A. Balasubramanyam Raju, Sethudamudran Project ;2For example, the distance between Tuticorin, a port southwest of Chennai, and Chennai will drop from 769 to 335 nautical miles, and that between Tuticorin to Kolkata will be reduced from 1,371 to 1,031 nautical miles.2 The direct navigation of ships is expected to save fuel costs and standing charges associated with longer voyages. The SSCP also includes plans to develop the Tuticorin port and promote economic development of the

backward areas of the Ramanathpuram and Tirunelveli districts of Tamil Nadu. The SSCP also hopes to promote coastal shipping and generate employment opportunities for the area, and to increase foreign investment in the Tuticorin district. More recently, a case was filed in the Supreme Court of India on cultural and religious grounds, protesting that Ram Sethu, also known as Adam's Bridge—and considered an Indian national treasure—would be damaged by the dredging process of the SSCP. There is also concern that even if the canal were deepened it could not accommodate the bigger shipping vessels that must navigate from east to west and vice versa. As a result, their need to circumvent Sri Lanka would continue. Also, dredging cannot stop once the work of the SSCP is over. It will be a continuous process to clear the seabed of sand that is redeposited in the dredged area over time.

[14] Joint Press Statement of the 6th Session of the Sri Lanka–India Joint Commission, June 10, 2005, 3. Colombo, Sri Lanka. 13 on the environmental concerns and addressing them. The objective of the consultations is to formulate measures to monitor and mitigate any adverse impacts of the SSCP. The Bilateral Experts Meeting, which met in both India and Sri Lanka, focused on these concerns as well as on strategic and marine ecological issues. Recommendations included joint monitoring and assessment of any adverse implications, creating a mechanism for exchanging information, joint assessment of risks through.

[15] Geethangani de Silva, "Indian Ocean Resource and Governance Challenges" in Ellen Laipson, Amit Pandya ed; *Maritime Issues in South Asia*, The Henry L. Stimson Center, 2009.

[16] Nong Hong, "Charting a Maritime Security Cooperation Mechanism in the Indian Ocean: Sharing Responsibilities among Littoral States and User States", Strtegic Analysis, Volume 36, Issue 3, Articles May 2012.

[17] McPherson, K., 'SAARC and the Indian Ocean', South Asian Survey, Vol. 9, 2 (2002), pp. 258, 260, also see 'Indo-Srilanka Mritime cooperation: Implications for Bay of Bengal Region" in T. NirmalaDevi, ef BIMSTEC: Experiment in Sub-Regional Cooperation, Gyan Publishers, New Delhi 2007.

[18] Ananda Gunatilaka, "Hydrocarbon Deposits in the Indian Ocean around Sri Lanka—An Overview". www.slaas.lk/HYDROCARBON%20DEPOSISTS%20THE%20 INDIAN%20OCEAN%20AROUND%20LANKA%201.pdf

[19] Gamini Warushamana, "Oil Exploration in Mannar Basin Will Take Time," *Sunday Observer*, 11 November 2007.

[20] Dipanjan Roy Chaudhury Boosting Maritime Capabilities in the Indian Ocean, 23 August 2007, www.worldpress.org/Asia/2908.htm.

[21] For critical analysis see Kim, Inho (2010). 'Who Bears the Lion's Share of a Black Pie of Oil Pollution Costs?', *Ocean Development and International Law*, 41: 1, 55–76.

[22] Potgieter, T. and Schofield, C., 'Poverty, Poaching and Pirates: Geopolitical Instability and Maritime Insecurity off the Horn of Africa', *Journal of the Indian Ocean Region*, Vol. 6, 1, June 2010, p. 97; Murphy, M., 'Contemporary Piracy and Maritime Terrorism, Chapter Three: Assessing the Threat', Adelphi Papers, Vol. 47, 388, June 2007, p.

[23] Sarah Kent, "The Shipping Firms Facing New Security Challenges", *The Wall Street Journal*, Oct. 14, 2012.

[24] See V. Srilatha, "LTTE and India's Maritime Security" Indian Ocean Survey, Vol. 4, No. 2, Jan.–Dec., 2008.

[25] Gotabhaya Rajapaksa, "Lanka enjoys a strategically significant geographical position in the Indian Ocean", 15 November 2011, *Gotabhaya Rajapaksa's address at the inaugural session of the "Galle Dialogue"* November 14, 2011.

[26] Ibid.

[27] Geethangani de Silva "Indian Ocean Resource and Governance Challenges", in Ellen Laipson, Amit Pandya ed; Maritime Issues in South Asia, The Henry L. Stimson Center, 2009.

[28] Ship Mate' to streamline Lanka's shipping and Maritime Industry, www.sipa.lk/ news_archives_06.asp.

[29] Nilanthi Samaranayake, The Long Littoral Project: Bay of Bengal: A Maritime Perspective on Indo-Pacific Security, IRP-2012-U-002319-Final, September 2012, www.cna.org.

[30] Asif Fuard "Maldives, Sri Lanka and India conducts joint Naval Exercises", Haveeru online, 24 April 2012.

End Notes

i. The prospect of these changes on the international law of the sea set in motion attempts, in the 1970's and 1980's to delimit maritime boundaries amongst littoral and island states. In view of the relatively limited distances amongst states and conflicting claims, it is not surprising that a number of maritime disputes are prevalent in the Indian Ocean.

ii. Bank after 1979, as well as to one third of the Pedro Bank, and some areas to the north of it. These areas, which are now in Indian waters, were the only grounds in Sri Lanka known to be suitable for the use of large trawlers. The establishment of EEZs by Sri Lanka and other countries of the region led to Sri Lanka losing access to the Wadge.

iii. The article, however, was vague enough for the Sri Lankan government to argue, "[the] agreement did not give any fishing rights, but only the rights to dry their fishing nets, to rest, and to the right of pilgrims to visit the island for religious purposes." Until civil war broke out in Sri Lanka in 1983, the Indian fishermen did not find it difficult to operate near the islet for fishing. At times, attracted by good quality fish and prawns, the Indian fishing folk strayed into the Sri Lankan waters. In due course of time, however, the Sri Lankan Navy became unfriendly to Indian fishermen owing to their inability to distinguish between genuine fishing vessels and boats used for smuggling goods for Sri Lankan Tamil militants. Consequently, indiscriminate firing and killing of Indian fishermen became common. Despite various outcries, the humanitarian aspect of the problem was overlooked by both countries. Various options like issuing identity cards to Indian fishermen and letting the islet, in perpetuity, to India have been explored, but not converted into action.

iv. The British government now is trying to persuade Sri Lanka not to upset the new status quo has U.K. firms account for more than half of the 24 companies currently participating in the Security Association for the Maritime Industry's certification program, an industry standard that has gained traction in the absence of an international benchmark of quality for private maritime security firms. Sri Lanka's decision raises a difficult legal question for U.K. based maritime security firms, because arms licenses issued by the U.K. government don't authorize the use of offshore floating armories. Finding reputable alternatives to U.K. based firms may prove difficult for ship owners, as British companies are so numerous within the industry.

v. Mumbai was a key link in this supply chain as LTTE's conduits often used the city to bring in drugs from Mandsaur district of Madhya Pradesh, and the Rajasthan and Punjab border. The consignments were then transported to coastal towns in Tamil Nadu such as Tuticorin, Rameshwaram, Ramnad, Nagapattinam, Kochi and a host of localities inhabited by fishing communities on the south-east coast. From there, the drugs would be shipped to Velvettiturai, a township located along the northern coast of Sri Lanka and formerly under LTTE control.

vi. The Indian Register of Shipping (IRS) is an internationally recognized independent ship classification society, founded in India in 1975. IRS provides professionally competent, completely independent and highly efficient third party technical inspection and certification services for all types of marine craft and structures. These services have also been expanded to cover a range of offshore and industrial projects.

Ethnicity, Plurality, Diaspora, Economic Cooperation and Trade Relations

Plurality and Diaspora

Rajiva Wijesinha

It is clear that Sri Lanka stands today at a cross-roads. Following the successful conclusion of the war against LTTE terrorism, Sri Lanka has an opportunity to build up a prosperous pluralistic future. This however seems increasingly difficult in the light of continuing international criticism, which has in turn put Sri Lanka on the defensive. This has contributed to failure to move swiftly on inclusivity and reconciliation, and I fear that unless there is greater trust, and confidence building, on all sides, we can only look forward to greater tensions, with increasing difficulties for not only Sri Lanka, but also India and the entire SAARC region.

In this context it is also important for India to recognize that she too stands at a cross-roads. Given the remarkable economic development of recent years, India will obviously attract increasing attention on the world stage. In the prevailing state of international relations, this will involve enticements to fall in line with the oppositional approach to global relations that marked the post Second World War period. The Cold War was characterized by efforts to build up confrontational alliances, and this was accompanied by demonization of those who failed to play ball. This conceptual framework has unfortunately continued into an era in which it has no business.

The greatest victim of this approach was India. What I see as the idealistic but also immensely practical vision of Nehru, to position India as a leader of Non-Alignment, fell prey to the refusal of bigger powers to accept that balance was possible. The obvious fact that India was the biggest gap in the encirclement of the Soviet Union and its allies that the various Treaty Organizations of the forties and fifties set up led to hostility, and support for countries that were seen as a counterweight to India. The saddest victim of this theoretically positive, most favoured nation, type of approach was Pakistan, where the secular determination of Jinnah, perhaps misplaced but essentially liberal in spirit, was overtaken by fundamentalism and militarism, since these were seen in the dark days of the Cold War as the best weapons against evil Communist empires.

But India too suffered from this demonization, and deliberately so I fear. The continuing problems of terrorism it faces arose from this oppositioning tendency. It was no coincidence, after all, that when the United States ultimately awoke to the threat presented by the monster it had created, and bombed terrorist training camps after the attack on the USS Cole, the victims were Kashmiri terrorists being trained by the same dispensation as had trained terrorists against the Soviet backed regime in Afghanistan.

All that should be water under the bridge, and the greater enlightenment with regard to India that now characterizes the West is to be welcomed. But old habits die hard, and I fear that India is now being inveigled into similar involvement in oppositioning alliances, as Pakistan was in the old days. The enemy now is not the Soviet Union, with India seen as an acolyte that also has to be contained, but rather China, which of course had been used in the seventies and eighties as a counterweight to the Evil Empire that was seen then as stretching from Vladivostok to Berlin, and from the North Pole to Cape Cormorin.

The demonizing of China that is a necessary part of persuading India to get involved in this new Cold War has contributed to a perverse presentation of China's role in Sri Lanka. Thus Chinese involvement in Sri Lanka is seen as excluding India and a threat to its security. This is highlighted in discussion of the Hambantota Port development, whereas the project was of course offered to India first, and to China only after India was unable to take it on. The fact that India then began to fast forward the Kankesanthurai Port development, which it had pledged to do some years back, but held back on for a range of reasons, makes it clear that Sri Lanka has no plans for exclusivity, and Indian involvement in our development is seen as a necessity.

But there will continue to be propaganda suggesting the opposite, and this is apparent in the efforts of the diaspora to demonize Sri Lanka and China equally in Indian eyes. Having failed to persuade India to intervene on the side of terrorists in 2009, the diaspora has now developed a more sophisticated way of pressurizing India, and stresses what it claims is Sri Lankan reliance on China. This is of course a persuasive factor as far as the West is concerned too, and the combined efforts of diaspora detractors and Cold War warriors in Washington can well upset Indo-Sri Lankan relations.

The problem is compounded, I should add, by two types of Cold War warriors within Sri Lanka, where the Foreign Ministry has singularly failed to develop policy guidelines but is instead prey to old ideologies and youthful emotionalism. In the first place, just as India for a long time had officials obsessed by the events of 1962, who saw China as a continuing threat, so Sri Lanka has officials who are obsessed by 1987 and see India as the basis of all our problems.

This school of thought is led by those who entered wholeheartedly into the Jayewardene view of international relations, when we became a willing ally of the West, more Catholic indeed than the Pope, in trying to flog Trincomalee and its oil tanks to the Americans when they were not particularly interested. After all they had the use by then of Diego Garcia, following the horrendous shenanigans with regard to its inhabitants that Britain perpetrated during the last extraordinarily dark days of colonialism.

Those Sri Lankan Cold Warriors, instead of admitting that the threat Jayewardene tried to present to India extenuates, even if it does not excuse, the training of terrorists that India engaged in, hold India solely responsible for the debacle of 1987. Instead of attributing the absurdities of the 13th Amendment to stupid Sri Lankan drafting, without attention to principle, they claim that it is all India's fault. Supported by the prejudice and chauvinism of some Sri Lankan journalists, this world view naturally engenders resentment amongst Indians, and contributes to increasing suspicions on either side.

This is augmented by some Sri Lankans who fight the Cold War from the opposite side as it were. In part because of their understandable anger with the West for its efforts to prevent the eradication of terrorism, they forget India's support for our struggle, and lump both together, while promoting a polarization that exalts China as the principal trustworthy ally. The fact that this is not at all what China wants is forgotten. In Geneva and elsewhere China has advocated working together with India, in a very different manner from what the West advocated in the polarizing days of the Cold War.

We then should more consistently affirm the inclusive policies that the President has formally laid down, namely a return to the Non-Alignment that the SLFP traditionally followed, with our closest relationships being with our closest neighbours. We should not allow Asia to be a playground for other countries, and in that context we must play an active role in building up understanding within SAARC as well as amongst other Asian countries.

Unfortunately our Foreign Ministry is so dysfunctional at present that they cannot give a lead in this. It is essential therefore for India to foster more positive approaches in other branches of government as well as Civil Society, to encourage think tanks to develop policy documents in this regard, and to promote economic links that will strengthen ties between our peoples.

***

Several factors unfortunately contribute to continuing misunderstanding and a failure on both sides to understand how we need to work together solidly to promote peace and security in South Asia. The first is the failure on the part of both sides to understand what inclusivity and pluralism should mean in Sri Lanka.

This has necessarily to be different from what obtains in India. In both countries there were efforts to impose a hegemonic model of government, but the different circumstances in the two countries meant that this played out differently. In both countries language was the initial instrument of domination, but India soon enough realized that the imposition of one language was not going to work. I believe the absence of an efficient centralized school system contributed to this as much as the quasi-Federal structure of government. In addition the Nehruvian understanding of the need for advanced technological education meant that aspirations beyond the limitations of a single language were widespread, and prevented the chauvinism of monolingualism holding sway for a protracted period.

In Sri Lanka unfortunately we are still stuck in monolingual mindsets, which militate against the full participation in government that all citizens should enjoy. This is especially tragic because all decision makers understand the need for change, and this government in particular has formalized the need for bilingualism, thus giving teeth to the change in language policy that was the single most important reform of 1987. Unfortunately the trilingualism that was originally agreed on then was defeated by the opposition of the old left, still stuck in its anti-colonial mindset. Thus the opportunity for wider activity that could provide dynamic incentives for all to move beyond monolingualism was minimized.

More seriously, the continuing incompetence of the Ministry of Education to fulfil the current trilingual policy of the President means that the empowerment through language rights which all agree on is still held up. This is an area in which, with its now enlightened language polices and the expertise in language education developed over the years, India could contribute much more. But unfortunately Indian assistance is passive, and thus straitjacketed by continuing statism, without encouragement of alternative models of teacher supply and development.

The same applies to training for public officials. I am aware that Indians too complain that their public service is not what it was, but comparing the capacity of Indian bureaucrats and their ability to conceptualize and initiate with those of Sri Lanka public servants makes clear how far we have fallen behind. This is especially sad, because the talent of our public servants is enormous, understandably so given the immense competition required to be appointed to established services. Unfortunately our training is limited, and suggestions to work together with India to develop collaborative mechanisms are confined to placements in India rather than the radical adjustments to our current training systems within Sri Lanka. In particular the need for better language and other soft skills is not yet understood here, which means that the capacity to study international developments and benefit from these is limited.

This is where SAARC could do much more, with institutions that work together to ensure high level skills in administrators, as well as common understanding of the political and social compulsions of the region. My understanding, from the brief period during which I served on the Board of one of the SAARC Centres, is that, with a few honourable exceptions, these contribute little to either development or mutual understanding. It is desirable therefore that SAARC commissions a serious study of the work of these Centres and tries to develop more effective systems of collaboration to share and develop best practice.

Whilst such collaboration may improve effectiveness, whilst also promoting mutual understanding, perhaps the single most important area in which such understanding is vital relates to political structures. The 13th Amendment to the Constitution, which was passed in 1987 following the Indo-Lankan Accord of that year, was intended to promote local empowerment, in a context in which centralized decision making had led to continuing neglect of many parts of the country. This was felt most strongly in Tamil majority areas, though the fact that we had two youth insurrections in Sinhala areas indicates that the sense of deprivation, and consequent bitterness, was nationwide.

This was exacerbated by a comparatively good general education system, which raised expectations, particularly in Tamil areas, only to find them shattered by our moribund and limited tertiary education system, and the statist control of the economy which left little room for independent initiative. Though the economic dispensation has changed, our education system has still failed to keep pace with modern employment needs, and this I fear will be what will lead to continuing unrest, amongst all communities. Here again we need to learn from India which, while its general education still lags behind ours, has encouraged the development of different mechanisms to increase opportunities for all segments of the population.

Unfortunately, instead of looking at practical needs, our politicians on all sides are obsessed with theoretical models and the protection of personal turf. This has prevented educational reform, and it stands in the way of meaningful political reform. I suppose this is understandable, since their primary concern is the power that they will wield, and to what extent this will have to be shared with others. But what the country as a whole should be concerned with is how power can be conferred upon the people.

Following a series of Divisional Reconciliation Committee meetings, I am now more than ever convinced that we need to work on the principle of subsidiarity, and ensure that power is exercised by the smallest unit possible for which power is relevant. While obviously there must be mechanisms to ensure that the exercise of such power does not harm other units, it will make much more sense to entrust governance of areas affecting the day to day lives of the population to a unit that can deal promptly with local problems.

Though clear conceptualization is not generally a characteristic of successful politicians, this approach has been suggested in many of the pronounce-ments of the President. From the need for regular consultation mechanisms, to the suggestion that educational appointments should be school based, there is understanding of the need to promote accountability to the people, along with responsibility for limited areas. Unfortunately this vision does not sit well with other politicians on all sides, whose idea of what politics means has been immeasurably corrupted by the preposterous electoral system with which we have been saddled for the last two decades.

This has been changed, at last, though only with regard to local government elections thus far. If the change is extended to other levels of government, we can look forward to greater responsibility, and greater responsiveness. In particular we can hope for the development of local teams, that will encompass both elected and appointed officials, to address local concerns expeditiously.

This does not mean that, while clearly the 13th amendment must be adjusted, power will be taken back to the Centre. That would be a mistake. Instead, while ensuring regulation as well as monitoring at Provincial level with regard to areas where understanding at that level is essential, responsibility for administration, with a concomitant requirement of accountability and transparency, should be entrusted to Divisions.

The benefits of such a dispensation, which would incorporate features of the Indian Panchayat system, should be made clear, and for this purpose the Indian and Sri Lankan governments should work together to make it clear that the main purpose of reform is to promote empowerment of the people and local communities. There should be resistance to reliance on formulaic approaches to devolution. Instead there should be study of best practice in other countries, and appreciation of the fact that the focus of reform, so as to provide better services to the people, should be local government. In this context, I hope very much that the study team from Sri Lanka that has recently visited South Africa has looked at the local government reforms that followed the initial constitutional model established during the negotiations leading up to the transfer of power from the old apartheid regime. That experience suggests the need, once the formalities of recognizing the need to share power are gone through, to move towards practical measures to make sure that people can share in government at meaningful levels.

At the same time we must do much more to include all our population in decision making at all levels. The failure of anyone in government to advance the commitment of the President to set up a Second Chamber, with equal representation for all Provinces, is symptomatic of the wholesale absence of a sense of urgency in our politicians. We have got used to doing nothing until pressures mount, and then making adjustments, which seem far too little far too late, when some swift action on measures agreed by everyone would have helped to create confidence in the first place. Unfortunately we have grown used to thinking in terms of comprehensive packages, whereas basic problem solving skills would have made us understand that dealing with simple problems expeditiously often reduces the magnitude of seemingly insurmountable problems.

I should note in this context that the failure of our experts in the field to build on the agreement of the major Tamil political party, that empowering small units of government was also desirable, seems to me as reprehensible as the failure to have moved on a Senate. The latter, by ensuring active and weighted participation in national issues by representatives of the regions, would have strengthened the sense of involvement in decision making which is a vital component of national integration; while the former would have allowed for greater understanding of local issues, and provided opportunities for simple solutions to problems, without threatening structures at central or provincial level.

The other area in which we need to do better, while also making clear what has already been achieved, is ensuring greater involvement of the minorities in the administration. This should include the security forces and, while the increasing numbers of Tamil and Tamil speaking policemen are welcome, we should also ensure recruitment at officer level, as well as in the ranks, in army and navy and air force. Proactive measures for this purpose should be put in place, including cadet schools and other educational initiatives—which would also help to improve general educational standards, whilst assisting with the promotion of trilingualism, since such schools could be models for language learning.

***

Putting in place inclusive educational and employment policies as a priority would be an effective way of involving the diaspora in the reconciliation process. Thus far there has been no concerted effort to involve the diaspora in nation building which is a tragedy because, at the conclusion of the conflict, there were many in the diaspora who welcomed the quelling of the terrorism that had caused so much misery to Tamils as well as other Sri Lankans.

Unfortunately the clear intention of the President, to use the victory to build up an inclusive nation, was stymied by political power plays that strengthened the position of extremists on either side. On balance the decision to advance the Presidential election, while initially intended to affirm the moderate stance of the government, led to polarization based on prejudice rather than principle. The encouragement of Sarath Fonseka by shadowy forces, culminating in support for his candidature by the major Tamil political party, suggested that regime change rather than reconciliation were the priorities of those opposed to the President. This in turn strengthened the position of those supporters of the President for whom pluralism seemed a threat.

India, it should be stressed, was no part of this strange maneuver, and indeed the vast majority of the international community was bemused at what was going on. But it has left scars, and the continuing determination to confuse advocacy of restorative justice for the minorities with determination to demonize the architects of military victory has destroyed the mutual confidence that should have been developed. In this context it is a pity that India allowed itself to be drawn into power politics at the Human Rights Council session in March 2012, though it should be noted that pronouncements by individual Sri Lankans also did nothing to promote confidence.

The impression then is that the agenda is being set by the more extreme voices in the diaspora, playing on the predilections of politicians in the

West and in Tamilnadu who benefit from their support. In Britain David Miliband made clear in 2009 that policy towards Sri Lanka was dictated by electoral considerations. The fact that this policy involved support for a terrorist organization and efforts to prolong its existence was skated over.

Similarly, in Tamilnadu, the antics of extremist politicians, who see separatism in Sri Lanka as their passport to political success, has had an unfortunate effect on mainstream politicians who have necessarily to compete with each other for votes. Meanwhile our Foreign Ministry has failed to concentrate on getting across to Tamilnadu politicians the work being done to promote pluralism—and that it does not see this as a priority is apparent from the fact that we no longer have a Tamil speaking Deputy High Commissioner in Chennai.

This deficiency, I should note, is widespread, as can be seen from the transfer of Tamil speaking officials out of London, just when it became vital to work with moderate elements in the diaspora. We should also be working with the younger generation to promote understanding, but whereas concerned NGOs are making an effort in this regard, as can be seen from the excellent report produced by a cross-party group of Parliamentarians who visited Britain recently, the Foreign Ministry has failed to build on such initiatives. The promotion of projects that will enhance connectivity is not thought of, even though encouragement of educational support, and volunteer teaching assignments that bring together young people of different ethnicities from the diaspora, could do much to enhance understanding of the actual situation in Sri Lanka.

Instead we leave it to extremists to set an agenda, and then respond. Whereas we should have told the story of the war soon after it finished, in 2009, we waited for the scurrilous attacks of Channel 4 and Gordon Weiss, and the Darusman Report that fed on similar sources, and then produced reports that were not precise rebuttals. Thus we allow myths to develop, whereas a careful use of statistics, with reproduction of documents from agencies that worked with us at the time, would have made clear the inaccuracy of much that has been alleged. At the same time, as the Lessons Learnt and Reconciliation Commission has made clear, where there is prima facie evidence, we should investigate and publicize the results of our findings, with judicial action where appropriate.

Obviously we are not going to win over the whole of the diaspora. We have to recognize that feelings run deep in those who have left a country because of ill treatment (as is most obviously the case with Irish Americans). In the Sri Lanka case, this is especially destructive because of the undoubted abilities of many of those who left Sri Lanka after suffering from the racist persecution of 1981 and 1983 which was encouraged, or at least not forcefully dealt with, by the Jayewardene government.

In this context our failure to atone for that persecution, through declaration of a national day of mourning, as has indeed been suggested by the LLRC, is regrettable. We should remember all victims, of violence as well as terrorism, and the best day for this would be July 23rd. I have suggested this, but even the normally sensitive Ministry of National Languages and Social Integration has not taken up the idea.

We must recognize that closure requires remedial action. Though the suffering all our people had gone through meant that it was essential to destroy the terrorist movement that had held us all in thrall for so wrong, and though we can show that the force we used in fighting was proportionate and sanctioned by international law and norms, we must also recognize that the reasons for terrorism developing to such monstrous proportions lie, at least to some extent, in the excesses of successive Sri Lankan governments, and in particular the government of 1977 to 1987. Unless this is acknowledged, it will not be easy to convince the more moderate elements in the diaspora that Sri Lanka is truly committed to pluralism.

In this regard India has a seminal role to play. The message to the diaspora must be clear, that separatism, even if divorced from terrorism (which in practice it never can be), is unacceptable. Instead of confrontation, there should be cooperation, but in terms of positive initiatives. Encouragement of these is vital and, with the agreement of the Sri Lankan government, India must support initiatives that bring people together for education and training and multicultural activities.

Some of this can be achieved through SAARC Centres that fulfil the aims of the SAARC Social Charter. This should involve non-governmental activities and community led efforts, and India, with its experience of local activism divorced from political imperatives, should foster such work. Funding for programmes of agencies such as the Gandhi Centre could do much to promote the respect and understanding that communities must be given. Indian involvement would encourage the diaspora also to contribute to such initiatives, and through such support we could move towards the shift in attitudes that is imperative.

Some of this may sound idealistic. But in the current context, ideals are perhaps the most practical way forward.

Impact of Sri Lankan Tamil Diaspora's Activism on India-Sri Lanka Relations

Tulika Gaur

ABSTRACT: Diasporas are the group of people who migrate from their homeland and settle in another territory due to various reasons. They seek to maintain cohesion and a sense of separate identity in the host country, and work actively through various political and economic channels in its host country to promote the interests of their kin groups living in homeland (Axel 2002: 411). Hence, they have become an integral part of homeland politics and international politics as well and it seems to be inevitable to avoid them as a factor impacting the political scenario at both levels. In this context, the Tamils of Sri Lanka serve as a useful example of a population whose many migrations have created a worldwide diaspora. The Sri Lankan Tamil diaspora is one of the largest diaspora communities in the world and has been quite active in exerting its influence both in Sri Lanka and in its host lands abroad. From the ethnic, cultural, religious, economic, and political perspectives, it is a highly heterogeneous entity, like most other established diasporas. Despite various basic similarities to other diasporas, it has its own uniqueness. Its size, scope, and complexity make the Sri Lankan Tamil diaspora a noteworthy subject for academic research. In South Asia, we find that the Sri Lankan Tamil diaspora in the West has been active in their homeland affairs by supporting the Tamil insurgents fighting for their right to self-determination against the Sinhalese government forces in Sri Lanka.

The Sri Lankan Tamil diaspora identifies itself as the "victim diaspora" because majority of its members fled the country in the wake of ethnic violence in Sri Lanka mainly after 1983. This group is largely made up of refugees and former refugees who are literally scattered around the world, but concentrated in certain countries in the West. About 170,000 Sri Lankan Tamils live in Tamil Nadu, whose coast line is less than fifty miles from the northern Sri Lanka. About 65,000 of them live in camps, and about 100,000 Sri Lankan Tamils are considered as non-camp refugees. These refugees have been actively playing a dominant role in deciding the shape of the regional as well as national politics in India. Hence, they have been a crucial factor in shaping the relationship between India and Sri Lanka as their huge presence in the Indian territory has been a significant factor for both these countries in shaping their foreign and domestic policies.

DEFINING DIASPORA

The term "diaspora" is derived from a Greek word *diaspeirein,* meaning the 'dispersal or scattering of seeds'.[1] Safran (1991) uses a rather strict definition of diaspora, defining them as expatriate minority communities:

1. that are dispersed from an original 'centre' to atleast two 'peripheral' places;
2. that maintain a memory, vision, or myth about their original homeland;
3. they believe they are not-and perhaps cannot be- fully accepted by their host countries;
4. that see the ancestral home as a place of eventual return, when the time is right;
5. that are committed to the maintenance or restoration of their homeland; and
6. of which the group's consciousness and solidarity are importantly defined by this continuing relation with the homeland.

Since the concept and nature of diasporas varies, it remains difficult for one to come up with a universal definition of diasporas. Hence, Bercovitch (2007: 19) defines diasporas as "the transnational communities created as a result of the movement of people, living in one or more host countries, organized on the basis of solidarity, shared ideas and collective identities, and showing loyalty to, and affinity with, their host country as well as their original homeland".

Since time immemorial the process of movement of people has been a significant part of our life. With changing times, the wave of globalization has brought this movement to a level where it has become hassle-free and easier. This has led the people move more freely, safely and above all more frequently across the borders. With these people moving, their identity, culture and faith and most importantly, their political ideology also crosses borders. Besides all these they bring along with them certain memories that remain crucial in framing their identity and political status in their host land or maintaining their old identity and connections with their homeland. Hence, national identities and political experiences, both of which are imparted before migration, make diasporas political activity in their homeland as well as host land a salient feature of the immigrant experience. The political activism of the diasporas includes efforts to create new states, change existing regimes, alter nationality or voting laws in ways that would facilitate migrant participation in homeland politics, defend homelands' beleaguered by enemies or disasters, or lobby host land on homelands' behalf etc. Home country national loyalties are widely felt, with sufficient intensity to consistently impel the diasporic community into activism. Hence, they make their political activity, a concept beyond borders which remains no more confined within the territorial boundaries of their homeland. Bercovitch (2007) argues that the process has now reached the level where the diasporas have "de-territorialized" their identity and have become global actors.

DIASPORA AND POLITICS

With the advent of globalization, politics has become unbounded and de-territorialized, and since then every other person could be a part of the political affair. Diasporas were recognized as international actors and today they have proved to be an important actor, real actor, and real entities with real interests in the global politics. They are no more 'virtual', today they make a count of themselves both in their homeland as well as host land as a different group altogether. And this number is continuously increasing day by day. They have started making their presence felt among the other international actors, in their host land as well as homeland. They are now the connecting link or the binding thread between their host land and their homeland at every front, be it political, economic or socio-cultural.

Diasporic participation in its homeland politics has been a noted phenomenon. The moment a migration takes place, it doesn't disconnect an individual from all the emotional connections and bonds with his homeland. Rather, there are cases when these bonds get all the more strengthened than they were prior to the migration of the individual. According to Waldinger (2008), "...migration has proved to be an important transnational process that has been contributing to 'politics' beyond the territorial limitations. Whereas it might be more accurate to say that the immigrants are really "the transplanted," almost all scholars agree that to say international migration has cross-border connections. Given the uncertain, transitional nature of the migration process, connections linking origin and destination places are inevitable". Hence, the diaspora is supposed to be an independent political entity, who while migration has taken the response-bility of their kin groups, hence, they continue to be a part of politics at all the three levels: host land politics, homeland politics and international politics.

The boundaries between the host and homeland have become blurred with increased transnational linkages such as human mobility across national spaces and the de-territorialized nature of social relations and political practice (Cheran and Vimalarajah 2010). However, it can be said that diaspora communities have multiple homes (Cheran 2006: 4–8) and thus have significant role to play in all their home and host land politics. This form of political engagement is considered as a subset of the "transnational political practices" of migrant communities (Ostergaard-Nielsen 2001). Diaspora remains at the critical juncture of both homeland as well as host land politics, *i.e.* it can equally participate, affect and in turn get affected by changes in any of them.

Since the diaspora has been extremely close and connected to its erstwhile homeland, transnationalization of homeland politics is bound to happen. It is due to this that the erstwhile homeland politics come to host land and diasporas become the driving force for it. However, with changing times, these transnational ties and homeland politics have received a major setback in the wake of 9/11 terrorist attacks and are now seen as the problematic features in host land security matters.

FACTORS AFFECTING DIASPORIC INVOLVEMENT IN POLITICS

The modern world has witnessed a higher frequency in the movement of people both voluntarily and involuntarily. Statistics suggest that approximately 175 million people *i.e.* 2.9 per cent of the whole world population have opted for moving out of their homeland for some or the other reason and this number is increasing day by day (Lyons 2004). This, in turn, has resulted in transfer of ideas and harmonization of cultures, making the diasporas to sustain with others who are both similar and different from themselves. Also it has strengthened the bond between them and their past as it has helped in sustaining and maintaining the links with their people residing in their homeland and their soil. Diasporas in politics, do not act as singular agents, but are instead characterized by diversity apart from their host land. In terms of identities, interests and capabilities, both on the individual and organizational levels (Bercovitch 2007:36; Brinkerhoff 2008:70–73; Faist 2007:35; Vertovec 2005:4). However, there are several factors that condition this involvement of diasporas in political affairs both in positive as well as negative ways:

• Globalization

Globalization has tended to increase the pace at which the diaspora used to participate in their homeland as well as host land politics in earlier times. This can be illustrated in three ways:

1. Globalization has smoothened the process of communication through which the dispersed population is able to act internationally without any interference from the host country. These diasporas keep in touch with their other people through various ways which include internet and publications etc. (Bercovitch 2007: 20).

2. Since globalization has removed the boundations, it has led the diaspora to keep their connection to their homeland even stronger. Now the diaspora can see whatever is happening in their homeland on television and hence it makes them more interested in their homeland political and social affair (Bercovitch 2007: 20).

3. As globalization has limited the confinement of the boundaries it has also let the people across borders connect through various ways. This in turn has enabled the diasporas to raise their voice on behalf of their kin groups in their homeland if they feel that injustice is done[2] (Bercovitch 2007:20).

Hence, globalization has given immense space for these diasporas to become an important international political forces. There has been an increase in the intensity of the diasporic groups' ties with their homeland and, hence, an increase in their involvement in homeland politics. Since they remain a connecting link between the host country and homeland, they remain an integral part of regional and international politics as well. With greater access to cheaper, more efficient travel and communication, more recently established diaspora-communities have been able to strengthen the diaspora-homeland nexus. Meanwhile, the proliferation of insurgencies and intrastate conflicts around the world, have produced growing numbers of refugees and migrants, seeking a new home. This, in turn, has created a huge number of diasporas that have a more recent, stronger, and arguably more emotional connection with developments in their erstwhile homes, especially when there is social or political upheaval.

• Pre-Migratory Experiences and the Homeland Background

The patterns of diasporic engagements in homeland politics are generally shaped by prior experiences, which involve the institutions that transmit political ideas, values, and norms, and the practice of political participation itself. A pre-migration political participation is bound to generate continued interest in homeland matters even after migration.[3] As membership in civic and political organizations imparts political dispositions as well as skills, diasporas with a prior record of activism or membership will have a stronger homeland orientation than those lacking such an experience. Similarly, it is obvious that higher the level of pre-migration activism, the greater the level of post-migration homeland interest (Waldinger 2008). Maintaining their hatreds developed during war and displacement, the structural integration empower these diasporas to pursue transnational activities which may impact homeland and host land politics in both positive and negative manner.

• **Relationship with their Host States**

The process of integration in the host land is directly proportional to diaspora's attitudes and activities in political affairs. The host land context provides opportunity and access to resources important to determining diasporas' impact on homeland affairs (Anderson 1992: 8–9; Collier 2000: 14). This is a consequence of a combination of three things:

1. absence of homeland government control,
2. acquiescence of host land government authority, and
3. the wealth and modernity of host land society.

Diasporas remain under the protective shield of their host land where they are provided with freedom of speech and expression that is generally absent in their homeland and has led them to migrate. They feel secure as the host land is responsible for their shelter and hence, they don't have to fear the state.

On the one hand, the political parties in the host states give the diasporas numerous options for civic engagements,[4] by making policies for them, which eventually boosts the morale of the diaspora for homeland political involvement (Zolberg 1999), on the other, it gives the newcomers access to the wealth thereby providing the migrant community with a material base that it can use to exercise leverage back home. The diaspora groups take advantage of these freedoms and lobby the host government and the international community to implement desired foreign policies towards the homeland. They are able to maintain resources and have access to some powerful factors[5] that can influence their homeland politics. Their ability to do so is affected by their social or political status, the views of their host-society and the homeland leadership, and the political and social character of their kin-state (Bercovitch 2007).

• **Growing Trends of 'Suspicions' about Diasporic Activities**

Since the 9/11 terror attacks in the United States, there has been an emergence of 'Homeland Security' as a major ideology that has led to serious consequences for diasporic involvements in their homeland affairs. In a security-dominated paradigm, the diaspora communities are often viewed as breeding grounds for terrorism and thus, their involvement in their homeland political affairs may be seen with an eye of suspicion which, in turn, may impact their involvement in their homeland affairs. The notion that diaspora communities automatically represent security threats[6] and therefore are appropriate targets for law enforcements attention seems to be predominant (Cheran 2003). Thus, we can say that the new linkages between the diasporas and terrorism have actually reduced the efficacy of the diasporas to participate in their homeland politics to a great extent.

• **Long-Distance Politics and Governance of the Homeland**

The long-distance politics in homeland, whose state uses embassies and high commissions in the host countries, and monitors and gathers intelligence about its diaspora population and their activities and thereby, essentially co-shape the diasporic involvement in their homeland affairs. There are possibilities that these institutions may not support their people in host countries and may trouble them, hence, diapsoric involvement in its homeland politics depends upon these institutions' attitude towards them.[7] The effects of homeland politics on diasporas economically, socially or in terms of their self-image ensure their high stakes for in continuation of their involvement in homeland politics (Baechler 2002).

Thus, we can see that the diasporas are both motivated as well as hindered to get involved in politics by a number of factors. How do they respond to these factors, however, remains to be the crucial thing as it depends on what interests diasporas have and to what extent can they be fulfilled by their actions.

IMPACT OF THE SRI LANKAN TAMIL DIASPORA'S ACTIVISM ON INDIA-SRI LANKA RELATIONS

The Sri Lankan Tamil diaspora identifies itself as the "victim diaspora" because majority of its members fled the country in the wake of ethnic violence in Sri Lanka mainly after 1983. This group is largely made up of refugees and former refugees who are literally scattered around the world, but concentrated in certain countries in the West. About 170,000 Sri Lankan Tamils live in Tamil Nadu, whose coast line is less than fifty miles from the northern Sri Lanka. About 65,000 of them live in camps, and about 100,000 Sri Lankan Tamils are considered as non-camp refugees. These refugees have been actively playing a dominant role in deciding the shape of the regional as well as national politics in India. Hence, they have been a crucial factor in shaping the relationship between India and Sri Lanka as their huge presence in the Indian territory has been a significant factor for both these countries in shaping their foreign and domestic policies.

Currently the Sri Lankan Tamil diaspora consists of more than 700,000 people settled in North America, Europe, India, Canada and Australia. Most of them have migrated since the mid-1980s, primarily as a direct or indirect result of the civil war in Sri Lanka. India has been the foremost destination for the Tamils who fled Sri Lanka during this period. Their number remains to be around 170,000 of which approximately 65,000 have been interning in camps and rest have integrated into Tamil Nadu and do not intend to return to Sri Lanka (Krishna 2000: 91). India does not only serve as the host country but also as the transit route to the West for these migrants. The Lankan Tamil diaspora residing in India accuse India of supporting the Sri Lankan government and ignoring the atrocities committed by the Sinhalese state to their ethnic kin. They expect India's greater support and say in the matter of providing autonomy to the Tamil nationalists. This section prefers to call the LTTE as 'part of the problem' and not 'the problem' (Cheran 2001: 4; Bose 1994: 84).

A huge number of Sri Lankan Tamils had migrated to India during the eelam war I due to a number of reasons: (Sivarajah 1995: 257).

- Being the 'regional big brother' and an ally of Sri Lanka, India gave some hope to the Sri Lankan Tamils for some help for themselves.
- Most of the Sri Lankan Tamils who migrated were poor and hence going far away to western countries was impossible for them.
- The presence of their ethnic kin group in Indian state of Tamil Nadu made them a bit comfortable rather than going to a whole new place.

Hence, all these factors are the proof of the hopes and expectations of the Sri Lankan Tamils from New Delhi in dealing with their homeland and supporting their cause. In other words, it was the pressure of the Sri Lankan refugees and their ethnic kin group residing in Tamil Nadu on the state government that resulted in pressurizing the central government to intervene in the ethnic conflict in Sri Lanka (Sivarajah 1996: 176–184).

"Signing of the Indo-Lanka Accord in 1987 was a big relief for them and they hoped for more. Following the Indo-Lanka Accord there was a ceasefire which led many of the refugees to return to their homeland. The first repatriation took place after the signing of the Indo-Sri Lanka Accord in 1987 and between 24 December 1987 and 31 August 1989, 25,585 refugees and non-camp Sri Lankan nationals returned to Sri Lanka"[8] (Sivarajah 1995: 257).

As a consequence of the accord, stationing of the IPKF made the situation a bit better for the Tamils as it kept the Sri Lankan army away from the Tamil areas, hence saving the Sri Lankan Tamils from further atrocities. However, the Tamil hopes were shattered when the IPKF indulged in a direct war with the LTTE and eventually many Tamil civilians were targeted by the IPKF. Furthermore, the agitation among the Tamils increased all the more when the Indian government decided to withdraw its forces and let the Sri Lankan government handle the situation. This move of the Indian government was perceived as a mere act of "appeasing thy neighbourhood" by the diaspora community and hence, the stance of India was criticized heavily. After getting disappointment from the Indian government, the diaspora activity in their homeland conflict increased. Funding the war, lobbying their host governments continued but this time it was at a greater pace.

"The Tamil Diaspora, who fled the country to save their children, sold their assets and consolidated their financial position. Many then used this as opportunity to provide financial support for the LTTE to the extreme. The Tamil Diaspora celebrated every victory by the LTTE as the Eelam, without using wisdom and vision for the future. They praised Prabhakaran as the greatest leader that Tamils had in the living memory. The Tamil daispora used their finance to modernise the LTTE armoury. They made Parabhakaran as the "Sun God" and funded his underground kingdom-like lifestyle. Their agenda remained to be the demand for separate eelam and the efforts to gather support for it continued on their behalf" (International Crisis Group Report 2010).

Political and material support from India, particularly Tamil Nadu, was the key to the growth of Tamil militancy in Sri Lanka during this phase. At least on two occasions, Prabhakaran was saved from annihilation, thanks to Indian intervention. But after he carried out the assassination of Rajiv Gandhi in 1991, popular support in Tamil Nadu for the LTTE dried up. And the Eelam Tamil cause was pushed to the backseat even in political rhetoric. However, they still stood for the support of the Tamils and have been raising their voices against the inhuman activities of the Sri Lankan government.

One of the most critical way of reaction from the diasporas to the last phase of war in their homeland occurred in form of self-immolation acts.[9] In India, at least eight people self-immolated, including a family man and a worker of ruling Congress party. In Malaysia, a Tamil man of Sri Lankan origin also self-immolated himself, calling on US President Barack Obama to stop Colombo's war (Tamilnet 2010). These acts demonstrated the desperation of the Sri Lankan Tamil diaspora suffering from the helplessness and inability to stop killings, nor spur government intervention. This was the first time that the Tamil diaspora had resorted to such extremes. Those self-immolating were well educated, deeply concerned members of the diaspora community. They ultimately felt they had no option other than to take their own lives, in this extreme and non-violent form of protest.

However, it has to be noted that the Tamil community cannot be considered as a unitary being that advocates for the cause of Tamil Eelam: not every Tamil supported the Tigers during the war and not every Tamil in the diaspora considered him or herself to be part of the civil war. Since the defeat of the LTTE, the diaspora has been more divided than ever. The basic goals of the diaspora have shifted from merely supporting the armed struggle to a non-violent struggle for an independent Tamil state. This shows that even though the war is over, the scepticism of the diaspora regarding the safety of their countrymen under the authoritarian government there remains the same. As they haven't drifted apart from their goal but it's just that they have changed their path. There are different responses from different groups on the central issue of Tamil Eelam. There are some ardent Tamil nationalists, especially in the West, who have not yet given up hope for Tamil Eelam. There are others who are ready to settle for a federal solution. In contrast, the poor Sri Lankan Tamil refugees living in Tamil Nadu refugee camps, any solution that ensures them livelihood and security seems acceptable.

Unfortunately, this plight of the Sri Lankan Tamils has been the triumph card well used by the political leaders in Tamil Nadu in attaining the power in their state and also to influence the New Delhi-Colombo relations. As was seen recently in the elections in Tamil Nadu, AIADMK under the leadership of Ms. Jayalalitha had used the Sri Lankan Tamils issue to gain leverage over the existing government of DMK. The huge influx of refugees during the last Eelam war and the New Delhi's stand over the whole war crime issue in Sri Lanka had given a chance to Ms. Jayalalitha to show their sympathetic attitude as well as criticize the Indian governments' ignorant attitude towards the suffering of people in the neighbourhood. This had to work as the entire Tamil Nadu had been the only state that had supported the Eelam movement since its start and has stood for their ethnic kin groups in Sri Lanka.

According to Col. Hariharan, a retired Military Intelligence officer of the Indian Army, "Ms Jayalalitha's approach to Sri Lanka Tamil issue in the past had been lukewarm though she had periodically been demanding the return of Kachativu to India. One of the main reasons for this was the rise of the Liberation Tigers of Tamil Eelam (LTTE) for whom she had no love lost. This was to be expected as her mentor and the founder of the AIADMK, MG Ramachandran had fully backed Rajiv Gandhi and the India-Sri Lanka Agreement 1987. In fact in 2002 during her earlier term as chief minister of Tamil Nadu, she had arrested Vaiko, leader of the Marumalarchi Dravida Munnetra Kazagham (MDMK) for his vociferous supporter to the LTTE and its leader Prabhakaran as LTTE, was a banned organisation in India. However, her attitudes to the LTTE-led Eelam struggle took an about-turn after she struck a political alliance with Vaiko in 2006. Though she abandoned Vaiko in the recent election while cobbling up the AIADMK-led front, she appears to have retained her strong sympathy for Sri Lankan Tamils."

Since the war has ended, it hasn't led to any reduction in the importance of the Sri Lankan Tamils in affecting the India-Sri Lanka relations. In fact, now it has been more evident that New Delhi has to take a strong position against Colombo despite the fact that they have been good allies and had a special status for each other, just because New Delhi-Chennai nexus has got more complicated. The ruling UPA coalition has DMK as one of its coalition partner which now sits in the opposition in Tamil Nadu. And AIADMK, that has got the power, leaves no chance to pull their opposition down and pressurize the centre to do as they desire. The significance of the Tamil issue has been so much that it eventually resulted in passing of two resolutions by Tamil Nadu assembly during June 2011. The first resolution unanimously passed on June 7 demanded the imposition of economic sanctions against Sri Lanka for its alleged crimes against Tamils. The second motion was to implead the State in a case filed by Chief Minister J. Jayalalithaa in her individual capacity for retrieval of Katchatheevu Island, ceded to Sri Lanka by India in 1974 by way of an agreement. The case is pending in the Supreme Court of India.

As noted by Col. Hariharan, "there are four issues in her Sri Lanka agenda on which she wants New Delhi to act: holding of a referendum for creation of Tamil Eelam, international action against Sri Lanka army personnel and political leaders for alleged war crimes against Tamils, pressurize Sri Lanka for a political solution to bring equity to Tamils, and impose economic embargo on Sri Lanka till it complies. These issues reflect the concerns of the Tamil Diaspora as well as the Tamil refugees in India at the cavalier way Sri Lanka had been handling Tamil affairs in the post war period. New Delhi's reticence even to discuss these issues in public domain has added to the suspicion that its acts of omission are partly to blame for the plight of Tamils."

In an interview with the media, India's Prime Minister Dr Manmohan Singh admitted the their government had been in dilemma in handling Sri Lanka Tamil issue. In the context of newly coming up of New Delhi-Chennai nexus he said "we have to find a difficult balance because what happens in Sri Lanka has a domestic dimension also. The Tamil Nadu government and the Assembly have often shown great worry about what is happening in Sri Lanka". He emphasized that India's emphasis would remain to persuade Colombo to ensure all ethnic groups were treated equally and "they can lead a life of dignity and self respect." Calling the decimation of the LTTE was "good," Dr Singh said the Tamil problem had not disappeared with that. As observed by Col. Hariharan, "the Prime Minister's expression of public concern on Sri Lanka was also probably triggered by reports that President Mahinda Rajapaksa told a high-powered Indian delegation his government was not able to concede land and police powers to provincial councils in accordance with the 13th Amendment to the Sri Lanka Constitution. From the beginning India had been emphasizing this aspect, which was fundamental to the India-Sri Lanka agreement 1987. Sri Lankan rebuff was not unexpected, but probably India had better expectations as the Sri Lanka foreign minister Dr GL Peiris had agreed that a "devolution package, building upon the 13th Amendment, would contribute towards creating the necessary conditions for such reconciliation" in the joint statement issued during his visit to New Delhi in May 2011."

With Ms Jayalalitha giving the issue a big push and the international campaign spearheaded by the Tamil Diaspora demanding action against Sri Lanka for alleged war crimes and human rights violations committed during the closing stages of the Eelam war two years back has continued to gain more and more ground and in turn, the Sri Lanka Tamil issue has figured more prominently in Tamil Nadu politics. This was evident from the big turnout at the candle light procession held in memory of the Tamil war victims and fighters of Eelam war on June 26. The day is observed UN day in commemoration of victims of torture—at the Marina in Chennai in memory. The Tamil Nadu Chief Minister Ms. Jayalalitha's strident demand for holding Sri Lanka accountable for its failure to meet Tamil aspirations and war crimes has found widespread opposition support. The Sri Lanka issue was brought up by the main opposition party the Bharatiya Janatha Party (BJP) in the monsoon session of Indian parliament. The BJP wants strong action by Indian government on this count. The Communist Party of India (Marxist) has also taken up the litany. The mood in Tamil Nadu got worse as over 30 fishermen were reported injured when Sri Lankan navy attacked them in continuing confrontations between the two sides. Recently, 25 Sri Lanka soldiers who were sent for training at the Madras Regimental Centre, Wellington in Tamil Nadu had to return home after public protest was mounted over their presence. Ms Jayalalitha's demands bear remarkable similarity to those of some of the human rights bodies and Eelam lobbies of the Tamil Diaspora, and the TGTE. And these organisations would not miss any political opportunity in India to muster Tamil Nadu's support to add to their 'legitimacy' and strengthen their credentials in the internecine fight for leadership among rival groups of the Tamil Diaspora. The TGTE for its part "is engaged in building a power base among the world Tamil community, particularly in Tamil Nadu, and with sections of the international civil society." The TGTE has already shown keen interest in furthering its linkages in Tamil Nadu. In April 2012 the TGTE nominated five persons from Tamil Nadu as "members" of TGTE "parliament." A TGTE Solidarity Centre with Prof Saraswathi Rajendran, a TGTE parliament member as convener, operates in Tamil Nadu.

Viewed in this background, India's vote for the U.S. resolution is supposed to be the peer pressure of Tamil Nadu to ask for a strong position against the atrocities done to the Tamils in Sri Lanka. The internal political compulsions as well as the growing strategic interests of the Chinese have been the main reasons for such a stand. Explaining it immediately after voting, Prime Minister Dr Manmohan Singh said: "one has to weigh the pros and cons. What we did was in line with our stand on Sri Lanka. We did not want to infringe on the sovereignty of Sri Lanka, but concerns should be expressed so that Tamil people can get justice and lead a life of dignity." There is a large Tamil constituency in India which has been concerned at Sri Lanka's insensitivity and callousness in not responding to international concerns on allegations of human rights violations and war crimes perpetrated against Tamils in Sri Lanka. The ethnic reconciliation process is also making tardy progress. Actually India's vote for the UNHCR resolution reflected these concerns; however, Sri Lanka does not seem to be very keen to address these concerns with any urgency.

Later on, there was a direct involvement of the Tamil diaspora organisation named TGTE (Transnational Government of Tamil Eelam) in the DMK proposal of reviving the Tamil Eelam Supporters Organization (TESO) in August 2012. Making an effort for a comeback to political power, this was basically aimed at having a get together meet up of all the Tamil organizations and sympathisers of the Tamil Eelam particularly with participation from Tamil Diaspora members. However, due to the Centre's pressure they had to drop the word Eelam as it would had created strong anti-Indian lobbies in Sri Lanka and further strain the relations between India and Sri Lanka. If the DMK would have fully activated TESO, its link up with TGTE would be firmed up. The Centre has sent a clear message "thus far and no more" on its stand on Tamil Eelam to Tamil Diaspora by not allowing some of the de-striped Tamil Tigers and pro-Eelam lobbyists to participate in the conference. This was done not only to maintain India's objection to Tamil separatism but also to act upon Sri Lankan concern on Diaspora Tamil separatists gaining a foothold in India. When pushed, New Delhi would probably take action to crack down on LTTE supporters in Tamil Nadu. New Delhi did not allow a few others from Sri Lanka to attend the conference. This showed that despite India's sympathies for Tamils, it was averse to allow the Tamil issue to eclipse its larger in interest in Sri Lanka.

Despite the surfacing differences between the two countries, the Indian Prime Minister is reported to have agreed to visit Colombo at the invitation Sri Lanka President; this would indicate that relations continue to remain cordial. But in the context of New Delhi's piquant political equation with Tamil Nadu's mercurial chief minister, in the coming months India-Sri Lanka relations could become gritty, hitting more troughs than crests.

CONCLUSION

To conclude we can say that diasporas and their participation in politics is something that cannot be judged at one instance. It has to be judged across several criteria and levels. Their involvement in homeland politics may be of a political, military, economic, social or cultural nature (Guarnizo *et al.* 2003; Snel *et al.* 2006). It includes either direct[10] or indirect action[11] and occurs either at the individual or organizational level (Al-Ali *et al.* 2001a: 581). Direct activities have an immediate impact in the homeland, while indirect activities influence the homeland via host land channels. The individual level refers to personal-to-person contacts and individual actions linking diaspora and homeland, while the organizational level refers interactions among formal associations, organizations or political parties. Thus, it is sure that it becomes inevitable for a state to ignore these groups and do not entertain them in their political affairs. They can be highly co-operative and dangerous at the same time. Hence, there definitely remains a need for the international community to recognise their presence and give them appropriate conditions in which they are free to assert themselves and have the power of decision-making for themselves as well as their brothers and sisters staying in their homeland.

The Sri Lankan Tamil diaspora remains connected to the Sri Lankan as well as Indian politics by its active involvement in various international forums and organizational affairs. However, the relationship between the diasporas and India- Sri Lanka bilateral relations doesn't seem to be that simple. It is a complex, and depends on various socio-cultural, political and economic norms. This remains to be the reason why diasporas have gained so much of importance in the wake of post war era in Sri Lanka. The answer lies in the fact that they keep affecting the politico-social norms both in their homeland as well as host land (including India and other European countries), and also affect the relationship between their host land and their homeland. Hence, they remain an inevitably important factor in global politics. The various aspects of their effects can be measured along the lines of conflict and peace situations both in their homeland as well as host land.

The Sri Lankan Tamils and the Indian Tamils in Tamil Nadu feel that Sri Lankan mainstream politics has been and will continue to revolve around the ethnic issue that has plagued the country since independence. They are pretty much sure that the Sinhalese government will never give the Tamils their full rights. The way the war was led and the way in which it ended and the destruction of the LTTE have deeply affected the Tamils in India and the Tamil diasporas and have shattered their confidence, regardless of whether they were members, sympathisers or opponents of the LTTE. Since, the Tamils in Sri Lanka still face hardships and feel lost, hence, the Sri Lankan Tamil diaspora community along with the Indian Tamils has become bound to take a role for themselves to continue with the struggle in a democratic manner that would ensure that the Tamil diaspora was and would continue to be an extremely vital element of their homeland, even if the Sri Lankan state refuses to recognize that. The active participation of the Tamil diaspora at the 2009 protests suggested that a new generation has come forward to carry on the struggle. However, the aim remains to be the same: 'their demand for autonomy'; as most of the Sri Lankan Tamil diaspora still believe that the Tamil rights are never coming to reality until there is rule of the Sinhalese in the island.

REFERENCES

[1] Axel, K.B. (2002). "The Diaspora Imaginary", *Public Culture*, 14: 411–428.

[2] _____ (2004). "The Context of Diaspora", *Cultural Anthropology*, 19(1): 26–60.

[3] Bandarage, Asoka (2010). "Diaspora and Post-conflict Developments in Sri Lanka", *Harvard International Review*, April 19, 2010.

[4] Basch, L., Schiller, N.G. and Szanton, C. (1994). *Nations Unbond*, Gordon and Breach.

[5] Bercovitch, Jacob (2007). "A Neglected Relationship: Daisporas and Conflict Resolution", in H. Smith and P. Stares (Eds.), *Diasporas in Conflict: Peace-makers or Peace-wreckers?* Tokyo: United Nations University Press.

[6] Bush, Kenneth (1990). "Ethnic Conflict in Sri Lanka", *Conflict Quaterly*, 10: 41–58.

[7] Byman, D.L. *et al.* (2001). *Trends in Outside Support for Insurgent Movements*, California: RAND Cooperation.

[8] _____ (2003). "*Diaspora Circulation and Transnationalism as Agents for Change in the Post Conflict Zones of Sri Lanka*". A Policy paper submitted to the Berghof Foundation for Conflict Management (http://www.berghoffoundation.lk/scripts/DiasporaCirc.pdf).

[9] Cheran, R. and Vimalarajah, Luxshi (2010). "Empowering Diaspora: The Dynamics of Post-war Transnational Tamil Politics", Berghof Occasional Paper No. 31.

[10] *Crisis Group interviews, TGTE officials, September and November 2009.

[11] Collier, P. (2000). "Economic Causes of Civil Conflict and their Implications for Policy", Washington, World Bank Development Research Group Report.

[12] Collier, P. and Hoeffler, A. (2004). "Greed and Grievance in Civil War", *Oxford Economic Papers*, 56: 563–595.

[13] DeSilva, Chandra R. (2007). "Sri Lanka in 2006: Unresolved Political and Ethnic Conflicts amid Economic Growth", *Asian Survey*, 47(1): 99–104.

[14] Effendi, Maria Saifuddin (2007). "Role of Third Party in Conflict Resolution: A Case Study of India and Norway in Sri Lanka", Policy Paper published by *Regional Centre for Strategic Studies*, Colombo: Sri Lanka.

[15] Fair, Christine. (2005). "Diaspora Involvement in Insurgencies: Insights from the Khalistan and Tamil Eelam Movements", *Nationalism and Ethnic Politics*, 11(1).

[16] _____ (2007). "The Sri Lankan Tamil Diaspora: Sustaining Conflict and Pushing for Peace", in Hazel Smith and Paul Stares (eds.) *Diaspora in Conflict: Peacemakers or Peace-wreckers?* New York: United Nations University Press.

[17] Fuglerud, Oivind. (1999). *"Life on the outside: The Tamil Diaspora and Long-Distance Nationalism"*, London, Sterling, Virginia: Pluto Press.

[18] Fuglerud, O. (2001). "Time and Space in the Sri Lanka-Tamil diaspora", *Nations and Nationalism*, 7 (2): 195.

[19] International Crisis Group. (2010). 'Sri Lanka: A Bitter Peace'. ICG, Asia Briefing, no. 99. Colombo/Brussels.

[20] _____ (2010). 'The Sri Lankan Tamil Diaspora after the LTTE'. ICG, Asia Report no. 186. Colombo/Brussels.

[21] Krishna, Sankaran. (2000). *Post-colonial Insecurities: India, Sri Lanka and the Question of Nationhood*, New Delhi: Oxford University Press.

[22] Lyons, T. (2004). *"Engaging Diasporas to Promote Conflict Resolution: Transforming Hawks into Doves"*. Unpublished paper. Institute for Conflict Analysis and Resolution. Arlington, VA: George Mason University.

[23] _____ (2006). *"Conflict-Generated Diasporas and Peace building: A Conceptual Overview and Ethiopian Case Study"*. Paper presented at the: University for *Peace Expert Forum on Capacity Building for Peace and Development: Roles of Diasporas. Arlington, VA: George Mason University.

[24] Nandakumar, Thusiyan. (2011). "Political Activism in the Tamil Diaspora", *Diaspora Dialogues for Development and Peace Project*, Berlin: Berghof Peace Support.

[25] Orjuela, Camilla. (2006). *"Distant Warriors, Distant Peace Workers? Multiple Diaspora Roles in Sri Lanka's Violent Conflict"*, Background paper of the High Level Expert Forum on 'Capacity Building for Peace and Development: Roles of Diaspora' (Toronto: University for Peace, 19-20 October 2006).

[26] Ostergaard-Nielsen, E. (2006). "Diasporas and Conflict Resolution—Part of the Problem or Part of the Solution?" DIIS Brief, March 2006. Copenhagen: Danish Institute for International Studies.

[27] Ropers, Norbert. (2008). "Systemic Conflict Transformation: Reflections on the Conflict and Peace Process in Sri Lanka", in Berghof Handbook Dialogue Series 6: Berghof Conflict Research.

[28] *Sangam: archive selection January 2009– December 2011.

[29] Schiller, N.G. *et al.* (1995). "From Immigrant to Transmigrant: Theorizing Transnational Migration", *Anthropological Quarterly*, 68(1): 48–63.

[30] Shain, Yossi and Tamara Cofman Wittes. (2002). "Peace as a Three-Level Game: The Role of Diasporas in Conflict Resolution", in Ambrosio, Thomas (ed.) *Ethnic identity groups and U.S. foreign policy*, Praeger Publishers.

[31] Sheffer, G. (1986). *Modern diasporas in international politics*, London: Croom Helm Publications, p 349.

[32] Skrbis, Z. (1997). "Homeland-diaspora relations: from passive to active interactions", *Asian and Pacific Migration Journal*, 6 (3): 439–455.

[33] Smith, Hazel (2007). "Diaspora in International Conflict", in Hazel Smith and Paul Stares (eds.) *Diaspora in Conflict: Peace-Makers or Peace-Wreckers?* New York: United Nations University Press.

[34] Stokke, Kristian and Anne Kirsti Ryntveit (2000). "The Struggle for Tamil Eelam in Sri Lanka", *Growth and Change*, Vol. 31: 285–304.

[35] *Tamilnet: archive selection January 2009– December 2011.

[36] *Transnational Governemnt of Tamil Eelam. (2010). *Formation of a Provisional Transnational Governemnt of Tamil Eelam: Final report based on the study by the Advisory Committee,* 15th March 2010.

[37] *United Nations. (2010). *Displacement after April 2008,* Joint Humanitarian Update North East Sri Lanka, report no. 24, 10–23 April 2010.

[38] Velamati, Manohari. (2008). "Sri Lankan Diaspora Itching for a Greater Tamil Eelam: Views from the UK and India", *Journal of Peace Studies.* Vol. 15, Issues 3–4, July–December.

[39] Vertovec, S. (2005). "The Political Importance of Diasporas", Centre of Migration, Policy and Society Working Paper No.13, University of Oxford.

[40] _____ (2006). "Diasporas good? Diasporas bad?" Centre on Migration, Policy and Society Working Paper No. 41, University of Oxford.

[41] Wahlbeck, Ö. (2002). "The concept of diaspora as an analytical tool in the study of refugee communities", *Journal of Ethnic and Migration Studies,* 28 (2): 221–238.

[42] Waldinger, Roger. (2008). "Between "here" and "there": Immigrant cross-border activities and loyalties," *International Migration Review,* 42(1).

[43] Wayland, Sarah. (2004). "Ethnonationalist Networks and Transnational Opportunities: The Sri Lankan Tamil Diaspora", *Review of International Studies.* 30: 405–426.

[44] Wickramasinghe, Nira. (2008). "Sri Lanka in 2007: Military Successes, but at Humanitarian and Economic Costs", *Asian Survey,* 48(1): 191–197.

[45] Wilson, J. (2009). "Sri Lanka in 2008: Waging War for Peace", *Asian survey,* 49(1): 59–65.

Websites

- www.berghof-peacesupport.org
- www.crisisgroup.org
- www.colhariharan.org
- www.diaspeace.org
- www.diaspora-centre.org
- www.diasporamatters.com
- www.diasporastrategies.wordpress.com
- www.foreignpolicy.com
- www.foreignpolicyblogs.com
- www.globaltamilforum.org
- www.idsa.in
- www.lankaweb.com

- www.sangam.org
- www.tamilnet.com
- www.tgte-us.org

NOTES

1. The concept was originally used to refer to the dispersal of the Jews from their historical homeland. Today we speak of Koreans, Palestinians, Chinese, Kurds, Armenians, Mexicans, Tamils and numerous other groups as constituting the new diasporas (New Webster's Dictionary, 1993: 264).

2. The modern world has seen many uprisings in a particular country that has been initiated by the diasporas. For example Sikh movement for an independent 'Khalistan' in India was basically an initiation from the Sikh diaspora and not from the state of Punjab in India.

3. For example, voting history is a powerful predictor of future behaviour. While migration may disrupt the norms that support continued voting, it is anticipated that voting, as a symbolically important act undertaken in public, generates other commitments, such that persons with a pre-migration experience of voting will retain greater interest in home country politics than those without (Plutzer 2002).

4. This is done by establishing special diaspora ministries to manage relations with diasporas, and giving similar mandates to existing foreign affairs ministries and departments. These new structures create formal contacts with diaspora organizations and also create opportunities for diaspora influence on the individual level. In many countries legislative seats are reserved to represent diaspora voting preferences (Spiro 2006: 214).

5. These factors are access to international media and organizations and also their powerful or significant host-government. All these contribute in making the diaspora an actor at the global stage and impact the events going on in their host land as well as homeland.

6. Refugees and non-citizens are particularly vulnerable in the terrorism discourse. The fear that newcomers may hold sympathies for rebles fighting against a state that oppressed them also prevails in the host states and hence the law enforcement is a natural way to curb the diasporic activites that link them to their homeland.

7. For instance, in case of Sri Lankan Tamil diaspora, since they have been identified by their homeland as "enemies", the Sri Lankan High Commission has been making efforts to curb any activity that questions the Sri Lankan state. In this effort it has been noted to provide false informations to the hostland authorities about the illegal activities of its diaspora. As a result, the recently held referendum process in the United Kingdom and Canada witnessed absence of the Sri Lankan Tamil diaspora as they feared negative repercussions for their families and friends (Baechler 2002).

8. The second wave of repatriation began in 1992, after the assassination of Rajiv Gandhi during which 54,188 refugees were voluntarily repatriated to Sri Lanka, until March 1995. Eelam War III commenced in April 1995 starting the third wave or refugees. By 12 April 2002, nearly 23, 356 refugees had come to Tamil Nadu. The flow of refugees had stopped in 2002 because of the cease fire agreement.

9. "In Chennai in January 2009 a 26-year old Tamil activist, K. Muthukumar, doused himself in petrol and set himself on fire as an act of protest against the Sri Lankan government and the failure of the Indian government to save the Eelam Tamils. He died after 90 minutes. When asked by a doctor 'why an educated person like himself had committed self-immolation?', he had replied that "several thousands of more intelligent and educated Tamil people were dying" in Eelam and that he "intended to save thousands of lives by sacrificing himself." Muthukumar's death sparked off a series of immolations, mainly in India, but also in Malaysia" (Tamilnet 2009).

10. In terms of direct impact, through homeland constitutional reforms and new legislation there is an increasing trend in dual citizenship and political representation for diasporas, allowing them an unprecedented influence in political affairs (Guarnizo *et al.* 2003:1214; Vertovec 2005: 4–5).

11. Beyond voting, diasporans may have indirect influence in homeland elections by impacting homeland contacts. Voters in the home state often depend on remittances from their relatives abroad, and this economic influence spills over into ideological influence (Itzigsohn *et al.* 1999: 328–9; Lyons 2004: 534–537).

Tamil Diaspora Nationalism in Post-Conflict Era

Shreya Upadhyay

ABSTRACT: Sri Lanka's present political situation has been described as the beginning of a "post-conflict" era by domestic as well as international actors. This post-conflict logic believes that the main driver of the conflict has been defeated with the dismantling of the LTTE and its leader's Vellupillai Prabhakaran's death.

This paper seeks to examine the trends in the long-distance nationalism of the Sri Lankan "stateless" Diaspora groups in the post-conflict homeland politics. The stateless Diasporas are those that are not desirous of leaving their past behind and carry on being concerned about the homeland politics. The focus of this paper is thus to map the activism, protests and propaganda reports of Sri Lankan Tamils in several parts of the world in the post-LTTE era. Even as the LTTE has been defeated, the ethnic conflict continues and peace has not been restored. The paper attempts to understand the dynamics of the role of Diaspora groups in today's conflicts ranging from their participation in peaceful marches, electoral process to extreme steps such as self immolation in order to garner attention to their cause in the global arena.

The paper will analyze Diaspora view of endorsing the call for a separate state. Whether the Diaspora identity remains divided among different groups and members? Whether there is a divide between Tamil Diaspora groups and Tamils residing in Sri Lanka on the issue of a separate state? Whether the reluctance on the part of the Sri Lankan government to include minority groups in the power sharing process is engendering future waves of violence? What are the post war opportunities for peace in Sri Lanka?

INTRODUCTION

The term Diaspora is derived from the Greek *diaspeirein,* meaning "dispersal or scattering of seeds". The ideal type representation of Diaspora, according to William Safran, is expatriate minority communities, dispersed from an original "center" to at least two "peripheral" places. They maintain a memory or myth about their original homeland. They believe they are not, and perhaps cannot, be fully accepted by their host country; and they see the ancestral home as a place of eventual return and a place to maintain or restore. The collective identities of these Diaspora communities are defined by this continuing relationship with the homeland (Safran 1991: 1).

Diasporas, much like ethnic groups, are imagined (transnational) communities, and the product of interactive processes of identification and ascription. People identify with certain diasporic imaginations of community for a plethora of reasons, and with a variety of degrees of commitment. As with all identifications, Diaspora-identity is dynamic and contextual. Not everyone living outside the homeland is bound to see herself as part of the Diaspora. Specific events or developments, however, may trigger such identification (the so-called "diasporic turn"). Thus Diaspora identity does not automatically result from migration but as the product of discursive constructions of community (Demmers 2007: 8).

Charles Taylor suggests that Diaspora while located abroad still have their primary concerns turned towards their home countries (Rafael and Sternberg 2002: 330). Even as they interact with the host community, deal with the exchanges and exclusions between various segments, fight against discrimination and take advantage of opportunities they have a considerable interaction with the communities of origin. At times, the Diaspora is also involved in the direct participation in effectively charged ethno nationalist movements, religious revivals, and fundamentalist causes that erupt in home countries. Diaspora activism can be seen in terms of political support to insurgent movements, sending remittances back home and participating in homeland affairs. This has especially been true with groups that have been prosecuted in the homeland like that of Tamil Diaspora.

Ranganathan has explained that this ethno nationalism at distance has further been facilitated through modern information and communication revolutions. "The integration of text and images, the replicator technology, the cloak of anonymity it provides, the phenomenal physical reach, the facility to incorporate instant feedback and voluminous and varied information in hypertexts and the ability to flag identity through its very address (URL) are key elements that have transformed the Internet into an alternative medium for the Sri Lankan Tamils" (Ranganathan 2010: 710–711). This is especially true in the cases of political activists who have to leave their nations for the fear of persecution and seek refuge in other countries. For them communication technologies and electronic transfers of money serve as a vehicle for their nationalism and allow them to continue their long distance activist nationalism safely from foreign soil.

The post- 9/11 period has particularly drawn attention to such connections and the tag of "home grown terrorists" accorded to immigrants in the host lands. The World Bank in 2003 claimed, "If a country which has recently ended a conflict has a large Diaspora in the USA, its risk that the conflict will resume is sharply increased and that Diasporas tend to be more extreme than the populations they have left behind" (Demmers 2007: 4). Noted human rights advocate and scholar Ignatieff has suggested that, "…Diaspora nationalism is a dangerous phenomenon because it is easier to hate from a distance: You don't have to live with the consequences—or the reprisals" (Ignatieff 2001). A 2006 Human Rights Watch report on LTTE intimidation and extortion in the Tamil Diaspora added to the image of Diasporas as radical hard-line with a pro-violence and conflict perpetuating impact.

However, such a view homogenises Diaspora nationalism and fails to understand and appreciate the distinction between terrorist groups like Al-Qaeda on one hand and other non-state actors engaged in their struggle for self determination, even though they might or might not be resorting to illegitimate tactics of different frequencies, like that of Kurds, Tamils, Palestinians etc. Diaspora organizations are also engaged in developing social networks to accommodate newcomers and find housing, jobs, and asylum. They often form religious groups, set up language courses and are engaged in all sorts of social events to celebrate national holidays, rituals and ceremonies. Events like the colourful Chariot Festival organised by the Sri Manicka temple in Paris arrondissement and 'Heroes Day' celebrated throughout the Tamil Diaspora play an important role in staging Tamil identity.

It is important to place emphasis that even the Diaspora is not uniform. It is heterogeneous and has multiple identities in terms of class, caste, gender, occupation and religion (Smith 2007: 5). For example there is a Sri Lankan Diaspora and a Ceylonese Diaspora. Ceylonese Diaspora associates itself to be belonging to a time when the country was full of educated and talented members of Sinhalese, Tamils, Burghers and Moors communities and each one of them contributed to the development of the nation. Prior to the escalation of the ethnic conflict, there was no such thing as a 'Tamil Diaspora'. Those who migrated during the colonial era regarded themselves as Ceylonese, irrespective of different ethnicities. The shift in the domestic policies in Sri Lanka following independence from Britain compelled members of the Diaspora to reconsider their notions of home and reconfigure their identity in view of the burgeoning ethnic strife in their homeland. Thus Ceylonese identification dissociates itself from the baggage of civil war. Sri Lankan Diaspora also disregards ethnic diversities of the island nation and is used as a blanket term for Sinhalese, Hindus, Moors and Malays. Other important minority groups include the Burghers, Colombo Chettys, etc. All these myriad groups who make up Sri Lanka have migrated overseas over differing periods of time in search of better livelihood and thus make a Sri Lankan Diaspora.

The Tamil Diaspora on the other hand has a strong identification with 'Tamil Eelam Diaspora'. Their identification is similar to communities like that of Jews who are regarded as a de- territorialized victim and define themselves in reference to exclusion and discrimination. The Sri Lankan Tamils retain an idealisation of the supposed ancestral home— Tamil Eelam—where "just order, meritocracy and the individual rights" are believed to reside. The quest for a resolution of war crimes, equal rights to education and employment opportunities shapes the psyche of this displaced community. The retention of collective memories of this nature and myth about their homeland has led to strong identifications with the 'Tamil Eelam Diaspora'. Yet the members of Tamil Diaspora can also be differentiated according to when they migrated, the means by which they gained residence in the host countries and the extent to which they integrated into the host country. There are also pre-migratory cleavages along the lines of caste, class, gender and religion. The majority of Diaspora Tamils are from the Northern Province (indeed, mostly from the Jaffna peninsula), from upper-caste and lower-middle or middle-class backgrounds. The poor, those from Dalit or lower-caste communities, and those from more marginalised areas (such as Mannar, Amparai or Batticaloa) have left in much smaller numbers. These other groups of Tamils do not feature prominently within the nationalist lobby in the Diaspora—and express doubts about the current nationalist campaigns. Thus, LTTE's claim regarding the sole representation of all Tamils, despite its stronghold on the community even before the 2009 events unfolded, remained contested (Sriskandarajah 2004: 499). Adding to this the Sri Lankan government has also not been a bystander to the Tamil Diaspora mobilization. Sinhala Diaspora also engages in counter protests.

FORMATION OF TAMIL DIASPORA

Over 18 million people inhabiting Sri Lanka are divided into four ethno-religious group. The Sinhalese comprise 74 per cent of the population and control the government. They are primarily Theravada Buddhist, speak the Sinhala language, and populate the central and southern parts of Sri Lanka. Sri Lankan Tamils make up 11 per cent of the population. They are mostly Hindus. They are settled in the northern part of the island around the city of Jaffna. Another seven per cent of Sri Lanka's population consists of 'up country' Tamils, the lower caste offspring of tea estate workers imported by the British from India in the late nineteenth century. Because of their more recent origins in Sri Lanka as well as their lower caste status, Sri Lankan Tamils do not share a sense of co-ethnicity with up-country Tamils. They live in the central highlands by the Sinhalese. Lastly, there are the Sri Lankan Moors, seven per cent, who are Muslims.

The northern-eastern and central units of Sri Lanka were administered separately until the arrival of the British who conquered Trincomalee, Batticaloa and Jaffna in 1795; Colombo in 1796; clubbed the coast with the Madras Presidency in 1798; made Ceylon a Crown Colony in 1802; and finally took the Kandyan kingdom in 1815. In 1833 the British placed both the Sinhalese and Tamil-occupied areas under a centralised government. Both the communities continued maintaining and perpetuating their separate identity and nationalism. This was further aided by the British government's policy of facilitating communal representation in the Legislative Council. British officials in the first half of the twentieth century established a network of schools in the northern Jaffna Peninsula. These schools introduced western education and the English language and oriented a number of Tamils towards graduate degrees, university positions in Europe and Ceylon Civil Services. A rift between the Sinhalese and Tamil political leadership occurred in 1924 over the issue of territorial representation and a reserved seat for the Tamils of the Western Province. In 1931, there was an introduction of universal suffrage, which worked to the disadvantage of Tamils. However, in 1946 the Sinhalese and Tamil political elites agreed on a constitutional settlement for independence. However, after Lankan independence the social, economic and political space for Tamils and other minorities in Sri Lanka narrowed. Elections produced Sinhalese governments that discriminated against Tamils and other minorities. In 1956, a Buddhist-backed coalition called the Sri Lankan Freedom Party (SLFP), favouring Sinhala as 'sole official language of government affairs', was elected in 1956. The SLFP was largely elected by the non-Westernised Sinhalese Buddhist majority who no longer wished to be controlled by an English speaking elite, many of whom happened to be Tamils. Sinhala Buddhism became a unifier of the mass of urban poor. Encouraged by Buddhist monks, the new political leaders espoused the values of traditional culture and religion that had been abandoned by the British-educated elite. In 1956, 'Official Language Act' was passed that recognized Sinhala as the sole official language of the state. Several other constitutional manipulations and policies throughout the 1960s and 1970s such as introduction of the new system of standardisation in admission to universities, adoption of new constitution making Sinhala the only official language and Buddhism the state religion further alienated Tamils from power sharing, getting state employment and education.

A series of agreements were signed between Tamil politicians and subsequent Sinhala governments for the protection of the rights of minority Tamils. However, these largely remained ineffective leading to disenchantment among Tamils. During the late 1970s and early 1980s, several insurgent organizations came up. These groups included the Tamil Eelam Liberation Organization (TELO), the People's Liberation Organization for Tamil Eelam (PLOTE), the Eelam Peoples' Revolutionary Liberation Front (EPRLF), and the Liberation Tigers of Tamil Eelam (LTTE). The LTTE secured dominance among these groups through massive violence and coercion. While some groups still exist at various levels, the LTTE has established itself as the principal and most lethal voice of militant Tamil aspirations (Fair 2005: 138). Its leader Velupillai Prabhakaran hit the news headlines in 1975 when he assassinated Jaffna mayor Alfred Duraiappah. The LTTE in course of time had taken charge of the movement for Eelam. In 1976, with the signing of the Vaddukkodai Resolution, the demand of the Tamils changed from a federal constitution to a sovereign state. During that time the number of Tamils leaving Sri Lanka was relatively small confined to those who could afford the cost of travel and study abroad and were lucky to find jobs. However migration rose to new levels as ethnic tensions reached a point in July 1983, known as 'Black July', when Tamil militants ambushed and killed thirteen soldiers in Jaffna. This led to mass killing of Tamils by Sinhalese mobs. In 1981, two years before the riots, the island's Tamil population was estimated at two million. By 1995 almost three quarters were displaced either as direct or indirect consequence (Asia Report 2010:3). At least 110,000 Sri Lankan Tamils were known to be living in the Tamil Nadu state of southern India at the end of 1998 (Bose 2000: 12). According to UNHCR, between 1980 and 1999, 256, 307 people of Sri Lankan origin applied for asylum in Europe (UNHCR 2001). There are substantial Diaspora populations in Canada (200,000–300,000),

Great Britain (180,000), Germany (60,000), Australia (40,000), Switzerland (47,000), France (40,000–50,000), the Netherlands (20,000), the U.S. (25,000), Italy (15,000), Malaysia (20,000), Norway (10,000), Denmark (7,000), New Zealand (3,000) and Sweden (2,000). It is likely therefore that one in every four Sri Lankan Tamils now lives in the Diaspora. There is a long tradition of Tamil migration from the Jaffna peninsula.

This mass migration after 1983 strengthened the Tamil Diaspora. Not only did the Diaspora grow in numbers, but the sense of oppression and injustice that was experienced during the pogrom strengthened their ideas of nationalism and the need for a collective identity. While thousands of Tamil youth joined the emerging militant movements, those who fled overseas carried with them the sense of injustice and anger that drove the militants.

The Sri Lankan Diaspora engaged in political activities to bring out their voices against suppression in their homelands. At the 12th World University Games in Edmonton, Canada in 1983, Tamils partnered with Vietnamese, Pakistanis and Polish protestors to demonstrate in front of the 50,000 attendees against repression in their respective homelands. In Switzerland 1,000 Tamils protested before the Swiss Parliament, seeking asylum as they escaped persecution in Sri Lanka (Nandakumar 2011: 5). Such protests were markers that Diaspora would mobilise into a political force. As explained earlier, Internet played an important role to mobilize the dispersed Tamil audience in order to sustain the fight for rights in Sri Lanka. Anderson has explained how communication movement dramatically changed the experience of the migrant. The same technology, which helped migrants stay in touch with their lands and people even after moving thousands of miles away, also promoted long-distance nationalism (Anderson 1998). This long distance nationalism was not answerable to the judicial system of the parent country, did not need to conform to the citizenship requirements, no fear of prison, torture of death. The Diaspora, safely positioned in a foreign land could send money and guns, circulate propaganda, and build intercontinental computer information circuits (Ranganathan 2010: 6).

POWER OF TAMIL DIASPORA

During a conference of Sri Lankan Diaspora organized by a pro-LTTE group, taking place in the year 1989, LTTE leader Prabhakaran sent a chastening message to the conference, describing the Diaspora as the 'lost generation' (Brun and Hear 2012: 66).

This negative view was directed at those who had left the homeland. However, with escalation of violence more and more people left the homeland, the Diaspora expanded and its potential to contribute to the struggle back home became more and more significant. At the same time those remaining in the north and east of Sri Lanka grew increasingly war-weary and their capacity and willingness to provide support wilted. Then the LTTE turned to the Diaspora.

From holding small peaceful protests, the Sri Lankan Tamil Diaspora became a fundamental component of Tamil insurgency. It has been the backbone of the LTTE's global operations and financial and ideological lifeline of the LTTE. The movement of immigrants and refugees from a situation of persecution and absence of political rights to open societies characterised by democratic governance, freedom of expression, and anti-discrimination laws has profound political implications. Thus, the Sri Lankan Tamil Diaspora migrating from a closed society to an open society was able to capitalise on newfound freedoms to publish, organise, and accumulate financial resources to an extent that was impossible in the homeland. In some countries of settlement, Diaspora funding even supported various forms of ethnic media and organisations (Wayland 2004: 417).

Sri Lanka is among the top 20 developing countries that receive large amounts of remittances from its Diaspora. It received $1,056-million dollars in 2001. This amounts to 7.0 percentage of the country's GDP (World Bank 2003). The relatively small number of Tamils from Sri Lanka living in Canada and Europe provided substantial resources that sustained both the armed struggle for a separate Tamil state and the Tamil refugee communities that are spread across the war-torn areas in Sri Lanka (Cheran 2003). The LTTE network straddles the globe and has offices in 54 countries, including Burma and Botswana. At the height of the conflict, which claimed over 100,000 lives, the Diaspora contributed an estimated $200 million a year to the Tigers (Asia Report 2010: 1). Tamil Diaspora, especially in Canada has been known for fundraising. Tamils living abroad are expected to pay a minimum of $50 a month per person to the LTTE, and Tamil businesses in Sri Lanka and abroad are reportedly forced to pay the Tigers as well (Sri Lanka: Alien Smuggling 1996). Another means of fundraising is the production and sale of Sri Lankan-made videos in the Diaspora. These videos feature footage of the war, the hardships of life under the Sri Lankan government, and pro-LTTE events. It is alleged that Tamils are also asked to buy items like calendars, newspapers etc. to support the separatist cause from Tamil stores that support the Tigers. Initially the funds raised from Diaspora were used for sustaining Tamil societies in war affected areas. But as the civil war dragged on, the humanitarian aid started being used to procure weapons and other war-related materials.

The mobilisation of the Diaspora was manoeuvred by the LTTE to gain financial support. This was done by waging continuous wars against rival Tamil militant groups or moderate groups in order to be the sole voice of Tamil aspirations and grievances. Dissidents were tortured and killed. The absence of alternate voices within the country helped LTTE in maintaining a tight hold on the Diaspora. The LTTE even attacked individuals and forums in the Diaspora to instil fear and ensure its total control. The assassination of activist Sabalingam on May Day 1994 in Paris along with attacks on journalists and forums organised by dissident activists sent a chilling message to the Tamil Diaspora. Despite such overwhelming power of the LTTE, dissent was never completely crushed. Actors like the University Teachers for Human Rights (Jaffna) continued to document and report on the abuses and destructive politics of the LTTE inside the country and literary groups in Europe continued to meet regularly and keep some forums independent of the LTTE (Kadirgamar 2010: 24–25).

DIASPORIC NATIONALISM FOR TAMIL EELAM IN THE POST-LTTE ERA

By way of violence, force, institutional developments and physical presence among Tamils in Sri Lanka and in the Diaspora, the LTTE had over the years gained acceptance as the sole representative of the Sri Lankan Tamil population. After the defeat of LTTE, there has been a profound shift in the relationship between people and locations in the Tamil political field when the relationship between agents operating inside Sri Lanka and outside changed. This led to a rupture between the Diaspora politics and homeland politics (Brun and Hear 2012: 68). LTTE's defeat in the year 2009 brought an abrupt end to the long ethno-political violence in Sri Lanka. This was preceded with a failed attempt to usher an internationally facilitated peace process which lasted till January 2008. However, the violent hostilities had begun in 2006 that gradually transformed into an open undeclared war and then into a full outbreak of violence in 2007. The war claimed more than 40,000 civilians which extended the total number of deaths over the past 35 years to more than 140,000 (Vimalarajah and Cheran 2010: 5).

From January 2009 to June 2009, Tamils residing in cities like London, Toronto, Sydney and Chennai staged sit-ins, chanted slogans, blocked public spaces and even immolated themselves to protest the inactivity of the UN, the US and the European Union. These protests have been unprecedented in the political mobilization of the Sri Lankan Diaspora. The protests saw active involvement of a second generation of Tamils, mainly the children of those forced to flee Sri Lanka, rather than those who chose to leave. Sri Lankan Tamils organized several petitions on various subjects as well. In May 2009, there was a petition organized by the Diaspora members to stop the IMF loan to Sri Lanka. The Tamil Diaspora activists in the UK also launched a "Key Campaign" which brought the conditions in Sri Lanka to the eyes of the British public and received attention from UK Parliamentarians, human rights activists, councillors and members of the community organizations. The idea was to stress the Diaspora's demand to "unlock the Concentration camps in Sri Lanka" (Go Petition 2009).

The defeat of the LTTE brought the spotlight on Diaspora. The LTTE's only surviving leader, S. Pathmanathan reportedly stated in an email audio file that had circulated around the Tamil Diaspora, that the goal of a separate Tamil state would be pursued from abroad (Ranganathan 2009: 709). On June 7, 2009, Tamilnet.com's editorial board wrote: *While not denying the fact that the nature of politics is going to be determined by the ground realities of oppression in the homeland, a parallel political stream in the Diaspora is not a liability but contributory to the Tamil nationalist cause. It is noteworthy that while the LTTE has been defeated and dismantled, the majority of Tamil Diaspora still aspires for a separate state.*

Even though the Diaspora has mixed feeling regarding the LTTE, it was seen as the only group fighting for the rights of Tamils. With LTTE's crushing defeat and enormous death toll, the Tamil Diaspora has been feeling powerless. The Diaspora politics has also undergone internal shifts. The groups that in the past had been the opponents of the LTTE have joined hands with LTTE sympathizers. Several LTTE representatives dissolved their structures and withdrew from the politics leaving the space to be filled by other Tamil nationalists.

The fact that the present Sri Lankan government has hardly taken any step to include Tamils in the power sharing procedure has been responsible for the continuing Diaspora nationalism. The election promises during the presidential campaign included the development of a strategy for conflict resolution and a strategy for sustainable economic development.

However, after election the strategy has been to consolidate the power base of the President. Thus, rehabilitation of the Tamil war-victims, or IDPs [internally displaced persons], and reconstruction of war-ravaged Tamil areas, do not find much space in media and societal discourse. The present political environment in Sri Lanka is highly volatile and tense. It illustrates some of the most flammable factors in ethnic relations: language, religion, divergent historical narratives and continuing separatist agitation (Arambwela and Arambwela 2010: 367–368).

Recently, the administration built a victory memorial base of a soldier standing with gun in one hand with a pigeon hovering over it and in the other hand the Sri Lankan national flag. This has been constructed at the very same place in northern Sri Lanka which was once a Tamil Tiger Territory. The war memorial situated next to it has an assortment of LTTE artillery, guns and sea tiger suicide boats on display. Such tactics by the government have been damaging to the so called talks about inclusiveness and Tamils being a part of the Sri Lankan state. Tamils who have not been LTTE supporters also view the memorial as "a reminder that for all the sacrifices that Tamils had to make, we are nowhere today." The continued presence of the entirely Sinhalese Army across Northern Sri Lanka, including in the Jaffna peninsula also add to Tamil woes. Of the 19 divisions in the Sri Lankan Army, 14 are based in the Northern Province. Tamils have the concern that army camps in the North will be converted into cantonments, soldiers will bring their families, and Tamil areas will become Sinhalised (The Hindu 2012).

Violence against Tamil people is yet to cease and the prospects of economic progress looks bleaker. The few steps taken by Rajapaksa government to reduce tensions with Tamil Diaspora also appear cosmetic. Efforts like the Sri Lankan Expatriate Forum 2009 are motivated to encourage the Diaspora to invest but hardly make any attempt at addressing their grievances. The Lankan administration has sponsored the visit of hundreds of expatriate Tamils in Sri Lanka to highlight its efforts to improve security and resettle over 300,000 displaced Tamils, visitors have come away unsatisfied and sceptical about the future (Asia Report 2010: 10).

Most Tamils living outside the country remain committed to Tamil Eelam. While they have realised that militancy has failed, they still want to continue with the struggle for an independent state. They are seeking new forms of struggle to pressurise the western governments to accept an independent state for Tamils. They endorse the call for a separate state, boycott against products made in Sri Lanka and advocate the support of international investigations into alleged war crimes by the Sri Lankan state. In March 2012, several Tamil Diaspora organisations such as Representatives of the Transnational Government of Tamil Eelam (TGTE), the British Tamil Forum (BTF), the Tamil Centre for Human Rights (TCHR), and the Global Tamil Forum (GTF) lobbied with the various diplomatic missions of the 46 UNHRC countries for the passing of UN Resolution on Sri Lanka. They have collected evidences for alleged war crimes by the Sri Lankan government against the Tamils during the war. These organizations work with other community groups, human rights organizations, trade unions and women organizations in their fight for self determination and in the process convince Western governments to pressure Colombo to negotiate a political deal with Tamils. These initiatives were born of the belief that Tamil politicians in Sri Lanka were not equipped to express their real political views—including continued support for a separate state—and that was up to the Diaspora to push the ideas they could not safely espouse.

The international community, however, still treats the Diaspora groups at an arm's length due to its pro-LTTE attitude.

TRANSNATIONAL GOVERNMENT OF TAMIL EALAM (TGTE)

Still in the nascent stage, the TGTE wants to act as a non-violent democratic political body in the Diaspora. It hopes that its democratic credentials would provide it with a moral authority to compel the international community to support an independent state for Sri Lanka's Tamils. The elections for the provincial TGTE took place in 11 countries on May 2, 2010. However, TGTE has been unable to be an acceptable option along several quarters. One of the main reasons has been that the name creates a picture of government in exile. While the founders disagree with such a stamp, the western governments remain sceptical as many see it as the last breath of LTTE. On the other hand the hardliner Tamil Diaspora groups such as Nediyavan faction accuse TGTE for not espousing full support to Tamil Eelam. Nediyavan faction has the potential to not only re-ignite militancy but also as strong links back home with the groups that survived the military offensive. Thus, it has the ability to pressure the TGTE into at least tacitly support violent activities taking place in future.

Referenda

The referenda are seen mainly as political mobilization and a tool for self affirmation in the Diaspora. The Tamil Diaspora groups in Norway, France, Canada, Germany, Switzerland, the Netherlands and Britain have held a series of referenda to gauge support for an independent Tamil Eelam, which signified vast support for an independent state. Interestingly, the polls were held when the LTTE's grip on Tamils was at its weakest. The June 2012 referenda organised by eleven Diaspora groups called for stopping the genocidal processes occurring in Sri Lanka. It stated, *"The Sinhala racist government which has intensified the process of genocide is currently destroying the traditional homeland of the Tamils, along with land grabs, destruction of economic resources, and assaults on the identity and cultural sites of the Eelam Tamils. As a result, the rights of our people in the homeland are trampled upon and their daily life passes under constant duress. Besides working to prevent and put a permanent stop to this process, we shall also endeavour to restore a dignified life and a humane existence to our people in the homeland"* (Tamil Guardian July 2012).

Such referenda indicate an emergence of a democratic non-violent political struggle. The relatively high turnout has reiterated the Diaspora's mobilisation capabilities. The process on one hand has been inward looking that sought to mobilise the disparate Tamil voices while also outward looking in its appeal to the international community to prevent further erosion of Tamil identity in the island (Vilamaraja and Cheran 2010: 24).

Global Tamil Forum

The GTF was formed with its constitution in August 2009 in Paris and formally launched in January 2010 in London. Its vision statement proclaims:

> *"Evolve an independent international organization, which adheres to the principal of democracy and non-violence and derives its strength from grassroots organization of the Tamil Diaspora that will be in solidarity with Tamils in Eelam and other communities in Sri Lanka to restore Tamil people's right to self determination and democratic self rule."*

The GTF is a conglomeration of pro-LTTE organisations from 14 countries that claim to speak on behalf of their respective Tamil populations. It aims to be a quasi-advocacy and humanitarian organisation based in London.

GTF also lobbies with Western governments to focus on the immediate humanitarian concerns of Tamils in Sri Lanka, such as closure of the internment camps, etc.

Democratically elected Tamil national councils and country councils are also constituted in countries like Norway, France, and Switzerland, etc. where there is a large Tamil Diaspora. The fall of the LTTE has also resulted in springing up of new social and political formations with contesting political agendas and political philosophies. The internal debates on politics, strategies and concepts have grown. For example the proposal to establish a provisional TGTE led to a lively debate among the Diapora on the core vision, the name itself and the long term outlook of the organisation.

Even while the LTTE was active, many in Diaspora, especially the pro-Tiger elements, focused on working within the system, especially in Toronto and London by getting Tamils elected to office and using electoral clout and money to influence policymakers. For the past several years, organisations like the BTF and Canadian Tamil Congress (CTC) have organised Tamil votes for parliamentary candidates sympathetic to their cause. Tamils are also seeking public office themselves. Several have already been elected to a variety of local government bodies in Canada, Norway and France. There is a hope among the Diaspora that representation at the local levels will ultimately translate into Tamil representation at higher levels.

ROLE OF THE YOUTH IN THE PRESENT DIASPORA POLITICS

With the end of LTTE and removal of several supporters and activists of the LTTE, some space opened up for the middle guard and the youth. People of this age group were mostly born in the host lands or had left Sri Lanka as children. They grew up hearing the story of their parents' exploitation and hardships, their difficult journeys through illegal traffickers. On the other hand many of them consider themselves as citizens of the host lands and to a large extent integrated in the culture of their place of birth or growing up. This second generation Diaspora emerged as important players in political organizing efforts especially through social networking and modern modes of communication during and after the events of 2009. Most of them have espoused democratic and more moderate nationalism with non-violent means of protests.

They also used symbols such Tamil Eelam flag and sat on hunger strikes to show solidarity with the Lankan Tamils and putting forward the demand of a separate state. They exploited modern tools of communications such as Facebook and Twitter. A trend that emerged early on and still continues is the use of Facebook profile photos. Thousands of the Tamil Facebook users changed their profile photos to either Eelam flag or pictures of civilian casualties as their main profile image.

TAMIL DIASPORA IN INDIA, POST-LTTE

India is only 35 kilometres away from Sri Lanka and a 45 minute boat trip by speed boat. It is considered to be home to roughly 65,000 refugees from Sri Lanka. Thus any political developmental in both the countries leaves a profound effect on the other. In the post-LTTE era there have been new signs of radicalisation among the Tamil population in India, especially the youth.

In 2009, a 26-year-old Tamil activist, K Muthukumar, immolated himself as an act of protest against the Sri Lankan government and the failure of the Indian government to save the Eelam Tamils. When asked by a doctor 'why an educated person like himself had committed self-immolation?' he had replied that "several thousands of more intelligent and educated Tamil people were dying" in Eelam and that he "intended to save thousands of lives by sacrificing himself." Muthukumar's death sparked off a series of immolations in India (Nandakumar 2011: 8).

Apart from the radicalisation resulting in sit-ins and protests there are also efforts at mobilising the Diaspora community. The TGTE for its part "is engaged in building a power base among the world Tamil community, particularly in Tamil Nadu, and with sections of the international civil society." In April 2012 the TGTE nominated five persons from Tamil Nadu as "members" of TGTE "parliament." A TGTE Solidarity Centre with Professor Saraswathi Rajendran, a TGTE parliament member as convener, operates in Tamil Nadu. The Diaspora groups were also instrumental in lobbying with Indian leaders shoring their support regarding passing of the UN Resolution against Sri Lanka in March 2012.

On the other hand, the political parties in Tamil Nadu have also been exploiting the present situation to their advantage by harnessing pro-Tamil sentiments and pursuing Tamil agenda. On several occasions hundreds of pro-LTTE activists, led by Marumalarchi Dravida Munnetra Kazhagam (MDMK) leader V Gopalswamy (Vaiko), have waved pictures of slain LTTE chief Prabhakaran and held protests in Chennai against President Mahinda Rajapaksa's visit. The political parties and the public have remained consistent in their support to Tamil Eelam if not the outright LTTE. Marumalarchi Dravida Munnetra Kazhagam (MDMK) started the campaign for the creation of a Tamil state in India which is now being reinforced by Vaiko that his party will unite with the Tamil Diaspora to carry forward the Tamil struggle. (Arambawela and Arambawela 2010: 365) DMK chief M. Karunanidhi has also announced the revival of the defunct Tamil Eelam Supporters Orgranisation formed in 1986 to pursue the Tamil Eelam agenda. The support of Tamil politicians legitimises the separatist cause and provides political space to pro-LTTE fringe parties in Tamil Nadu. If the DMK fully activates TESO, its link up with TGTE would be firmed up.

TAMIL DIASPORA AND LANKAN TAMILS

It is important to explore the dynamics of relations between the local and Diasporic community and to track shifts in the political field over the course of the conflict. The political field shows how the groups emerge in different fields and struggle for power and influence (Bourdieu 1991). It thus becomes a site of competition for power which takes the form of mobilising the right to speak and act in the name of others. In terms of the 'Tamil political field', there are groups of people within Sri Lanka and in the Diaspora. The political field in Sri Lanka (the 'local political field') and a political field in the Diaspora (the 'Diasporic political field') are linked to form the 'transnational political field' (Brun, Hear 2012: 62). Different actors operate from different locations within it. Power is accumulated, transferred, and at times shifts between these fields. In the recent years, especially in the post war period, there have been ruptures in all three fields—local, Diaspora and transnational—resulting in such shifts in power relations within and among them.

The Sri Lankan Tamils and the Tamil Diaspora at present are not on the same page regarding carrying forward LTTE's fight. The Lankan Tamils do want a separate state but are not willing to fight and die for it. Exhausted with decades of war they are now interested in rebuilding their lives rather than continuing to struggle for an independent state. The Tamil leaders in Sri Lanka are instead asking for reforms and power sharing within the country. This has not gone down well with Diaspora leaders who consider themselves deeply committed to Tamil Eelam.

The January 2010 Presidential elections in Sri Lanka showed the dissonance between the Diaspora and island Tamils. While the Diaspora organizations called for a boycott the Tamil National Alliance (TNA), the most important Tamil political party, extended its support to the head of the army Sarath Fonseka that carried out the attacks on Tamil civilians over Mahinda Rajapaksa who had ordered these attacks as the head of the government. This showed Tamil leaders' desire for independent political decision to not boycott elections under the pressure of Diaspora.

CONCLUSION

The events of 2009 jolted both moderate and uninterested Tamil Diaspora to become ardent supporters of Tamil struggle. The lack of condemnation from the western powers strengthened the resolve for an independent state. The protests during and in the aftermath of war charged the second generation Diaspora. The presence of 'Transnational Government of Tamil Eelam' indicates that the struggle for a separate Tamil Eelam is now being orchestrated from abroad.

The ties between Diaspora and Tamils staying in the country though weakened with the end of the LTTE still continue through internet and phone links, visits, participation in weddings and other events, and private and community-based remittances and other transfers of resources. While the end of the LTTE has ushered in a more democratic space within the Diaspora as well as the Tamils in the island state their goals point in a different direction. The Diaspora today more than ever aspires for a separate nation state, believing that it can achieve self determination and independent nationhood for Tamils through diplomacy. While in principal many Tamils in Sri Lanka want a separate state but the war weary population at present wants peace and reconstruction. This has not gone down well with the Diaspora that blames the Tamil leaders within Sri Lanka for being traitors to the liberation struggle or considering them too weak to stand for their rights and thus want to fight on their behalf. Diaspora's claim to stand as representative of Tamil people back home is, however, reminiscent of LTTE's assertion of it being the sole representative to fight for Tamil Eelam. It is important to bring home the point that while the Sri Lankan government and majority politics played on its part, the total political disenfranchisement and subjugation of the Tamil people was wrought by the LTTE, with the backing of the Diaspora, over the war years. There is also a doubt that this nationalism push within the Diaspora might actually be a money making tactic. The use of referenda and democratic process to conjure international support of a separate state will fall flat if the Diaspora is reminded that none of the nations condemned the use of force on civilians by the Sri Lankan government during the crackdown on LTTE. The main reason for this has been international community's scepticism regarding voices within the Diaspora due to LTTE's separatist and illiberal tendency. In order to conjure host-lands' support, the Diaspora leaders should reject violence. Once confidence is established between the Diaspora community and host government, than there is a hope of international support to increase pressure on the Sri Lankan government to address Tamil grievances. Thus, wwhat is needed of Diaspora is to bring about a change in its policy and extend its support in peace building efforts in Sri Lanka.

The chance for peace, however, depends largely on the Lankan state. The present administration's strategy thrives on use of fear of the Diaspora to mobilise nationalist sentiments within Sri Lanka and oppress Tamils within the state. This also allows the government to continue militarisation; open camps in Tamil dominated areas and harass the minority population. In order to bring peace it is required that all the parties concerned should have long period of constructive political engagement. From the state front it is required that there is a support for civil society peace activism and economic improvements with focus on contested areas. The Sri Lankan government needs to address the longstanding sense of marginalization, disrespect, and insecurity amongst the Tamil minority which essentially gave rise to the LTTE. The political solution in Sri Lanka requires taking into the consideration the needs of not only Tamils inside and outside Sri Lanka but also other minority communities such as Muslims, etc. There is also a need to address concerns of Muslims, Dalits and women that are often sidelined and have to suffer horrifically from all sides. What is important is creating a movement for democracy.

The Diaspora nationalists need to understand that its members are not the protagonists in this theatre of politics. Instead, it is the people of Sri Lanka who need to play a central role in any such endeavour.

REFERENCES

[1] (2012). Tamil Diaspora organisations call for referendum on Tamil Eelam. Tamil Guardian. 31 July 2012. Retrieved 24 October 2012 from http://www.tamilguardian.com/article.asp?articleid=5416.

[2] Arambewela, Nadeeka and Arambewela, Rodney (2010). Post-war opportunities for peace in Sri Lanka: an ongoing challenge? *Global Change, Peace and Security: formerly Pacifica Review: Peace, Security and Global* Change. 22(3). 365–375.

[3] Brun, Catherine and N.V. Hear. (2012). Between the Local and the Diasporic: The Shifting Centre of Gravity in Wartorn Sri Lanka's transnational politics. *Contemporary South Asia*. 20(1): 61–75.

[4] Bose, Tapan (2000). Protection of Refugees in South Asia: Need for a Legal Framework. *South Asia Forum for Human Rights*. Retrieved October 18, 2012 from http://www.safhr.org/index.php?option=com_docman&task=doc_download&gid=61 2&Itemid=562

[5] Cheran, R. (2003). Diaspora Circulation and Transnationalism as Agents for Change in the Post-Conflict Zones of Sri Lanka. *Department of Sociology and Centre for Refugee Studies*. Toronto: York University Publications.

[6] Cheran, R. and Luxsi Vilamarajah (2010). Empowering Diasporas: The Dynamics of Post War Transnational Tamil Politics, *Berghof Peace Support*, 31: 1–39.

[7] Demmers, Jolle (2007). New Wars and Diasporas: Suggestions for Research and Policy, Journal of Peace Conflict and Development Issue.

[8] Fair, Christine (2005). Diaspora Involvement in Insurgencies: Insights from the Khalistan and Tamil Eelam Movements. *Nationalism and Ethnic Politics*. 11:125–156.

[9] Ignatieff, Michael (2001). The Hate Stops Here. *The Globe and Mail*. October 25, 2001. Retrieved 15 October 2011 from http://www.balkanpeace.org/index.php? index=/content/library/misc1/hate_stops.incl

[10] Immigration and Refugee Board of Canada, *Sri Lanka: Alien Smuggling*, 1 May 1996, Retrieved 19 October, 2012 from URL: http://www.unhcr.org/ refworld/docid/3ae6a8660.html

[11] International Crisis Group (2010). *The Sri Lankan Tamil Diaspora after The LTTE*: Asia Report N 86.

[12] Immigration and Refugee Board of Canada (1996). *Sri Lanka: Alien Smuggling*, Published 1 May 1996. Retrieved 20 October 2012 from http://www. unhcr.org/refworld/docid/3ae6a8660.html.

[13] Jones, Sam (2009). Tamil Killed Himself 'to guide others to liberation. *The Guardian*, 19 February 2009, http://www.guardian.co.uk/world/2009/feb/19/tamil-suicide-protest-geneva.

[14] Kadirgamar, Ahilan (2010). Classes, States and the Politics of the Tamil Diaspora. Economic Political Weekly, XLV (31): 23–26.

[15] Nandakumar, Thusiyan (2011). Political Activism in the Tamil Diaspora. *Berghof Peace Support*.

[16] Radhakrishnan, R.K. and Suramanian, N. (2012). Near Site of LTTE's Last Stand, a Victory Memorial that Tamils Don't Visit. *The Hindu*, 21 October 2012, Puthukudiyiruppu.

[17] Rafael, E.B. and Sternberg, Y. (2002). *Identity Culture and Globalisation*. Netherlands.

[18] Ranganathan, Maya (2010). *Eelam Online: The Tamil Diaspora and War in Sri Lanka*. News Castle: Cambridge Scholars Publishing.

[19] Ranganathan, Maya (2009). Understanding Eelam through the Diaspora's online engagement. Continuum: Journal of Media and Cultural Studies, 23(5): 709–721.

[20] Rajasingham, Nirmala (2012). The Simulated Politics of Diaspora. *Sri Lanka and Diasporas*. Retrieved 23 October 2012 from file:///C:/Users/admin/Desktop/lanka/

The%20simulated%20politics%20of%20Diaspora%20by%20Nirmala%20Rajasinga
m%20%20%20SRI%20LANKA%20&%20DIASPORAS.htm

[21] Safran, William (1991). Diasporas in Modern Societies: Myths of Homeland and
Return. *Diaspora: A Journal of Transnational Studies,* 1(1): 83–99.

[22] Sriskandarajah, Dhananjayan (2004). Tamil Diaspora Politics. *The Increasingly
Urban Map for Global Capital and Global Diasporas,* 493–501.

[23] Nadarajah, Suthaharan and Sriskandarajah, D. (2005). Liberation Struggle or
Terrorism? The Politics of Naming the LTTE. *Third World Quarterly.* 26 (1): 87–100.

[24] GoPetition (2009). Stop IMF Loan to Sri Lankan Government. Retrieved 23
October 2012 from http://www.gopetition.com/petitions/stop-imf-loan-to-sri-lankan-
goverment.html

[26] Wayland, Sarah (2004). Ethnonationalist Networks and Transnational Opportunities:
The Sri Lankan Tamil Diaspora. *Review of International Studies,* 30(3): 405–426.

Ethnic Conflict in Sri Lanka and Its Impact on India-Sri Lanka Relations: The Intervention of SAARC

Chalamalla Venkateshwarlu

ABSTRACT: India and Sri Lanka share common values and traditions as well as a common commitment to democratic governance. India-Sri Lanka relations are based on a deep and abiding friendship on shared historical experience and common civilization. Both countries have taken a similar trajectory in international relations, having emerged from the colonial oppression. Since then, the two independent nations of India and Sri Lanka have proceeded to renew and reinvigorate age old cultural, commercial and strategic links for the mutual benefit of the two nations and their peoples. India is concerned at the ongoing hostilities in Sri Lanka which has taken its toll on civilian casualties and resulted in an exodus of refugees. India is of the view that the only way out is a negotiated, political settlement which meets the legitimate aspirations of all communities while respecting the unity, sovereignty and territorial integrity of Sri Lanka. There was progress in the negotiations between India and Sri Lanka on a CEPA, which would build on the success of the FTA. The specific geo-strategic location of Sri Lanka in the Indian Ocean has been the most important factor in their relations. The Sri Lankan ethnic conflict had caused tensions and pressure on India-Sri Lanka relationship. India involvement in Sri Lanka's ethnic provides ample testimony to the wrench of closeness. The history of ethnic conflict in Sri Lanka is the history of emergence of consciousness among the majority community, the Sinhala, which defined the Sri Lanka society as Sinhala-Buddhist, thus denying its multi-ethnic character. The growth of this consciousness impinged on the minorities in Sri Lanka to the extent that internal resolution of the problems becomes impossible. In asserting a Sinhala identity and in legitimizing Sinhala control of the country's polity, the leaders of the Sinhala. In recent years, one was the evacuation of over 100,000 refugees from the northern regions of the island to Tamilnadu in South India; these were primarily civilians who had become victims of the government's drive against Tamil militants. The Indo-Sri Lanka Agreement also has many implications for the security of South Asian region. It is a known fact that all of India's neighbors' have problems which involve India in some way. The Indo-Sri Lanka Agreement can be read by all these countries as a signal that their internal and foreign policies must be so adjusted as to not to affect significantly India's security concerns. In this paper an attempt has been made to discuss the historical background of India-Sri Lanka relationship and focuses on ethnic conflict in Sri Lanka and its impact on Indo-Sri Lanka relationship. It argues that the intervention and the role of the SAARC in addressing ethnic conflict.

INTRODUCTION

India and Sri Lanka share common values and traditions as well as a common commitment to democratic governance. India-Sri Lanka relations are based on a deep and abiding friendship on shared historical experience and common civilization. Both countries have taken a similar trajectory in international relations, having emerged from the colonial oppression, India in August 1947 and Sri Lanka five months later in February 1948. Sri Lanka, the pear-shaped island, is a Republic of the British Commonwealth, to the South-East of India. Since then, the two independent nations of India and Sri Lanka have proceeded to renew and reinvigorate age old cultural, commercial and strategic links for the mutual benefit of the two nations and their peoples. Sri Lanka and India have been related to each other for millennia and a love-hate relationship had developed due to historical circumstance. However, it is acknowledged that culturally, linguistically, philosophically, and ethnically that both share more similarities than differences. Therefore, in the context of the evolving New International Economic Order struggling to be born a relationship of mutual interdependence must be forged and reinforced by every means possible. It should also be noted carefully that healthy relationships cannot be built on a foundation of apprehension but on a foundation of transparency and cordial mutual respect. Whilst we look to India as 'big brother' it behooves India to look upon us as 'little sister' and help us to protect our independence, sovereignty and territorial integrity inviolate.

Sri Lanka and India has at the moment quite friendly relations based upon mutual understanding. Although there have been minor disputes and differences in the past, they seem to have been slowly resolving by now. India should also understand that Sri Lanka, along with it, is one of the founder members of the Non-Aligned Movement (NAM) that told the two major power blocs that it would remain independent and uninvolved in their struggles for global supremacy. If anything, that was the major thrust of the NAM. Then, we co-operated in forming the South Asian Association for Regional Co-operation (SAARC) as a viable forum to prevent conflict, enhance economic co-operation, and discuss our common problems in a civilized manner. When a dispute arose about the possession of *Kacchativu* Island which to all purpose belonged to India. India was gracious enough to hand over the possession of this island to Sri Lanka. India did not want Sri Lanka to become a pocket of America on this score, for then. Colombo would have become an American Military base both India and Sri Lanka are active members of the Colombo Plan and the Non-Aligned Movement. And now, India and Sri Lanka seem to have amicably settled the issue of the Tamil immigrants in Sri Lanka after the signing of the India-Sri Lanka Agreement drawn in July, 1987.[i] Both countries are also members of several other multilateral groups and the overarching United Nations system. This means dynamic engagement. It also means that besides economic co-operation and engagement that the social context of people-to-people engagement also be greatly increased.

In the recent past India is concerned at the ongoing conflict in Sri Lanka which has taken its toll on civilian casualties and resulted in a migration of refugees. India is of the view that the only way out is a negotiated, political settlement which meets the legitimate aspirations of all communities while respecting the unity, sovereignty and territorial integrity of Sri Lanka. There was progress in the negotiations between India and Sri Lanka on a Comprehensive Economic Partnership Agreement (CEPA)[ii] which would build on the success of the Free Trade Agreement (FTA). The specific geo-strategic location of Sri Lanka in the Indian Ocean has been the most important factor in their relations. A free trade agreement was signed between both the nations in 2000. Since then the two neighbors have witnessed positive growth rate in trade. Further, both the nations being members of organizations like South Asia Co-operative Environment Programme (SACEP) of SAARC, South Asian Economic Union (SAEU) and Bay of Bengal Initiative for Multi Sectoral Technical and Economic. Cooperation (BIMSTEC)[iii] are making effort to strengthen commercial and cultural ties. India has willingly cooperated with Sri Lanka for the latter's development in areas of education, health, etc.

THE ETHNIC PROBLEM IN SRI LANKA

The ethnic problem in Sri Lanka dates back not to one year or the decade only, but it has its roots deep in century's old history. The rivalry between the Sinhalese and the Tamils is at the root of the genocide of the civilian population that has shaken the very roots of the entire political structure of Sri Lanka. It is difficult to say for certain who are the original natives of Sri Lanka—the Sinhalese or the Tamils, both staking claim to this privilege. In this ethnic rivalry both the Dravidian races conveniently forget that they both originally hail from India and that Sri Lanka was once part of the Indian peninsula. Religion and language have no small share in creating the division. Theologically, the Tamils follow Hinduism whereas the Sinhalese worship Buddhism. Surprisingly both the religions preach Ahimsa and religious Forbearance and tolerance. In Sri Lanka they have become so intolerant as to shed the blood of each other sect. Linguistically, the official language of the Sinhalese (as also of the administration) is Sinhalese, while the official language of the Tamils is Tamil.

The central question that will occupy the world attention concerning Sri Lanka is will there be a political solution to the ethnic conflict in the aftermath of the government's military success over secession? Sri Lanka's president has repeatedly emphasized that once the LTTE is defeated, his government would introduce a political solution. However, moving in that direction will not be an easy proposition. A one-sided military victory in an ethnic civil war is not likely to open up new political space for the government to initiate political reforms giving the ethnic minorities any measure of self-rule, which had dominated the agenda of the defeated rebellion. Branding the LTTE insurgency as terrorism and crushing that terrorism should not obviate the fact that the secessionist rebellion, despite its defeat, represented Tamil political aspirations for equality and autonomy. Tamils in Sri Lanka devastated in their thousands need facilities and help for economic reconstruction and development. Pro-LTTE Tamil Diaspora must be severely warned by their respective governments to desist from fanning Tiger terrorism in their new homelands. Two years ago a six-decade civil conflict of cold-blooded communal contentions and controversies and thirty years of a horrendous civil war came to conclusion with an intolerable loss of thousands of innocent civilian lives. This is the toll Prabhakaran and his terror contraption extracted as they finally got wiped out. His obdurate obstinacy and opulent lifestyle never gave a chance for a political solution. Historians for decades will comment and contend whether such an awesome price was needed to bring to end the ruthless campaign of the Liberation Tigers of Tamil Eelam (LTTE).

Sri Lanka Ethnic Groups

Sri Lanka is the 53rd most populated nation in the world, with an annual population growth rate of 0.73%. Sri Lanka has a birth rate of 17.6 births per 1,000 people and a death rate of 6.2 deaths per 1,000 people. Population density is highest in western Sri Lanka, especially in and around the capital. Sinhalese constitute the largest ethnic group in the country, with 74.88% of the total population. Sri Lankan Tamils are the second major ethnic group in the island, with a percentage of 11.2. Moors comprise 9.2%. Tamils of Indian origin were brought into the country as indentured labourers by British colonists to work on estate plantations. Nearly 50% of them were repatriated following independence in 1948. They are distinguished from the native Tamil population that has resided in Sri Lanka since ancient times. There are also small ethnic groups such as the Burghers (of mixed European descent) and Austronesian peoples from Southeast Asia. Moreover, there is a small population of Vedda people who are believed to be the original indigenous group to inhabit the island.

Ethnic Issue in Sri Lanka

Sri Lanka has three major communities which include Sinhalese, Tamils and Muslims. Muslims in Sri Lanka prefer to identify with their religion than ethnicity. Sinhalese are a majority with a minority complex and Tamils are a minority with a majority complex. Tamils constitute 18 percent of the total population in Sri Lanka and they have an ongoing common active link and brotherhood with Tamils in Tamil Nadu. Sinhalese in comparison to Tamils feel that they do not have any other place to live in the world. They are heir to a well-preserved Buddhist civilization that seems to have vanished from the sub-continent. Therefore, the feeling of being beleaguered builds a complex behaviour among the Sinhalese. Sinhalese feel isolated and this is one critical tool in understanding the ethnic conflict in Sri Lanka. Nevertheless, over the years there has been an earnest effort to mitigate the majoritarian tendencies of Sinhalese, which is a result of their insecurities. Sri Lanka needs to work out a package or political dispensation that would make every Sri Lankan comfortable with each other and this remains a challenge before the government. As Benedict Anderson suggests, many of the primordial identities, nations and traditional homelands espoused y various ethno-nationalist groups are only imagined communities formulated in response to modern circumstances rather than primordial entities based on historical facts.[iv] The traditional Tamil home-lands thesis manufactured the Sri Lankan Tamil elites is a case in point.[v]

The *Sri Lanka Freedom Party* (SLFP) government declared Sinhalese as the official national language.[vi] After a stiff challenge from the Tamil leader Selvanayakama, a pact was arrived at in 1957 between Prime Minister Bandamaike and Selvanayakama whereby Tamil was recognized as the official language of the Tamil minorities of the eastern peninsula. However, the pact was not implemented. In 1972, the new constitution of Sri Lanka was framed and Sri Lanka was declared a Republic with Sinhalese as the Official language and Buddhism as the official religion of the country. The Tamils boycotted the entire process of the framing of the constitution. This paved the way for the formation of the Tamil United Front (TCJF) with 6-point demands for decentralized structure of the government at the basis of religion and languages. In fact, there had been a planned move on the part of the Sri Lankan government to downgrade the Tamils as 'second grade citizens' under the guise of standardization and regionalization of education, there began a gradual elimination of Tamils from engineering, medical, science and technical education and minimization, of Tamils in government employment. This naturally created a strong wave of discontent and rebellion among the Tamil militant youths. The year 1976 proved to be a milestone in the history of the Tamil Movement; it saw establishment of Tamil United Liberation Front (TULF) and the institutionalization of the Tamil Movement. The TULF pressed forward the demand for seven Tamil Eelam districts in the north eastern Jaffna peninsula, including Jaffna Vavunia, Trincomalls and Batticaloa. In 1977 the TULF fought the general elections with 'Tamil Eelam as their manifesto. When the United National Party (UNP) comes into power with President Jayawardene, the Sri Lanka President promised to give adequate representation to Tamils in education and employment. However, when in 1978 the new Constitution was passed, Sinhalese was recognized as the official language, with recognition to Tamil as second language for official administrative work in Tamil majority areas. But all this was a paper exercise and a ploy. So discontent went on brewing among the Tamils against this discrimination. By now several underground terrorist groups of Tamils had sprung up—LTTE (Liberation Tigers of Tamil Eelam); EROS, EPRLF, TELO and PLOT.[vii] The government passed stringent laws to neutralize and liquidate the legitimate demands of the Tamils and gave unlimited powers to the armed forces to deal with the Tamil militants by declaring emergency in May 1983. Ethnic conflict in Sri Lanka and regional security, By Kumari Jayawardhana, His paper, given a historical summary of ethnic conflict in Sri Lanka, and trace the many ways in which the conflict became a matter of concern in Tamilnadu, in India and internationally, resulting in a swiftly concluded agreement between the governments of India and Sri Lanka, over the heads of combatants.

The violent ethnic conflict that has ravaged Sri Lanka for a decade resulted in an agreement between the governments of Sri Lanka and India—the 'Indo-Sri Lanka Agreement—to establish peace and normalcy in Sri Lanka' (signed on 29 July 1987) and the Provincial Councils Act (providing for regional autonomy) passed in parliament in November 1987.[viii] What has begun as an essentially domestic problem, arising from a minority ethnic group's attempts to overcome acts of discrimination and oppression, acquired over time a regional and an international dimension; it had ultimately to be resolved by the intervention of a regional power with the support of all the major world powers, but with opposition from both Sinhala and Tamil militants in Sri Lanka.

It is perhaps ironic that one of the most unfortunate ethnic wars of recent times should occur in Sri Lanka, an island reputed to have had a peaceful transition from 'model colony' to stable Third World state achieving international praise for its excellent quality of life and democratic institutions. These were factors which made Sri Lanka a 'country of concentration' for several aid donors, and after 1977, increased private foreign investment. All these expectations were seriously eroded by years of carnage and destruction when the 'emerald isle' of tourists literature turned blood red. The civil war not only killed off thousands of innocent people (Sinhala, Tamil, and Muslim) and brutalized civil society, giving rise to a climate of chauvinist hysteria and intolerance, but also left in its wake little alternative except outside intervention. Ultimately a civil war erupted from 1983 to 2009. In 2009 Sri Lankan armies defeated the LTTE to end the civil war. Even after the civil war, there were conflicts between different ethnic groups. There was also a conflict for chief minister post and majority of power in Eastern province council between Muslims and Tamils. Also Tamils resisted the Sinhalese settlements in districts of North province—*Mannar, Vavuniya, Kilinochchi, Mullaitivu* which have the lowest population densities in Sri Lanka.

Watchdog groups have accused both the Sri Lankan military and the LTTE of engaging in widespread human rights abuses, including abduction, conscription, and the use of child soldiers. In August 2007, Human Rights Watch released a report that catalogues alleged abuses on both sides of the conflict. Amnesty International made similar accusations in its2008 report on the state of the world's human rights. Increased fighting in the country's north in early 2009 left more than 250,000 displaced; both the LTTE and the government were accused of placing civilians at risk. The fighting between the government and the militants resulted in huge civilian casualties and censure from the international community.[ix]

INDIA'S ROLE IN THE ETHNIC CONFLICT

India's intervention in the ethnic conflict in Sri Lanka began as a genuinely mediatory role. The conflict had become significant factor in the politics of Tamilnadu and it was necessary that its influence on the inflammatory Tamil separatist tendencies be minimized. It was not in the India's interest, nor that of Tamilnnadu state, to allow Sri Lanka to crush Tamil opposition and assert Sinhala hegemony over them. Such a situation would have been unacceptable to Tamils of India. Indian tolerance of Tamil militant groups has to be seen in that light—an effort to prevent a military victory by the Sri Lankan government. However, a victory by the Tamil militants and the establishment of a separate state would not be in India's interest either. The Indian state itself is plagued with a number of separatist and secessionist struggles and in this context, the emergence of a small state in Northern Sri Lanka would not have been a desirable precedent. It could also exert an influence on the volatile sentiments of Tamilnadu; an independent Tamil state might have become an attractive magnet for separative sentiments.

Thus India would have wished neither for a Sri Lankan military victory nor military success for the Tamil militants. Its best interests would be served by a resolution of the conflict whiched recognized Sri Lanka's unity and territorial integrity, but which also allowed for democratic, political and economic rights of the Tamil people as a collectivity.

During the 1970s, India's external intelligence agency, the Research and Analysis Wing (RAW) helped to train and arm the LTTE, but after the group's terrorist activities grew in the 1980s—including its alliances with separatist groups in the southern Indian state of Tamil Nadu—RAW withdrew this support. In 1987, India made a pact with the Sri Lankan government to send peacekeeping troops to the island. The Indian forces were unable to end the conflict and instead began fighting with the LTTE. India was forced to withdraw by Sri Lankan President Ranasinghe Premadasa in 1990. Rajiv Gandhi, prime minister of India at the time of the peacekeeping force deployment, was killed by an LTTE suicide bomber in 1991. Premadasa met a similar fate in 1993. India has been wary of getting involved in Sri Lanka since then, but trade between the two countries has been on the rise. Bilateral trade increased from $658 million in 2000 to $ 3.2 billion in 2008, and India remains one of the country's leading foreign investors. Sri Lanka is also in talks to form a partnership (Bloomberg)with India's National Stock Exchange, which may include offering India a stake in Sri Lanka's bourse. The Asian Development Bank in 2008 said the rise in violence had not yet had an impact on growth

(PDF), which has been driven by strong domestic demand and a robust private sector. But it says the escalating conflict could hamper economic growth. The United Nations Development Program's 2008 statistics show Sri Lanka ranks 104 out of 179 countries on the Human Development Index, which measures education, standard of living, and life expectancy.

India remains concerned about the conditions of the Tamil minority in Sri Lanka, as it stirs protests and tensions among its own Tamil population in the south. In February 2009, India's foreign minister expressed concern over the safety of civilians in Sri Lanka and said the only way forward would be the devolution of power from the center to the provinces. Under the 1987 accord with India, which was followed by the thirteenth amendment to the Sri Lankan constitution, Colombo agreed to devolve some authority to the provinces and make Tamil an official language of the state. But no government has fully implemented the provisions, say experts.

This conclusion would also assume that Sri Lanka's movement away from a non-aligned policy in its foreign relations would have been no more than an irritant in the eyes of India. It was unwelcome, but posed no immediate threat to India's security interests. That India looked on this problem as one of human right is also evident from the fact that the only international forum at which she raised it was the US Commission for Human Rights.

However, the course of developments during the escalation of the conflict was instrumental in pushing Indian security concerns to the fore. These were the growing military relationship between Sri Lanka and Pakistan, Israel and certain Western countries, the growing influence of such countries on Sri Lankan security forces, the linkages seen to be developing between Sri Lanka, Pakistan and China. Taken together these indicated s security threat on India's southern flank, an area which had previously appeared secure. Thus the resolution of the ethnic conflict in Sri Lanka became bound up with the safeguarding of India's security interests.

It is the contention of many that India's security interests played a larger role in the accord than the actual resolution of the ethnic conflict. V. Prabhakaran, the leader of the most powerful Tamil militant group, the LTTE, has openly declared that he has no alternative but to acquiesce in the Agreement, even though it sacrifices Tamil aspirations and hopes to India's security concerns; he expressed dissatisfaction with the temporary nature of the merger between the northern and eastern provinces and said that LTTE would continue to work towards a separate state. There have been equally vehement attacks on the Agreement from the Sinhala side. The Jayawardena government has been accused of accommodating

Indian security concerns to the extent of seriously compromising Sri Lanka's sovereignty and independence. This view rests on an analysis of the Agreement that places greater emphasis on the security issues; it argues that India was prepared to dismantle Tamil militant camps in India only when Sri Lanka agreed to give in on the security issues.

The Indo-Sri Lanka Agreement also has many implications for the security of South Asian region. It is a known fact that all of India's neighbours have problems which involve India in some way. Nepal is faced with internal unrest led by movements which evoke some sympathy in India; while expecting Indian support in meeting these threats, Nepal is at the same time attempting to modify some of the provisions of the Treaty of Peace and Friendship entered into with India in 1950, particularly those with regard to security affairs. Bangladesh has problems with its Chakma ethnic group in the Chittagong hill areas and has been flowing a foregin policy favourable to the US. The problems between Pakistan and India are so familiar that it is not necessary to summarize them. The Indo-Sri Lanka Agreement can be read by all these countries as a signal that their internal and foregin policies must be so adjusted as to not to affect significantly India's security concerns. In this connection it is interesting to note that, while most countries were not happy with India's violation of Sri Lankan air space in dropping food supplies, most countries have expressed their support for the Peace Agreement. The two countries to have voiced reservations have been Pakistan and China.

In effect, in signing the Peace Agreement, Sri Lanka has recognized the necessity of formulating its foreign relations so as not to affect its big and powerful neighbour, India. It is an acceptance of India's role as the regional power. The Agreement has been welcome by both USA and USSR. This also signifies the acceptance by all of India's role in the South Asian region and of the general desire to remove a focus of instability in the region.

ETHNIC CONFLICT—INDIA-SRI LANKA RELATIONSHIP

The Sri Lankan ethnic conflict had caused tensions and pressure on India-Sri Lanka relationship. India involvement in Sri Lanka's ethnic provides ample testimony to the pangs of proximity. The history of ethnic conflict in Sri Lanka is the history of emergence of consciousness among the majority community, the Sinhala, which defined the Sri Lanka society as Sinhala-Buddhist, thus denying its multi-ethnic character. The growth of this consciousness impinged on the minorities in Sri Lanka to the extent that internal resolution of the problems becomes impossible. In asserting a Sinhala identity and in legitimizing Sinhala control of the country's polity, the leaders of the Sinhala. In recent years, one was the exodus of over 100,000 refugees from the northern regions of the island to Tamilnadu in South India; these were primarily civilians who had become victims of the government's drive against Tamil militants. It is well established that Sri Lankan security forces often turned against Tamil civilians in their attempt to flush out the militants. The Indo-Sri Lanka Agreement also has many implications for the security of South Asian region. It is a known fact that all of India's neighbors' have problems which involve India in some way. The Indo-Sri Lanka Agreement can be read by all these countries as a signal that their internal and foreign policies must be so adjusted as to not to affect significantly India's security concerns. Generally a friendly relation has existed between India and Sri Lanka. However, the Sri Lankan civil war and inefficiency of the Indian government in intervening during the civil war marred this amicable relation. Both the nations have maintained diplomatic ties since Sri Lanka's independence in 1948.

Ethnic riots broke out in Colombo on July 25, 1983, prompt, by the killing of 13 Sinhalese soldiers in an ambush by Tamil militants in Jaffna in northern Sri Lanka. Five hundred persons mostly Tamils were killed, hundreds of houses, shops, factories and places of worship belonging to the minority community were destroyed or damaged and 1,00,000 Tamils were left homeless in nine days of rioting across the island. Signs started emerging of possible solution to the Sri Lankan crisis three years after ethnic riots sparked a major increase in violence between Sinhalese and the Tamils. In 1985 Rajiv Government put forward fresh proposals of mediation when Jayawardene visited India in June 1985. An agreement was arrived at to the effect that India would assist in the suspension of the fight, and that India would cooperate in the talks between the Tamil militants and Sri Lankan government. There were two rounds of talks in July and August 1985, but the talks proved abortive with both the parties sticking to their guns. In December 1985, TULF made some alternative proposals, which were also turned down by the government. In April 1986, an Indian delegation under Mr. P. Chidambararn, the Central International Security Minister, discussed the Tamil issue with President Jayawardene. Consequently, Jayawardene proposed a peace plan which was endorsed by a conference of eight moderate political parties on July 26, 1986. This raised expectation of a settlement. The peace conference appealed to the Tamil militants to put forward their own proposals for a political solution within a undivided country. After the ten-day talks between the TULF leaders and Sri Lankan President the prospects to a settlement of the ethnic conflict improved. But once again the Government backed out of the pact. In January 1987, President Jayawardene imposed strict control and restriction on the Tamils' economic constraints in Jaffna and launched military action against the Tamil guerillas. In May and June 1987 more than 600 Tamils were slaughtered and thousands were injured as the invading Government troops rampaged through villages and towns and fired indiscriminately on civilians. There were heavy casualties when Sri Lankan Air Force bombed school buildings and temples where the civilians had taken shelter. This was genocide in the name of combating terrorism. India treads to send relief to the Tamils in a 20-boat Indian flotilla. But Sri Lanka threatened to 'shoot and sink' any Indian boat appro aching Sri Lankan waters. Appalled by the 'negative and obstructive attitude' of Sri Lankan government, India gave a stern warning to Sri-Lanka that it will not remain a silent and 'indifferent-spectator' to the plight of Tamils in Jaffna. Under the circumstances, the Indian government had no option but to paratroops the relief supplies. In a swift operation, the Indian Air Force flew into the war—torn Jaffna peninsula on June 4, 1987, over-riding Colombo's warning: Five AN- 32 transport aircrafts escorted by 4 Mirage 2000 fighters took off from Bangalore and were back in Indian airspace within an hour after completing their assignment. All this happened under the supervision of the Red Cross. Now, the 82 year-old President took the hint and relented. On 29 July, 1987 the India-Sri Lanka Agreement was signed between Prime Minister Rajiv Gandhi and the Sri Lankan President Jayawardcne. The TULF and other parties but the LTTE tigers did not favor this agreement.[*] India will also give military assistance to Sri Lanka to facilitate the implementation of the agreement. On the request of President Jayawardene, the Indian Peace Keeping Force (IPKF) was sent to Sri Lanka. Detailed talks were held on 23, 26 and 28 September, 1987 between the Indian Officials and the leader of LTTE to sort out various disputed points of the India Sri Lanka Agreement, particularly the surrender of arms and the formation of an Interim Administrative Council with greater representation to LTTE in relation to the other Tamil groups. Trouble again shot up about the nomination of the Administrator of the Interim Council, Jayawardene nominated Sivaganam; LTTE rejected their name and insisted on the nomination of Padmanatham, a native of the eastern peninsula. Even the intervention of the Indian government yielded no results. In the meantime Jayewardene committed a diplomatic blunder. The Sri Lankan forces apprehended 17 Tamil guerillas and as they were being whisked away to Colombo for interrogation they swallowed cyanide and committed suicide. This acted as an incendiary and the Tamil guerillas mounted attacks on the Sinhalese on all fronts. Left with no choice, the IPKF had to take an unpleasant decision to disarm the LTTE guerillas and to compel them to surrender, just to salvage their prestige. This debatable and dangerous step resulted in con—fusion worse confounded. Since then, the situation in Sri Lanka is going from bad to worse. The Tamil guerillas are fighting an interminable war with the IPKF, unknown to the local terrain and the

LTTE guerilla tactics the IPKF has been suffering heavy casualties, in addition to earning the wroth and animosity of the both the Tamils and the Sinhalese. Recently, President Jayewardene has announced a general election to be held in Sri Lanka early next year with Prime Minister Premadasa as the official UNP candidate for President ship. State—hood has been conferred on the eastern Jafina peninsula and a majority of political prisoners have been released in a bid to ensure peaceful elections. Still, hopes of the dawn of peace in this Island of the setting sun are very bleak and remote indeed with the India Sri Lanka Agreement, the Rajiv government has played in to the hands of the clever Sinhalese. And the fun of all this game is that in an interview published in New York Times on September 25, 1988, Jayewardene said that the ethnic problem had been abetted if not created by India. The latest development in the India-Sri Lanka relations is a probable flaring up of animosities as a result of the declaration made by Precedent Premadasa regarding the total withdrawal of IPKF from Sri Lanka by July 1989 and the refusal of the Indian Government to do so. The world is watching further movements with baited breath.

A healthy bilateral relation was established by the then Prime Minister of India- Indira Gandhi and Prime Minister of Sri Lanka- Sirimavo Bandaranaike. An agreement signed on 29th July, 1987 between the then Prime minister of India, Rajiv Gandhi and the then President of Sri Lanka, J.R. Jayewardene to address three controversial issues: people of Indian origin in Sri Lanka, strategic interests, rights of Tamil minority in Sri Lanka. The Rajiv-Jayewardene Accord, as the agreement is popularly known, led to some unfortunate events. With the signing of the agreement India got engaged in a war with a separatist organization of Sri Lanka called, Liberation Tigers of Tamil Eelam. A special peace keeping force called the IPKF was employed to curb the LTTE. Around 1200 Indian soldiers gave their life fighting. Further, India felt insulted when Sri Lankan President Ranasinghe Premadasa, demanded for the withdrawal of the IPKF even before the completion of the mission. India's sentiments received the hardest blow when Rajiv Gandhi was killed by the LTTE in May 21, 1991 at Sriperumbudur in Tamil Nadu. The killing was masterminded by LTTE chief, V. Prabakaran. Since, then the relationship of India –Sri Lanka tensions caused. The Sri Lankan ethnic conflict had caused tensions and pressure on India-Sri Lanka relationship. India involvement in Sri Lanka's ethnic provides ample testimony to the pangs of proximity. The history of ethnic conflict in Sri Lanka is the history of emergence of consciousness among the majority community, the Sinhala, which defined the Sri Lanka society as Sinhala-Buddhist, thus denying its multi-ethnic character. The growth of this consciousness impinged on the minorities in Sri Lanka to the extent that internal resolution of the problems becomes impossible.

Ethnic conflicts are essentially identity conflicts in which the definition or construction of threats, enemies and friends plays a pivotal role. Ethnic conflicts evolve according to how identities are defined, the definitions being predicated on the material condition facing the communities themselves in relation to the manifest practices of the state. In contrast to realist discourses that see only endless conflicts and an invariable security dilemma for groups, and liberalism that defines ethnic peace (or conflict) in terms of transaction costs and utility calculations, the constructivist reading of ethnicity enables International Relations to interrogate ethnicity in cultural-ideational terms. By using constructivist propositions to a select set of ethnic conflicts in South Asia, ethnicity as a pervasive mode of conflict in the subcontinent.

Today, only 15 per cent of Sri Lanka's population resides in the North and East. The case in the East is different from that in the north; Sinhalese, Tamils and Muslims harmoniously live in the East in equal proportions. A majority of Tamils live along with the Sinhalese in all other provinces. In Colombo, Tamils are the majority, not the Sinhalese. Therefore, any merger of two provinces on ethnic lines would not solve the question. There is also a need for a more enlightened Tamil leadership from those war torn provinces to consolidate peace. Power should be shared, however, and it should be to the satisfaction of all Sri Lankans. Any solution should encourage Tamil leaders to engage in the political system on a national basis while discouraging ethnic affiliations among political parties. Diaspora politics should not be imposed on the innocent Tamils of Sri Lanka who live peacefully. The situation is complex but it is a good sign that the majority of Tamil politicians agree with the political leadership on many facets of governance. Therefore, a home grown solution is ideal provided India generously supports its implementation.[xi]

In asserting a Sinhala identity and in legitimizing Sinhala control of the country's polity, the leaders of the Sinhala. In recent years, one was the exodus of over 100,000 refugees from the northern regions of the island to Tamilnadu in South India; these were primarily civilians who had become victims of the government's drive against Tamil militants. It is well established that Sri Lankan security forces often turned against Tamil civilians in their attempt to flush out the militants. The Indo-Sri Lanka Agreement also has many implications for the security of South Asian region. It is a known fact that all of India's neighbors' have problems which involve India in some way. The Indo-Sri Lanka Agreement can be read by all these countries as a signal that their internal and foreign policies must be so adjusted as to not to affect significantly India's security concerns.

THE TAMIL FACTOR IN POLITICS –IMPACT ON INDIA SRI LANKA RELATIONS

The Tamil ethnic group sought to counter this growing discrimination by demands at a political level. Before independence, the Tamil Congress unsuccessfully demanded balanced representation - 50% seats for the Sinhala and 50% for the combined minority ethnic groups. Later, in the face of continuing discrimination, a Federal Party emerged which asked for a federal political structure that would give Tamils a degree of autonomy in the areas inhabited by them, as well as adequate representation at the centre. It was in this period of accelerated demands and rejection that Tamil political leaders concluded in 1976 that only a separate state could ensure the security and welfare of the Tamil people, a state carved out of the northern and eastern provinces of Sri Lanka to be called Tamil Eelam.[xii] The demands of the Tamil people had by this time become a major factor in Sinhala Politics. Sinhala political hegemony was also becoming institutiona-lized.

While the established political party of the Tamils—the Tamil United Liberation Front (TULF)—was demanding a separate state and using parliamentary democratic processes towards obtaining it, some Tamil youth, dissatisfied with the non-violent policies of the TULF, formed groups which took up arms in the same cause. It is only necessary to state that it led to a protracted and bitter war in the northern and eastern parts of Sri Lanka during the course of which the state security forces were guilty of severe excesses, attacks on civilians and serious violations of human rights of the Sri Lankan citizens, while the armed groups in turn resorted to brutal killings of both the Sinhala civilians and those Tamils thought of as 'informers'. The number of deaths has been estimated at 6000 by the government and 15000 by Tamil groups; damage to property has been incalculable.

At the ideological level, the response to Sinhala chauvinism was the emergence of Tamil chauvinism and extreme forms of nationalist mythmaking. According to Radhika Coomaraswamy, these include the myth that the Tamils are pure Dravidian by race, that they are heirs to the Mohenjadaro and Harappa civilizations of India, that they are the original inhabitants of Sri Lanka, that the Tamil language in its purest forms is spoken only in Sri Lanka and that the "Saiva Siddhanta" form of Hinduism has 'a special homeland' in Sri Lanka [Coomaraswamy 1987:79]. Many of the Tamil militant groups have also been sustained by such ideologies, and expressions like 'Dravidian Drive' and 'Chola charisma' have been used in their literature to mobilise support for armed struggle.

Another effect of the Sinhala-Tamil strife has been that the class solidarity among workers of all ethnic groups has been replaced by a sense of trans-class ethnic solidarity on the part of both the Sinhala and Tamils. As Gunasinghe has observed, in both the Sinhala and Tamil ethnic formations "class contradiction are over determined by ethnic conflict", while among the Tamils, "class contradictions are softened and even submerged" in the face of a perceived "danger to its collective social existence"; among the Sinhalese masses, "dissatisfaction with the existing state of affairs has taken a false external direction against what is perceived to be the unreasonable demands advanced by already privileged Tamils." [Abeysekera and Guna-singhe 1987: VI]

It is against this historical background that the regional and international dimensions of ethnic conflict in Sri Lanka have to be investigated and understood. The pogrom against Tamils in July 1983 and the resulting clashes had two very important demographic consequences. One was the exodus of over 100,000 refugees from the northern regions of the island to Tamilnadu in South India; these were primarily civilians who had become victims of the government's drive against Tamil militants. It is well established that Sri Lankan security forces often turned against Tamil civilians in their attempt to flush out the militants. The second consequence was an exodus of Tamils living in southern parts of the island amidst the Sinhalese, to their 'traditional homes' in the north and east. Paradoxically as it may seem, the violence of July 1983 convinced many Tamils that they could be safe and secure only in their own areas, this despite the presence and operations of the army. These moves immediately strengthened, one the one hand, the notion of a Tamil homeland in which Tamils would have their own state, and on the other, it established a close link between the Tamils of Sri Lanka and the Tamils of India, resulting in the Sri Lanka Tamil issue becoming the major issue in Tamilnadu politics. The presence of Sri Lankan Tamil political and militants leaders and a large number of refugees in Tamilnadu necessarily had an impact on the politics of that state. Tamilnadu was extremely conscious of its cultural heritage and its role vis-a-vis Tamil communities in the other parts of the world. It had also been the scene of separatist demands for an of Tamil nationalism were kept alive by independent state in the 1960s. Although these demands died down, the embers the "Dravida Munnetra azhagam"(DMK) which was in power between 1967 and 1977. [Kodikara 1983] After July 1983, the DMK, which was by then in opposition, wholeheartedly took up the cause of Sri Lankan Tamils. It described the actions of Sri Lanka as genocide against the Tamils and called on the Indian government to send its armed forces to Sri Lanka in order to save the Tamils. By 1983 the ruling party in Tamilnadu was the All-India Anna Dravida Munnetra Kashagam (AIADMK), a split from the DMK, and its leader, M.G. Ramachandran also spoke out on the behalf of the Tamils of Sri Lanka. It accorded a measure of state patronage to the TULF and militant leaders as well as Sri Lankan refugees. It also mobilized public opinion by first organizing a state-wide stoppage of work, protesting against the oppression of tamils by the Sri Lankan government; a resolution was passed in October 1983 in the Tamilnadu State Assembly condemning the violence of Sri Lanka and urging the United Nations to intervene in the pursuit of a peaceful solution. Even though the AIADMK's support for the Sri Lanka Tamil cause stopped short of support for a separate state, the Sri Lankan Tamil Issue became a focal point in the internal politics of Tamilnadu itself.

It has sometimes been said that it was the pressure emanating from Tamilnadu that forced the Indian central government to intervene in the matter. The Tamilnadu government was no doubt concerned to see the divisive issue was settled, but it is now apparent that the central government of India was also motivated by reasons of national security as much as the pressure from Tamilnadu. Mediation by the central government began very shortly after July 1983. Prime Minister Indira Gandhi offered India's good offices in order to facilitate a political solution and this was accepted by Sri Lanka. G. Parthasarathy, a well known Indian diplomat and advisor to Indira Gandhi, visited Sri Lanka, discussed issues with leaders of the government, political parties, including the TULF, and by December 1983, had developed a set of proposals to resolve the conflict. These were presented to an All Party Conference in January 1984 which, however, ended inconclusively in December 1984. This ended India's first mediation effort. It was activated on the premise that a conscious on the ethnic issue among the major political groups was desirable. Hereafter Indian mediation efforts were primarily to concern the Sri Lankan government and the Tamil parties and groups. During 1984 and 1985, while negotiations towards a peaceful solution were proceeding rather desultorily, the military conflict intensified, claiming ever more civilian casualities on both sides. The Sri Lankan President and the Indian Prime Minister met in early June 1985 in New Delhi and this produced a quickening of efforts at mediation. Peace talks followed between the Sri Lankan government and Tamil political and militant organizations in Thimpu in Bhutan, but these failed too.

From August 1986 and in the subsequent months, officials of the two governments held talks in Delhi and arrived at what were described as 'draft terms of Accord and understanding'. These terms envisaged a system of devolution at three levels, divisional, district, and provincial. Powers at the provincial level were defined allowing broadly for devolution with respect to law and order, agriculture, land settlement and other functions. This framework was the object of discussions between the two governments as well as the government of India and the Tamil groups in Madras and produced an expansion of some powers devolved at the provincial level.

Many attempts in 1986 to solve the conflict proved abortive but the next stage in this process of resolution moved with amazing rapidity. A car bomb exploded at a busy bus station in Colombo at the end of April 1987, killing 113 people. The government, faced with popular outrage, launched what it called an ' all-out offensive' on the Jaffna peninsula and by the end of May captured a large part of it at great cost in terms of life, property and the massive dislocation of inhabitants in these areas. It was at this stage that the Indian Government intervened directly and decisively. Arguing that army offensive had rendered the people of Jaffna totally destitute, it decided to send in 'humanitarian relief'. When a flotilla of boats carrying relief supplies were turned back by the Sri Lankan navy, India dropped relief supplies by air and then negotiating with the Sri Lankan government for the further supplies.

The idea of resolving the ethnic conflict through an understanding between the two governments had been in the air for a few months. Moreover, Sri

Lanka found itself under great pressure from donor countries to solve the conflict—especially in view of economic devastation the war has caused and increased military expenditure. The Indian government thus found itself in a position it could enforce willingness both from Sri Lankan government and from the main military group, the Liberation Tigers of Tamil Eelam (LTTE). The Agreement which signed in July 1987 was the result. India had moved from the position of mediator to that of direct participant, a participant with separate and specific interests of its own. The agreement had three components—first, the 'modalities' of settling the ethnic conflicts through devolution of power to a Tamil region combining the northern and eastern provinces; second, the guarantees and obligations of the government of India with regard to the implementation of the accord; third, (in letters exchanged alonged with the Agreement), the undertakings given by the government of Sri Lanka to India which are not related to the ethnic conflict but concern India's security interest's in the region.

SRI LANKA: INDIA-SRI LANKA RELATIONS CONTINUED TO DEVELOP FROM 2006

India-Sri Lanka relations continued to develop in 2006. India is concerned at the ongoing hostilities in Sri Lanka which has taken its toll on civilian casualties and resulted in an exodus of refugees. India is of the view that the only way out is a negotiated, political settlement which meets the legitimate aspirations of all communities while respecting the unity, sovereignty and territorial integrity of Sri Lanka.[xiii] There was progress in the negotiations between India and Sri Lanka on a Comprehensive Economic Partnership Agreement (CEPA) which would build on the success of the Free Trade Agreement (FTA).

The recent increase in top level Indian delegation visits to Colombo indicates that India has entered a new and more comprehensive phase of bilateral relations with Sri Lanka. However, a highest level political visit from India is yet to materialize, while Sri Lankan counterparts have already visited Delhi twice in the recent past. What underlies these frequent diplomatic visits? The global power configuration is changing in favour of Asia, particularly China and India. The United States, and the West in general, are losing the pre-eminent position that they have had for centuries. Moreover, smaller regional countries are also emerging with strong identities. In this setting, India finds its rivals making inroads into Sri Lanka.

The Indian External Affairs Minister Mr. S.M. Krishna's statement during his visit to Sri Lanka in November 2010 that "The relationship between India and Sri Lanka need not to be at the cost of other countries, our ultimate objective is to see a prosperous, stable Sri Lanka," is a testament to this. Sri Lanka's largest market is the United States. Even so, affirming a strong partnership with India, President Rajapakse recently stated that all countries are friends of Sri Lanka but India is Sri Lanka's relation. Sri Lanka will not initiate any action with any other country against India as it would be a self-defeating act. Sri Lankans do not see India's prosperity and power as detrimental to them. In fact, Sri Lanka stands to benefit from India's prosperity.

All efforts by the government to bring the LTTE to the mainstream and accommodate their grievances within a united Sri Lanka failed. They used violence to assert their demand for a separate state for Tamils. When terrorism became unbearable and uncompromising, the government had no option but to resort to strong actions. It is essential to eradicate violence when it is used as a tool for political purposes anywhere in the world. Presently, Sri Lanka is in the process of consolidating peace through reconciliation and re-democratization of the North and the East. Sri Lanka's effort to find peace for all communities has resulted in the 13th Amendment to the Constitution. Further, there is an idea for power sharing at the centre by having a second chamber.

The end of terrorism in Sri Lanka has given rise to new opportunities for improved relationship between India and Sri Lanka. One important aspect of this relationship is to reinvigorate lost contacts with Tamil Nadu. It is essential for Sri Lanka's security, well being and peace. Sri Lanka is determined to rebuild the relationship with the Tamil population in India. The decade old free trade agreement between India and Sri Lanka is witnessing massive increases in trade. Today, India is the second largest investor in Sri Lanka. Sri Lanka has always been with India. It was one of the earliest supporters of India's bid for a permanent seat in the Security Council.

Mr. Krishna's visit was also significant for a number of trade and financial deals he signed and the two Indian consulates he opened. One consulate is in the former LTTE stronghold of northern Jaffna and the other in southern Hambanthota. The aid package also included funding for post war construction, electricity power projects, north-south railway development and the resumption of a ferry service between India and Sri Lanka.[xiv]

The visit by an Indian external affairs minister to Sri Lanka is always an important affair. Sri Lankans of all communities and political leanings watch it carefully. They listen to the statements and read between the lines. To many, especially for the Sri Lankan Tamils and the committed democratic sections of the Sri Lankan and Indian polity, these are moments of hope.

However what Tamils and democratic groups' world over are really looking at are the key words that Krishna uttered and how will India uphold these ideals he committed to on behalf of the Indian people. Krishna hoped that the positive recommendations of the Lessons Learnt and Reconciliation Commission (LLRC) would be implemented and said that India was hoping for a 'genuine political settlement based on a devolution of power' that would be 'building upon the 13th amendment' and lead to a lasting political settlement. He also said that 'India will do anything possible to assist in this process'.

But what is the government of Sri Lanka really doing to bring back peace, build confidence and reconciliation between alienated communities; to deliver justice to the victims, the displaced and the missing of this civil war? International bodies that have legitimacy and credibility in recording conflict and post-conflict reconciliation like the International Crises Group, the Human Rights Watch, United Nations bodies, and Sri Lankan democratic and human rights groups as well of many Western governments say that the peace process in Sri Lanka is completely inadequate; that human rights have not been addressed. What is worse is that anyone who takes up these issues is targeted and an atmosphere of fear continues.

The most recent visit to Sri Lanka was the three day trip by Indian Defence Secretary Mr. Pradeep Kumar in late December 2010. The establishment of a bilateral defence dialogue and joint naval exercises, strengthening of coast guard services, extension of more military training and assistance for military infrastructure construction were all topics of discussion, affirming that India will work with Sri Lanka to cater for the latter's defence. The decision to empower the Sri Lankan Naval Commander to deal directly on urgent matters with Indian naval authorities on issues in the maritime domain is a step in the right direction, as the misbehaviour of a single fisherman on either side could create a bilateral issue. There is hope that this new approach in particular will be an effective mechanism to tackle human smuggling and the illegal entry of arms and drugs. As the narrow sea stretch is hardly an obstacle to smugglers it could be worthwhile to similarly empower ground military commanders along the same lines. India's recognition of Sri Lankan Security Forces Commander Jaffna as an honorary General in India and his Tamil Nadu equivalent vice versa in Sri Lanka would be an important confidence-building measure as well.

"Should Indian foreign policy to a neighbour like Sri Lanka be based on such ... and east for its rehabilitation packages to ensure that aid gets to where it is most needed."—India clearly plays a big role in the local politics of Sri Lanka. Sri Lankan Tamils have ethnic links with India's south despite the fact that are very distinct with their own different traditions and culture. India would like a stable, democratic and territorially integrated Sri Lanka and any conflict there in the past or future flows over and impacts India. The tragic and futile episodes of the Indian Peace Keeping Forces and the assassination of Rajiv Gandhi seem to be written into the foreign policy psyche and are often cited as reasons for non-intervention.[xv]

But current reality should also be taken into account. The LTTE and insurgency are clearly over. There is no secessionist movement. The Tamil parties and leadership are committed like India is to an integrated, democratic and secular Sri Lanka, but one that also guarantees political and economic power to its north and east where Tamils live. So India needs to play a more pro-active role and put pressure for devolution through the 13th amendment with self-governance. This pressure is not hegemonic or interventionist but moral and normative. It will not go against India but ensure stability in favour of India and South Asia.

India is a great power in the region and aspires for this status worldwide. But what is it doing with this power? India should not deal with Sri Lanka through the prism of a geostrategic competitor like China but use its power for the common good of the region. India will have to show to Sri Lanka that its own success and integration is because of the democratic, federal, secular institutions that have enabled it to resolve many existential crises. The idea of minority rights is deeply ingrained in India's constitution. Why should it not ask Sri Lanka to implement this in a fixed time-frame, especially since its minority community has suffered so much?

The world is looking to India to use its power judiciously in the region. If India can give millions of dollars in development assistance, it should be matched with accountability in terms of democratic rights by the Sri Lankan government. Nothing less should be acceptable.

Sri Lankan President and Indian Prime Minister met in the Addu Atoll to discuss a host of bilateral issues and strengthening regional cooperation. Both leaders took the opportunity to raise issues related to the escalation of fishermen's issues, poaching piracy and maritime terrorism in the Indian Ocean. They also discussed Sri Lanka's political process for ethnic reconciliation and resettlement of displaced.[xvi]

INDIA-SRI LANKA RELATIONS IN THE CONTEXT OF THE SAARC SUMMITS

SAARC is a project that India needs to nurture. India should be able to use SAARC as a regional instrument to consolidate cooperation and peace. Sri Lanka believes that it is a natural leadership that India has within SAARC. Through SAARC India could venture to provide benevolent leadership in the region. This would make the neighboring countries in the region comfortable with India's dominating geographical volume and profile.

The South Asian Association for Regional Cooperation (SAARC) is an organization of South Asian nations.[xvii] The Indo-Sri Lanka Agreement has implication for Regional Co-operation as well. The South Asian Association for Regional Co-operation (SAARC) excludes from consideration purely bilateral issues. Sri Lanka, however, has on many occasions attempted to override this and bring up the ethnic issue for discussion. These efforts have generally been supported by other members like Pakistan, who have also argued that the SAARC forum should be open to the consideration of bilateral issues. India has always opposed this view, maintaining that issues between any two countries of the region could best be settled on a bilateral basis and not be allowed to cloud issues of regional co-operation.

Another area of concern on which the Agreement may have some impact is the project to keep the Indian Ocean as a zone of peace. This idea was first advanced by Sirimavo Bandaranaike at the Non-aligned summits at Nairobi and Cairo, and later at the United Nations in 1971 where it was generally received with favour. India too supported the project, seeing it in a way of keeping the Indian Ocean free from naval deployments by both superpowers. The US has established a naval base on the island of Diego Garcia in the Indian Ocean. Although most countries still back the proposal in principle, it has been found difficult to get to the next stage of the project—namely a meeting in Colombo to work out the details. India has shown herself deeply suspicious of Sri Lanka's stand and refused to attend meetings in Colombo of technical groups concerned with research into aspects of Indian Ocean activities. India still appears keen to pursue this project and Sri Lanka's re-structured relationship with India will possibly be of help.

The SAARC established on 8 December 1985, the first summit was held in Dhaka, Bangladesh on 7–8 December 1985, and was attended by the

Government representative and president of Bangladesh, Maldives, Pakistan and Sri Lanka, the kings of Bhutan and Nepal, and the prime minister of India. They signed the SAARC Charter on 8 December 1985, thereby establishing the regional association, and established study groups on the problems of terrorism and drug trafficking, as well as planning a ministerial-level meeting about GATT, and a ministerial-level conference on increasing the participation of women at the regional level. The summit also agreed to establish a SAARC secretariat and adopted an official SAARC emblem.[xviii]

The Seventeenth Summit was held from 10-11 of November 2011 in Addu City, Maldives. H.E. Mohamed Nasheed was elected as the Chairperson of the 17th SAARC Summit. In his inaugural address President Nasheed highlighted three areas of cooperation in which progress should be made; trade, transport and economic integration; security issues such piracy and climate change; and good governance. President also called on the Member States to establish a commission to address issues of gender inequalities in South Asia.

The Head of States of all the SAARC Member States addressed the Meeting. The inaugural meeting was attended by Foreign/External Ministers of SAARC Member States, the Secretary General of SAARC, the Heads of Observer Delegation, Cabinet Ministers of the Maldives, Ministers in the visiting delegations and other state dignitaries.

In her address Secretary General stated that the Summit being held under the theme of "Building Bridges" provides further impetus and momentum to build the many bridges that needs to be built: from bridging the gaps created by uneven economic development and income distribution, the gaps in recognizing and respecting the equality of men and women, the closing of space between intent and implementation.

In this Meeting, the Foreign Ministers of the respective Member States signed four agreements; SAARC Agreement on Rapid Response to Natural Disasters SAARC Agreement on Multilateral Arrangement on Recognition of Conformity Assessment SAARC Agreement on Implementation of Regional Standards SAARC Seed Bank Agreement In addition, the Addu Declaration of the Seventeenth SAARC Summit was also adopted.

From first summit Dhaka, Bangladesh on 7–8 December 1985 to Seventeenth Summit from 10-11 of November 2011 in Addu City, Maldives, several themes were discussed and made agreements for instance trade, transport and economic integration; security issues such piracy and climate change; and good governance. But none of summits discussed in Sri Lankan ethnic conflict issues in thoroughly and cannot be made any conclusions on ethnic conflict issue. Thus, the Institute of Peace and Conflict Studies (IPCS), India-Sri Lanka Relations in the Context of the SAARC Summit.[xix] Chaired by Amb Salman Haidar, Speaker: HE Mr CR Jayasinghe, High Commissioner, Sri Lanka. On of the speaker Salman Haidar raised the conflict issue. This discussion is being held at a time of conspicuous changes in Sri Lanka, some of which are worth probing further. Militarily, matters had appeared to be stuck as the rebels gained authority and the central government continued to be engaged in a stand-off with little possibility of any major change. This conventional thinking has now been challenged. At the political level, some settlements such as devolution of powers were being worked on. Has this process stalled in light of the changing military situation or does it continue? On the economic plane, a notable development has been the Free Trade Agreement (FTA) between India and Sri Lanka that could bring both countries closer and change the dynamics of South Asia in important ways. Finally, it would be worth exploring what more could be done to realize SAARC objectives and agreements. Would the India-Sri Lanka FTA make it easier to achieve a SAARC FTA?

CR Jayasinghe, speaks amidst a distinguished and well informed audience at IPCS the ground situation has changed dramatically in Sri Lanka. A ceasefire agreement between the government of Sri Lanka and the rebels was operationalized in February 2002 under the aegis of the Norwegians. It collapsed after four years in light of the assassination of the Sri Lankan Foreign Minister, Lakshman Kadiragamar on 12 August 2005, attempt on the life of the army commander Lieutenant General Sarath Fonseka and targeting of civilians seen in bus bombings in Kebitigollawa, Nittambuwa, Seenigama and Cheddikulum. Two attempts by the Sri Lankan President Mahinda Rajpaksa to engage the LTTE through dialogue at Geneva failed to yield a positive outcome.

In fact, the LTTE's militarism increased by abusing the ceasefire to acquire new weapons systems such as the Ultra Light Aircraft that is believed to have been smuggled into the island by the LTTE sometime in 2004. The LTTE leaders utilized their travel overseas for political dialogue to places such as Norway, Thailand, and Japan and to reach out to the Tamil Diaspora in order to mobilize money. The LTTE's game plan was to pressure the government into releasing their eastern operative Karuna who had broken away from the LTTE chief Parbhakaran. Many also felt that the dismantling of the security check points around Colombo, as part of the ceasefire, was used by the LTTE to push through suicide bombers.

The international community on its part kept urging the Sri Lankan government to come up with innovative solutions to the crisis while ignoring the political realities of the day. The government of Sri Lanka did not enjoy a majority, while the population remained extremely skeptical about the motives of the LTTE.

However, Sri Lanka has shown that despite facing tremendous internal upheaval it possesses the capacity to take things forward in South Asia. A good case in point in this respect is the gains made at the SAARC summit in Colombo—coinciding with which the LTTE made a shrewd but unsuccessful unilateral ceasefire offer. The fallout of India's gaffe in Sri Lanka was so immense that even the ministerial level meetings for launching SAARC were adversely affected. The most obvious example cited as a justification of India's hegemonic aspirations is the Indira Doctrine. The origins of the Doctrine are traced to the Sri Lankan crisis of 1988 and laid down that India would consider the presence or influence of an external power in the region as adverse to its interests. India's justification for the policy was an attempt to insulate the region from the adverse effects of the Cold War, but the neighbours viewed it as a policy to abolish any challenge to India's regional position. In the recent years India has not only allowed but in fact aligned with extra-regional powers to address regional issues, but the regional perceptions fail to take cognizance of these developments.

People SAARC memorandum 2011 submitted to the 17 SAARC official SAARC process emphasized that the; We call for the South Asian states to recognize the universality of opportunity, and equality in rights and dignity of all people including so far excluded groups and minorities on the basis of ethnicity, gender and the physical/mental ability. Therefore, we urge the; SAARC states to recognize the prevalence of patriarchy, masculinity, religious extremism and caste-based discrimination that deny human rights, human dignity, socio-economic and political equality, justice and peace to the millions of marginalised groups and classes, in the SAARC countries. In the 17th SAARC Summit: President Rajapaksa meets regional leaders in Maldives President Mahinda Rajapaksa concluded bilateral talks with his regional leaders this morning on the sidelines of the two day SAARC Summit which is been held in Maldives from 10 November.

SAARC's success is likely to bring enormous economic and security benefits to Bhutan and the Maldives, the two smallest South Asian countries. It is, therefore, not surprising that these two countries have shown, and continue to show, a great deal of interest in the growth of regional cooperation in South Asia. In this section, I will briefly discuss the political and economic interests and concerns of the India and Sri Lanka countries and their effects on the prospectus of the growth of regional cooperation in SAARC.

However, India will be more inclined to play a much greater role and make bolder initiatives in order to make SAARC more effective and visible? Indian policy makers are aware of the fact that any bold initiatives or a greater role by India in SAARC will strengthen the South Asian neighbours' perception of Indian hegemonism, and thereby jeopardize prospects for further regional cooperation. On the other hand, India's lack of initiatives may be interpreted as a lack of sincerity for SAARC. As India's support is crucial for the growth of SAARC, India needs to take moderate policy initiatives with respect to SAARC activities and pursue accommodative diplomacy more vigorously to inspire confidence in her neighbors.

Basically, there are two main problems between India and Sri Lanka: (1) Sri Lanka's denial of citizenship to a large number of Tamils and their repatriation to India despite the latter's protest of discrimination; and (2) the spillover effect of Sri Lanka's Tamil ethnic conflict since 1983 and the impact of the India factor in Sri Lanka's domestic problem. The last factor appears to be the most serious one. From 1986 to 1990, Indo-Sri Lanka relations suffered the most because of the active Indian intervention in the Sri Lankan civil war. Not surprisingly, Sri Lanka's response to the growth of SAARC during this period was lukewarm. However, with India showing support toward the Sri Lankan government's efforts to achieve peace in the island, the Indo-Sri Lankan bilateral relationship has improved substantially in the post-1990 period. Since Sri Lanka has no major bilateral disputes with other states of South Asia, the improved Indo-Sri Lankan relationship has revived the latter's enthusiasm for SAARC.

CONCLUSION

Sri Lanka was one part of the Indian mainland from which it separated by Palk Strait. It is an extremely important focal point of Indian Ocean trade routes owing to its position near the southern end of the Indian peninsula which divides the Bay of Bengal and the Arabian sea. By virtue of its geographical location on the map of Asia, Sri Lanka holds a position of supreme strategic importance in the Indian Ocean. Both the super-powers have an eye on Sri Lanka and U.S.A. has succeeded in establishing a major naval base in Diego Garcia very little island near Mauritius. It is in the interest of both the countries that India remains a nuclear free peace zone. India clearly plays a big role in the local politics of Sri Lanka. Sri Lankan Tamils have ethnic links with India's south despite the fact that are very distinct with their own different traditions and culture. India would like a stable, democratic and territorially integrated Sri Lanka and any conflict there in the past or future flows over and impacts India. The tragic and futile episodes of the IPKF and the assassination of Rajiv Gandhi seem to be written into the foreign policy psyche and are often cited as reasons for non-intervention.[xx]

But current reality should also be taken into account. The LTTE and insurgency are clearly over now. There is no secessionist movement. The Tamil parties and leadership are committed like India is to an integrated, democratic and secular Sri Lanka, but one that also guarantees political and economic power to its north and east where Tamils live. So India needs to play a more pro-active role and put pressure for ensure stability in favour of Sri Lanka and South Asia. India will have to show to Sri Lanka that its own success and integration is because of the democratic, federal, secular institutions that have enabled it to resolve many existential crises. The idea of minority rights is deeply ingrained in India's constitution. The world is looking to India to use its power judiciously in the region. Hence it is important that India looks at these developments with great caution and ensure a proper policy toward her closest southern neighbor. India needs to invest in Sri Lanka to keep the latter in its zone of influence. India's timely help during the Tsunami has proved to the world that we are capable of handling challenges facing the region. Having proved ourselves, it is important that India should consolidate the good will amongst the neighbors. India and Sri Lanka should also work pro active role to strengthen SAARC. There are number of challenges which seek the intervention of SAARC. Not only ethnic conflict but also most of these challenges such as climate change are increasing without considering the borders of the member countries. In addressing these challenges, it is not only the SAARC secretariat, but the member governments must also be aligned with what the new Secretary-General proposes for. For instance, it would be detrimental to the economic interest of India, Pakistan, and Sri Lanka if they do not seek access to the markets in Central Asia, Southeast Asia, the Gulf region, and the Organisation for Economic Co-operation and Development (OECD) countries. The key to the development of a pragmatic strategy to increase economic interdependence among the South Asian countries is to promote intraregional trade by lowering tariffs without delinking from extra regional and global economic relations. Despite progress made by SAARC in recent years, a number of challenges continue to confront the organization. To play an effective role as a regional grouping, challenges such as poverty alleviation, the energy crisis, combating terrorism, and effects of globalization, among others, should be tackled jointly. SAARC countries, in general, need assistance in all these fields owing mainly to their weaker economies. Observers, having closer relationship with SAARC members, may be instrumental in meeting these challenges.

Given the low level of mutual trust, spillover effects of the ethnic and religious conflicts, and the magnitude of bilateral disputes in South Asia, it is unrealistic to believe that any substantial growth of regional cooperation is possible without easing political tensions. To the extent that political tensions remain unresolved, SAARC is likely to experience only a "stop-and-go" pattern of growth in which limited pragmatic cooperation on specific techno-economic issues is possible over a period of time. In the post-1990 period, there appears to be some realization among the South Asian leaders that the future of SAARC, like any other regional grouping, lies in concentrating on economic cooperation in specific areas. The SAARC leaders' renewed emphasis on increasing intraregional trade at three consecutive SAARC summit meetings (Colombo, 1991; Dhaka, 1993; and New Delhi, 1995), the ratification of SAPTA, and the discussion to create SAFTA in future are evidence of their growing willingness to enhance regional economic cooperation in South Asia.

REFERENCES AND BIBLIOGRAPHY

[1] From SARC to SAARC: Milestones in the Evolution of Regional Cooperation in South Asia (1980–88), Vol. I, SAARC Secretariat, Kathmandu.

[2] Sri Lanka Watch, Wednesday, 21 November 2012. http://srilankawatch.com/index.php?option=com_content&task=view&id=960&Itemid=

[3] Annual Report, Ministry of External Affairs, Government of India, 1999–2000, POT Bangladesh, Vol. XII, No. 7, January 10, 1987.

[4] SAARC Survey of Development and Cooperation, 1998–1999, Research and Information System for Developing Countries, New Delhi.

[5] Cheema, Iqbal, Pervaiz (1999). 'SAARC Needs Revamping', in Nancy Jetly and Eric Gonsalves ed., Dynamics of South Asia Regional Cooperation and SAARC, New Delhi: Sage Publications.

[6] Stephen P. Cohen and Richard L. Park, India: Emergent Powers? New York, Crane, Russak and Co. Inc, 1978.

[7] Kant K. Bhargava, India and its South Asian Neighbors- Obligations and Privileges, paper presented during CASAC National Seminar on India's Pivotal Role in South Asia, in New Delhi, 2000.

[8] Benedict Anderson, Imagined Communities, London, Verso, 2006.

[9] Ashoka Bandarage, The separatist conflict in Sri Lanka, terrorism, ethnicity, political economy, IUniverse, Inc, New York Bloomington, 2009.

[10] Pervaiz Iqbal Cheema, "SAARC Needs Revamping", in Nancy Jetly and Eric Gonsalves edited Dynamics of South Asia Regional Cooperation and SAARC, Sage Publications, New Delhi, 1999, p. 95.

[11] Muni, S.D., "India in SAARC: A Reluctant Policy Maker", in Bjorn Hettne, Andras Inotai and Osvaldo Sunkel, National Perspectives on the New Regionalism in the South, Vol. 3, Macmillan Press Limited, Great Britain, 1998, pp. 127–128.

[12] Mohan, C. Raja, 'The 12th SAARC Summit and the Future of SAARC', *BIISS Journal*, Vol. 25, No. 4, October 2004.

[13] Chaturvedi, Ravi and Singleton, Rian, Ethnicity and Identity, Gloal Performance, Rawat Pulications, New Delhi, 2005.

[14] Abeysekera, C. and Gunasinghe, N. (eds)—"Facets of Ethnicity in Sri Lanka", Social Scientist Association, Colombo, 1987.

[15] Abeysekera, C., 'Ethnic Representation in Higher State Services' in "Ethnicity and Social Change", Colombo, 1985.

[16] Bandaranayake, Senake, 'The Peopling if Sri Lanka' in "Ethnicity and Social Change", Colombo, 1985.

[17] Bastian, Sunil, 'University Admission and the National Question', in "Ethnicity and Social Change", Colombo, 1985.

[18] Coomaraswamy, Radhika, 'Myths without conscience: Tamil and Sinhalese Nationalistic Writings of 1980's', in "Facets of Ethnicity in Sri Lanka", Colombo, 1987.

[19] Gunawardena, R.A.L.H., 'The People of the Lion' Sinhala Consciousness in History and Histography in "Ethnicity and Social Change", Colombo, 1985.

[20] Jayawardena, Kumari, "The Rise of the Labour Movement in Ceylon", Durham, N.C., 1972.—"Ethnic and Class Conflicts in Sri Lanka", Colombo, 1986.

[21] Kodikara, Shelton, 'Internationalisation of Sri Lanka's Ethnic Conflict', Paper presented at a Social Scientists Association Seminar, 1983.

[22] Social Scientists Association (SSA), "Ethnicity and Social Change in Sri Lanka", Colombo, 1st printing 1984, 2nd printing 1985.

[23] Siriwardena, Reggie and Coomaraswamy, Radhika, 'Ethno-Populism', paper presented at the International Center for Ethnic Studies, Colombo, 1987.

[24] The Hindu, August 3, 2012.

[25] Jayadeva Uyangoda, Sri Lanka Sans the LTTE? Economic and Political Weekly, Vol. XLIV, No. 7, February 14, 2009.

[26] Uyangoda, Jayadeva, LTTE and Its Separae State Project, EPW, December 29, 2007.

[27] Down the spiral in Sri Lanka, EPW, December 8, 2007.

[28] Ravi Vaitheespara, Sanmugathasan, The unrepentant left and the ethnic crisis in Sri Lanka, EPW, October 27, 2007.

[29] The New Indian Express, Jan 26, 2012.

[30] Nirupama Subramanian, Lessons to learn from Geneva, The Hindu, April 7, 2012.

[31] See W. Howard Wriggins, "South Asian Regional Politics: Asymmetrical Balance of One-State Dominance?" in Wriggins, Dynamics of Regional Politics.

[32] Mukherjee, I.N., "Regional Trade, Investment and Economic Cooperation among South Asian Countries," Paper presented at the International Conference on South Asia as a Dynamic Partner: Prospects for the Future, New Delhi, May 25–27, 1992.

[33] Perera, W.R.H., Perspective for the Development of Himalayan Resources (Colombo: Marga Institute, 1984).

[34] Thomson, William R., "South Asia: The Challenges and Opportunities of the 1990s" (Report presented at the International Conference on South Asia as a Dynamic Partner: Prospects for the Future, New Delhi, May 25, 1992).

[35] The Hindu, May 2, 1995.

[36] The Hindu, May 2, 1995.

[37] The Hindu, April 7, 2012.

[38] The Hindu, 20-5-2012.

[39] The Hindu, 28-7-2012.

[40] India Not anti Lanka, Its pro reconciliation, The Asian Age, 27-3-2012.

[41] Meenakshi Ganguly, *Srilanka takes the wrong road to peace*, The Asian Age, 16-5-2011.

[42] *SAARC: Moving Toward Core Areas of Cooperation*, Report by the Independent Group on South Asian Cooperation, United Nations University South Asian Perspectives Project (Columbo, December 1991).

[43] Rohini Hensman, *Democracy as solution to Sri Lanka's Ethnic Crisis*, EPW, August 9, 2008.

[44] Rohini Hensman, *The Way forward in Sri Lanka*, EPW, Vol. XLIV, No. 31, August 1, 2009.

NOTES

i. Twenty five years ago on 29th July 1987, when the Indian Prime Minister Rajiv Gandhi and the Sri Lanka President J.R. Jayawardene signed the Indo-Lanka accord, it was a day of mourning in the South of Sri Lanka, a day of confusion in the North and East and a miraculous day for India, especially for the Gandhi family. In the South, half of Colombo was on fire.

ii. Comprehensive Economic Partnership Agreement—CEPA. There appears to be a great deal of the public domain concerning the Indo-Sri Lanka CEPA. First, it should be understood that this greatly expanded free trade agreement between the two neighbours has been worked-out through exhaustive negotiations that have taken years of study and consultation to ensure a 'level playing field' that does not give undue advantage to the numerically bigger partner. India-Sri Lanka Free Trade Agreement signed in 1998 and became operational in 2000. The signing of Comprehensive Economic Partnership Agreement (CEPA) would bring more investment and services into Sri Lanka.

iii. Bay of Bengal Initiative for Multi Sectoral Technical and Economic Cooperation (BIMSTEC) is an International organisation involving a group of countries in South Asia and South East Asia. The member countries of this group are: Bangladesh,

India, Myanmar, Sri Lanka, Thailand, Bhutan and Nepal. In the first Summit on 31 July 2004, leaders of the group agreed that the name of the grouping should be known as BIMSTEC.

iv. Benedict Anderson, Imagined Communities, London, Verso, 2006.

v. Ashoka Bandarage, The separatist conflict in Sri Lanka, terrorism, ethnicity, political economy, IUniverse, Inc, New York Bloomington, 2009.

vi. *In 1956, Sri Lanka Freedom Party (SLFP) as formed, professing Sinhalese as the official language as its motto.* The republican Constitution of 1972, while proclaiming Sinhala as the official language, declared that Buddhism had the 'foremost place' in Sri Lanka, thus almost affirming a Sinhala-Buddhist state. It is precisely this history that persuaded the Tamils that co-existence with the Sinhala in a single polity was no longer possible.

vii. LTTE (Liberation Tigers of Tamil Eelam), EROS (Eelam Revolutionary Organisation), EPRLF (Eelam People's Revolutionary Liberation Front) TELO (Tamil Eelam Liberation Organisation) and PLOT(People's Liberation Organization of Tamil Eelam (PLOTE, also PLOT) these are all Guerrilla organizations seeking to establish an independent Tamil state in northern and eastern Sri Lanka. Read more: http://www.answers.com/topic/liberation-tigers-of-tamil-eelam#ixzz2DUaBTzLG and www.tamilarangam.net

viii. The Indo Sri Lanka Agreement signed by Prime Minister Rajiv Gandhi of India and President J.R. Jayawardene of Sri Lanka on 29 July 1987 in the context of India's geo political interests and the impact of the subsequent offensive launched by the Indian Peace Keeping Force on the Tamil people—it is a revised version of two speeches delivered in London in January and March 1988."...The Indo Sri Lanka Agreement refuses to structure a federal constitution where power may be shared between the Tamil nation and the Sinhala nation. The Agreement does not even create a 'Tamil Nadu like' constitutional structure for the Tamils in the island of Sri Lanka.

ix. European Union foreign ministers called for an independent inquiry into alleged war crimes (BBC) by both Tamil Tiger rebels and Sri Lanka's government. Watchdog groups also accused both sides of violating international laws of war. In April 2009, Human Rights Watch reported while rebels were preventing civilians from leaving the last tiny strip of land where they were fighting the government forces, the government forces repeatedly and indiscriminately shelled the area.

x. The following are the terms of agreement: Rejection of the demand for a separate Eelam with a view to strengthening the integrity, sovereignty and regional supremacy of Sri Lanka. Sri Lanka was declared as Multi-ethnic and Multi lingual society; (2) English and Tamil given a status equal to Sinhalese as official language; (3) Northern and Eastern regions to be recognized as joined administrative units with separate elected council, Governor, Chief Minister and Ministry. It was also decided upon to hold a plebiscite to whether the people want a joint administration or not; (4) Tamil guerillas must stop violence within 48 hours of the Agreement, and must surrender their arms to the Sri Lankan authorities; (5) General political reprieve to all political prisoners and rehabilitation of the Tamil militants to bring them back in the main—stream of the nation; (6) The Indian Government to guarantee the implementation of the Agreement proposals and to assist the Sri Lankan Govern ment in its implementation. India will take firm steps in not allowing the Indian territory for any anti-Sri Lanka activities.

xi. Hemantha Dayaratne, A New Phase in India-Sri Lanka Relations, Share on facebookShare on twitterShare on emailMore Sharing Services, January 3, 2011.

xii. The main political parties were not totally insensitive to this process, S.W.R.D. Bandaranaike, Prime Minister and leader of the SLFP (Sri Lanka Freedom Party) arrived at an understanding with the leader of the Federal Party (the Bandaranaike—Chelvanayakam Pact of 1958) which gave Tamils a degree of regional autonomy, including control of the land settlement in their areas. However, Bandaranaike had to abandon the pact in the face of opposition from the United National Party (UNP) and was killed by a monk in 1959. Likewise, when the UNP was again in power, Dudley Senanayake, the Prime Minister, worked out a somewhat similar understanding in 1967; this too was scuttled in the face of opposition, this time mainly from the SLFP.

xiii. Sri Lankan President Mahinda Rajapakse visited India in November 2006. Prime Minister Ratnasir I Wickramanayake visited India in January 2007 to attend the Satyagraha conference. Sri Lankan Foreign Minister Rohitha Bogollagama visited India in end January 2007. From India several ministerial and official level visits took place. External Affairs Minister Pranab Mukherjee visited Colombo in January 2007 to handover the SAARC Summit invitation to the Sri Lankan President. Bilateral trade for the period April to October 2006 amounted to US$ 1 billion and annualized figures are expected to touch US$ 2 billion. India became the second largest investor in Sri Lanka. Bilateral tourism received a boost as the weekly frequency of flights between the two countries increased and Indians formed the largest group of tourist arrivals in Sri Lanka.

xiv. These projects will help heal differences between two domestic communities separated by war while enhancing people-to-people contact between Sri Lankans and Indians through the new ferry service. Moreover, Krishna's remarks as to the need for a political solution to the Tamil ethnic question varied little from the official Sri Lankan government's standpoint; there is merely disagreement on how to get there. India urges devolution of powers based specifically on the 13th amendment while the Sri Lankan government favours a home-grown solution. This is a matter to be handled with great care since the outcome of any ill-conceived design would impact on bilateral relations.

xv. Anuradha M Chenoy, The New Indian Express.

xvi. President Rajapaksa met Indian Prime Minister Dr. Manmohan Singh at Hotel Shangri La in the Addu Atoll to discuss a host of bilateral issues and strengthening regional cooperation. Both leaders took the opportunity to raise issues related to the escalation of fishermen's issues, poaching piracy and maritime terrorism in the Indian Ocean. They also discussed Sri Lanka's political process for ethnic reconciliation and resettlement of displaced. Sri Lanka and India haven't had a bilateral engagement at the top-most levels in governance, reflecting the changing priorities in New Delhi towards its immediate neighbourhood. A series of issues between Sri Lanka and India since the close of the Eelam war IV in May 2009, which saw the demise of the Tamil Tigers, has seen New Delhi cold-shoulder Colombo for over two years. That leaves out Sri Lankan President Mahinda Rajapaksa as the only leader in the region whom Dr. Singh hasn't consciously met in a formal bilateral forum—the two leaders have met on the sidelines of the 2011 SAARC summit in Addu City in the Maldives, and the last session of the United

Nations General Assembly. These meetings are necessarily hurried and short, and nothing of substance can be discussed at any length. The last time an Indian Prime Minister visited Sri Lanka was in 2008—that too wasn't for a bilateral meeting; it was for the SAARC summit.

xvii. SAARC established on 8 December 1985 when the government of Bangladesh, Bhutan, India, Maldives, Nepal, Pakistan, and Sri Lanka formally adopted its charter providing for the promotion of economic and social progress, cultural development within the South Asia region and also for friendship and cooperation with other developing countries. It is dedicated to economic, technological, social, and cultural development emphasizing collective self-reliance. Its seven founding members are Sri Lanka, Bhutan, India, Maldives, Nepal, Pakistan, and Bangladesh. Afghanistan joined the organization in 2007. Meetings of heads of state are usually scheduled annually; meetings of foreign secretaries, twice annually. It is headquartered in Kathmandu, Nepal.

xviii. The second summit was held in November 16–17 Bangalore, India in 1986. The third summit was held in Kathmandu, Nepal on 2–4 November 1987, The fourth summit was held in Islamabad, Pakistan on 29–31 December 1988 It was also agreed to hold regular "South Asian Festivals" with the first being hosted by India. The fifth summit was held in Malé, Maldives on 21–23 November 1990 The sixth summit was held in Colombo, Sri Lanka on 21 December 1991 The seventh summit was held in Dhaka, on 10–11 April 1993. The eighth summit was held in New Delhi, on 2–4 May 1995.The ninth summit was held in Malé, on 12–14 May 1997. The tenth summit was held in Colombo, on 29–31 July 1998. The eleventh summit was held in Kathmandu, on 4–6 January 2002. The twelfth summit was held in Islamabad, on 4–6 January 2004. The thirteenth summit was held in Dhaka, on 12–13 November 2005. The fourteenth summit of SAARC was held in New Delhi, on 3rd–4 April 2007. The fifteenth summit of SAARC was held in Colombo, Sri Lanka on 1–3 August 2008. The sixteenth summit was held in Thimpu, Bhutan on 28–29 April 2010. The Seventeenth Summit was held from 10–11 of November 2011 in Addu City, Maldives. The Meeting, which was held at the Equatorial Convention Centre, Addu City was opened by the outgoing Chair of SAARC, Prime Minister of the Royal Government of Bhutan, H.E.Lyonchhen Jigmi Yoezer Thinley.

xix. Report of the IPCS Seminar held on 29 September 2008

xx. Anuradha M Chenoy, *Ensure Sri Lanka Delivers*, The New Indian Express, Jan 26, 2012.

India-Sri Lanka Relations:
A Dark Past, But a Bright Future

Samarth Trigunayat and Venkat Siddarth

ABSTRACT: The relationship between India and Sri-Lanka is nearly 2500 years old and is built on the annals of cultural, religious, economic and trade colloquy. The two countries have a common history and many of the former kings of these nations have established good economic and trade relations with one another. The relationship between the two countries is a polymorphous concept and has developed with the passage of time. Both countries are the member of various regional associations, SAARC being the most important of all. In present scenario, with the end of Lankan civil war in 2009 both countries must look forward to establish better relationships for mutual development and growth. India's foreign policy has always been friendly towards the island country and has never dominated over its sovereignty. The bone of contention between the two countries has always been the conflicts between the Indian-origin Tamils and the Sinhalese population of Sri Lanka.

Both countries have been a victim of economic recession. In Lankan case it is more serious because it has witnessed a civil war too in the recent history. This has adversely affected the development and growth of the island country. Sri Lanka has always been a trade dependent country and 62% of its exports are to the EU and the US mostly comprising tea and garments, but recent reduction in demand of Sri-Lankan items in the EU and US has degraded the Lankan economy. The Free Trade Agreement (FTA) signed between India and Sri-Lanka in 2000 accelerated the trade percentage increasing the trade by 128% in just four years. Indian exports to Sri Lanka contribute to 14% of the total global Lankan imports. Sri Lanka is also the 5th largest export destination of India comprising a total of 3.5% of Indian exports. Recent collaborations in almost all the fields between Sri Lanka and India will definitely take the relationship between both the countries to a new level.

Both India and Sri-Lanka are the signatories of South Asian Free Trade Agreement (SAFTA). India has also given three lines of credit to Sri-Lanka for developmental projects. There is a necessity for both countries to come together for mutual development. The research paper will deal with the following things: **Trade between India and Sri-Lanka after the signing of Free Trade Agreement**—this will deal with the present scenario of trade relations between both the countries; **Impact of Sri-Lankan Civil war on**

Sri-Lankan economy—this will deal with the Sri-Lankan economy during the period of the Sri Lankan civil war and the post war effects; **Developmental projects in Sri-Lanka with Indian assistance**—this includes the collaborations between the two countries; **Future perspectives of the trade and economic relation between the two countries**—the growth in trade and commerce recently has opened gates for expansion of this relation between two countries in near future; And lastly the author will put his points after the analysis of the above mentioned topics.

INTRODUCTION

India and Sri Lanka have always shared a *'Love-Hate'* type relationship with each other. The relationship has been through diverse stages. The relationship between the two countries is more than 2500 years old and is built on the annals of cultural, religious, economic and trade colloquy. The two countries have always managed to maintain their bilateral relations even in the worst of times. The failure of Indian Peace Keeping Forces (IPKF) to end the civil war in Sri Lanka has affected the relations adversely. Despite all the odds the two countries have developed good relations.

The relationship between the two countries has a history dating back to pre-colonial era. In the colonial era both of them produced goods for the colonial powers. They also acted as a market for the goods manufactured by them. Even after the independence, up to 1970s[1] the trade between the two was not remarkable. Trade was limited as both the countries newly got independent and they focused mostly on manufacturing goods for their own consumption. Not much was exported or imported between the two.

With the Indian Economic reforms of 1991, the scenario changed and the reforms gave a strong acceleration to the manufacturing sector of India, ultimately giving a push to the trade relations between the two countries. The most remarkable increment in the trade was seen after the signing of Free Trade Agreement (FTA) also known as ISFTA *i.e.* India Sri Lanka Free Trade Agreement, in 1998. This agreement came into force from 1st March 2000.

At present the two countries share a good relationship. With Indian assistance many new projects are being set up in Sri Lanka. India has also provided Sri Lanka with many lines of credits for developmental projects. The two countries aim at increasing the trade between the two to $15 billion by 2015.

The two countries are tied historically, culturally and religiously. The proximity makes it important for both the countries to develop sustainable and healthy relationship.

OBJECTIVES

The objective of this paper is to study following things:

- Trade between India and Sri-Lanka after the signing of Free Trade Agreement.
- Impact of Sri-Lankan Civil war on Sri-Lankan economy.
- Developmental projects in Sri-Lanka with Indian assistance.
- Future perspectives of the trade and economic relation between the two countries.

METHODOLOGY

The study is based on the data analysis approach. This study relies on primary as well as secondary sources. We have had to heavily depend on periodical literature, newspaper clippings, research journals, books and unpublished material and help from the Internet has been sought.

Hypothesis

The authors believe that the relationship between the two countries has been through very diverse situations. The relationship has been stagnant in the near past and a remarkable growth in is seen in the present scenario. The two countries have signed various agreements aimed at developing the infrastructure and the economy of one another. The growth in the trade and commerce between the countries and the changed nature and pattern of the relationships make it clear that the future relations are going to be at the highest level of trust.

A HISTORICAL BACKGROUND

The relations between two countries form subject of many interesting tales and stories. According to Ceylonese texts *Dipvamsa* and *Mahavamsa* an Indian Prince named Vijay Simha landed in Ceylon and after some minor resistance he was able to wrest power and thus the island was named after him as Simhaldvipa. One of the Ajanta's painting records this event, thus supplementing the narrative of the history.[2]

Another important event in the history of Sri Lanka was arrival of Prince Mahendra and Sanghmitra with a Bodhi Tree sapling and ever since then India and Ceylon have been communicating with each other in various fields of culture, trade, religion and economy at various levels.

Economic Cooperation between both the countries started much later. We often find mention of the fact that both the countries have competed in the near past for the supremacy of being the major tea exporter. India's Economic relation with Sri Lanka began expanding since 1966 when India extended a ₹ 2 crore loan to enable Sri Lanka to import food products.[3] Later in 1967 India also provided another credit worth ₹ 5 crore to Sri Lanka for financing general electronic and mechanical items.

After the visit of Indian Prime Minister Indira Gandhi in 1973, the trade and economic relations between the two countries got a boost. In order to correct the balance of Trade between the two countries, which was disturbed in 1971, the two countries readily accepted cooperation in five areas- sheet glass, rubber, graphite, refractory and mica. India also offered annual aid of 1 crore for 5 consecutive year to Sri Lanka for developmental projects. In 1974 the two countries agreed to set up several small industries in Sri Lanka and also a micro wave connection between the two countries. In 1975 a science and technical cooperation was also signed between the two countries.

A remarkable growth was seen between the countries in 1993. The total trade value was 1131 crores with exports to Sri Lanka of ₹ 1069 crores and imports of 62 crores. As compared to 1973 it was a remarkable growth, though it still lacked balance. The trade between the countries reached to new heights in 1995 with total trade of value 1252 crores. To check the imbalance of trade between the countries the Sri Lankan government demanded Indian assistance and investment. India also announced reduction in custom duties on 18 items.

Comparison of Facts and Figures

Parameters	India	Sri Lanka
Capital	New Delhi	Sri Jayawardenapura Kotte
Area	3,287,263 km^2	65,610 km^2
Population	1,210,193,422	20,277,597
Density	370.7/km^2	323/km^2
GDP	$ 4.457 trillion	$ 116.541 billion
Currency	Indian Rupee	Sri Lankan Rupee
HDI	0.547	0.691
Gini	36.8	36

TRADE BETWEEN INDIA AND SRI LANKA AFTER THE SIGNING OF FREE TRADE AGREEMENT

The Indo-Sri Lanka Free Trade Agreement (ISFTA), signed on 28th December 1998, aims at promoting economic linkage between India and Sri Lanka through enhancement of bilateral trade and investment. The agreement covers only trade in goods and requires the two countries to offer market access for each other's exports on duty free basis and concessionary tariffs. The ISFTA does not provide for elimination of non tariff barriers. The economic reforms implemented by India in 1990, helped a lot to strengthen the relations between the two countries. From post 1990 period, Indian economy is most dynamic and attractive with which Sri Lanka continues to have strong relations by reasons of shared historical experience, common civilization and cultural values sustained by geographically proximity and ethnic affinity.

Under ISFTA both the countries have agreed to offer Zero Duty on all the products except for the one's in their negative lists. Since the signing of the agreement trade between two countries has increased. Except for the year 2006, a growth is marked in the trade of products between the two countries. The restoration of political stability in Sri Lanka in 2008 is expected to ensure much better trade relations between the countries in the near future.

The India -Sri Lanka Free Trade Agreement was signed with an objective to promote trade and economic relations between the two countries and promote FDI. It entered into force from March 1, 2000. Being a larger and much resourceful nation in comparison to Sri Lanka, why did India find a need to pledge to a strategy of reciprocity through the ISFTA? There could be two possibilities. First, the security relationship between the nations involved does have a role to play. It has been argued that trade among allies adds to a collective economic power whereas the same among adversaries increases interdependencies. Thus India's improving security relations with Sri Lanka plays a huge role in the build up to the FTA. Second, India views trade as an important developmental strategy, and hence global economic interdependence becomes important.

ISFTA has been one of the few very successful FTA. It has also proved that the size difference of the nations become insignificant if the interests of the smaller nation is taken into account with a favorable treatment. After signing of the FTA both nations have granted tariff concessions on various products. Both the parties have their own list of negative items (no concessions), positive list (immediate full concessions) and a residual list (phased tariff concessions).

After signing of the ISFTA, trade between the two South Asian nations has increased manifold. In 1999 India's import from Sri Lanka was USD 47 million which accounted for 0.1% of its total imports. By the end of 2007, the imports reported a rise of 838% to USD 516 million. Also, India had become the third largest export destination for Sri Lanka. India's export to Sri Lanka amounted to USD 499 million in 1999 which reported a rise to USD 2,785 million by the end of 2007. The total trade between India and Sri Lanka increased from USD 646 million in 2001 to USD 3,301 million in 2007.[4] The export volume increased slower than the import volumes and the bilateral trade balance increased in favor of India from USD 531 million in 2001 to USD 2,234 million in 2007. Nevertheless, Sri Lanka's exports to India grew faster than imports during the initial period of 2001–2005. During 2006–2007 the deficit increased as a result of increased petroleum imports and decreased exports of vanaspati and copper. This way India became one of the major trading partners of Sri Lanka after the signing of the agreement.

India and China have been the two major export destinations for Sri Lanka. Comparing the two we can see that since 2000 *i.e.* after the ISFTA, Sri Lanka's share in India's total imports have been on a rise. On the other hand Sri Lanka's share in China's total imports has been constant. Export items from Sri Lanka to India increased from 505 in 1996 to 1062 in 2006. The major products exported by Sri Lanka to India in 2006 included—Fats and Oils (22.3%), Copper and Articles of Copper (8.6%), Electrical Machinery (8.6%) and Spices, Coffee, Tea (6.2%). Similarly, India exported Mineral Fuel, Oil (22.44%), Vehicles (18.08%), Iron and Steel (4.54%), Machinery, Reactors, Boilers (4.22%) and Pharmaceutical Products (4.13%) to Sri Lanka. if we analyse this, there is a visible shift from agricultural products to manufacturing goods.[5]

Due to awareness to partners' market, smoothening of custom issues and easy access to ports, there has been considerable rise in imports of the negative list items as well from 0.5% in 2001 to 1.19% in 2006. But the trade of the items under the positive list has been stagnant. The reason for this is that both the nations have provided those items under the positive list in which they do not have a comparative advantage. This strategy also helped the FTA to become a workable agreement. The above facts are a clear indication to a marked increase in trade between India and Sri Lanka after the implementation of the ISFTA.

IMPACTS

Since the FTA came into force in 2000, the bilateral trade between India and Sri Lanka has been on a rise. At the end of 2007, the overall trade turnover between the two nations stood at USD 3.2 billion. The FTA also resulted in a 10 fold growth of Sri Lanka's exports to India and a 5 fold growth of India's exports to Sri Lanka. The FTA facilitated a two way trade. India became the largest exporter to Sri Lanka and most importantly India became the 3rd largest export destination for Sri Lanka, rising from the 16th spot. Hence the FTA helped India to emerge as Sri Lanka's most balanced trading partner since it's all other leading partners are predominantly exporters or importers. The FTA has also contributed to reduce the import-export ratio from 10.5:1 in 2000 to 5.3:1 in 2007. The trade of items under the FTA has been fairly equal. In 2007, Sri Lanka exports of items under the FTA were around USD 450–500 million and India's export of the similar items were USD 600–700 million. But the non FTA exports of Sri Lanka in 2007 were negligible. It amounted to only USD 50 million. On the other hand India's exports to Sri Lanka of the non FTA items were around USD 2 billion. This means, had the FTA not been implemented, the Sri Lankan exports would have remained stagnant. Hence the FTA has benefited Sri Lanka by creating its present export credentials. Had the FTA not been implemented, the import-export ratio would have stood at 40:1. Overall, as a result of the FTA India now is the largest trade partner of Sri Lanka. Also, Sri Lanka displaced Bangladesh as India's biggest trade partner in South Asia.

The Following graph shows the total trade between the countries for last one decade.

Year	Imports	Exports	TOT (Total Trade)	BOT (Balance of Trade)
1999	499	47	546	−452
2000	568	55	623	−513
2001	577	69	646	−508
2002	835	169	1,004	−666
2003	1,076	241	1,317	−835
2004	1,358	385	1,743	−973
2005	1,399	559	1,959	−840
2006	1,822	494	2,316	−1,328
2007	2,785	516	3,301	−2,269
2008	3,007	418	3,425	−2,589
2009	1,710	325	2,035	−1,385
2010	2,463	470	2,933	−1,993

All in USD mn.   *Source:* Customs/DOC/EDB

ECONOMIC IMPACTS OF SRI LANKA CIVIL WAR:

In spite of continuous period of confusion and chaos and turmoil, for over 25 years, Sri Lanka has managed to maintain an average growth rate of 5% in last few years, though we cannot neglect the impacts of the war on the Sri Lankan economy. The economic growth could have been more in the absence of internal war. In 2007, the government borrowed $181,449 worth of defense loans from international financial markets, virtually double the amount used in the previous year. In 2008, the Sinhalese government designated $1.5 billion for defense, a 20% increase from last year's budget. This year, Sri Lanka expects to allocate $1.64 billion to war efforts, a 6.4% year-on-year increase. War costs currently consume around 30% of the government's budget, and have been estimated to have cost the country over $200 billion over the years.[6]

The Civil war also affected the infrastructure of the country. Due to the indulgence in the war the Government couldn't pay heed to the planning and development of the infrastructure of the country. Government could also not take effective measures against the natural calamities. The railway network, roads and the ports were also not up to the mark of contention.

Since 2004, there has been a decrease in the growth rate of the country. The national trade deficit has also increased to 78%. Rajapakse's considerable efforts have ended the civil war by increasing the military power but some measures are needed to be taken in the field of infrastructure development.

The victory of Military over the LTTE has definitely put an end to the chaos and tension, but the government needs more new plans to ensure economic growth in the long run. The growth of infrastructure is one of the most important factors which the country has lacked in the near past. Investment in infrastructure is required for economic stability and growth of the country.

Education is also lacking in the country at present. As per a report, in 2008–10, only 2% of young people went for higher education, which is very low for a country. Education is an empowerment tool and is required as it will create a strong workforce of skilled and educated workers. Corruption and lack of transparency is another factor which is affecting the economy. These two remain significant issues in the country and could substantially affect investment levels and approvals of international loans. Sri Lanka is extremely dependent on foreign assistance, with the World Bank, the Asian Development Bank, Japan, and other donors providing loans totaling $1.4 billion in 2007. Due to its inability to provide transparency, Sri Lanka has already lost its EU concessions for the following year, compromising 2% of its annual GDP growth. The depreciation of Sri Lankan currency has also led to further economic instability. The current overvalued currency is draining foreign reserves and could impose severe damages in Sri Lanka's annual financial statement.

Sri Lankan population is 70% Sinhalese, 25% Tamil and 5% are those who are not Sinhalese ethnically. The purely military action to the Tamil revolt and government's inability to consider few of their demands may lead to another guerilla style uprising in the near future as suggested by analysts and in future they may hit economic and political centers which can further lead to economic depreciation of the country.

The past 25 years of civil war followed by Global recession have resulted in Sri Lanka's high public debt load. Economists expect the country to need investments levels of around 30% of GDP and 1–8% economic growth rates in order to successfully reduce unemployment and poverty. Political instability and lack of security caused by the conflict have led to investment levels averaging around 25% in the last ten years.[7]

Now it is totally up to the future actions taken by the Sinhalese government, which will play an important role in the higher level of investments and economic growth of the country. With the military's victory over the LTTE, Sri Lanka's economic prosperity primarily depends on infrastructural and educational reforms, transparency, political stability and a return to peace. It is crucial for the government to achieve unification and stability by focusing on social, economic political solutions to a sustainable long-term conflict resolution by bringing new reforms and their proper implementation.

INDIA SRI LANKA COLLABORATIONS

In order to increase the pace of development and to build up a better infrastructure in Sri Lanka (this could not be built due to Sri Lankan civil war) the two countries have entered into many collaborations. Few of them are listed below.

Collaboration for manufacture of Auto Components

India will help Sri Lanka to establish a special economic zone to manufacture auto components in Trincomalee. The SEZ will also help to promote exports to the production chains in India. A joint task force on SEZ would be set up and will submit its report in 90 days.[8]

Collaboration for Pharmaceutical Hub

Announcement for setting up of a pharmaceuticals manufacturing hub in Sri Lanka was also made by Anand Sharma. He said that soon a team from India will visit Sri Lanka to work out on the details. India is aiming at doubling the bilateral trade between the countries by the year 2015, which for the last year was around $ 5 bn.[9]

Comprehensive Economic Partnership Agreement (CEPA)

CEPA would bring more investments and services into Sri Lanka. The Indian Commerce Minister, Anand Sharma, said that the two commerce secretaries would resume dialogue on CEPA and resolve all the related issues. He asserted that Sri Lanka would be given preferential access to the 'big Indian Market'.

Design Development and Student Exchange Program

Anand Sharma on Sri Lanka's record of highest per capita apparel exports in the region said that, "India can offer synergistic partnerships in design development and student exchange programmes through its premier design institutes like NIFT, NID and FDDI." Two Sri Lankan apparel business houses- Brandix Apparels and MAS Holdings- have already partnered with India in setting up two integrated textile parks at Vizag and Nellore to provide expertise to India in green manufacturing processes.

Housing Projects

US $ 270 million Indian Housing project for displaced Tamils in Sri Lanka is now on track. The Pilot phase of the project for construction of 1,000 houses has been completed. The next phase of Indian Housing Project for 43,000 housing units under owner driven mode in the northern and eastern provinces has been launched. After the initial obstacles the pilot project of building 1000 houses was completed in July this year.[10].

Collaboration for Railway Development

The Indian Railways and Sri Lankan Government's agreement for a US $ 149 million reconstruction project of railway line between Kankesanthurai and Pallai has been already agreed upon and the implementation is on its way. General Manager of Sri Lanka Railways, BAP Ariyaratne and Managing Director of Ircon Mohan Tiwari, signed the agreement.

The project covering 56 km is likely to be completed in two years. Besides, Ircon is also executing other rail projects in Sri Lanka including the restoration of 106 km land Medawachchciya- Talaim annar section, 90 km long Omanthai- Pallai section and supply and installation of signaling and telecommunication system on the entire railway network in the Northern Province.

These collaborations show that the nature and intensity of relations between the countries have changed up to a great extent. The restoration of trust and confidence between the two has led to development and growth. The economic cooperation and trade relation between the two have always been subject to the different political strategies of the two, but now as they have realized that the aims for both are same, thus they have united themselves and are jointly working towards the aim of becoming a developed and prosperous country in the near future.[11]

Future Perspective

In last few years significant changes have taken place in Indo-Sinhalese Relation. These changes, positive in nature, are the result of mutual steps taken by both the countries to develop economic cooperation and trade relation between each other. The relationship between the two in last few years has shown the world that relationships are not subject to the difference in the sizes of the countries but to the level of mutual understanding.

The changed nature and pattern of relationship between the countries has for sure made it clear that in the near future the two countries are going to pace up their development rate by mutual cooperation in various fields. The credit of this goes to the leaders of both the countries for taking the bilateral relationships to new heights. The end of mutual misconception and the increase in mutual understanding are responsible for the desired change.

Sri Lanka's real threat is not its only neighbor but the dissatisfaction of the internal minorities. The two countries now need to work together to end up the remaining evils in the countries which have external linkages. History has proved that the mistrust and misperception between the countries in the past was the major cause of strategic divergence which led to the insecurity of the country. Undoubtedly, development of trust will promote a constructive bilateral engagement between the two countries for the mutual benefit of both.

The lack of communication and awareness in the Sinhalese population has generated a fear of India in the minds of people. The lack of awareness of India's stand in Sri Lankan civil war has led the people to follow and grow this fear. Man to man conversation and proper awareness will lead to end of this misconception and fear. So far there has been no initiative by any of the countries to bring people of both the countries in direct contact. The image of India as a de-stabilizing and a hostile neighbor must be replaced with a friendly and cooperative power which believes in peaceful co-existence. At the same time Sri Lanka's image of intolerant society dominated by chauvinistic forces needs to be changed.[12]

Tamil Nadu is another important factor between India-Sri Lanka Relations. Tamil Nadu plays a significant role in declaration of bilateral relations between the two countries No ties can be made by Delhi without considering the benefits of state of Tamil Nadu. Thus the Indian Government must take the Tamil Nadu factor seriously into account while framing new laws and statutes regarding relationships between the two countries in future.

One more hope for further strengthening the relationship comes from the Palk Strait. In spite of fighting over the border issue both countries can jointly explore and exploit the resources of that area. This will further help the countries to meet up the demands of raw materials and will also increase their production.

In past, both countries have experienced same problems. So in future they must work together to end them up. To increase the economic growth rate both countries must come together and must increase their trade. Militancy and terrorism is another problem which has always been an obstacle in the way of development. This must be dealt together. Illiteracy, poverty, ill-health, disaster management are the other problems which can only be dealt with cooperation and mutual trust.[13]

The problems faced by the two countries are nearly same so in future the two countries must deal with it together. The previous relationships are the examples which show that the only way to end up the problems is by development of mutual trust and mutual confidence. Such bilateral ties will definitely help the countries to increase their growth and will lead to development.

For e.g., The FTA, by expanding traditional exports and bringing new exports to Sri Lanka's trade basket, was able to reduce India's import-export ratio from 16:1 to 5:1 between 1998–99 and 2002–03. The same figure was further reduced to 3.7:1 in 2004–05. This experience has increased Sri Lanka's confidence in a positive sum trade relationship with its large neighbor and at the same time has promoted India's trade.

Rohita Bogollagama said, *"Bilateral Ties with India are at highest levels of trust, friendship and confidence…'Continuous dialogues' at the bilateral level had helped us to communicate better towards finding solutions effectively and towards sustaining our relationship at the highest leve[14]"*

CONCLUSION: AN ANALYSIS

This part of the research work is based totally on the analysis of the data collected by the researchers.

The relationship between the two countries has generally been friendly. The major factor influencing Indo-Sinhalese relation is security and shared ethnicity of Tamils living in the Southern India and in Northern and Eastern Sri Lanka.

The relations between Sri Lanka and India improved somewhat in the early 1990s, as the government attempted to expand economic, scientific and cultural cooperation. This happened after the assassination of Rajiv Gandhi and the economic reforms brought up by Indian government. Before the assassination of Rajiv Gandhi by LTTE group India's intervention in Sri Lanka's fight was indirect, but with assassination of Rajiv Gandhi, India started to end the presence of LTTE in Tamil Nadu, which benefitted Sri Lanka. And this in turn brought them together against a common enemy.

After the signing of FTA in 1998, there was a remarkable increase in trade and cooperation between the two countries. The overall trade between the countries has grown five times since its implementation in 2000. The ratio of imports and exports of both the countries has improved after the signing of this FTA.

India Sri Lanka agreements will help both the countries to develop at a faster rate and will also increase their growth rate. It is evident from the past experiences that the two countries have shown a remarkable growth whenever they have worked together for a common cause. Except for the year 2009, every year the Indian export to Sri Lanka has increased. This shows that the FTA was a success and has helped the two countries to come together and understand the real motive of each other. The Indian image of a dominant neighbor has changed to a helpful power in the minds of many Sri Lankan people which is a great achievement. India's stand on terrorism and other militant groups has made it clear that the two countries share the same ideology, *i.e.* eradication, for these purposes.

India is the most important and the most potent country in Indian Subcontinent. In Asia also it is next to China and is competing well with China to get the top position. The different political and foreign philosophies of the two countries have made them enemies of each other. India has lost one of its most important neighbors Pakistan to China. It is believed that now India shares whole of its land border with China because of the Chinese presence in Pakistan, Nepal and Arunanchal Pradesh. This makes it very serious for India. Now India needs to maintain healthy relations with its neighbors in order to stay safe and to reduce intruders in its border areas. In order to compete with China's growing power it is very much essential for India to counter it by getting more countries in good faith. China's ideology of providing weapons to these neighbors of India at very small price will make India's neighbors a slave of Chinese arms and politics.

Thus an action is required by India. As India is not a big Manufacturing Economy as China, thus it needs to expand its presence through such bilateral agreements only. At present it is mandatory for India to get into such agreements in order to ensure its security.

It can be said that a relationship is not based on size of the countries but on the level of trust they have. We have come so far with this relationship but this is not the end. The two countries have to work more and have to achieve more in the long run.

Yet there are differences between them and they need to be sorted out. The trust needs to get increased as every relationship is based on trust and belief. The two countries share a glorious history and they need to work together to make their present and future much more prosperous. The dreams which they have seen together must be accomplished as that is the only way to restore trust and confidence in them.

BIBLIOGRAPHY

Books

- Sridharan, E, International Relations Theory and South Asia.
- Shah, Giriraj, Indian Heritage.
- Khanna, V.N., Foreign Policy of India.
- Roy, Meenu, India and her Subcontinent Neighbors.
- Websites
- www.lankabusinessonline.com
- www.sldhcchennai.org

- www.asiaecon.org
- Newspapers
- The Hindu, 15th August, 2012.
- The Hindu, 12th September, 2008.
- The Hindu, 3rd August, 2012.
- The Economic Times, 18th November, 2011.
- The Indian Express, 4th August, 2012.

NOTES

1. Sridharan, E, International Relations Theory and South Asia, Oxford University Press, New Delhi, 2011.
2. Shah, Giriraj, 'Indian Heritage', Abhinav Publications, New Delhi, 1982.
3. Khanna, V.N., 'Foreign Policy of India', Vikas Publishing House, Noida, 2007.
4. http://www.lankabusinessonline.com/fullstory.php?nid=1480523226, accessed on 17th October 2012.
5. http://www.sldhcchennai.org/images/stories/Tenders/Trade%20Stata.pdf, accessed on 18th October, 2012.
6. http://www.asiaecon.org/special_articles/read_sp/12556, 'Economic Impacts of Sri Lankan Civil War', accessed on 3rd October, 2012.
7. http://www.asiaecon.org/special_articles/read_sp/12556, 'Economic Impacts of Sri Lankan Civil War', accessed on 3rd October, 2012.
8. India to set up manufacturing, export hubs in Sri Lanka, The Indian express, 4th August 2012.
9. India to help Sri Lanka set up SEZs, The Hindu, 3rd August 2012.
10. Indian housing project for Tamils in Sri Lanka on track, The Hindu, 15th August 2012.
11. Indian Railways to undertake $149 million project in Sri Lanka, The Economic Times, 18th November 2011.
12. Roy, Meenu, 'India and Her Subcontinent Neighbor', Deep and Deep Publications, 2010.
13. Roy, Meenu, 'India and her Subcontinent Neighbors', Deep and Deep Publications, 2010.
14. Interview, The Hindu, September 12, 2008.

Health Care Performance of Sri Lanka and Indian State of Kerala: Lessons for SAARC Nations

Feroz Ikbal

ABSTRACT: Quality of health of the people is one of the indicators of peace and prosperity of any country. Many of the countries of south Asian regions have poor health indicators comparable with sub-Saharan African countries. But among the SAARC countries, Sri Lanka has health care performance comparable to that of middle income countries or even rich countries. Again among the various Indian states, Kerala stands ahead and its health care indicators are comparable to middle income countries as well to Sri Lanka. This paper intends to examine the healthcare performance of Kerala and Sri Lanka, which is comparable to that of rich countries and much ahead of low income countries. Textual data pertaining to health care pertaining to Kerala and Sri Lanka has been used for this study. Content analysis is used for data analysis. Study reveals that Kerala and Sri Lanka didn't follow a particular model or structure to improve the health care. But various historical and social dimensions have played a crucial role in their achievements. The experience of Kerala and Sri Lanka will be of great use to other SAARC countries to develop their own strategies and policies to improve the healthcare systems and better outcomes. Strong government interventions and focus on social determinants of health like high women's literacy have contributed to the better performance. But since 1990's there has been stagnation in the healthcare indicators, though there is much scope of improvement. At the same time few unhealthy trends also crept into the healthcare scenario of both Kerala and Sri Lanka like increase in suicide rates, increased caesarian sections, proliferation of private sector without much regulation, and decline in the share of public expenditure in healthcare.

INTRODUCTION

Countries like Costa Rica, Cuba, Sri Lanka have impressive health indicators, even when they face adverse economic conditions. Similarly among the various Indian states Kerala has made remarkable achievements in the field of health status of its population measured in terms of life expectancy at birth, mortality, health transition and utilisation of health services (Kannan *et al.*, 1991; Gangadharan, 2008; Panikar PGK and Soman

C R, 1985; Navaneetham and Thankappan, 1999). Despite the political turmoil and ethnic war, Sri Lanka has impressive healthcare indicator among the south Asian countries.

But today both Sri Lanka and Kerala are facing new challenges in healthcare. Several policy makers have expressed serious doubts whether both the societies can sustain their achievements. Government's role is coming down and the out of pocket expense in healthcare is increasing in both the places. Adding to the woes, both Kerala and Sri Lanka are facing new epidemiological challenges

This paper is a descriptive and analytical study. Textual data regarding the health care performance of Kerala and Sri Lanka was obtained. Content analysis is used for data analysis.

HISTORICAL PERSPECTIVE

If we examine historically, Social and political interventions have played a crucial role in the better health care performance of Sri Lanka and Kerala. Influence of missionaries and progressive role played by the native rulers played a crucial role in the better health care performance of Kerala and Sri Lanka.

At the time of independence the present state of Kerala composed of two princely states of Travancore and Cochin as well Malabar district of the madras presidency. The rulers of the princely states had taken seriously the issues of health and education than the rulers of other princely states of British India. Just after 15 years of discovery of small poll vaccination, it was adapted in Travancore. Though Malabar region was laggard in healthcare indicator it was much better than other districts of Madras presidency.

Various governments along with missionaries played an important role in improving the education particularly women's education even from the beginning of twentieth century. Social reformers like Sree narayana Guru, Chattambi swami, Ayyan kali, Mohammed Abdul rahman and Moidu mouvalavi along with the rise of left movement paved the way for strong social churning in the Kerala's civil society which provided base for the future achievement in health and education. Missionaries also laid the strong foundation for education particularly of girls. The first primary health centre in India was established in south Kerala in late 1920's with the support of Rockfeller foundation.

Table 1: Select Healthcare and Social Indicators of Kerala *vs* India

Indicator	Kerala		India	
	1992–93	*2005–2006*	*1992–93*	*2005–2006*
Vaccination DPT (percentage of Children aged 12–23 months)	NA	84	46.9	55.3
School attendance (percentage of Children 6–10 years)	94.8	98.4	68.4	82.9
Literate persons (percentage of total population aged 15–49)	89.8	93.5	52.3	63.4
Under nutrition prevalence, Weight for age (percentage of Children under 5 years)	28.5	22.9	53.4	42.5
Total Fertility Rate (Births per Women)	2.0	1.9	3.4	2.7

Source: National Family Health survey Survey and Census data.

Following the independence also Kerala continued to maintain its good record in social and health indicators under the democratically elected governments when compared with other Indian states (Table 1)

Sri Lanka has a long experience of healthcare focused on the primary care. The first health unit in Asia was established at *Kalutara-Totamune*, Sri Lanka, in 1926, which soon became the training center for public health personnel for the expanding health units across the country. As the health unit program succeeded in controlling infectious diseases and reducing mortality rates in Sri Lanka, the Rockefeller Foundation introduced this program to other countries in South and Southeast Asia as part of its global campaign to promote health. The health unit program attracted renewed interest in the early 1980s, when the Rockefeller Foundation and the World Bank campaigned to promote *selective* primary health care as opposed to *comprehensive* primary health care advocated by the *Alma-Ata Declaration* of the World Health Organization (WHO). The Rockefeller Foundation cited the outstanding health achievements in Sri Lanka (and the State of Kerala in India) as examples of successful community-based primary care programs, which contributed to "good health at low cost." Following political independence in 1948, the health unit system became an integral part of the multi-pronged approach to health and development in the country. The *Kalutara*health unit was expanded, and the National Institute of Health Sciences was created in 1979, which today is the country's premier training center for public health personnel.

Selective primary health care model will be more cost effective in achieving better health indicators.

Table 2: Select Healthcare and Social Indicators of Sri Lanka

Indicators	1985	2008
Vaccination DPT (percentage of Children aged 12–23 months)	70	97
Primary School completion rate	83	98.4
Poverty gap at 2 dollars a day	16.1	11.9
Adult literacy rate	86.8	90.6
Under nutrition prevalence, Weight for age(percentage of Children under 5 years)	29.3	21.1
Total Fertility Rate(Births per Women)	2.92	2.33
Life expectancy at birth	69.0	74.1

Source: World Bank Documents.

WAR AND CONFLICT AS SOCIAL DETERMINANT OF HEALTH

Kerala is a state in India where conflicts are relatively less. With few exceptions of communal tensions like in Marad and Thalassey and occasional violence among political parties the state is relatively peaceful.

But Sri Lanka saw one of the toughest civil wars which had tremendous effect on the health care. Civil war rapidly progressed from a low intensity ethnic conflict involving multiple parties in multi-ethnic Sri Lanka during the 1980s to an intractable civil war between the Government of Sri Lanka (GOSL) and the Liberation Tigers of Tamil Eelam (LTTE) in the 1990s. By 2001 the war consumed over 50 percent of the annual budgetary allocations of the state, threatening to reverse Sri Lanka's widely acclaimed achievements in health and social welfare

Even though active armed conflict was largely restricted to parts of Northern and Eastern Provinces, ramifications of the ethnic conflict engulfed the whole of Sri Lanka. The countrywide ramifications included devastating suicide attacks by the Liberation Tigers of Tamil Eelam on southern civilian and military targets, army reprisals in the form of rampage on Tamil civilians, violent outbreaks of ethnic riots and an overall breakdown of the law and order situation. The 25 year war left more than 75,000 people killed, at least 20,000 people disabled, an unknown number of men, women and children traumatized, an economy, physical infrastructure and livelihoods in the war affected areas completely disrupted, over one million civilians displaced, and an exodus of Sri Lankan refugees to India, Europe and North America The health services in particular suffered due to shelling or military occupation of health facilities, displacement or flight of health human power, logistic difficulties as well as security concerns in delivery of urgent medical supplies to LTTE-controlled areas and war-induced pressure on available health facilities. The attack on the Jaffna Hospital by the Indian Peace Keeping Force (IPKF) in October 1987 killing an unknown number of hospital staff and patients was one of the worst episodes in the early phase of the war in Sri Lanka. As Tamil Tigers tended to take control of local hospitals for treating injured rebels at times of heavy fighting, hospitals themselves sometimes became military targets.

In spite of the war, the Sri Lankan Government maintained skeleton services inclusive of health facilities in all conflict-affected areas, including LTTE held territory. This was difficult due to staff turnover, restrictions imposed by armed forces and the LTTE on mobility of people and goods and war-related disruption of services. Clearly showing the pronounced legacy of Sri Lanka as a welfare state, the GOSL sought to maintain at least rudimentary health services in rebel held areas. These services however were grossly inadequate to meet the demand stemming from the war situation. In the LTTE held areas humanitarian agencies such as ICRC and MSF conducted mobile clinics to supplement the state-run health services. On the other hand, as large numbers of Tamil, Muslim and Sinhala civilians became displaced due to escalation of war, humanitarian assistance to the affected populations became a joint responsibility of GOSL, NGOs and inter-national donors. The Jaffna Rehabilitation Project and the Integrated Food Security Project implemented by GTZ demonstrated that some donors were willing to go beyond relief work in areas where security situation permitted rehabilitation work.

Following a peace initiative mediated by the Norwegian government, an MOU was signed between the GOSL and LTTE in February 2002, open hostilities ended and a series of peace talks between the government and LTTE was held between April 2002 to March 2003. This peace process, however, suffered a major setback when the LTTE withdrew from peace talks in April 2003, claiming that the government has failed to implement certain agreements already reached. In 2006 war was resumed in Eastern and later Northern parts of Sri Lanka. But with the killing of the LTTE leader velupillai Prabhakaran in May, 2009 the civil war came to an end. But the plight of the people particularly in the LTTE dominated areas still continues. The episode of Tsunami in December 2004 also had tremendous impact on Sri Lankan coast.

The outcomes of the war included destruction of health infrastructure, flight of health workers, and scarcity of medical supplies and massive displacement of people resulting in increase in the demand for emergency health care. As of 2001, over 50% of cadre positions were vacant in many categories of health workers. Many of the qualified health professionals moved out of the area and proceeded abroad in some instances during over two decades of war. Although many efforts have been made to fill the remaining vacancies in the Northeast since the ceasefire agreement, not many qualified health professionals have come forward due to continuing insecurity, instability of the peace process, lack of facilities including staff quarters, lack of opportunities for private practice (government doctors being permitted to do private practice after hours), lack of language skills to work in the Northeast among many of the health professionals from the South and a variety of other constraints. Even the doctors passing out of the Jaffna Medical School, the only medical school in North East until recent establishment of a medical school in Eastern University of Sri Lanka, want to secure postings outside the CAAs, due to limited career prospects and insecurity, including taxes imposed by the LTTE. In order to fill many vacant positions in preventive health services in the NEP, a crash programme to recruit and train Tamil speaking Family Health Workers has been initiated. A nationwide campaign to recruit the relevant category of workers did not succeed in 2003 due to lack of suitable applicants. Subsequently the government lowered entry requirement in view of the limited supply of potential applicants from the North-east. This resulted in better response but even in 2005 less than 50% of the vacancies in FHW cadres had been filled. This lowest category of preventive health workers is given a specialized training in addressing war-related health problems such as trauma. By 2004 WHO had initiated scheme whereby medical specialist from outside, including retired personnel, were posted in selected institutions in the North-east, under an attractive salary package offered to them. The specializations supported included psychiatry, surgery and ophthalmology with the demand for the relevant services increased in the postwar 'period. Many of the NGOs active in the North-east (e.g. Populations Services Lanka,) relied on trained health volunteers recruited from the local areas in their health education and service delivery programs. There was an incipient private health sector making inroads into the North-east, particularly in border towns such as Vavuniya, but private investments were limited and staff turnover was rapid due to the same factors that inhibited the government health services.

CURRENT HEALTH ISSUES IN KERALA AND SRI LANKA

Surprisingly the achievements which Kerala and Sri Lanka made in health care all these days have become the base of their current healthcare problems. The increased life expectancy has brought a shift in disease patterns from communicable diseases to life style diseases. Coronary artery diseases, Diabetes, neurological disorders are rising in both Sri Lanka and Kerala. Morbidity of diseases also increased in both the places.

Incidences of Emerging and Re-emerging infections are of serious concern in both Sri Lanka and Kerala. Last few years saw several episodes of Chikungunya, leptospirosis and Dengue fever in Kerala. Re- emergence of malaria in certain pockets of Kerala has been reported. In Sri Lanka the incidence of Dengue Hemorrhagic Fever (DHF) rose from 7.9 per 1,00,000 in 1990 to 28.4 in 2006 and the incidence in TB increased from 39.2 (per 1,00,000) in 1990 to 48.4 in 2006.

The societies of Kerala and Sri Lanka carries heavy burden of Mental Illness and Suicides. Kerala State mental health authority has reported incidence of mental disorders as high as 20 per 1,000 populations. According to W.H.O in Sri Lanka over four lakh people are reported to have mental illness per year particularly due to the trauma caused by civil war and Tsunami. Kerala (26.8per lakh) and Sri Lanka (23.9 per lakh) recorded highest rate of suicide in the world as per the records of National crimes record bureau of India and WHO report.

LESSONS FOR OTHER SAARC COUNTRIES

Kerala and Sri Lanka gives lessons which can be followed by other SAARC countries to improve their health indicators. These include:

1. Focus on social determinants of health like education, food safety.
2. "Good health" can be obtained at "low cost". There is a need to innovate the healthcare delivery models suiting the local requirements. Countries and states with limited economic resources, but with strong political commitment, can effectively address the most serious health problems, which creates sustainable economic growth contributing to low mortality and high life expectancy.
3. Develop manpower for health care. Also there is a need to focus on competency than mere qualifications.

CONCLUSION

Kerala and Sri Lanka has shown that better health care performance can be obtained at lower cost. But to sustain the achievement and to better it they need to develop next practices in Public health. Today health has become a purchasable commodity in Sri Lanka and Kerala with increased private sector participation and high out of pocket expenditure. But strong social interventions and public policy is the need of the hour in both Kerala and Sri Lanka. The lessons both positive and negative from these two societies will be of great relevance to other SAARC countries. Also Kerala and Sri Lanka needs to take lessons from other societies in the region. Particularly lessons from the state of Tamil Nadu of India will be of great help in improving the health care delivery. Kerala, Sri Lanka and other SAARC nations can take lessons from Bhutan which has conceived the idea of Gross National Happiness (GNH). The concept of GNH will reduce the suicidal tendencies and degradation of environment.

REFERENCES

[1] Balabanova, D., Mc Kee, M. and Mills, A. (eds). *'Good Health at low cost 25 years on. What makes a successful health system?* London School of Hygiene and Tropical Medicine, 2011.

[2] Good Health at Low Cost. Proceedings of the Bellagio Conference, Bellagio, Italy, The Rockefeller Foundation, 1985.

[3] Kannan, K.P., Thankappan, K.R., Ramankutty, V. and Aravindan, K.P., *Health and Development in Rural Kerala.* Kerala Sastra Sahitya Parishad, Trivandrum, 1991.

[4] Panikar P.G.K. and Soman, C.R., *Health Status of Kerala: The Paradox of Economic Backwardness and Health Development.* Centre for Development Studies, Trivandrum, 1985.

India-Sri Lanka Economic Cooperation and Trade Relations

Antaryami Beriha

ABSTRACT: This paper assesses economic and trade relations between India and Sri Lanka, which has strengthened more after the new economic policy adopted by India in 1991. Even though in 1977 Sri Lanka was first South Asian country to open its market or adopt the liberalisation policy but due to political tension between both countries the economic relations remained neglected. Therefore, this paper will examine initiatives taken by both the countries to strengthen the economies and trade relations since 1991. This has reinforced their respective economies as well as established economically South Asian Association for Regional Cooperation (SAARC) as a potent regional cooperation. At the same time this paper also highlights the initiative of SAARC taken to form the South Asian Preferential Trade Agreement (SAPTA) and later it also formulated the South Asian Free Trade Agreement (SAFTA) to improve the economic relations between the members of SAARC. It also examines the India-Sri Lanka Free Trade Agreement (ISLFTA) and highlights the Comprehensive Economic Partnership Agreement (CEPA), which has been paving the way for expansion of trade relations between both the countries. The implementation of the ISLFTA has been observed as well as incorporated the asymmetry between the two countries. Economic cooperation through the bilateral FTA, between a large South Asian economy and small economy has benefitted not just the large but also the smaller economy of Sri Lanka.

BACKGROUND

The legacy of relations between India and Sri Lanka began to change in the 1991s with the opening the market of both economies. Although, in 1977 Sri Lanka became the first South Asian country to liberalize its economy, opening it up to the rest of the world. However, partial liberalization of Indian economy during the 1980s and further liberalization in 1991, trade began to pick up particularly in favour of India. But from 1993 and 1996 there were two way trades. In 1995 India replace Japan as the largest source of imports to Sri Lanka accounting for 8–9 percent of total imports (Kelegama and Mukherji 2007).

Before proceed to the economic and trade relation of India and Sri Lanka, there is need to understand the objective of Sri Lanka to integrate with India. The main goal of Sri Lanka was to increase trade ties with most dominant economic power of South Asia particularly with India. The purposed of Sri Lanka was to induce the transformation of exports from low value added goods to high value added goods aimed at position in market. At the same time it also attract more export oriented Foreign Direct Investment (FDI) from third countries by promoting itself as an effective entry point into the Indian market.

However, this paper is constituted in the five sections; in the initial section of this paper try to analyse the economic relations of the India and Sri Lanka. In the second part of this paper it has discussed the trade relations of both countries and focus on the India-Sri Lanka Free Trade Agreement. In the third section of this paper basically focus about the Comprehensive Economic Partnership Agreement (CEPA) and in the fourth section of this paper focus on the India-Sri Lanka role to strengthen the South Asia Association for Regional Cooperation (SAARC) and finally there is the concluding remark.

ECONOMIC COOPERATION BETWEEN INDIA AND SRI LANKA

Economic linkages between India and Sri Lanka have a long history with recorded commercial links going back many centuries. After the independence the political and economic ties has weakened the relation of both countries. As both countries had initiated inward-looking economic policies. However, these ties once again started to strengthen, when Sri Lanka embarked on a liberalisation policy in 1977 that subsequently encompassed other South Asian countries including India. Economic links between the two once again started to strengthen. Moreover, there is important institutional mechanism, political factor, and strategic issue are responsible for strengthening the economic cooperation between both the countries, which is discuss below.

Institutional Mechanism for Trade and Economic Cooperation

Joint Commissions and Sub-Commission

The 1961 trade treaty an Indo-Sri Lanka joint committee on economic cooperation was set up in 1968 with the objective of increasing cooperation in trade industry, agriculture, and tourism. From 1977 till 1990 the joint committee was brought to life by upgrading the committee to a full-fledged joint commission headed by the foreign Minister which presently it has constitute three sub Commissions, one the trade investment and finance, the second on social, cultural and education matters and third on science and technology. However, the joint commission and sub Commission has set up for promote the economic relation between India and Sri Lanka.

Joint Business Council

The Memorandum of Understanding (MOU) between the Federation of Indian Chamber (JBC) of Commerce and Industry (FICCI) and the Federation of Chambers of Commerce and Industry of Sri Lanka (FCCISL) was signed in 1981. The main propose of JBC is to provide a forum for interaction between policy makers, business persons and association to interact and discuss both opportunities and progress of bilateral trade in the changing economic environments resulting from the FTA. The Sri Lankan government has identified some problems regarding the issue of rules of origin of FTA for products such as tea and vanaspati, heavy thrust on few products like copper, low value addition in certain products in Sri Lanka, imposition of discriminatory taxes by Tamil Nadu governments and unhelpful by the customs authorities and non recognition of bilateral standards. A detail presentation had been made by the Sri Lankan Board of Investment (BOI) on measures taken by the host country for attract foreign investment. On issue of investment has discussed by the Indian and Sri Lankan business men to attract more foreign investment in South Asia.

Economic and Technical Cooperation

Under the Indian Technical and Economic Cooperation (ITEC) programme, India is providing the technological assistance by Indian experts to provide or on the provision of training facilities to Sri Lankan nationals and supply of necessary equipment. The major courses under this scheme are financial managements, auditing and accounting, rural development, parliamentary studies, rural banking, insurance, plantation managements, teacher training, textile, engineering and railway. There is also a separate programme of cooperation of science and Technology. India has also assisted Sri Lanka through technology transfers including setting up of an automatic met data receiving station in Sri Lanka. Under the ITEC programme India has provided agricultural seed and equipment a microwave link project and animal husbandry project to Sri Lanka. From this number of Sri Lankan official received training in various fields in India every year. India has also signed bilateral agreement in the fields of science and technology with Sri Lanka.

Technological Transfers

Apart from joint-venture Indian companies have transferred technology to Sri Lanka through licensing and technological collaborations, export to turnkey project, capital goods and machinery consultancy service and management contracts. For instance on Indian company KCP Ltd constructed sugar factory in Sri Lanka on turnkey basis under an Asian Development Bank (ADB) project. Three Indian companies have been operating public sector textile mills in Sri Lanka under management contract, one of which viz pugoda textile mill has been finally converted into a joint venture after the transfer of ownership. Similarly Oberoi Hotel of India has the management contract of Hotel Lanka Oberoi in Colombo. Indian consultancy organisations have rendered consultancy services to Sri Lanka for improvement of railway system and have constructed oil-storage tanks on turnkey basis.

So this technical institutional mechanism helps India and Sri Lanka to strengthen the economic relation. These mechanisms help resolve the problems which are related to the bilateral trade. Since 1991 the economic relation between India and Sri Lanka has reached a new image. Since 1991 or after the end of cold war and the introduction of liberal economic reforms, India's policy has furthered economic engagement with the South Asian countries and rest of the world.

Political Factors of Motivating for Economic Cooperation

India and Sri Lanka trade was vulnerable before 1998; and some of the weaknesses[1] had impeded the progress of the joint commission since 1968. There had been fears for Sri Lanka that the more liberalized trade with India would lead to the Indian products flooding Sri Lankan market which hamper the Sri Lankan domestic industry. So that Sri Lankan government was apprehensive to sign the bilateral agreement with India. And at the same time, after the end of cold war Sri Lanka was more concentred on the western countries during the J.R. Jayawardane presidency. Before cold war India's market was not open but after 1991 and its economic opening up. She was more concentrate on the South East Asian countries through its 'Look East Policy'. However, the East Asian Crisis of 1997–98, gave a lesson to India to develop its trade relation with South Asian countries also.

The constructive relations between India and Sri Lanka improved signi-ficantly after Narasimaha Rao became the Prime Minister. Subsequently, Prime Minister Gujral, Vajpayee continued the positive relation between two countries. Another reason was the departure of the Indian peace keeping Force that was followed by an extraordinary level of activity within the joint Commission.

The removal of the security irritant was accompanied by India's pursuit to increase its trade. The U.S trade sanctions in the aftermath of the Indian nuclear test and the Asian financial crisis increased India's resolve to have a successful sub-regional trade agreement with Sri Lanka. India was willing to grant more than reciprocal concessions to Sri Lanka.[2] Sri Lanka also had reasons like, India large market and potential benefits from the Indian market. The success of India's economic liberalization program had already India overtaking Japan as Sri Lanka's leading source of imports in 1996. India supplied 10.4 percent of Sri Lanka imports compared with 9.2 percent coming from Japan. In 1997 out of a total trade of US $ 560 million Sri Lanka exports to India were US$ 42.7 million. Sri Lanka exports to India as share of its exports declined from 1.1 percent in 1990 to 1.0 percent in 1996 (Mukherji 2000).

Strategic Issues for India-Sri Lanka Economic Cooperation

The emerging geo-political reality relating to the sharing of water on the Indian Ocean neighbours involving India and Sri Lanka is major strategic and political concern for both countries. The Chinese presence in the Indian Ocean has helped to develop the better relation between India and Sri Lanka. On the other hand global attention on securing the energy sea-lanes from the oil-rich Gulf region to the rest of the world has created greater awareness about the need for both the countries to work together.

There is frequently concern of the Indian side on the involvement of China in Sri Lanka. China made to the setting up ports in Sri Lanka and Beijing has funded a coal-fired thermal power project in western part of Sri Lanka. Chinese funds are growing enormously in Sri Lanka. However, the Chinese centric concern in certain sections of Indian strategic is thinking real for both the countries. Hence the existing mechanism of the two countries have evolved measures to ensure consultation mechanisms and information sharing processes that are required for better relations and management of the further problems.

Apart from the political forces and strategic issues that have helped to promoted trade relations between Sri Lanka and India. Trade liberalization of India and Sri Lanka in 1991 was another facilitating factor for the development of trade agreement or trade relations between two countries.

TRADE RELATIONS BETWEEN INDIA AND SRI LANKA

The trade relation between India and Sri Lanka has been improving since 1991 when India fully liberalized their economy. Before 1991, both the countries (India and Sri Lanka) were more concentred on the western countries, its means both the countries were deepened on the European countries to promote their economy. But the time was changed, when South Asia Preferential Trading Agreement (SAPTA) was formulated in 1993 by the member of South Asia region. But the SAPTA was suspended from 1999 onwards, as the political situation between India and Pakistan became tense. South Asia Free Trade Agreement (SAFTA) was announced only in 2004 and implemented in 2006.

In the period in between there emerged bilateral Free Trade Agreement (FTA) in South Asia. For instance India-Sri Lanka bilateral FTA in 2000. The bilateral FTAs have provided more trade integration between both countries and has led the member countries to liberalise their own economy. The intra regional trade of South Asian countries as a share of total trade even after SAFTA was implemented in 2006 has remained low, but the bilateral trade between member countries has increased.

India-Sri Lanka FTA was signed in December 1998 and came into operation in March 2000. The FTA marked an important milestone in India Sri Lanka relations. It concretized and paved the way for closer economic integration between the two South Asian countries. The SAPTA agreement was signed in 1995, and was only based on the 'positive list' but ISLFTA was formulated on the 'negative list' approach where each country extends preference concessions to all commodities except those indicated in its negative list. The ISLFTA follows the trade liberalization rule set by the (WTO). It has been considered as a relatively strong agreement with substantial product coverage, (about 80 percent of tariff lines coming under the product classification code at 6 digit level), significant tariff cuts, and simple rules of origin. From India's point of view the agreement countered its isolation in international arena from the economic sanctions as in 1998; India had lunched her second nuclear test. On the other hand from the Sri Lankan perspective there were political and economic objectives such as reducing prevailing political tensions between two countries and increase the benefit of economic liberalisation (Kelegama and Mukherji 2007).

Sri Lanka's Trade with India

After the implementation of the India-Sri Lanka FTA there was a significant improvement in trade relation between the two economies. India and Sri

Lanka shared a vibrant and growing economic and commercial partnership, with bilateral trade growing rapidly in the last decade. By the year 2007, Sri Lanka's export to India was only US$ 515 million that is 6.6 percent of total exports of Sri Lanka to India. But it changed in 2009 because of the global financial crisis. By 2010, Sri Lanka's exports to India stood at US$ 471.23 million compared to US$ 333.54 million in corresponding period in 2009, and registered a growth of about 30%. The bilateral trade in the first eleven months (Jan.–November) of 2011 amounted to US$ 4.46 billion, which is 71.94 percent higher than the corresponding year of 2009.[3] Over the ten years following the FTA, bilateral trade multiplied nearly five-fold. Bilateral trade in 2010 reached US$ 3.04 billion, which was US$ 2.07 billion in 2009. Significantly, the rate of growth of exports has increased rapidly than the imports (De Mel 2008).

By year 2006, about 96 percent of Sri Lankan exports to India came under zero duty list of the ISLFTA and Sri Lanka's exports to India consisted of 94 products. The ISLFTA played an important role in enhancing the exports of Sri Lanka four times from the previous amount. The preferential exports under the FTA were not for direct final consumption but were intermediate products which are required by the Indian industries. The main Sri Lankan exports to India are metal products, electronic products, general machinery and electrical products, paper and paper products, pepper, chemical and plastic products, food, beverages and tobacco, wooden products, cloves and woven fabrics. The most important products which contributed to exports growth include copper ingots, wire bars and billets, tyres, furniture and Dual Inline Memory Modules (DIMMs). Export of these items to India rapidly increased from 2002. The FTA, thus, greatly enhanced trade between two countries, and specially beneficial for Sri Lanka. The trade creation is visible from the number of products entering into the Indian market from Sri Lanka through ISLFTA.

Imports of Sri Lanka from India

Sri Lanka became the main importer goods from India after implementation of the FTA. India's export to Sri Lanka stood at about 13.81 percent of total imports of Sri Lanka from India in 2002, which amounted to US$ 835 million. By the year 2007, it had reached US$ 2750 million of imports of Sri Lanka from India, which was 24.43 percent of total imports. By the year 2010, the import of Sri Lanka from India reached US$ 2571 million. During 2007–08, the amount of imports was high, but after the global financial crisis, Sri Lanka was more focused on the exports to India and other South Asian countries.

Provision of Quota for Readymade Garment and Tea

Under the ISLFTA, Sri Lanka had limited amount of tea exports to India. India allowed import of 15 million kilogram of tea per annum and 8 million pieces of garments from Sri Lanka. However, the utilization of quota for tea and readymade garments remained at a miserable level of below 5 percent of the quota. Therefore, exports of these items under the ILSFTA increased only marginally in 2001, and it reduced in 2002.

Especially the exports of tea reduce because the two main ports of India, Kolkata and Cochin have not been supportive of tea exports entering the Indian market. And also because these two ports are located in tea growing areas. But garments have been accessed through Mumbai, Chennai, and Kolkata. The Sri Lankan government was unable to fill the quota allocations for tea and garments under the ISLFTA. The main reason was because Sri Lanka was not able to compete with developed countries in Indian market in textile exports as the developed countries had position to exports their products to the Indian market.[4] So, Sri Lanka failed, as a result of rigid competition in its traditional garment markets. Furthermore, it required Sri Lanka to negotiate with India's policy makers to remove non-tariff barriers and also increase exports of value added tea to Indian market.

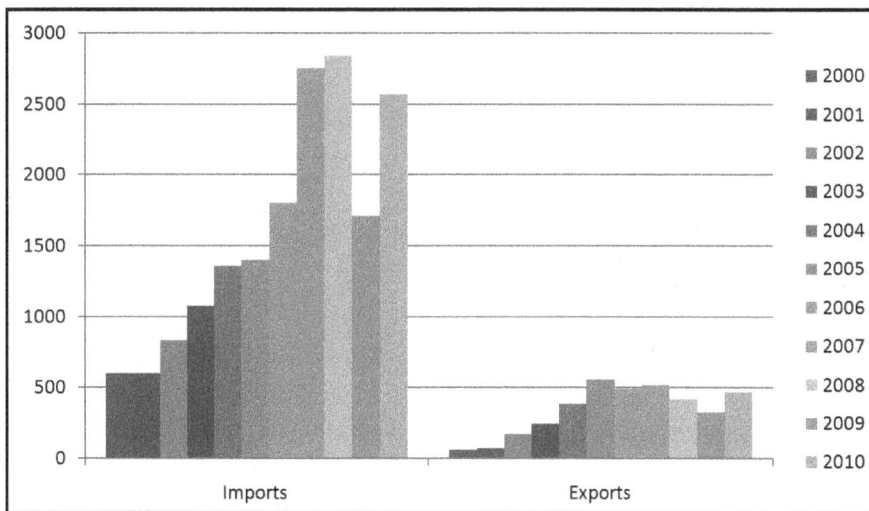

Fig. 1: Sri Lanka Exports and Imports to India (amount in US$ Million)

Source: Sri Lankan Custowww.customs.gov.lk. ms.

The imports pattern of Sri Lanka shows that the Indian imports rapidly increased in the years since the FTA came into effect. The major imports of Sri Lanka from India are agricultural products, textiles, transports goods, machinery, and base metals. The new products entered as a result of the FTA.

India's Trade with Sri Lanka

Since the ISLFTA there has been a drastic change in the trade pattern of both countries. India's exports to Sri Lanka rose from US$ 641 million in 2000–01 to US$ 2827 million in 2007–08. And by the year 2010, the amount of exports has reached to US$ 2170.35 million. Thus, the total trade between the two economies more than quadrupled from 2000–01 to 2007–08. The major products exported by India to Sri Lanka were petroleum and petroleum products, pharmaceutical products, two wheelers vehicles, woven cotton products, vegetables including onion etc.

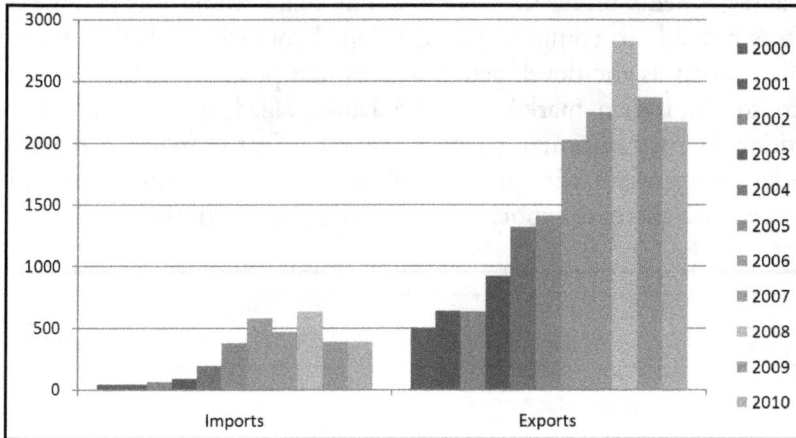

Fig. 2: India's Trade with Sri Lanka (amount in US$ Million)

Source: India Trades, CMIE cited (Nags 2011)

India Imports from Sri Lanka

India's imports from Sri Lanka were marginal, it was US$ 45 million in 2000–01 and it rose to the US$ 631 million in 2007–08. By the end of 2010, the total amount of imports of India rose to the US$ 390 million. After the year 2007, the imports of India decreased. The main reason was the financial crisis and the problem of quota utilization on tea and garments. Thus, the total trade taking place between the two economies increased more than four times during 2000 to 2008. However, India's import growth of 27 percent was much higher than exports growth 14.5 percent in 2000, on Compounded Annual Growth Rate (CAGR)[5] (Nag 2011). By 2006–07, India achieved a share of 17.33 percent from Sri Lanka imports and became the largest importer.

The main products in India's import basket are rubber products, spices (cloves, papper etc.), animal feed, refrigerating equipment, electric wires etc. Imports of copper products like wire increased after the implementation of FTA. Refined copper (H.S heading 7403) and wire and cables of copper (H.S. heading 7413) accounted for 16 percent of total copper imports from Sri Lanka in 2008. But the copper imports from Sri Lanka slowed down in the next two years. Another product that witnessed a big surge in India's import was edible oils. In 2007, 26 percent of total imports were that of the animal/vegetable fats and oil (H.S. 1516) but this decreased to 16 percent in 2009. Thus, the export of vegetable oil and copper products from Sri Lanka have come down in recent time and the new products such as refrigerating machineries, tugs and pusher craft, glass product have taken higher share in 2009–10.

Investment

Indian investment into Sri Lanka has increased substantially because Sri Lanka served as a production and profit centre for Indian companies for seeking access to regional and global markets. Sri Lanka has long been a priority destination for direct investment from India. Over 60 percent of Indian joint ventures and wholly owned subsidiaries in the South Asian region are located in Sri Lanka. By the year 1998, Indian investment was Rs 165 million and it had increased to US$ 125.925 million[6] by the year 2008. The total investment of India by the year 2010 was US$ 600 million. The principle sector of investment were petroleum, retail, steel, cement, rubber products, tourism, computer software, IT training, textile and garments, food products, automobiles components, plaits products, construction, chemicals, electricity equipment, printing, shipping, financial and non financial services. India was the top investor in Sri Lanka by the year 2010. Out of total FDI of US$ 516.30 million, India's investment share stood at US$ 110.24 million, constituting about 21 percent of the total investment. The well-known Indian companies such as IOC, Tatas, Bharthi Airtel, Piramal Glass, LIC, Ashok Layland, L&T, and Taj Hotel are present in Sri Lanka.

From the last six or seven years, the leading Indian companies such as Gujrat Ambuja, Indian oil, Apollo Hospitals, Asian Paints, Larsen and Toubro, CEAT tyers, Taj Hotels, Mudra Communications, National Diary Development Board, Ashok Layland, Exide Inductries, Tata Tea, Cadile pharmaceuticals, Ansal Housing, Arvind Mill etc., have made much investments in Sri Lanka. Furthermore, the operation of ISLFTA has forced Indian companies to set up their ventures in Sri Lanka with a view to buy

back the duty free Indian market mainly in South India. So such investments encouraged the entry of Sri Lankan made products to the Indian
market. Such products included copper, vanaspathi, and marble industries.

Table 1: Top Ten Investor in Sri Lanka 2000–2003

2000		2001		2001		2003	
Country	*$Mn*	*Country*	*$mn*	*Country*	*$mn*	*Country*	*$mn*
Singapore	273	UK	290	UK	329	UK	354
UK	260	Singapore	253	Singapore	237	Singapore	283
Japan	244	Japan	209	Japan	204	Japan	205
Korea	190	Korea	165	Hong Kong	137	Hong Kong	193
Sweden	99	Australia	107	Australia	140	Korea	155
Australia	96	Sweden	83	USA	113	USA	135
Br. Virgin Is	55	USA	63	India	89	India	115
Netherland	52	India	53	Sweden	48	Netherland	68
Finland	52	Finland	45	Netherland	43	Sweden	53

Source: Board of Investment of Sri Lanka cited by (Kelegama and Mukherji 2007).

Table 1 shows the major investor that invested in Sri Lanka during 2000–
03. But, much of the investment that came into Sri Lanka was associated
with products such as vanaspati and copper industry. Taking advantage of
the FTA, third party got an opportunity to break into Indian market in Sri
Lanka (kelegama 2009). Therefore, 40 Indian manufacturing projects are
currently operating in the Sri Lankan market and it was only made
possible by the ISLFTA. Sri Lankan investment in India was small before
implementation of FTA. For the last few years there was increase in

Table 2: Manufacturing Project in Sri Lanka under ISLFTA

Products	*Country*	*No. In Operation*
Copper and Copper based Products	India/USE	10
Vanaspati	Singapore/Malaysia	9
Electricity and electronic Products	India/USA	7
Lead and Lead based products	India	2
Zinc Oxide	India	1
other Chemical and chemical based products	India/Sri Lanka/USA	3
Marbal Products	India	3
Pine resins	India	2
Rubber-Base milk Cream	India	1
Ghee from milk cream	India	1
Diamond cutting tips	India	1

Source: Board of Investment (BOI) Sri Lanka Cited by (Kelegama and Mukherji 2007).

Sri Lankan investment into India. For instance, Ceylon Biscuit (Munchee brand), Carsons, Cumber batch (Caresherg), Brandix (about US$ 1 billion to set up a garment city in Vishakhapatnam in south India), MAS holding John keels, Hayleys and Aitken Spance (Hotel) apart from other investment in the freight servicing and logistic sector.

Services

Unilateral services liberalization was adopted by Sri Lanka and India in 1977 and 1991 respectively, and Sri Lanka has gained much from this initiatives. Sri Lanka has opened FDI in various service sectors for India especially retailing sector, even though it is a sensitive area that neither India nor Sri Lanka liberalized under General Agreement of Trade in Service (GATS) during the Uruguay Round of WTO talks. Moreover, the service sector provides a positive component for the two countries mainly through franchise arrangements. Such franchise led retail services are Titan, Usha, Godrej, Bajaj, etc., from India. Initially, FDI from Sri Lanka was not allow in the Indian market because the Exports Development Board of Sri Lanka (EDB) with Reserve Bank of India (RBI) made way for Sri Lankan firms to engage in exhibition-cum retail sale.

The commercial service exchange between the two countries has increased. The largest number of tourist arrivals to Sri Lanka is from India. This was largely due to Sri Lanka's unilateral measure of issue of visa upon arrival of Indian citizens. Also, many Sri Lankan students and patients travel to India to purchase education and health services. Each year, approximately 70 percent of the Colombo ports income is from transhipment earning from India. Approximately 40 percent of the Sri Lankan airlines revenue is from Indian market. Indian airliners such as Jet wing, Sahara Airlines and Kingfisher have operations in Sri Lanka. Sri Lankan information technology firms have provided technical solutions to Indian companies.

Sri Lanka is looking very closely into improving its professional service sector. The country is currently experiencing a shortage of English teachers, nurses in hospitals in the North and East and professional in geriatric care. Under the Comprehensive Economic partnership Agreement (CEPA) India has been given preference to provide these services. This agreement was planned between the professional body of Sri Lanka Medical Council and the Indian Medical Council for the inflows of nurses. In case of educational sector, there is also mutual recognition between the Sri Lanka University Grants commission and Indian University Grants Commission to fulfil the scarcities in Sri Lanka.

Table 3: Indian Service Suppliers in Sri Lanka

Sector	Service Suppliers
Health	Apollo Hospital, Escorts heath centre at Durban Hospital
Hotels and Restaurants	Taj Hotels, Barista, (fast food/coffee outlet, Amaravathi (restaurant)
Air Travel	Jet Airways, Air Sahara and Kingfisher
Retailing and Distribution	Indian oil company/Titan Watches, Usha (Electrical appliances, Godrej (consumer durables), Bajaj (Three wheelers/ scooter)

Source: Kelegama and Mukherji 2007.

COMPREHENSIVE ECONOMIC PARTNERSHIP AGREEMENT (CEPA) NEGOTIATION AND TRADE

After the successful of the India and Sri Lanka FTA, both countries want continue to improve their economic and trade relation. However, both the countries engaged themselves in the negotiation on the CEPA, which include trade, investment, and technology transfer etc. The CEPA negotiation was initiated in 2005 and concluded in 2008.

One of the major objective of CEPA negotiation is to reduced the negative list of both countries so that India and Sri Lanka access their market in more efficient way. Under the India-Sri Lanka FTA Sri Lanka had a larger negative lists (1180 tariff line) than India 429 tariff line. However, the negotiation of CEPA encourage to India to reduce its negative list by another 114 items while Sri Lanka would be reducing 32 items (Nag 2011). In the services sector also a number of unresolved disuses need to be addressed. It is by resolving these issues that the movement towards CEPA could be put on fast track to make it a reality in 2008. CEPA has the potential to break new ground in South Asia's forward movement towards economic prosperity. However, India-Sri Lanka trade in service agreement under the CEPA is expected to remove certain barriers. In this agreement India has provided flexibility especially to Sri Lanka for the development priority.

After the operation of the FTA, the Indian investment in Sri Lanka has been increased rapidly. The main reason behind the increase of investment is re-exports to India while benefiting from lower tariffs on raw materials in Sri Lanka. The most visible Indian investment in Sri Lanka is Lanka Indian oil Corporation, TATAs (Taj Hotels), Bharti Airtels etc. The FTA dealt on the goods sector and perhaps the CEPA can address the issue related to investment in much better way.

INDIA-SRI LANKA ECONOMIC AND TRADE RELATION TO STRENGTHEN THE SAARC

India-Sri Lanka economic and trade cooperation has been strengthening the South Asia region since 1991, even though the SAARC regional organisation was formulated by the years 1985. Since 1985 there has been lots of tension between the member countries of this region. The two major economic power India and Pakistan had always engaged on the political tension which impacts the economic development of the region. Apart of the two major actors, there was also the political tension between India and Sri Lanka' but both the countries has been more concerned on their economic development than the political issue.

From 1998, the economic and trade relations between India and Sri Lanka has been more strengthened. India-Sri Lanka FTA is one of the most effective and successful FTA in the South Asia. The FTA which has been playing important role to economically integrated the South Asia region. The trade development between India and Sri Lanka has been reflected from the FTA, which has provided more stable economic development between both the economy and same time for South Asia region.

So far the South Asia is concerned the economic relations of India and Sri Lanka are more consistences and it is visibly contributed in the intra regional trade of the region. But the trade amount between India and Pakistan is still low, although they are the large economy in the South Asia region. The main reason behind the low trade of both the countries are more concerned for their political conflict than the economic development which is impacted on the SAARC economic progress. But in the case of India and Sri Lanka it has not found to see because both the countries are more determined for the economic improvement and they economically more contribute to the South Asia region than the other countries.

CONCLUSION

So all the above discussion has reflected that the economic relations between larger and small economy will benefit not only the large country but also small country. And it has found in the case of India and Sri Lanka economic cooperation and trade relations. The second most finding in my research, both the countries are forgot their past political conflict and more determine to strengthen their economic. On the other hand the operation of FTA helps both the countries to accelerate their trade relations. As well as FTA is the trade creation and it's reflected the large number of new products of Sri Lanka has been entering into the Indian market. However, the amount of trade has been increasing rapidly between two countries, which have contributed efficiently to the intra region trade of the South Asia. Therefore, it is necessary for all the South Asian countries to actively participate in the regional development by integrated their respective economy with the member of the region, through which the economic situation will be more strengthened.

REFERENCES

[1] Adhikari, Ratnakar and Paras Kharel (2010). "Bilateral Trade Agreements In south Asia" *Trade Inslight*, 6 (2):14–19.

[2] Adihikari, Ratnakar (2009). "Intra-Regional Free Trade Agreements Implication for Regional Trade Integration in South Asia" Briefing Paper No. 9.

[3] Aggarwal, K. Vinod and Mukherji, Rahul (2007). "India's Shifting Trade policy South Asia and Beyond" www. basc.berkeley.edu.

[4] Athukorala, P. and Kelegama, Saman (1998). "The political economy of agricultural trade policy: Sri Lanka in the Uruguay Round", *Contemporary South Asia*, Vol. 7(1).

[5] Bandara, S. Jayatilleke and Yu, Wusheng (2001). "How Desirable is the South Asia Free Trade Area—A Quantitative Economic Assessment," *SJFI working Paper No. 16*.

[6] Batra, Amita (2005). "India-Country Perspectives" *South Asia Free Trade Area Opportunities and Challenges*, United States Agency and International Development, USAID.

[7] Batra, Amita (2007). "South Asia's FTA Strategies and Options," *Economic and Political Weekly*, Vol. XLII (38): P 3878–85.

[8] Baysan, T., Panagariya, A. and Pitigala, N. (2006). "Preferential Trading in South Asia", policy Research Working paper Series, No. 3813, Washington, DC: World Bank.

[9] Bhagwati, Jagdish (2002). *Free Trade Today*, London: Princeton University Press.

[10] Bhatta D. Chandra (2007). "Regional Integration and Peace in South Asia: An analysis", www.peacestudiesjournal.org.uk.

[11] Chowdhury, Mamta (2005). "Trade Reform and Economic Integration in South Asia: SAARC and SAPTA" *Applied Econometrics and International Development*, 5(4):23–39.

[12] Dash, Kishor C. (1996). "The Political Economy of Regional Cooperation in South Asia" *Pacific Affairs*, 69(2): 185–209.

[13] Gonsalves, Eric (2006). "Regional Cooperation in South Asia" *South Asian Survey*, 13(2): 203–209.

[14] Hrilal, K.N. and Joseph, K.J. (1999). "India-Sri Lanka Free Trade Accord" *Economic and political weekly*, 34 (13): 750–753.

[15] Jayaratne, Chandra (2007). "Regional Cooperation in South Asia: Sri Lankan Perspective" www. siteresources.worldbank.org

[16] Jayawardena, L.L. Ali and Hulugalle, L. (1993). 'Indo-Sri Lanka Economic Cooperation: Facilitating Trade Expansion through a Reciprocal preference Scheme', *Study Group Series No. 9 UNU/WIDER*. www.wider.unu.edu

[17] Joshi, Vivek (2010). "An Econometric Analysis of Indo-Sri Lanka Free Trade Agreement" *HEID* Working Paper No. 04. www.ideas.repec.org

[18] JSG (2003). "India-Sri Lanka Comprehensive Economic partnership Cooperation: Facilitating Trade Expansion through a Reciprocal Preferential and Impact", SANEI completed study, www.saneinetwork.net.

[19] Kelegama, Saman (1998). Indo-Sri Lanka Economic Relation: Trends and Outlook' in L.B. Associates (eds) *Sri Lanka 50 years: In Commemoration of the 50th Anniversary of Independence of Sri Lanka.*

[20] Kelegama, Saman (1999). "Indo-Sri Lanka Trade and the Bilateral Free Trade Agreement: A Sri Lankan perspective", *Asia-Pacific Development Journal*, 6(2).

[21] Kelegama, Saman (2001). "Impediments to Regional Economic Cooperation in South Asia", *Institute of Policy Studies of Sri Lanka.* www.fessrilanka.org

[22] Kelegama, Saman (2001). "Indo-Sri Lanka Bilateral Free Trade Agreement: Progress of Sri Lankan Exports in the year 2000", *Sri Lanka Exports*, Vol. 34.

[23] Kelegama, Saman (2003). "Sri Lanka Exports to India: Impact of Free Trade Agreement", *Economic and political Weekly*, 38 (30): 3153–3154.

[24] Kelegama, Saman (2006). "The Bilateral Track: The Case of the India-Sri Lanka Free Trade Agreement", *South Asian survey*, 13(2): 295–301.

[25] Kelegama, Saman (2007). "Towards Greater Economic Connectivity in South Asia" *Economic and Political Weekly*, 42 (39): 3911–15.

[26] Kelegama, Saman (2009). "India-Sri Lanka Bilateral FTA: Sri Lanka perspective on Emerging Issues", Bangkok: IDEAS, GSEI and ITD,

[27] Kelegama, Saman and Adhikari, Ratnakar (2007). "Repositioning SAFTA in the Regionalism Debate", In Anjum Siddiqui (eds.) *India and South Asia: Economic Developments in the Age of Globalization*, New York: M.E. Share Aromonk.

[28] Kelegama, Saman and Mukherji, I.N. (2007). "India-Sri Lanka Bilateral Free Trade Agreement: Six Years performance and Beyond", RIS Discussion paper No. 119, RIS New Delhi. www.eaber.org

[29] Mel De, Deshal (2008). "India-Sri Lanka, Pakistan-Sri Lanka Bilateral Free Trade Agreements" *Institute of Policy Studies of Sri Lanka.* www.ips.lk/saes

[30] Mel De, Deshal (2008). "India-Sri Lanka: Comprehensive Economic Partnership Agreement" *World Trade Net Business Briefing.*

[31] Mel De, Deshal (2008). "Indo-Sri Lanka Comprehensive Partnership Agreements", World Trade Net Business Briefing. [Online Web] URL: http:// www.economics webinstitute.org/essays/capaindiassrilanka.pdf.

[32] Mel De, Deshal (2008). "Indo-Sri Lanka Free Trade Agreements: Sri Lanka Perspectives", *Trade Insight*, 4 (2):11–13.

[33] Mel De, Deshal (2009). "Indo-Sri Lanka Trade Agreements: Performance and Prospects" in *Economic Review, International Trade and Some issue of Sri Lanka*, 35(6):23–28.

[34] Mel De, Deshal (2009). "The Role of Stakeholder in the Formulation of Inclusive Trade Policies: What Went Wrong the Indo-Lanka CEPA Negotiation" *Designed by Inclusive Trade* Policy Research paper No. 5. www.unescap.org

[35] Mel De, Deshal (2009). Bilateral Free Trade Agreements in SAARC and Implication for SAFTA, www.siteresources.worldbank.org

[36] Moorthy, N. Sathiya (2011). "India and Sri Lanka Continuing Inning, Construction Engagement", *Institute of Peace and conflict studies*, No. 140. www.ipcs.org

[37] Mukherji, I.N (2000). "Indo-Sri Lanka Trade and Investment Linkages: With Special Referencce to Sapta and Free Trade Agreement", *South Asia Economic Journal*, 1(53): 53–77.

[38] Mukherji, I.N. (1996). *South Asia Preferential Trading Arrangment: Assessing Trade Flows in the First Round of Trade Negotiation* 'New Delhi: Frieddrich Naumann Stiftung.

[39] Mukherji, I.N. (1998). "The South Asian Preferential Trading Arrangment: Identifying products in India's Regional Trade" *Asia-pacific Development Journal*, 5(1).

[40] Mukherji, I.N. (2000). "Charting a Free Trade Area in South Asia: Instruments and Modalities", paper presented at the Second Conference of the South Asia Network of Economic Research Institutes (SANEI), Kathmandu, August 26–29. www.uoit.ca

[41] Mukherji, I.N., Jayawardena, T. and Kelegama, Saman (2002). "India-Sri Lanka Free Trade Agreement: An Assessment of Potential and impact", *SANEI completed study*, www.saneinetwork.net.

[42] Nag, Biswajit (2011). "Comprehensive Economic Partnership Agreements between India and Sri Lanka: Where Does it Lead?", *Indian Institute of Foreign Trade*, Working Paper No EC–11–03.

[43] Orland, Brian (2008). "India's Sri Lanka Policy Toward Economic Engagement", Institute of Peace and Conflict Studies, No. 16, New Delhi, www.ipcs.org.

[44] Panchamukhi, V.R., Rao, V.L. and Kumar, N. (1993). "Indo-Sri Lanka Economic Cooperation: An Operational Programme, Research, and Information system for the Non-Aligned and other Developing Countries", New Delhi.

[45] Perere, M.S.S. (2008). "Impact of the Indo-Sri Lanka Free Trade Agreement on the Sri Lankan Economy: A Computable General Equilibrium analysis", *South Asia Economic Journal*, 9 (1): 1–50.

[46] RIS (2004). *South Asia Development and cooperation Report 2004*, RIS, New Delhi, India.

[47] Sarvananthan, Muttukrishan (2000). "Indo-Sri Lanka Free Trade: Hype and Reality" *Economic and political weekly*, 35(14): 1157–1158.

[48] Schiff, Maurice and Alan, Winters L. (1998). "Regional Integration as Diplomacy", *The world Bank Economic Review*, 12 (2): 271–293.

[49] Sikdar, Chandrima (2010). "India-Sri Lanka Bilateral Trade: A General Equilibrium Approach", *South Asia Economic Journal*, 11(2): 155–180.

[50] Sikdar, Chandrima and Debesh, Chakraborty (2011). "The Factor Content of Bilateral Trade between India and Sri Lanka", *XIX International Input-output Conference in Alexandria, USA*, www.iioa.org.

[51] Siriwardana, Mahindra (2000). Effects of Trade Liberalization in South Asia with Special Reference to Sri Lanka, *Paper presented at the third Annual Conference on Global Economic Analysis Monash University*, Melbourne Australia-2351. www.monash.edu.au

[52] Siriwardena, Mahinda (2004). "An Analysis of the Impact of Indo-Lanka Free Trade Agreement and its Implication for Free Trade in South Asia" *Journal of Economic Integration*, 19(3): 568–589.

[53] Srinivasan, T.N. (1994). "Regional Trading Arrangements and Beyond: Exploring Some Options for South Asia Theory, Emperies and policy." Report No. 142, World Bank Washington, DC. www.unige.ch.

[54] Suhail, P. and Sreejesh, S. (2011). "The Bilateral Trade Agreements and Export Performance of South Asian Nation s with Special Reference to India-Sri Lanka Free Trade Agreement", *The Romanian Economic Journal*, N–4.

[55] Taneja, N., Mukherji, A., Jayanetti, S. and Jayawardena, T. (2001). "Indo-Sri Lanka Trade Services: FTA II and Beyond", *SANEI completed study available at* www.saneinetwork.net.

[56] Taneja, Nisha; Muttukrishan, Sarvananthan and Sanjib, Pohit (2003). "India-Sri Lanka Trade Transacting Environments in Formal and Informal Tradeing", *Economic and Political weekly*, 38 (29): 3094–98.

[57] Thenuwara, H.N. (2005). "Beyond Indo-Sri Lanka Free Trade: Comprehensive Economic Partnership Agreement with India", *24th anniversary lecture of the centre for Banking Studies, Central Bank of Sri Lanka*, December 2005.

[58] Upadhyay, S.S. (2007). *India & Sri Lanka Economic, and political Relations*, Jaipur: ABD Publishers.

[59] Weerakoon, Dushni (2001). "Indo-Sri Lanka Free Trade Agreement: How Free Is It?" *Economicc and political Weekly*, 36(8): 627–29.

[60] Weerakoon, Dushni and Jayanthi, Thennakoon (2008). "India-Sri Lanka FTA: Lessons for SAFTA", *Commonwealth Seccretariat*, www.thecommonwealth.org.

[61] Weerakoon, Dushni and Jayanthi, Thennakoon (2008). "The South Asian Free Trade Agreement: Which Way Forward?", *Journal of South Asian Development*, 3 (1): 135–49.

[62] Weerakoon, Dushni and Wijayasiri Janaka (2002). "Regionalism In South Asia: The Relevance of SAPTA for Sri Lanka" *South Asia Economic Journal* 3 (1): 95–106.

[63] Weerakoon, Dushni and Wijayasiri, J. (2001). "Regional Economic Cooperation in South Asia: A Sri Lankan Perspective", *International Economic Series, No. 6*, Colombo: Institute of Policy Studies,

[64] Weerakoon, Dushni and Wijayasiri, J. (2001). "South Asian Regionalism: Sri Lanka Perspecctive", Institute of Policy Study of Sri Lanka. www.ips.lk

[65] Weerakoon, Dushni and Wijayasiri, Janaka (2002). "Regionalism in South Asia: The Relevance of SAPTA for Sri Lanka", *South Asia Economic Journal*, 3(1): 95–106.

[66] Wickremasinghe, Mineka (2006). "The FTA/CEPA" paper presented to the 9th meeting of the Sri Lanka-India joint Bussiness Council, Jointly organized by the FCCISL and FICCI, Taj Samudra Hotel, Colombo, 3–4 November (Mimeno).

[67] Witharana, Dileepa (2010). "An Act of Faith? Ten Years of The India-Sri Lanka Free Trade Agreement" Law and Society Trust Sri Lanka, www.lawandsocietytrust.org

[68] Yatawara, Ravindra A. (2007). "Exploiting Sri Lanka's Free Trade Agreements with India and Pakistan: A Exporter's Perspective", *South Asia Economic Journal*, 8(2): 217–247.

Internet Source

Sri Lanka Customs, www.customs.gov.lk
Board of Investment of Sri Lanka, www.investsrilanka.com
ITC Trade Map, www.intracen.org

DGCI&S, Kolkata www.commerce.nic.in
India-Sri Lanka FTA available at www.doc.gov.lk
India Trades, CMIE, www.cmie.com.
Department of commerce, Sri Lanka www.doc.gov.lk
FAPCCI Review of 2008, www.fapcci.in.

NOTES

1. The weakness is like, India's involvement in Sri Lanka ethnic issue.
2. Aggarwal, Vinod k. and Rahul Mukherji (2008). "India's Shifting Trade policy: South Asia and beyond", www.basc.berkeley.edu.
3. Sri Lanka Custom.
4. It had mentions in the reports of Secretariat of Central Bank of Sri Lanka.
5. The compounded annual growth rate (CAGR) is the rate at which something (e.g., revenue, savings, and population) grows over a period of years, taking into account the effect of annual compounding. A compound is composed of two or more parts. In the case of compound growth, the two parts are principal and the amount of change in the principal over a certain time period, which is called "interest" in some circumstances. This is sometimes called "growth on growth" because it measures periodic growth of a value that is itself growing periodically. If we are calculating the annual compound growth rate, then each year the new basis is the previous basis plus the growth over the previous period. During this CAGR India's exports to world was around 17 percent and imports from the world was 19.66 percent.
6. Board of Investment (BOI) of Sri Lanka (2008).
7. The Tamil ethnic conflict and India Peace Keeping Force in Sri Lanka.

Micro Finance:
Lessons for India and Sri Lanka

Ferhana Fatima, Mohammad Adbul Samad and Syed Moizuddin

ABSTRACT: Micro Finance (MF) implies provision of financial services to poor for inclusive financial system, low income people, micro entrepreneurs and small businesses who lack access to banking and related services, due to high transactions, cost associated with serving these clients, it is more of a social business than a profit maximizing business. This study investigates what lessons could be learnt by India and Sri Lanka regarding micro finance and whether micro finance is able to realize the dream for developing countries like India and Sri Lanka to eradicate poverty from the grass root levels in their societies. The true potential of MF through social intermediation can be realized by using the informal network of distribution channels already existing in India and Sri Lanka. The outreach of the MF institutions is quite high in some areas with 82.55% of households having used the services offered by financial institutions. MF institutions have been used mainly for purpose of credit taking and lesser for savings which can be opposite in the years to come. MF is predominantly used by female clientele and during emergencies only, MF will play a greater role in employment generation; improve life quality and GDP growth if MFI's operate efficiently. The governments of both counters should provide industry friendly environment, while the MF industry should avoid taking damaging actions like unreasonable interest and out of reach for the poor. The increased involvement of formal banking sectors in MF in future would also provide if MF were to meet its challenges and handles it well.

INTRODUCTION

Microfinance is more of a social business rather than a profit maximizing business. It is all about others, all about people who are deprived, neglected poor for a social cause, for a social benefit. If this concept is inserted into the economic theory, it becomes social business. It is a considered as a powerful tool for poverty alleviation. It implies provision of financial services to poor and low-income people whose low economic standing excludes them from formal financial systems. It should not be made as a huge money minting industry at the cost of poor and the help-less. The microfinance business can act as a 'miracle cure' for poverty and ensure smooth of economy.

The availability and access to financial services by the poor and the deprived is highly important for the success of market based and sustainable poverty alleviation programs. Access to services such as, credit, venture capital, savings, insurance, remittance is provided on a micro-scale enabling participation of those with severely limited financial means. The typical microfinance clients are low-income persons who do not have access to formal financial institutions. Microfinance (MF) is a powerful poverty alleviation tool. It implies provision of financial services to poor and low-income people whose low economic standing excludes them from formal financial systems. Therefore, there is a tendency among development thinkers and practioners to gauge the impact of MFIs purely in monetary terms, *i.e.* eradication of income poverty.

This is not only a partial view of the potential and purpose of microfinance but also a cause of unbridled growth of MFIs. MFIs have the capacity and responsibility to empower the most vulnerable and deprived sections of the society to allow the not-yet-economically-active to become so.

LITERATURE REVIEW

The condition of farmers in India and the scenario of suicides need to be examined in this context. Most conventional microfinance providers charge rates of interest that are found to be high when benchmarked against mainstream banking rates. Several reasons are usually given in defence:

- First, returns on investment in micro-enterprise are very high, by the standards of banks and other investors—the reason being the miniscule size of investments compared to the earnings numbers. Hence, entrepreneurs can "afford" to pay high interest rates as cost of funds (sometimes as high as sixty-seventy percent) as long as the same are lower than rates of return. And that interest rates are much less important to micro-enterprises than access, timeliness and flexibility.
- Second, interest rates on microfinance are pegged relatively higher, since they entail higher administrative charges, monitoring costs and are by definition, riskier than a traditional financing portfolio. (Obaidullah Mohammed and Khan Tariqullah, 2008).

Criticism of micro lending practices and the high interest rates they charge on loans to the poor has been accompanied by calls for stricter regulation of MFIs. There have been concerns that MFIs could find themselves laden with defaults because of the risk that multiple institutions may have lent to the same borrowers. There were three major allegations against the MFIs that came up during the crisis:

1. MFIs are charging exorbitant rates of interest. Not only that MFIs charge absolutely high interest rate upwards twenty percent;
2. MFIs are resorting to unethical ways of recovering loans by confiscating title deeds, using intimidation and abusive language, and combining multiple products like savings, insurance and loan to ensure prompt recovery.
3. MFIs are aggressively poaching from government and banks to capture their borrowers. They are luring the members of government supported SHGs by liberally financing them, leading to multiple financing (Shylendra, 2006).
   - It is argued that MFIs are causing a huge burden on the poor, leading to a vicious cycle of debt, poverty and even deaths [Kumar 2006]. Though there is no clear evidence to prove these allegations against the MFIs in AP; there is however some evidence from studies carried out at other places, which indicate that these allegations are to some extent true about MFIs in general [Hulme 2000; Mitra 2005; Rhyne 2001; Sinha and Matin1998].
   - The profitability of microfinance is driving a new wave of investment into the sector. Three deals alone in the past year would cause the size of the microfinance capital markets to increase substantially. Deutsche Bank announced the formation of its Global Commercial Microfinance Consortium, a $75 million fund that brings together over 25 institutional investors with an interest in microfinance. (Deutsche Bank, 2005).
   - The global recession which started in 2008 after the sub-prime crisis and the unprecedented default or rescue of many financial institutions has strongly affected the credibility of the international banking system, damaging also the real economy. Due to this joint crisis, the credit crunch is severely affecting the economy in Western globalized countries. Developing countries, not fully integrated with international markets, seem less affected and local microfinance institutions might also allow for a further shelter against recession, even if foreign support to donor driven NGOs or not fully independent microfinance banks is slowing down and collection of international capital is harder and more expensive. (Moro Visconti, Roberto, 2008).

—   The Microfinance industry in India is around ₹ 22,500 crores
    which is passing through one of its most difficult phases the
    controversy over issues of corporate governance at SKS Micro-
    finance Ltd and the recent Andhra Pradesh government ordinance
    banning the forced recovery of loans have raised doubts on the
    business model of microfinance institutions (MFIs). The stock
    price of SKS dropped below its issue price and analysts believe
    the uncertainty surrounding the sector could adversely affect the
    prospects of other micro-lenders looking to tap the capital market
    for funds. (Pramit Bhattacharya, 2010).

INCLUSIVENESS AND MICROFINANCE

In 2010, according to a survey, India had around 403 million mobile users,
out of which 46% i.e 187 million, did not have bank accounts. Reserve
Bank of India deputy governor K.C. Chakrabarty, in a recent presentation
on financial inclusion in Mumbai, said about 40% Indians have check-in
accounts. Going by his presentation, 51 out of every 100 Indians had
bank accounts in 1993. This has marginally gone up to 54 in 2007. Another
central banker, a few years ago said 59% of adult population in India has
bank accounts and that there is a large gap between the coverage of banking
services in urban and rural pockets. In rural India, the coverage among
the adult population is 39% against 60% in urban India. This, of course,
doesn't necessarily mean that 60 out of every 100 Indian adults in cities have
bank accounts as many people operate multiple accounts. According to
the survey conducted by British Bankers' Association, 92-94% of the
population in the UK has either current or savings accounts.

The low coverage is true for other financial services as well. According to
a survey, barely 45 million Indians invest in mutual funds. This is about 4%
of India's population. The comparable figure for the US is 31%. When it
comes to direct investment in equities, the number drops drastically and
only 15 million Indians hold DEMAT (electronic share) accounts that one
needs to buy stocks. Nearly 80% of the Indian population is without life,
health and non-life insurance coverage. While life insurance penetration
is 4%, non-life cover is even lower at 0.6%. The per capita spend on life
and non-life insurance is just about ₹ 2,000 and ₹ 300, respectively,
compared with a global average of at least ₹ 18,000 and ₹ 13,000. Some
other relevant data will help us understand the criticality of the issue. Only
5.2% of India's 650,000 villages have bank branches even though 39.7%
of the overall branch network of Indian banks, or 31,727, are in rural India.

A large number of studies on poverty reduction reveal that exclusion of the poor from the financial system is a major factor contributing to their inability to participate in the development process. In a typical developing economy the formal financial system serves no more than twenty to thirty percent of the population. The remaining seventy to eighty percent are those who are excluded. This majority are poor living below poverty line. With no access to financial services, these households find it extremely difficult to take advantage of economic opportunities, build assets, finance their children's education, and protect themselves against financial requirements and shocks thereby caught into a vicious circle of poverty. Building inclusive financial systems therefore, is a central goal of policy makers and planners across the globe. In this regard, microfinance has been recognized worldwide as an important policy instrument. Many failed MF programs owe their failure to inadequate evaluation of the client's financial condition. Provision of micro finance does not stand to reason for a person in need of social safety nets resulting in the funds being consumed away instead of being invested. The poor come in disparate categories with varying needs of consumption and productive investment and risk of delinquency and default.

A MACRO VIEW OF MICRO FINANCE

Table 1: State-wise Break-up of Microfinance Borrowers

State	No. of Microfinance Borrowers	Rank	Percentage of Total
Andhra Pradesh	62,50,000	I	23.42%
Tamil Nadu	45,70,000	II	17.12%
Karnataka	37,40,000	III	14.01%
West Bengal	35,20,000	IV	13.18%
Orissa	16,00,000	V	6.00%
Maharashtra	14,70,000	VI	5.50%
Uttar Pradesh	12,10,000	VII	4.53%
Madhya Pradesh	10,10,000	VIII	3.78%
Bihar	7,50,000	IX	2.81%
Chhattisgarh	4,60,000	X	1.72%
Other States	21,10,000	–	7.90%
Total	**2,66,90,000**		100%

Source: Association of Community Development Finance Institutions.

As per the data on microfinance borrowers (beneficiaries), shown in Table 1, Andhra Pradesh stands first with 62,50,000 clients which is nearly 10% of the total population of the state. Tamilnadu and Karnataka ranks second and third with a client proportion of 45,70,000 and 37,40,000 respectively. The total proportion of these states amount to more than half i.e 55% of the total consumer client share in India. But it is evident from various studies that the recovery system adopted by the lenders and the high rate of interests has been a major reason for the suffering of the MF clients.

Table 2: State-Wise Break-Up of Loans Outstanding

State	Loans Outstanding (₹ Crores)	Rank	Percentage of Total
Andhra Pradesh	5210.80	I	28.40%
Karnataka	2551.40	II	13.90%
Tamil Nadu	2387.10	III	13.01%
West Bengal	2108.30	IV	11.49%
Orissa	1200.40	V	6.54%
Maharashtra	967.10	VI	5.27%
Uttar Pradesh	951.1	VII	5.18%
Madhya Pradesh	593.8	VIII	3.23%
Bihar	496.5	IX	2.7%
Delhi	346.	X	1.89%
Other States	1530.7	–	8.34%
Total	18343.9	–	100%

Source: Association of Community Development Finance Institutions.

As per the data on microfinance loans outstanding, shown in table.2, the states of Andhra Pradesh, Karnataka and Tamil Nadu stood at ₹ 5210.80 Crores, ₹ 2551.40 Crores and ₹ 2387.10 Crores which collectively counts to 55% with an individual share of 28.40%, 13.90% and 13.01% respectively. This large industry has been criticized for high interest rates being charged and methods of recovery.

The client base of these institutions went up by 46% to reach 26.7 million active borrowers. Over 55% of the loans disbursed by MFIs are in southern India, where the industry took root, and the eastern region comes second, accounting for 25% of loans. India's once- booming Microfinance industry has fallen into the crosshairs of the country's murky politics, though the statistics seem to be very high. The fact that the client bases of MFIs are the most vulnerable sections of society makes them a target of political activism and regulatory intervention. The high profit growth of these firms is often seen to be at the expense of the poor. There are some real instances that speak about the reality.

The crisis in the southern Indian state of Andhra Pradesh over microfinance-induced suicides has taken an ugly turn (*Microfinance Focus*). The media report based on a fact-finding report prepared by the Gender Unit of SERP (Society for Elimination of Rural Poverty) said 54 deaths were microfinance-related, out of 123 cases of alleged harassment by some of the largest and well known microfinance institutions in the state.

ALTERNATE MODE OF FINANCE—MICRO-FINANCE: IN SRI LANKA

Sri Lanka has better socio economic indicators than other SAARC countries but poverty is still significant. 20.5 million people live there of whom 5.6% lives with below USD1 per day, 42% lives below USD2 per day and 15.2% of them is under the national poverty line. GDP per capita is USD 2,053 at market prices. Sri Lanka stands at position 102 in HDI ranking. There are several models of MFIs in Sri Lanka. Such as; Individual lending using a group (centre, cluster) as a focal point, Village banking, Self help groups and Individual lending. Loan guarantees are provided using two members guarantee method, Grameen type group collateral etc. However, recent trends involve less paper work, quick lending and recoveries in structured manner.

MFIs in Sri Lanka can be broadly categorized into two parts (1) Micro-finance as core business and (2) as an ancillary business. The first one covers MFIs National/Regional/local and NGO's/Private), Government MFIs (Samurdi/Agrarian Services), Village banks, Co-operative establishments and Specialized (Development) Banks; where the latter one covers Regulated Development Banks, Commercial banks and Finance/leasing companies.

In 2008, National/Regional/Local MFIs had the highest USD96 of average savings per member. However, CRB (deposit accounts) had the highest savings of 31,998 million SLR in 2007. RDB's had ₹ 32 billion savings, 50% of this estimated to have micro savings. In case of borrowers and loan outstanding in 2008, National/Regional/local MFIs topped at USD164 average loan outstanding per borrower. Loan outstanding of CRB (loan accounts) in 2007 was SLR21,711 million. Over 65% of members were females. Approximately 30% of the total population and 50% of the population below national poverty line was reached. Nonetheless, some critical issues are multiple borrowing, lack of accurate data, significant number of members in CRB and some members of VB and MFIs (less) are not poor, reach in North and the East are weak and reliable data is not available.

Acceptable data on the overall sector is not available. However, case load is very low; average 60 loans per staff member, ₹ 620,000 ($ 5,586) outstanding loan balance per staff member. Samurdi and village banks are at lower ends (17 loans) and CRB is at higher end (192 loans). Very few MFIs are financially and operationally sustainable. MIX reports 16 cents to maintain each Dollar in Sri Lanka MFIs. Lack of tools for sustainable operations like business planning and costing together with high level of investment in social mobilization and credit plus services mixed with credit are some of the reason. Nevertheless, the efficiency and sustainability are in increasing trends during the recent past. Certain level of information on impact of microfinance in Sri Lanka is available. It is evident that 71% of borrowers increasing income. Establishment of livelihoods, Improved housing and sanitary facilities, Household and business assets building, Empowering women and poor, Environmental impact (for example, Loans for solar panels reduced use of 19 million liters Kerosene, that is, 54.5 million Kg of CO), Reconstructing lives after Tsunami, Supporting living under conflict. However, systematic and much focused SPM is not commonly practiced by MFI's. But there is an increasing trend in willing to use SPM including use of PPI at present. Microfinance in Sri Lanka is financed by multiple methods. First of all, saving; that involves credit unions, cooperatives, Samurdi and certain NGO/private MFIs. Historically many MFIs received grants but depleted now due to unsuitability of MFIs. These are limited to certain TA's to MFI and sector development now. NDTF used to provide low cost funding but it is becoming very limited at present. Other lenders such as SMAGL and Etimose play a significant role today.

The microfinance movement in Sri Lanka dates as far back as 1906 with the establishment of Thrift and Credit Co-operative Societies (TCCSs) under the Co-operative Societies Ordinance introduced by the British colonial administration. These were the first credit co-operatives to be established in Sri Lanka. The societies fulfilled a wider role during the early decades of the 20th century, being involved also involved in procurement of inputs and distribution of products, a role eventually taken over by the Multi-Purpose Co-operative Societies (MPCSs) which were originally established during the 1940s as Consumer Co-operative Societies and renamed Multi Purpose Co-operatives in the 1950s. The network of TCCSs was weak and in decline by the late 1970s and there were plans to wind up many societies. It was that this time that a revival of the movement was initiated by the charismatic P.A. Kiriwandeniya, with the TCCSs being re-organized under a new name: SANASA. The SANASA TCCSs are member owned societies, grouped together as a Federation but coming under the purview of the Department of Co-operative Development. Parallel to the SANASA TCCSs are the MPCSs and their financial service arms, the Co-operative Rural Banks (CRBs). The MPCSs and CRBs also fall under the purview of the Department of Co-operative Development. Commencing in 1985 the Government established 17 Regional Rural Development Banks (RRDBs) through an Act of Parliament. These institutions were given the task of reaching remote rural areas and small-holders who lacked access to financial services from commercial banks. The RRDBs covered all districts of Sri Lanka with the exception of the North and East. Their success, however, was limited by internal structural weaknesses and excessive geographical fragmentation, which prevented them from reaching a critical mass. In addition, the banks lacked sound lending and monitoring policies, and operations were difficult to improve and standardize.

A significant restructuring and recapitalization took place in 1998–1999 and the RRDBs were consolidated into the six Regional Development Banks (RDBs) which exist today. This involved granting RDBs more autonomous management, allowing a broader ownership base, and having board members appointed by shareholders, also entered the sector after the tsunami and rapidly scaled up to become a significant player among NGOMFIs, achieving an outreach of 75,000 microfinance clients in just 4 years. A recently emerging trend is the entry of commercial banks and registered finance companies and other large corporate entities into the microfinance business. Hatton National Bank's "Gami Pubuduwa" ("Village Awakening") microfinance programme is probably the oldest microfinance programme among the licensed commercial banks, having been established in 1989 and disbursing over ₹3.5 Bn (approximately US$ 35 Mn) to around 70,000 micro entrepreneurs over the years. Some recent entrants are aggressively moving into the sector and have the resources and infrastructure to scale up rapidly.

However, for many commercial banks and finance companies, microfinance is more a Corporate Social Responsibility (CSR) or image building activity. As mentioned below in the section on regulation, the absence of a cohesive regulatory and supervisory system for the microfinance sector is one of the barriers to the future growth of the sector. With donors moving out of the Sri Lankan microfinance sector, funding becomes a key issue, especially for NGO-MFIs, which are restricted by law from accepting public deposits and further restricted from obtaining off-shore debt and equity funding due to prevailing exchange control restrictions. Accessing local funding is also somewhat of an issue as local banks and other funding agencies are still reluctant to lend to or invest in the microfinance sector due to the perception of high risk.

MAJOR MICROFINANCE PROVIDERS

Sri Lanka's microfinance sector is served by a diverse range of institutions. These can be segregated into the following broad categories.

Regional Development Banks and other licensed specialized banks	Thrift and Credit Co-operative Societies (TCCSs/Sanasa societies)
Co-operative Rural Banks and other co-operatives	Samurdhi Bank Societies (SBSs)
NGO-MFIs	Other financial institutions (this category includes commercial banks, registered finance companies

Depth of Outreach

The income distribution of microfinance clients according to data gathered in the MFI survey is presented in

Table 3: Income Profile of Microfinance Clients

Clients	< ₹ 3,000	₹3,000– 5,000	₹5,000– 10000	₹10000– 20000	₹20000– 40000	> ₹ 40,000
RDBs	19.3%	18.3%	24.2%	28.3%	7.5%	2.3%
SBSs*	85.0%	–	–	–	–	–
CRBs/WDCs	n/a	n/a	n/a	n/a	n/a	n/a
Sanasa/WDCs	20.1%	29.4%	26.3%	14.7%	5.3%	4.3%
Other MFIs**	50.4%	31.5%	13.3%	3.0%	1.6%	0.3%

From the available information, it appears that the SBSs and the NGO-MFIs have the greatest depth of outreach, with 85% and 50.4% of clients respectively having a monthly household income of less than ₹ 3,000/-. For the NGO-MFIs, nearly 82% of their clients have a monthly household income of less than ₹ 5,000. The RDBs clearly serve a different market segment, with over 50% of their clients falling into the ₹ 5,000–20,000 range of monthly household income.

Table 4: Distribution of Outlets Vs Poverty Distribution

Province	Outlets (%)	Contribution to Total Poverty (%)
Central	12.9	16.8
Western	107	20.4
Southern	25.4	12.1
North Weatern	10.8	12.2
North Central	4.1	6.0
Uva	11.4	12.3
Sabaragamuwa	11.8	16.6
Eastern	13.0	3.6

Source: MF NGO—Sri Lanka.

Product Portfolio

A diversity of products is not seen in the microfinance sector. Although many institutions have broad product portfolios, these essentially consist of a proliferation of loan and savings products which differ mostly in name but offer more or less the same features, although the loan period may differ. Licensed specialized banks such as the RDBs and Sanasa Development Bank are permitted to mobilize deposits. Institutions registered as cooperative societies are also permitted to accept member deposits. However, in practice, many NGO-MFIs do also accept deposits on a limited scale. Many microfinance providers impose compulsory savings requirements as a pre-condition to obtaining a loan.

Table 5: Loan Portfolio Deposit Base

Organization	Loans (₹ 000)	Deposits (₹ 000)
RDBs*	19,418,585	18,750,757
SBSs	7,785,081	20,810,360
CRBs**	14,620,570	25,311,550
Sanasa/TCCSs***	4,025,124	3,936,818

Donor Support for Microfinance

Donor support for Sri Lanka's microfinance sector increased substantially following the 2004 tsunami which left the country with over 35,000 dead and over 800,000 displaced. Large multi-lateral and bilateral agencies such as the ADB, JBIC and UNDP provided funding for microfinance through the Central Bank and the bulk financing apex agency, the NDTF. Some donors worked directly through existing NGOs and MFIs, but others created new microfinance programmes, especially in the south where existing MFIs already had a significant presence.

Key Challenges of Microfinance Macro and Micro Level for India and Sri Lanka

A key challenge is the lack of a long term vision and policy for the sector.

Macro Level

- The **lack of a regulatory and supervisory framework for microfinance** is a key factor which has been raised by practitioners, donors and other stakeholders. The absence of a unique supervisory and policy framework (for microfinance) has allowed the proliferation of fundamentally unsustainable MFIs **Politicization** is a fundamental issue affecting government owned and/or controlled microfinance institutions. Microfinance is often used as a political tool through institutions such as the Samurdhi.
- **Insufficient specialized microfinance training facilities** have contributed to many microfinance providers failing to meet the standards required for them to transform into financial institutions and attract the funding they require from commercial investors in order to scale up their operations in an environment where cheap donor funds are fast drying up.
- **Limited knowledge** transfer and information exchange within the sector Lack of credit information sharing is highlighted in the CLEAR Review as a challenge for the sector.

Micro Level

- **Quality of human resources.** The quality and skill levels of MFI staff seem to be issues that cut across the institutional types. In the GTZ survey of microfinance institutions, staff issues ranked among the top 5 challenges faced by most MFIs. The cause of the problem however, differs across institutional types. The SBSs face overstaffing as they are frequently used to achieve political objectives by providing employment for political supporters.

- **Involvement of government in retail credit provision** is widespread as more than half of microfinance clients are with government owned or controlled institutions.
- There is **limited focus on sustainability** as the sector has been protected by a large amount of subsidized funding, from government and foreign donors alike, although the latter source is now much reduced.
- **Weak corporate governance** is also a cross cutting issue in the sector
- **Organization culture** in most NGO-MFIs still leans towards a social welfare mentality. Many such MFIs still adopt an integrated approach, combining microfinance business with community development activities.
- **Lack of Transparency and Standardization.** There is an overall lack of transparency and reluctance to share even the most basic, non-financial operational information among MFIs, even those who are not direct competitors.

LIMITED USE OF TECHNOLOGY STRENGTHS

Diversity of Institutions

There is a long tradition of informal savings and credit in Sri Lanka, especially through grass root initiatives significant savings culture. The CLEAR Review estimates 15 million savings accounts in Sri Lanka with a value of ₹ 49 billion large outreach. A high proportion of the population has access to financial services Strong financial sector infrastructure.

Sri Lanka has strong financial sector market infrastructure in general: capital markets, stock exchange, debentures markets, credit bureau; auditors; rating agencies; a large pool of chartered accountants; ATMs even in rural areas; several training facilities; high level universities, well- qualified MBAs, etc.

Specialized Microfinance Training Emerging

The University of Colombo and Institute of Bankers have/plan to introduce microfinance diploma programmes.

Conclusion—Micro Finance Lessons for India and Sri Lanka
The interest rates prevailing in the microfinance sector are very high and are certainly much higher than the rates of formal agencies. Even SHGs

which are linked to formal banks normally charge 2 per cent per month to their ultimate borrowers. With regard to MFIs, though the rates are much lower than the informal sector, they have ended up creating an interest rate structure which is only second best for the poor. At times it becomes difficult to estimate the effective rate of interest charged by the MFIs. Not many MFIs make it clear to their borrowers what the effective rate would be. So, there is a need for an alternate system which from interest towards the upliftment of the deprived and needful at a very low cost to fulfill the expired expenses attached to such activity. It is a social business.

But there is a need to examine microfinance at three levels—micro level (microfinance institutions, contracts/products and resources), Meso level (financial infrastructures) and macro level (policy and regulatory framework). At a micro level, the major challenges to microfinance providers arise from their diverse organizational structures, lack of product diversification and poor linkages with banks and capital markets. Some strategic initiatives are suggested as solutions, such as, a move towards collective resolution of regulatory issues, enhancement of product range through research and financial engineering and increased participation of banks in microfinance through provision of credit guarantees and safety nets.

Microfinance should emphasize ethical, moral, social, and religious factors to promote equality and fairness for the good of society as a whole. Principles encouraging risk sharing, individual rights and duties, property rights, and the sanctity of contracts are all part of the code underlying the financial system. In this light, many elements of microfinance are consistent with the broader goals of finance. Both advocate entrepreneurship and risk sharing and believe that the poor should take part in such activities. Both focus on developmental and social goals. Both advocate financial inclusion, entrepreneurship and risk-sharing through partnership finance. Both involve participation by the poor.

Social performance measures are not nearly so well developed. That may seem ironic for an industry which was founded because of the social benefits that it can achieve. Yet the lack of well-developed social standards may be the product of that heritage. It may simply be presumed that a microfinance institution in India and Sri Lanka are providing significant social and economic benefits to the poor. These are exciting days to be involved in microfinance, but they are not easy. The managers of most microfinance institutions will continue to find difficulty as they try to meet the strong demand for their services by raising more capital. They will need to have a strong business model, a growing market and the ability to clearly communicate those successes in terms that are understood by both commercial and social investors. Like any emerging industry, the rewards will come to those with the discipline and perseverance to recognize its social responsibility, manage risk and understand the ethical aspects attached to the industry.

There are some ethical aspects of lending and borrowing loans in the larger interest of the society. In the current scenario and global economic conditions, where the interest-based system is towards its decline. An alternate model is needed to be developed which is free from interest and several other elements which are unethical and unsocial. Islamic concept of micro-finance can also be the best alternative. Islamic MF products must be free from interest and several other elements forbidden under Islamic law. Even if poverty decreases through micro-finance, albeit at a slow rate, poverty is rampant in a country that has the largest presence of micro-finance programs in the world. Micro-finance is not to blame for this high incidence of poverty. We must admit that micro-finance is only an instrument among a large number of poverty reduction strategies that policy makers must pursue to reduce poverty. Certainly growth is a significant factor in reducing poverty. Investment in human capital and other means to empower the poor are also important tools for reducing poverty. Similarly, micro-finance intervention reduces poverty for a small percentage of the poor, and certainly provides an institutional credit and savings facility to a large percentage of the poor, especially women. The role of micro-finance must be evaluated from such perspectives.

For microfinance, therefore there is ethical and economic justification for looking beyond income poverty or to move from financial intermediation to social intermediation. So today we not only need to introduce new products or services in the field of microfinance but also explore new frontiers of development towards social and economic cause. This results in human development in terms of infrastructure for health, education, skill and enterprise. The MFIs need to produce accurate and comparable reporting on financial performance (e.g., loan repayment and cost recovery) as well as social performance (e.g., number and poverty level of clients being served). To sum up, the principles broaden the definition of MF from micro-credit to provision of an array of financial services, such as, savings, insurance and remittance Microfinance institutions (MFIs) have turned the business of lending tiny amounts to the unbanked poor—from vegetable vendors and tailors in the cities to fishermen and farmers in the villages—into a thriving industry with assets estimated at almost ₹ 12,000 crore in fiscal 2009 according to a study. But MFIs involved in high profit making at the expense of the poor by charging interest rates as high as 24–36%.

At last it is concluded that these are some of the many unanswered questions regarding the beneficiaries of micro finance which reveal that it is not micro finance alone, it is not inclusion alone, it is not poverty reduction alone which is the solution to the problem. Minting money out of the deprived by providing short–term loans and charging interest rates that to a very high level which is almost two to three times higher than the normal rate of interest charged by any bank. This micro finance industry and practice prevailing today is proved to be a killing pill for most of the clients. In a world of globalization, liberalization and privatization, where there is a huge competition in any business, even if it is retailing business of fruits and vegetables, where a vendor cannot earn a profit of more than 10%, how is he expected to pay a interest of 2% to 3% per month which counts to almost 24% to 36% per annum. The economically strong and intellectual people should come up and take this challenge and work for the cause of society. Alternate models are needed to be developed, an interest-free environment should be created such that the deprived people are included and the society is benefited at large.

REFERENCES

[1] Hulme, David (2000). 'Is Micro-debt Good for Poor People? A Note on the Dark Side of Microfinance', Small Enterprise Development, 11(1), March, pp 26–28.

[2] Mitra, Subrata Kumar (2005). "Asking Price of Microfinance Loan to Poor Borrowers".

[3] Kumar, S. Nagesh (2006). 'The Making of Debt Trap in Andhra Pradesh', The Hindu, April 20.

[4] Shylendra, H.S. (2006). "Microfinance Institutions in Andhra Pradesh- Crisis and Diagnosis", Economic and Political Weekly, May 2006.

[5] Microfinance and Disaster Management, Trainer's Manual Stuart Mathison (Ed.), 2006, ISBN: 0-9586728-9-X.

[6] Moro Visconti, Roberto (2008), Global Recession and Microfinance in Developing Countries: Threats and Opportunities, Social Science Research Network SSRN Working Paper, March 2009.

[7] Obaidullah, Mohammed and Khan, Tariqullah (2008), Islamic Microfinance Development: Challenges and Initiatives. Islamic Research and Training institute Social Science Research Network SSRN Working Paper, May 2008.

[8] Obaidullah Mohammad (2008), "Role of Microfinance in Poverty Alleviation: Lessons from Experiences in Selected IDB Member Countries", Islamic Development Bank, 2008.

[9] Capacity Building for Partnerships in Microfinance Trainer's Manual Jamie Bedson (Ed.), 2008 ISBN: 978-0-9804698-1-3. ISBN: 978-0-9804698-2-0.

[10] Microfinance in Asia: Trends, Challenges and Opportunities Jamie Bedson (Ed.), 2009.

[11] Vijay Mahajan (2010), "Myths of Microfinance", Global South Development Magazine, Oct-Dec2010, pp. 12–17.

[12] Lykke E. Andersen (2010), "Microfinance and Development: Do the math", Global South Development Magazine, Oct–Dec2010, pp. 18–19.

[13] Microfinance Industry Report SRI LANKA 2009 Produced by GTZ ProMiS in collaboration with The Banking with the Poor Network.

[14] Micro Finance In SAARC countries, Updates 2011, Badruddoza, S, Institute of Micro Finance (InM), Dhaka, Bangladesh, 10. February 2011.

[15] Atapattu, Anura; State of Microfinance in Sri Lanka (Presented at the conference "Microfinance in SAARC Countries: Sharing Lessons and Way Forward", Kathmandu, Nepal. November–December 2010)

[16] Sinha, Sanjay; State of Microfinance in India (Presented at the conference "Microfinance in SAARC Countries: Sharing Lessons and Way Forward", Kathmandu, Nepal. November–December 2010) www.bwtp.org

[17] Online at http://mpra.ub.uni-muenchen.de/38011.

An Assessment of India-Sri Lanka Economic and Trade Relations: An Overview

R. Sidda Goud

INTRODUCTION

Economic links between India and Sri Lanka have a long history—with recorded commercial links going as far back as the 4th century—and with both countries falling under British rule during the 19th century, these links strengthened to the point where legal barriers to movement of goods and labour practically disappeared. But in the early years of the post-independence period, despite close political ties economic ties weakened as both countries implemented inward looking economic policies. However, with Sri Lanka initiating a liberalisation drive in 1977–78 that subsequently encompassed other South Asian countries including India, economic links between the two once again started to strengthen. This process has been further encouraged by the South Asian regional integration initiatives and by a bilateral Free Trade Agreement (FTA) between the two countries.

The bilateral trade agreement between India and Sri Lanka were initiated since early 1990s, the emergence of the possibility of Regional Preferential Agreement (RFA)—proposed by Sri Lanka and Nepal in 1990 and accepted by the South Asian Association for Regional Cooperation (SAARC) in 1993—effectively pushed a bilateral agreement to the background. This was reinforced by the implementation of the South Asian Preferential Trade Agreement (SAPTA) in 1995 and an agreement to forge ahead towards a South Asian Free Trade Agreement (SAFTA) in 1996, complemented by progressive unilateral liberalisation efforts of most South Asian economies, particularly from the early 1990s. Bilateral trade between the two countries had been expanding rapidly in the 1990s, driven primarily by unilateral liberalisation efforts with trade flows being largely in favour of India. In fact, India emerged as Sri Lanka's primary source of imports in 1996—overtaking Japan for the first time. However, regional efforts came unstuck in 1998 with the heightening of tension between India and Pakistan following nuclear test explosions by both countries. With the near halt of SAARC related efforts to push forward regional economic integration, India and Sri Lanka embarked on a bilateral agreement—the India Sri Lanka Free Trade Agreement (ISFTA)—signed in December 1998.

Notwithstanding such perceived benefits to Sri Lanka, there was little discussion on the proposed ISFTA at the domestic level. In fact, the ISFTA was signed in 1998, with both countries agreeing to negotiate and to finalise the finer points—in particular, the composition of the negative list of items—to allow full implementation to begin in February 1999. Opposition to the agreement was voiced from within Sri Lanka's domestic industrial sector (as well as from particular sectors within India) with regards to potential adverse implications from heightened competition from cheaper imports. Nevertheless, the agreement came into effect in March 2000 (with negotiations delayed as both governments attempted to address domestic interest pressure concerns) and has since continued to be implemented according to the schedules that were agreed upon.

In the backdrop of the SAFTA agreement implemented in July 2006, the ISFTA provides useful lessons for other South Asian economies, both in terms of the initial conditions prior to the negotiation of the bilateral agreement and in terms of the progress in strengthening trade and economic linkages post implementation. This report is intended to review the evolution and current status of the economic ties between India and Sri Lanka. It reviews the historical background, analyses trends in trade in goods and investment, and discusses these in the broad economic, policy and political context, with emphasis on the policy liberalization. This paper intends to analyse the nature and part of regional initiatives, such as SAFTA/SAPTA and bilateral cooperation between India-Sri Lanka relations/agreements with emphasis on the policy liberalization and moves towards regional integration.

While India's interests in furthering trade relations could be understood given its broader industrial base and ability to meet Sri Lanka's import needs, the key factors prompting Sri Lanka's interests were the prospect of 'early mover' access to a large market that would help the country to diversify its industrial base and the potential for to raise its profile as a destination for Foreign Direct Investment (FDI) on the basis of preferential access to a still relatively 'protected' Indian market.

BILATERAL TRADE COOPERATION BETWEEN INDIA AND SRI LANKA: HISTORICAL BACK GROUND

Sri Lanka's central position in the Indian Ocean and its geographic proximity to South India—and the resultant cultural and historical ties— were factors that influenced the early development of trade between the two countries. These links persisted till colonial times when economic relations between the two countries were geared very much towards producing goods for the colonial powers and meeting food requirements resulting from shortages. Existing trade links were strengthened during the colonial period, primarily on account of Indian labour that was brought Sri Lanka to work on the plantations. In 1938, for example, 42.5 percent of Sri Lanka's import bill was spent on imports from India and the larger share of such imports was related to plantation labour.

After independence, Sri Lanka made a concerted attempt to diversify such dependence by increasing production of certain previously imported items at home and securing alternative sources from a wider range of countries. By the late 1940s, Sri Lanka's imports from India had declined to around 15 percent of its total imports, while exports to India totaled around two percent of all Sri Lanka's exports—a trend that continued into the 1950s.

The composition of bilateral trade has changed over the years. During the 1960s textiles and agricultural products were the major Indian exports, but during the 1970s engineering products (in particular, transport equipment) became increasingly more important—a change facilitated by the Sri Lankan trade liberalisation process. Demand for cotton yarn and fabrics have been stimulated by the growth of Sri Lanka's export-oriented garment industry, but the free trade regime has broadened the range of imports. As a result, in addition to transport equipment, many light engineering products, pharmaceuticals, pulses, and a variety of other commodities became significant Indian exports to Sri Lanka.

The adoption of inward looking economic policies, *i.e.* stringent exchange controls, increasing state control over all areas of economic activity and reduced opportunities for private sector participation, and an unfriendly attitude to foreign investment, the ending of Indian labour inflows—all heralded a continuing steady decline in Indo Sri Lanka economic links. There were some attempts during this period to revive economic links, but they had little success. The idea of a formal arrangement to facilitate trade channels between the two countries was proposed in 1961. This took the form of a bilateral trade agreement, whose main aim was to promote the highest possible volume of trade between the two countries. However, the agreement had no noticeable impact on trade flows, prompting the establishment of an Indo-Sri Lanka Joint Committee on Economic Cooperation in 1968 with the objective of strengthening cooperation in trade, industry, agriculture and tourism.

Despite such pronouncements, bilateral trade between India and Sri Lanka remained stagnant since last two and half decades. In contrast, Sri Lanka's exports to India have been considerably less diversified, though they have become somewhat more diversified in recent years. Until the 1970s coconut products, together with natural rubber, accounted for the bulk of exports. With the development of the oil refining facilities in Sri Lanka, oil exports became an important item but by the mid-1980s, tea and rubber dominated exports. Scrap metal became an important export in the late 1980s.

Political tensions between India and Sri Lanka were also heightened with the outbreak of civil conflict in Sri Lanka in the mid1980s that culminated with direct military involvement of India. The perception of anti-Indian sentiment in Sri Lanka raised its riskiness in the eyes of Indian investors. It also diminished Sri Lanka's attractiveness as a holiday destination for Indians. Taken together, these factors had a dampening impact on bilateral economic ties. A clear upturn in bilateral economic ties started after the launching of the Indian policy liberalisation process in 1990–91, which coincided with a 'second phase of economic reforms' of policy reforms in Sri Lanka. Although the concept of strengthening bilateral trade cooperation between India and Sri Lanka was pursued once more in the early 1990s.

Particularly on the part of Sri Lanka, including the emergence of a regional initiative in the form of SAPTA, the implementation of SAPTA in 1995, and the decision to convert to SAFTA agreed on in principal in 1996, and the focus appeared to implement measures to improve intra-South Asian economic links as part of the SAARC process.

Though this was a period of general policy liberalisation, and also regional and bilateral initiatives to foster economic links, the SAPTA process offered only very limited liberalisation, while the transition to SAFTA stalled with the heightening of political tensions between India and Pakistan in the late 1990s. A critical outcome of the limited achievements of the SAPTA process was that it provided an impetus for countries to undertake 'fast-track' liberalisation on a bilateral basis. The original intent of fast-track liberalisation was primarily to permit countries willing to proceed at a faster place to do so within the SAPTA/SAFTA framework. However, as SAARC official activities came to a virtual standstill from the latter half of 1998, what emerged was bilateral FTAs amongst members, but wholly outside the SAARC process. In fact, there is little evidence of similar trends in other regional groups. The vast majority of regional blocs began from an agreed base on the intensity or degree of cooperation and has progressed from there, taking collective decisions with regard to either the speed of integration or admission of new entrants to the bloc.

Although there were already bilateral agreements between India and Nepal and between India and Bhutan—these were essentially nonreciprocal in nature with India offering market access on a unilateral basis. The defining bilateral FTA to emerge in the region was the India Sri Lanka FTA (ISFTA) signed in December 1998. It was a culmination not only of the slow progress made through the South Asian regional initiatives but also a mark of renewed political confidence between the two countries.

There were concerns that while some Sri Lankan exports (such as rubber products, ceramic products and leather goods) catering to particular niche markets in India and enjoying a comparative advantage may benefit from liberalisation, some Small and Medium Industrial Enterprises (SMEs), and producers of livestock and subsidized agricultural products not protected under the negative list will face stiffer import competition from Indian exporters, who arguably enjoy the advantages of a relatively sophisticated industrial and agricultural base, and economies of scale provided by the larger domestic market. On the other hand, it was also considered that in some products where current exports are nonexistent or minimal, there may be scope for expansion of Sri Lankan exports to the Indian market.

While it was obvious that the largest gains from trade would likely to come from opening up precisely those sectors where domestic industries will come under strong import competition, they were naturally also the sectors where domestic producers felt most vulnerable, where adjustment.

TRENDS IN TRADE FLOWS PRE AND POST ISFTA

The asymmetric treatment offered appears to have held out an advantage to Sri Lanka in terms of the volume of bilateral trade generated in the post implementation of the ISFTA. Sri Lanka's exports to India have seen a significant increase since the implementation of the ISFTA. In absolute terms, Sri Lanka's export earnings increased from US$58mn in 2000 to US$566mn by 2005. Export earnings dropped in 2006 with the disruption to Sri Lanka's exports of *Vanaspathi* following the trade dispute between the two countries. Nevertheless, in general growth in export earnings to India has far outstripped total export earnings for the country since 2001 and assisted significantly to closing the trade gap between the two countries in favour of Sri Lanka (see Table 1).

Table 1: India Sri Lanka Merchandise Trade (2000:2006)

	2000	*2001*	*2002*	*2003*	*2004*	*2005*	*2006*
Sri Lanka							
Exports to India $ mn	58	72	170	245	391	566	489
Imports from India $ mn	600	601	832	1076	1439	1835	2173
Share of total exports %	1.0	1.5	3.6	4.6	6.8	8.9	7.1
Share of total imports %	9.0	10.5	13.8	16.1	18.	20.7	21.2
India							
Share of total exports %	1.4	1.2	1.7	2.0	1.8	1.9	1.8
Share of total imports %	–	0.1	0.1	0.2	0.3	0.4	0.3

Notes: ... implies negligible. *Source:* IMF, Direction of Trade, various issues.

India is Sri Lanka's most important trading partner in the SAARC region. Though marginally less important than the Maldives in export trade it is, by far, the most important source of imports. On the other hand, Sri Lanka has long been a very minor trading partner from an Indian viewpoint. Recently, however, it has been more successful in raising its share of exports to India. Nevertheless, India's total imports from Sri Lanka still remain at a negligible 0.3 percent. The growing penetration of the Sri Lankan market by Indian exports, and the importance of India in Sri Lanka's imports (see Table 1).

The major liberalisation of the Sri Lankan economy in 1977 did little to change the volume of goods traded between the two economies. In fact, there was a continuing decline in the percentage share of Sri Lanka's exports to India, with the emergence of new industrial exports geared to markets in North America and Europe. Though there was also a sharp increase in Sri Lanka's overall imports following trade liberalisation, the corresponding increase in imports from India was quite limited. This can be attributed to several reasons. The most important of these, perhaps was the fact that

Indian produced goods were perceived as being of low quality *visàvis* similar goods from Japan, and other emerging East Asian economies like South Korea. Most consumer goods produced in India was geared to meet domestic consumption demand in the context of a highly protected economy, and was not quality competitive in international markets. It was only after the liberalisation process of the Indian economy (started in 1990–91) that this began to change. The push for export growth, combined with quality improvements with increased exposure to competition, and facilitated by the policy reforms undertaken in Sri Lanka at the time, rapidly raised the volume of Indian exports into Sri Lanka. But Sri Lanka's exports, though they too showed an initial increase, failed to keep pace.

The commodity composition of bilateral trade between India and Sri Lanka in recent years in Sri Lanka's exports appears to have changed quite substantially. Sri Lanka's total exports to India has shown a remarkable upward trend since 2002 and accelerated sharply from 2003 with the provision of duty free access to the Indian market as per the agreement. The growth is mostly visible in product categories of base metal, animal or vegetable fats and oils, machinery and mechanical goods and chemical products etc. For instance, the top exports to India in 2005, ranked in terms of value included vegetable fats and oils, copper products, aluminum wire, antibiotics, spices such as cloves, pepper, edible preparations of fats and oils and waste and scrap metal and paper, etc. A notable feature is that India has also increased its demand for imports from Sri Lanka which are currently being produced in the Indian domestic market. For instance, despite their domestic production, Indian demand for imported tyres and tubes from Sri Lanka has been increasing in recent years due to the raid expansion of the automobile industry in India.

Even before the implementation of the ISFTA, India had been a significant and growing source of imports for Sri Lanka for a wide variety of products. The major import categories before the 1990s were agricultural products, food and beverages, cotton and fibre, machinery and equipment, and base metal. However, this pattern changed quite visibly during the latter half of the 1990s. The most significant imports at present include motor vehicles and parts, mineral fuel, pharmaceuticals, and cement. The top imports from India in 2006 included petroleum oils, motor vehicles—such as motorcycles, diesel or semi-diesel motor vehicles, ambulances, prison vans, hearses and auto trishaws, etc.,—pharmaceutical products, residues and waste from the food industry such as oilcake and other solid residues of soya-bean and mineral products such as cement.

Table 2: Sri Lanka's Exports to India under ISFTA Categories

	Average						
	1999–2000	*2001*	*2002*	*2003*	*2004*	*2005*	*2006*
Negative List	10.5	6.9	3.6	2.7	5.8	2.4	3.3
No. of items	37	34	51	53	69	69	70
Zero Duty	77.6	86.0	94.0	94.3	92.0	95.7	92.7
No. of items	300	383	469	560	664	723	708
Residual List[a]	11.8	7.1	2.4	2.9	2.2	1.8	4.0
No. of items	63	73	100	99	154	162	156
Growth in Exports (%)							
Exports to India	15.7	27.5	143.3	43.1	59.9	45.1	−12.5
Exports to ROW[b]	19.8	−12.8	−2.4	9.2	12.2	10.2	14.4

Notes: a: Includes Tariff Rate Quotas on textiles and tea.
b: Rest of the world.
Source: Estimated using data from Department of Customs, External Trade Statistics, Sri Lanka.

Though, at first glance, this expansion of trade might appear as a clear sign of bilateral trade growth between India and Sri Lanka as a result of the ISFTA, a closer examination is warranted to ascertain whether, in fact, this growth is exclusively attributable to the concessions under the agreement.

In the post ISFTA years, there has undoubtedly been a significant expansion in trade, including greater product diversification on the part of Sri Lanka. At the time of implementation of the ISFTA, Sri Lanka's total products numbered around 400 items; this has risen progressively to around 930 products by 2006, though there was a sharp drop in export earnings growth to India in 2006. And in the case of Sri Lanka, much of the increase in exports has come in those products that progressively received significant tariff concessions from India to reach zero duty by 2003 (see Table 2). As a proportion of total trade, the share of Sri Lankan exports to India receiving such preferential treatment had risen to nearly 93 percent by 2006.

Similarly, the total number of imports from India has risen from 2906 in 2000 to 3409 by 2006. Looking at the overall distribution of concessions granted by Sri Lanka, of the total products exported by India, nearly half of the products in terms of value are subject to the Sri Lanka's negative list, and only around 10 percent benefit from zero tariffs. India's traded exports enjoying zero tariffs are to be found in a few categories such as chemical products, base metal and machinery and mechanical goods where the category of base metal accounts for nearly half of the total. The top 10 imports from India enjoying duty free access to the Sri Lankan market in 2006 were select chemical products.

Table 3: Imports from India under ISFTA Categories

	Average						
	1999–2000	*2001*	*2002*	*2003*	*2004*	*2005*	*2006*
Negative List	41.4	42.4	48.8	56	55.1	46.6	50.5
No. of items	593	588	673	694	747	721	712
Zero Duty	13.6	14.4	15.5	11.8	10.7	13.1	12.8
No. of items	750	739	809	856	873	888	918
Residual List	45.0	43.2	35.8	32.2	34.1	40.	36.7
No. of items	1517	1531	1636	1687	1747	1786	1779
Growth in Imports (%)							
Imports from India	3.7	5.9	46.0	31.4	26.2	6.1	25.3
Imports from ROW[a]	5.6	–8.8	14.4	9.4	19.59	5.5	16.0

Notes: [a] Rest of the world.
Source: Estimated using data from Department of Customs, External Trade Statistics, Sri Lanka.

A breakdown of the composition of Sri Lanka's trade receiving zero duty preference suggests that the increase of Sri Lanka's exports has been concentrated in a handful of export items (see Tables 4 and 5). The most significant expansion has come in the sector of base metals where predominantly Indian investors established manufacturing bases in Sri Lanka to export copper to make use of the preferential tariff treatment afforded under the ISFTA. Copper and copper articles had jumped from accounting for just 3.5 per cent of Sri Lanka's total exports to India in 2001 to account for nearly a half of all exports by 2003.

The other item of significant export expansion has been in vegetable oil which increased its share of exports to India from one per cent in 2002 to 25.6 percent of total exports by 2005. Again the main export item of interest is *Vanaspati* (a hydrogenated vegetable oil similar to ghee) where Indian investors established processing plants in Sri Lanka to make use of the preferential tariff treatment to export to India.

Table 4: Significance of *Vanaspathi* and Copper in Sri Lanka's Exports to India

Category		2000	2001	2002	2003	2004	2005	2006
Animal or Vegetable								
Fats	US $ mn	2.4	1.3	1.6	5.7	17.5	143.1	108.2
Copper and Articles	US $ mn	1.1	2.4	71.2	118.7	12306	155.1	103.0
Other Exports[a]	US $ mn	50.9	65.5	95.7	116.8	244.4	261.0	278.3
As a share of total exports to India	%	93.6	94.6	56.8	48.4	63.4	46.7	56.8
Total Exports to India	US $ mn	54.3	69.3	168.5	241.1	385.5	559.2	489.5
Growth in Exports								
Article 15 and 74	%	14.3	7.1	1855.8	70.8	13.4	111.3	−29.2
Other Exports[a]	%	14.0	28.8	46.0	22.0	109.3	6.8	6.6
Total Exports to India	%	16.8	27	143.3	43.1	59.9	45.1	−12.5

Note: a: Exports to India excluding Article 15 and 74.

Source: Estimated using data from Department of Customs, External Trade Statistics, Sri Lanka.

Table 4 shows the significance of Article 15 (vegetable fats and oils) and 74 (Copper and articles) in the total export earnings of Sri Lanka. Excluding these items, Sri Lanka's total exports to India have increased only from US$51mn in 2000 to US$ 278 mn in 2006. The significance of vegetable fats and copper is evident from the fact that the share of other exports to India declined sharply from 93.6 percent in 2000 to around 57 percent by 2006.

Exports under Articles 15 and 74 reached its peak in 2005 accounting for over half of the total exports to India and with a 111 per cent annual growth, but reported a sharp fall in 2006 with a negative growth as a result of interruptions to shipments following the imposition of quotas/canalisation by India. The overwhelming dominance of *Vanaspathi* and copper exports in the post-ISFTA export basket has generated some concerns as the growth in these export products are not considered to be sustainable in the longer-term. Sri Lanka has no real comparative advantage in either product.

Table 5: Composition of Sri Lanka's Exports Receiving
Zero Duty Treatment under ISFTA[a]

	Sector	Average						
		1999–2000	2001	2002	2003	2004	2005	2006
Live Animals, Animal								
01–05	Products	1.7	0.5	0.1	0.3	0.2	0.2	0.1
06–14	Vegetable products	40.5	28.1	26.3	9.0	7.3	6.2	6.9
15	Animal or vegetable fats and oils	5.0	1.9	1.0	2.4	4.5	25.6	22.1
16–24	Prepared foodstuffs	1.0	1.2	0.4	0.8	0.9	0.6	1.8
25–27	Mineral products	5.0	24.4	5.2	0.5	0.3	0.5	0.5
28–38	Chemical products	0.7	1.2	1.1	2.7	5.3	6.3	4.9
39–40	Plastics and rubber	0.9	0.7	0.9	1.6	1.7	1.1	2.0
41–43	Leather products	0.0	0.1	0.7	0.6	0.7	0.4	0.5
44–46	Wood products	0.1	0.0	0.7	1.7	2.3	2.0	2.1
47–49	Paper products	7.6	8.4	3.8	3.8	3.3	2.7	3.4
50–63	Textile articles	0.0	0.0	0.0	0.0	0.0	0.0	0.0
64–67	Footwear	0.2	0.1	0.0	0.0	0.1	0.0	0.0
68–70	Stone, plaster, cement	0.7	2.4	0.8	2.3	3.6	1.7	5.5
71	Pearls	0.2	0.1	0.1	0.3	0.4	0.5	0.4
72–83	Base metal	11.6	11.2	47.6	55.1	43.8	39.9	29.6
	Copper and articles thereof	(1.5)	(3.5)	(42.3)	(49.2)	(32.1)	(27.7)	(21.0)
Machinery and Mechanical								
84–85	Goods	2.0	4.0	3.4	12.2	15.5	6.8	10.5
86–89	Transport equipment	0.1	0.4	0.3	0.1	0.8	0.1	0.8
90–92	Optical, photographic Equipment	0.1	0.1	0.4	0.1	0.1	0.1	0.1
93	Arms and ammunition	0.0	0.0	0.0	0.0	0.0	0.0	0.0
94–96	Misc. manufactured articles	0.3	1.4	1.1	0.9	1.1	1.2	1.6
97–99	Works of art	0.0	0.0	0.0	0.0	0.0	0.0	0.0
	Total Zero Duty List	77.6	86.0	94.0	94.3	92.0	95.7	92.7

Notes: As a percentage of total exports to India.

Source: Estimated using data from Department of Customs, External Trade Statistics, Sri Lanka.

Sri Lanka's traded exports in recent years placed on the Indian negative list are to be found mostly in the categories related to plastics, rubber articles, pulp of wood, scrap of paper, and textile and textile articles (an explained in table 6). Products that were among the top 50 exports from Sri Lanka to India in 2005 and 2006—but treated under the negative list—included articles of apparel and clothing accessories, smoked sheets and printed paper and paperboard labels of all kinds.

Even though product items under the negative list are less significant in terms of numbers, since 2002 there has been a notable increase in exports subject to negative list treatment. The total value of exports on the negative list exceeded that on residual list in 2002 and continued the pattern until 2006. In 2005, the value of total exports falling under the negative list was around US$13.6 mn while exports treated under the residual list stood at only US$10.3 mn. Though exports under the negative list category have not recorded a steady and significant growth during the period under review, there has nonetheless been a steady growth in products related to plastics and rubber and related articles, waste and scrap of paper, textile articles, etc., under the negative list. Thus, the momentum in bilateral trade generated by tariff preferences appear also to have spilled over—albeit in a moderate way—to trade in products not directly offered preferences as well.

Table 6: Composition of Sri Lanka's Exports under India's ISFTA
Negative List (As a percentage of total value of negative list)

Sector (% share)	1999	2000	2001	2002	2003	2004	2005	2006
Vegetable products	0.0	3.2	0.3	1.0	7.1	47.9	7.8	0.6
Plastics and rubber	78.1	57.8	75.2	88.7	75.9	43.2	72.8	84.4
Paper products	6.8	8.9	14.8	9.3	15.1	7.1	15.0	9.2
Textile articles	15.1	30.1	9.8	1.0	2.0	1.5	4.2	5.6
Total Exports under								
Negative list (US $ mn)	4.7	5.9	4.8	6.1	6.6	22.2	13.6	16.1
No. of items	30	36	34	51	53	69	69	70

Source: Estimated using data from Department of Customs, External Trade Statistics, Sri Lanka.

A chapter-wise analysis of Indian exports facing Sri Lanka's negative list is given in Table 6. As it appears, items of export interest to India are subject to Sri Lanka's negative list. Of those Indian exports falling under the negative list, vegetable products, transport equipments and mineral products account for nearly 80 percent, and increasing over time. In 2006, nearly 11 percent were in the category of vegetable products, 48 percent in mineral products, 19 percent in transport equipment, and six percent in paper products. However, Sri Lanka will permit free access to more than a half of all Indian exports—these items currently entering Sri Lanka on a concessionary base—with the phased tariff reduction to zero duty by 2008.

INDIA-SRI LANKA AGREEMENTS

With the objective of further enhancing the current economic relations, the Governments of Sri Lanka and India, at the highest political level, have agreed to conclude a Comprehensive Economic Partnership Agreement (CEPA). The CEPA aims at promoting trade in both goods and services, facilitating greater investment flows and enhancing mutual cooperation in the sphere of overall economic relations. The existing Indo-Sri Lanka Free Trade Agreement (ISFTA) will become the "Goods Chapter" of the CEPA, with further improvements.

To assess the current status of the bilateral relations and make recommendations on how to move the two economies towards greater economic integration through the conclusion of a CEPA, the then Prime Ministers of Sri Lanka and India in 2002 appointed a Joint Study Group (JSG). The (JSG), co-chaired by Mr. Rakesh Mohan of the Reserve Bank of India and Mr. Ken Balendra of Sri Lanka, concluded in 2003 that the accomplishment of the CEPA would take the two countries to a qualitatively new level of engagement by intensifying and deepening bilateral economic interaction.

The JSG recommendations include improvements to the current ISFTA, binding commitments in identified sectors in services, facilitation of investment flows and enhanced cooperation in the fields of education, culture, ocean resources exploration, health and medicine, agriculture, ferry services, development of railway etc. However, the two sides agreed at the Commerce Secretaries level meeting in August 2004 to refer to the JSG report as a useful reference document in the CEPA process, as it contains valuable recommendations, but not as the basis for Negotiations. The two sides also agreed on two fundamental principles viz, to take in to account asymmetries of the two economies in all elements of negotiations and progressive and sequencing of liberalization in the Services sector.

The binding commitments on trade in goods under CEPA would primarily relate to (a) reducing the size of the negative lists, in the current FTA, (b) more flexibility on rules of origin criteria, (c) elimination of non-tariff barriers, and (d) mutual recognition of products standards and conformity assessment.

As regards the binding commitments on trade in services, the bilateral negotiations will cover pre-identified service sectors, using the WTO General Agreement on Trade in Services (GATS) as the negotiating framework and its positive list approach. The service sectors that are being considered by Sri Lanka for liberalization at the initial stage include information and communication technology, tourism and leisure industry, financial services and transport and logistic services. It is proposed that high priority be given to the infrastructure development and the future growth areas which will facilitate making Sri Lanka a service-hub in the region of South Asia. Sri Lanka would not consider any binding commitments on liberalisation of professional services (*i.e.*, medical, legal, architecture, accounting etc.) until proper regulatory mechanisms are put in place in respect of such service sectors.

INDIA-SRI LANKA BILATERAL RELATIONS

In recent years India and Sri Lanka relationship has been marked by close contacts at the highest political level, growing trade and investment, cooperation in the fields of development, education, culture and defiance, as well as a broad understanding on major issues of international interest.

The nearly three-decade long armed conflict between Sri Lankan forces and the LTTE came to an end in May 2009. During the course of the conflict, India supported the right of the Government of Sri Lanka to act against terrorist forces. At the same time, it conveyed at the highest levels its deep concern at the plight of the mostly Tamil civilian population, emphasizing that their rights and welfare should not get enmeshed in hostilities against the LTTE. The conclusion of the armed conflict saw the emergence of a major humanitarian challenge, with nearly 300,000 Tamil civilians housed in camps for Internally Displaced Persons (IDPs). The Government of India put in place a robust program me of assistance to help these IDPs return to normal life as quickly as possible. In June 2009, Prime Minister Dr. Manmohan Singh announced a grant of INR 5 billion (SLR 12 billion) for relief and rehabilitation in Sri Lanka. In the immediate aftermath of the end of armed conflict, India provided a total of 250,000 family relief packs for the IDPs. It also established an emergency medical unit in the IDP camps, which treated over 50,000 IDPs and carried out over

3000 surgeries from March to September 2009. Medicines worth SLR 225 million (INR 9.2 crores) were also supplied to Sri Lankan authorities.

India also consistently advocated the need for IDPs to be resettled to their original habitations as early as possible. In order to help with this, India provided shelter assistance by way of supplying 10,400 tonnes of galvanized iron (GI) sheets (a total of over one million sheets) between August 2009 and May 2011 for constructing temporary housing for IDPs. In addition, 95,000 starter packs of agricultural implements were supplied to help resettling families begin livelihood generating activities. The Government of India also supplied 400,000 bags of cement to help IDPs rebuild their shelters. Since the requirement of de-mining was a major constraint on the speed of resettlement, the Government of India fully financed seven Indian de-mining teams, engaged in various sectors in northern Sri Lanka to help expedite resettlement.

With the shift from relief and rehabilitation to reconstruction and development, the Government of India turned its attention to the housing requirements of the IDPs. During the visit of President Mahinda Rajapaksa to India from 8–11 June 2010, an announcement was made by Prime Minister Singh that India would support a program me to reconstruct 50,000 houses in Sri Lanka. The groundbreaking ceremony of the pilot phase of the Project for one thousand houses covering all the five districts of Northern Province was held during the visit of the Minister of External Affairs of India Mr. S.M. Krishna to Sri Lanka in November 2010 at Ariyalai near Jaffna. The work on the pilot phase is in advanced stages of completion. The first lot of completed houses was handed over to beneficiaries during the visit of Minister Krishna to Jaffna on 18 January 2012. An MoU with the Government of Sri Lanka on the modalities of implementation of the next phase of the Project for remaining 49,000 houses was also signed during this visit. The next phase, which is expected to be launched soon, will cover the Northern, Eastern, Central and Uva Provinces in terms of its spatial spread and involve construction of new dwelling units and repairs of existing houses.

Since agriculture is the primary means of livelihood in the areas affected by the conflict, Government of India has focused its attention on supporting this sector with a view to jumpstart the revival of the local economy through a wide-ranging program me for agricultural renewal. The proposals that were taken up for urgent implementation include supply of seeds for the Maha and Yala seasons in Sri Lanka in 2010–11 and supply of tractors and other machinery to farmer organizations in northern Sri Lanka. 500 tractors with four implements each (renovator, tiller, cage-wheel and disk plough) have been supplied to farmer organizations and agrarian service centers in the Northern Province. The total cost of the project is SLR 600 million (INR 25 crores approx). To cater to the transportation needs of persons being resettled and to aid revival of their livelihoods, India has also undertaken a project for supply of 10,000 bicycles to returnees in Northern Province.

Education is a core area of cooperation between India and Sri Lanka. Both countries agreed to launch an India Sri Lanka Knowledge Initiative during the visit of President Rajapaksa to India in June 2010. During the visit of Minister of External Affairs Mr. S.M. Krishna in January 2012, a nearly three-fold increase in scholarship support to deserving Sri Lankan students was announced. The expanded scholarship program me would benefit not only regular undergraduate studies but would also provide opportunities for higher research. In addition, under the Indian Technical and Economic Cooperation Scheme and the Colombo Plan, India offers nearly 200 slots annually to Sri Lankan nationals for short and medium term training courses in a wide variety of technical and professional disciplines.

Tourism also forms an important link between India and Sri Lanka and India is the largest source market for Sri Lankan tourism. India is the largest contributor with every fifth tourist being from India. In 2010, out of the total 654,976 tourists, 126,882 were from India constituting about 20%. In the period from January to November 2011, the tourist inflow to Sri Lanka increased to 758,458 from 570,349 in the corresponding period of 2010 showing an increase of about 33 %. Out of this number of 758,458, 153,919 tourists were from India giving a share of about 20 %. Sri Lankan tourists too are among the top ten sources for the Indian tourism market. In 2011, nearly 200,000 visas were issued by the High Commission in Colombo to facilitate travel between Indian and Sri Lanka.

Today, the India-Sri Lanka relationship is strong and poised for a quantum jump by building on the rich legacy of historical linkages and strong economic and development partnerships that have been forged in recent years.

IMPACT OF ISFTA ON BILATERAL TRADE

- The overall trade turnover has grown five times since the entry into force of the FTA and stands at USD 3.2 billion in 2007. India is now the largest trade partner of Sri Lanka. Sri Lanka has also emerged as India's largest trade partner in South Asia, displacing Bangladesh from that position a few years ago.

- Sri Lankan exports to India have grown 10 times while Indian exports, mostly on the non-FTA route, have grown by 5 times.
- FTA has facilitated two way trades between India and Sri Lanka. India was the second largest exporter to Sri Lanka before the FTA and is now the largest exporter to Sri Lanka. But, more important, India became the third largest export destination for Sri Lankan products (rising from 16th rank) as a result of FTA. We can, therefore, say that FTA has enabled India to emerge as Sri Lanka's most balanced trade partner with both exports and imports returning substantial figures. All other leading partners of Sri Lanka are either predominantly exporters or importers.
- FTA has enabled Sri Lanka to export new products where Sri Lanka did not traditionally have capacities.
- While the trade gap has expanded due to faster growth rate of Sri Lankan exports, the export-import ratio has come down from 10.5.1 in 2000 to 5: 3: 1 in 2007.
- Non-FTA exports from Sri Lanka to India in 2007 are negligible at about US$ 50 million, around the same figure as it was when FTA came into force. Non- FTA exports from India to Sri Lanka in 2007 are substantial standing at about US$ 2 billion, up from about US# 500 million in 2000. This would imply that without the FTA, Sri Lankan exports to India would have remained stagnant while Indian exports, which are largely on the non-FTA route, would have grown four times from the 2000 level. In other words, FTA has benefited Sri Lanka by creating 90% of its current export potential.
- The import-export ratio which has come down from 10.5.1 to 5.3.1 In 2007 could have been 40:1 if the FTA was not there.
- Yet another way is to look at size of the economies. Indian economy is about 40 times larger than Sri Lanka. The export of India to Sri Lanka vis-a-vis exports of Sri Lanka to India is only 5 times larger. The ratio of exports and imports without FTA in place as stated above would have been 1:40. It could imply that Sri Lanka's current export potential is much more than should have been given the ratio of size of economies and this is largely due to the FTA.

Services Trade

The initial phase of the cooperation between India and Sri Lanka focused on trade in goods both in the context of SAFTA (South Asian Free Trade Agreement) and Indo-Sri Lanka Free Trade Agreement. In recent years' service sector has gained much importance in terms of its share in GDP and total trade. Sri Lanka concentrated mainly in the export of trans-shipment services as port of Colombo is a major hub port for India and tourism. India however focused in the export of both traditional services (construction, engineering, tourism) and knowledge based services (like software, education, health). Both the countries show much larger engagements in services trade in recent times. Increasing number of Sri Lankan students and patients travel to India to receive education and health services each year. Many Indian services companies such as VSNL, NIIT have already invested in India. Sri Lankan Airlines and Indian private airlines are now flying to each other's cities. Approximately 40% of Sri Lankan airlines' revenue is from the Indian market. IT firms in Sri Lanka are providing technical solutions to Indian companies. Sri Lankan has set up small hotels in different parts of India to cater to tourists coming to India.

The liberalisation of trade in services refers to the removal of barriers that obstruct trade across these modes. Unlike trade in goods where tariffs and taxes are the major trade barriers, government regulations comprise the major barriers to trade in services. These include limitations on foreign investment in services, limits on number of foreign workers permitted, restrictions on remittances of salaries and profits of foreign establishments and so on. The Indo-Lanka trade in services agreement under the CEPA is expected to remove certain barriers in this direction. As the negotiation mainly went on the basis of positive list approach, it should have given flexibility to India and especially to Sri Lanka for commitment, considering the developmental priority. India has agreed to larger and deeper openings than Sri Lanka. India will open far more sectors upfront (about 80 sub-sectors) and grant deeper concessions in each of these areas. In return, Sri Lanka will take up more gradual approach, open only selected areas (about 20 sub-sectors), and restrict openings in these sectors up to the levels it is comfortable with.

ISSUES IN INVESTMENT

Indian investment into Sri Lanka has increased significantly since the FTA came into operation, major reason being the ability to re-export to India while benefiting from lower tariffs on raw materials in Sri Lanka. Between 1978 and 1995, Indian investment accounted for only 1.2% of total FDI. Cumulative Indian investment which was a mere US$ 1.44 million in 1998 increased to US$ 126 million by 2008, contributing to 14% of total FDI flows to Sri Lanka and securing the position of second biggest investor (exceeded by Malaysia). Some of the most visible Indian investments are

Lanka Indian Oil Corporation, TATAs (TajHotels) VSNL, Watawala tea plantations, LIC, L&T (now Aditya Birla Group), Ambujas, Jet Airways, Bharti Airtel etc. Five Indian Human Resource and education companies like ICFAI, banks like ICICI have also entered in Sri Lankan market. Axis Bank, Bank of Baroda etc. are also looking at the opportunity in Sri Lanka. Almost 63% of Indian investment is in the sectors such as telecommunication, health, retail service, energy, hospitality and aviation sector. By the end of 2007, Indian investment resulted in close to 100 projects, employing 6747 individuals 6. Kelegama identifies that during the FTA period job creation by Indian investment has been limited7. FTA has been mainly concentrated on goods sector and perhaps CEPA can address the issue related to investment in much better way. Beyond service sector much of the investment in Sri Lanka especially in the manufacturing sector came from India and third parties in sectors such as vanaspati and copper. This has been to export products back to India and some other countries. CEPA proposes that the Investment Agreement will provide an institutional framework to create an enabling environment for greater flow of investments between the two countries. There will be an MRA on standards. This Agreement on Mutual Recognition/equivalence will facilitate recognition of each other's standards, assessment procedures, equivalence arrangements etc. It also proposes for an MoU on Harmonisation of Ayurvedic medicines which is expected to enable both countries to cooperate in traditional system of medicines. Several studies identifies that Indian investment in Sri Lanka helps domestic entrepreneurs to develop JVs with Indian players for exploring market access possibility in other countries through efficient production system and exploiting economies of scale.

INFRASTRUCTURE DEVELOPMENT

India is active in a number of areas of development activity in Sri Lanka. The last four years have witnessed extension and utilization of credit lines amounting to US $ 281 million. These credit lines have been utilized for wheat, buses, petroleum products, commodities and consultancy services. India is participating in infrastructure development in Sri Lanka. A line of credit of US$ 100 million has been extended for the refurbishment of the southern railway corridor from Colombo to Matara. The project involves track laying on the Kalutara-Matara sector by IRCON and provision of training and rolling stock by RITES. The total cost of the project is likely to be around US$ 167 million and is likely to be implemented in two phases.

In the power sector, as mentioned earlier, NTPC Ltd. is in discussion with Government of Sri Lanka to set up a 500 MW coal based thermal power plant in Trincomalee as a joint venture with Ceylon Electricity Board (CEB). An MoU was signed between NTPC, CEB and GoSL on December 29, 2006 at Colombo. The project would involve investments of US$ 500 million and would be implemented by a JV company to be formed with a stake of 50% each by NTPC and CEB.

Another power related project relates to setting up an interconnection of the electricity grid between India and Sri Lanka to enable Sri Lanka to source electricity from India. The two sides have set up a Steering Committee at Power Secretary level and a Task Force to carry out negotiations on the modalities of implementation.

Lanka Indian Oil Corporation has invested in Sri Lanka and now operates 170 petrol pumps in Sri Lanka and has successfully raised money through an IPO to fund expansion of its activities, including the setting up of a lubes plant in Trincomalee with an investment of US and 5 million.

DEVELOPMENT CO-OPERATION

In Sri Lanka, a number of development projects are planned and also implemented with maximum efforts under the Indian government.

India and Sri Lanka have also signed a MoU in April 2008 for creation of vocational training centre in Puttalam which is under implementation. During the Joint Commission meeting in 2005, EAM announced a scheme for Small Development Projects. A MoU on Cooperation in small development Projects has been signed. India has started work on several such projects at a cost of ₹ 40 million each and the numbers are likely to increase with the period of time. Some of the projects being implemented include providing fishing equipments to the fishermen in the North and East of Sri Lanka, Solar Photovoltaic Aided Computer Education in Uva Province of Sri Lanka, creation of an Ayurveda faculty in the Eastern University of Sri Lanka, supply of 4 Air Quality Monitoring Stations to Government of Sri Lanka and renovation of a Railway Station in Colombo.

In the health sector, India has assisted with supply of equipment and renovation of OT at Dickoya, and work is on for implementation of a project for construction of a 150-bed hospital at Dickoya and for upgradation of the hospital at Trincomalee. A proposal for supplies of equipment to the medical faculty in Eastern University is also under consideration. This is in addition to donation of medicines to the hospital in Point Pedro, supply of 4 state of the art ambulances, a cataract eye surgery programme for 1500 people and donation of equipment to hospitals at Hambantota and Point Pedro.

In continuation of this process, during 2008, India and Sri Lanka entered into necessary arrangements to provide a line of credit of US$ 100 million for the upgradation of Southern Railway corridor in Sri Lanka between Colombo and Matara. This project, once implemented, will reduce the time taken in travelling on this sector and improve the overall quality of travel experience on this sector.

India is also assisting in development of the core sectors like power and energy Talks between NTPC and CEB have progressed on setting up a joint venture to set a coal based thermal power plant in Sampur in Eastern Sri Lanka. The plant would have a capacity to produce 300 MW and would involve and investment of US$ 500 million. India and Sri Lanka have also finalised a MoU on conducting a feasibility study for establishing inter connection of electricity grids between the two countries. The MoU is likely to be signed shortly.

As part of our bilateral assistance program India implemented a number of projects last year. Under the Small Development Project scheme, fishing boats and equipment at a cost of Sri Lanka ₹ 110 million were granted to IDPs in Eastern Sri Lanka. A similar programme is currently under consideration. Another program to set up a faculty of AYUSH medicine in Eastern University of Sri Lanka is under implementation. A project to supply equipment for establishment of 20 Nenasalas (e-learning centres) in Eastern Province is also under implementation. India had, earlier set up 20 nenasalas all across Sri Lanka. In order to improve connectivity of Battichola and Trincomalee with Colombo. India is currently implementing a project to supply 5 Rail Buses to the Eastern Province. India is also examining the possibility of rehabilitation of some schools in the Eastern Province through supply of equipment and study materials.

CONCLUSION

The relationship between India and Sri Lanka has undergone a period of significant recuperation since 1990. In the post 1990 period consistent efforts have been made by India and Sri Lanka to upgrade bilateral economic relations. India and Sri Lanka have established a dense bilateral network of institutions and mechanisms so as to ensure sustained cooperation irrespective of domestic politics and changes in the external environment of the two countries. The year 1998 saw the biggest boost in economic relations when both the countries signed ISLFTA. ISFTA has resulted in rapid expansion of trade volume, growth in investments, better connectivity, and a more intensive economic and development cooperation between both the countries. ISLFTA has promoted mutually beneficial bilateral trade and strengthened intra-regional economic cooperation. Following the success of ISFTA, the governments of India and Sri Lanka felt that more action was required to unleash the full potential of bilateral economic relations. Accordingly, both the governments decided to set up a JSC to explore possibilities of starting negotiations for a CEPA. CEPA is expected to build on momentum generated by the ISFTA. CEPA seeks to extend two economies beyond trade in goods, to include services, investment and overall economic co-operation. It will address some of the issues that have come up in the implementation and operation of the ISLFTA as well. It will also impart renewed impetus and synergy to bilateral economic relations. Economic relationship between India and Sri Lanka are at the highest level of cordiality. India and Sri Lanka will develop development partnership in the coming years. Economic relations can go a long way in building and cementing stable and peaceful political and strategic relations. India-Sri Lanka relationship is heading towards model relationship which can be emulated by other smaller states in Indian Ocean countries as well as South Asia.

REFERENCES

[1] Mel, De. Deshal 2008, "Indo-Sri Lanka Free Trade Agreement Sri Lankan Perspectives", Bilateral Trade, Trade Insight, Volume 4, No. 2.

[2] Mukherjee, I.N., T. Jayawardena and S. Kelegama (2002), "India-Sri Lanka Free Trade Agreement: An Assessment of Potential and Impact", SANEI completed study available at www.saneinetwork.net.

[3] R. Hariharan India's concerns in Sri Lanka: Update No. 199 South Asia Analysis Group 6th June 2010.

[4] Central Bank of Sri Lanka (2005) Annual Report.

[5] Grarer, F., and A. Mattoo, eds., (2001). *India and ASEAN: The Politics of India's Look East Policy*, New Delhi: Manohar Publishers.

[6] International Monetary Fund (IMF), Various Issues, "Direction of Trade Statistics", IMF

[7] Kelegama, S., (1999). "Indo-Sri Lanka Trade and Bilateral Free Trade Agreement: A Sri Lankan Perspective", Asia Pacific Development Journal, Vol. 6, No. 2.

[8] Kodikara, S., (1965), *Indo-Ceylon Relations since Independence*, The Ceylon Institute of World Affairs, Colombo Apothecaries Co.

[9] Mukherji, I.N., (2000). "Indo-Sri Lanka Trade and Investment Linkages: With Special. Reference to SAPTA and Free Trade Agreement", South Asia Economic Journal, Vol. 1, No. 1, March 2000.

[10] Panchamukhi, V.R., V.L. Rao and N. Kumar, (1993). "Indo-Sri Lanka Economic Cooperation: An Operational Programme", Research and Information System for the Non-Aligned and Other Developing Countries, New Delhi.

Computer Monitoring and Right to Privacy: A Comparative Analysis of Sri Lanka and India

Prathiba Mahanamahewa

INTRODUCTION

It is no secret that governments worldwide are going "online" (*i.e.*, accessing the Internet and establishing Web sites) at a very rapid rate. The United States leads all countries with most of their agencies online. Canada and Australia online agencies follow the United States. In Sri Lanka, the government embarked on an ambitious program that established e-mail and Internet in all government sector organisations under the guise of World Bank in 2003. Under this project public sector employees are equipped with a computer and wide access to e-mail and Internet in the workplace. This transformation of workplace to on-line environment has raised numerous privacy related questions for both employers and the employees. In particular, the issue of e-mail and Internet usage and employee monitoring in the workplace is a significant matter. It was demonstrated here that many countries around the world are competing rapidly to maintain a policy to govern this issue in respect of employee privacy in the workplace. Finding the balance point for many public managers means developing, implementing, and enforcing an acceptable use policy for the e-mail and Internet. But what are the key components of such a policy? How and why do the components vary from organisation to organisation? This paper analyses the issue of electronic surveillance in the workplace and its impact on employee privacy rights. This paper will commence with a discussion of E-government and its various stations and in particular its implementation in Sri Lanka and India. It will then consider the information privacy as a human right in international and regional instruments. This will be followed by an evaluation of the regulatory framework for protection of privacy in Sri Lanka and India. Finally it highlights the importance of an e-policy in an organisation to balance the competing interests of employer and employee and proposing a convention for the SAARC region.

E-GOVERNMENT

E-Government initiatives can be seen to operate at various levels (O'Flaherty, 2000). The first level comprises simple government to citizen communication through which government information such as reports, policy documents, legislation and case law is made available direct to the public through electronic means. In the second stage, citizen to government communication becomes possible allowing citizens to make electronic submissions concerning government proposals for example or to provide government agencies with new information about themselves, such as change of address, by electronic means. Third-level services facilitate more complex interactive transactions. These often involve legally binding procedures and/or online payments. Examples of such transactions include voter and motor vehicle registration or the submission of formal objections to applications for building permits. Fourth level services focus on the delivery of access to a wide range of government services across a whole government administration through a single contact point. At the fifth stage, yet to be fully realized in practice, government applications become intertwined with commercial applications and users are facilitated in building their own interfaces designed around their personal interactions with both government services and commercial entities.

INTERNET USAGE AND ELECTRONIC PRIVACY

There are four primary categories of Internet usage: sending and receiving electronic mail (Known as e-mail), accessing and posting documents on the World Wide Web, sending and retrieving computer files (known as file transfer protocol or FTP),and joining electronic discussion groups (such as news groups, listservs, and Internet relay chat groups). E-mail is the most widely used Internet service, although many users are active in all categories. In general the workplace presents a unique arena for privacy analysis. Two competing interests exist in the employment context: the employer's right to conduct business in a self-determined manner is matched by the employee's privacy interests or the right to be let alone.

For managers, monitoring is necessary. It is argued that workplace e-mail and Internet monitoring are the most effective means to ensure a safe and secure working environment and to protect employees. In addition, some contend that monitoring may boost efficiency, productivity and customer service and allows more accuracy to evaluate performance (DeTienne, 1993; Sipior and Ward, 1995; Orthmann, 1998; Sipior *et al.*, 1998). The impact of monitoring of these workplace relationships is the focus of this thesis. If used reasonably it may enhance efficiency without "trenching on" employees rights.

However, critics of monitoring point to research evidencing a link between monitoring and psychological and physical health problems, increased boredom, high tension, extreme anxiety, depression, anger, serve fatigue and musculoskeletal problems (Amick and Smith 1992; Kidwell and Bennett, 1994; Chalykoff and Kochan, 1989; OTA, 1987; Working Women Education Fund 9 to5, 1990; Stanton, 2000). More seriously, critics point to violations of their fundamental right to privacy (Stone *et al.*, 1983; Bylinsky, 1991; Culnan, 1993; Smith, 1993; Vest *et al.*, 1995; Alge, 2001). Unless an acceptable remedy is soon found, workplace productivity may rapidly deteriorate and employee morale may disintegrate.

INFORMATION PRIVACY AS A HUMAN RIGHT

International Instruments

The most significant international human rights instrument is that of the *Universal Declaration of Human Rights of 1948* (UDHR). Its provisions which deal expressly with privacy are set out in article 12, which states:

> No one shall be subjected to arbitrary interference with his privacy, family, home or correspondence, nor to attacks upon his honour and reputation. Everyone has the right to the protection of the law against such interference or attacks.

In almost identical terms, article 17 of the *International Covenant on Civil and Political Rights, 1966* (ICCPR) provides that:

> No one shall be subjected to arbitrary or unlawful interference with his privacy, family, home correspondence, nor to unlawful attacks upon his honour and reputation.

> Everyone has the right to the protection of the law against such interference or attacks.

Regional Instruments

Whereas the above provisions are framed essentially in terms of a prohibition on "interference with privacy", the equivalent provisions of article 8 of the *European Convention on Human Rights, 1950* (ECHR) are phrased in terms of a right to "respect for private life":

Everyone has the right to respect for his private and family life, his home and correspondence.

There shall be no interference by a public authority with the exercise of this right except such as is in accordance with the law and is necessary in a democratic society in the interests of national security, public safety or the economic well-being of the country, for the prevention of disorder or crime, for the protection of health or morals, or for the protection of the rights and freedoms of others.

The Charter of Fundamental Rights of the European, 2000 Union reaffirms the recognition of fundamental rights in the context of EU. Article 7 of the Charter states that:

Everyone has the right to respect for his or her private and family life, home and communication.

Article 8 of the Charter states that:

1. Everyone has the right to the protection of personal data concerning him or her.
2. Such data must be processed fairly for specified purposes and on the basis for the consent of the person concerned or some other legitimate basis laid down by law. Everyone has the right of access to data which has been collected concerning him or her, and the right to have it rectified.
3. Compliance with these rules shall be subject to control by an independent authority.

The intention of the drafters of this article was to follow the traditional wording of article 8 (ECHR) while at the same time adapting the former to modern developments and technological change. This was done by replacing the term 'correspondence' (article 8, ECHR) with 'communications'. Article 7 guarantees protection against the intervention or interference of public authorities in the private sphere.

Article 8 of the Charter recognises Data Protection as an innovative fundamental right. The Draft Treaty establishing a Constitution for Europe ('European Constitution'), as proposed by the European Convention on the Future of Europe reproduces article 7 of the Charter of Fundamental Rights under article 7 and article 8. Article 50 of the Draft Treaty is intended to establish a single legal basis for the protection of personal data, both for the protection of data which is processed by the European institutions. The protection of privacy may take on new meaning as a consequence of the Charter of Human Rights and the adoption of privacy provisions in a future European Constitution. Other than article 11 of the Inter-American Convention on Human Rights, the major regional human rights catalogue omits express protection for privacy or private life.

These international and regional instruments recognise privacy as a fundamental human and civil right. If article 12 of the Universal Declaration of Human Rights is taken in conjunction with article 8 of the Convention for the protection of Human Rights and Fundamental Freedoms, as well as with the concepts outlined by international organisations and individual countries, a fairly clear and broad definition of privacy can be identified, setting a standard of privacy that clearly protects the individual. That which is private should be respected, only to be breached in the case of very clearly set criteria, a notion reinforced with the European Convention of human rights. It is against these fundamental codes and declarations of human rights that this consideration of e-Work and monitoring is set. All actors considered are clearly covered by the definition and should, therefore, be respectful of and compliance with the protection provided by them. Although electronic surveillance is yet to be considered under the ICCPR, it has been taken up under the equivalent privacy right (article 8) contained in the ECHR, as well as in the draft European Constitution.

THE COUNCIL OF EUROPE AND THE DATA PROTECTION DIRECTIVES

The Council of Europe Convention for the *Protection of Individuals with regard to Automatic Processing of Personal Data 1981* seeks to protect individual rights and freedoms. The convention is particularly relevant because it provides for a right to privacy. In 1995, the European Union enacted the *Data Protection Directive (95/46/EC)* in order to harmonize member states' laws in providing consistent levels. The Directive provides for a basic or fundamental level of privacy that not only reinforces current data protection law, but also establishes a range of new rights. The twin objectives of the Directive expressed in Article 1 were: to protect the rights of individuals with respect to the processing of their personal data; and to facilitate the free movement of personal data between member states. The first objective received much attention and it was the second that hold out the prospect of major economic benefit. The EU Directive (1995) is motivated by economic considerations, particularly the need to harmonise data privacy laws in the Union. However, the Directive also stresses the importance of fundamental human rights. The economic impact of the EU Directives has been far greater than any other instrument given its legal effect within the EU and its approach towards third countries. One of the fundamental economic objectives of the Directive was to enhance the free flow of data within the EU by removing barriers caused by internal borders.

In 1997, the European Union supplemented the 1995 directive by introducing the *Telecommunications Privacy Directive (97/66/EC)*. On June 25, 2002 the European Union Council adopted the new privacy and *Electronic Communication Directives (2002/58/EC)*. In the context of the spread of ICT at work and its associated risks, new concerns are arising in respect of the relationships between employers and employees to address these special issues related to workplace privacy. The European Commission is due to enact a Directive on workplace data protection in 2004 or 2005. The next section analyses information privacy defined in agreements of International organisation.

INTERNATIONAL ORGANISATIONS

Organisation for Economic Cooperation and Development (OECD)

In the late 1980s, the OECD issued a set of guidelines concerning the privacy of personal records. Although broad, the OECD guidelines set up important standards for future governmental privacy rules. Unsurprisingly, the organization had economic considerations in mind when it issued its guidelines. These guidelines underpin most current international agreements, national laws, and self-regulatory policies, and are voluntary and address the collection limitation principle, purpose specification principle, use limitation principle, openness principle and accountability principle. Clarke (1988) argues that the expression of privacy guidelines was shown to have been motivated by the protection of business activities, rather than of peoples privacy.

The primary reference for privacy protection is located in the OECD *Guidelines on the Protection of Privacy and Transborder Flows of Personal Data in 1980* and Implementing the OECD 'Privacy Guidelines' in the Electronic Environment: Focus on the Internet', Committee for Information, Computer and Communications Policy. This instrument is a set of guidelines. It is not a convention; and it merely "recommends" that member countries consider the principles into their domestic legislation. Greenleaf (1996) contends that existing legislations having incorporated privacy guidelines do not provide sufficient protection against new monitoring technologies coupled with highly bureaucratic administrative practices.

International Labour Organisation (ILO)

The ILO has no convention to protect privacy but has adopted a *Code of Practice on Protection of Workers Personal Data 1997*, which covers general principles about protection of personal data and specific provisions regarding the collection, security, storage, use and communication of such data. Unlike other ILO instruments, the code is not legally binding like other international treaties. It provides employers and workers with the basis for rules to be designed by them. The code was intended to provide guidance in the development of legislation, regulations, collective agreements, work rules, policies and practical measures in the workplace.

According to an ILO survey (ILO, 1993), workers in industrialized countries are gradually losing privacy in the workplace as technological advances allow employers to monitor nearly every facet of time on the job as a remedial measure and to protect employee privacy. The ILO introduced, therefore, guidelines on employee monitoring at the workplace. To further protect workplace privacy the ILO introduced a code of practice called the *Protection of Worker's Personal Data* (1997). Its purpose is to provide guidance on the protection of workers personal data and is not as a binding force. The code does not replace national laws, regulations or other accepted standards. It can be used in the developments of legislation, regulations, collective agreements, work rules, policies and practical measures at enterprise level. According to the ILO Code, secret monitoring is permitted only if there is suspicion on reasonable grounds of criminal activity or other serious wrongdoing. The ILO recognises that workers rights to privacy should be treated as a fundamental human rights issue, but the new technology can pose dangers to privacy, even as it is improving all of our lives. The ILO calls the problem the "chemistry of intrusion", a combination of threats to informational privacy, increasing encroachments on physical privacy and increased physical surveillance.

There is a certain consistency among these principal instruments. Each seeks to establish consistent rules to protect the recognized right to privacy in order to pre-empt incompatible national rules that would damage the economic benefits of free flow of information.

It is now a quarter of a century since key data privacy instruments were adopted by the OECD (1980) and Council of Europe (1981). These were followed by the United Nations Guidelines (1990) and EU Directives (1995). Most of these instruments have had reviews of one or another sort. Nonetheless, there are people who wonder whether the various national laws, and these instruments, really achieve their objectives of protecting privacy and whether achieving the supposed benefits is worth the cost. The time to define the exact nature and extent of privacy protections is long overdue. Unless privacy is asserted as a human right, fundamental protecttions for individuals and institutions will decline leading to a breakdown of social and economic processes.

The EU Directives requires that "Each member State shall provide that one or more public authorities are responsible for monitoring the application within its territory of provisions adopted by the Member states pursuant to the Directive" (EU 1995, Article 28.1). The OECD Guidelines fail to require the creation of privacy protection agency. However, the public expectation is that a specialist body will exist to supervise government agencies and corporations, and the OECD Guidelines fail to fulfil that expectation. The OECD Guidelines fail to specify the measures needed to ensure that privacy protection regime is achieved. The OECD Guidelines appear to be silent on this matter. They clearly need to be enhanced to require the privacy protection agency to make the maximum information available to the public, and to establish working relationships with privacy advocates and representatives of the public. Therefore, need to define a new the exact nature and extant of privacy protections.

Is There any Legal Protection for Data Privacy in Sri Lanka?

The concept of privacy is not clearly defined unlike the European Union, where most people seem to know what to expect, which makes the work of the judicial bodies easier as issues of interpretation are quickly settled. Conventionally, general privacy concerns have been addressed through the law of torts (breach of confidentiality, trespass and nuisance) and criminal law. Like many other Commonwealth countries the common law of Sri Lanka is based on principles of English law. In addition, some of the principles of law of contract are governed by Roman-Dutch law like in South Africa. The lack of a framework on data protection prevents e-business from the European Union and affects Sri Lanka's economy. Therefore, privacy norms and procedures are expected to arrive from the United Kingdom.

Therefore, legislative measures or other measures, such as the adoption of "Codes of Practice", embodying privacy principles would ensure workplace privacy protection on employees' personal information. This would mean that Sri Lanka is in a similar position with the West. The question remains whether these arrangements can meet the extra demands brought about by electronic communications.

Information about an individual's tastes and leisure activity has economic value, and the exchange of such information helps to grease the economy. Sri Lanka has never banned the sale of such data, despite the potential impact on privacy. There are, however, many different levels of legal protection for privacy when websites and e-commerce firms, without consent, use private information for commercial purposes. No comprehensive protection exists. In many countries there is a general law that governs the collection, use and dissemination of personal information by the public and private sectors. An oversight body then ensures compliance. This is the preferred model for most countries adopting data protection laws and was adopted by the EU to ensure compliance with its data protection regime.

Legislation to Protect Privacy in India

Like in Sri Lanka the Indian Constitution does not expressly guarantee a right to privacy. Therefore, on the face of it, it may seem that the law both in India and Sri Lanka has placed less emphasis upon this right. However there are several legal cases recognized Right to Privacy in India recently.

In M.P. Sharma and Others v Satish Chandra, District Magistrate, Delhi and Others It was stated,

> *When the Constitution makers have thought fit not to subject such regulation to constitutional limitations by recognition of a fundamental right to privacy, analogous to the American Fourth Amendment, we have no justification to import it, into a totally different fundamental right, by some process of strained construction.*

Though, initially, the Indian courts took a stringent stance against regarding the right to privacy as a fundamental right, with the passage of time a more liberal approach was taken and perhaps the landmark decision of *Kharak Singh v The State of Uttar Pradesh and Other*[1] is a manifestation of this change in judicial thinking. However, it must be pointed out that the Indian courts were not willing to expressly recognise a fundamental right to privacy. This becomes apparent from the words of Justice Subba Rao in *Kharak Singh*, which are as follows:

Further, the right to personal liberty takes in not only a right to be free from restrictions placed on his movements, but also free from encroachments on his private life. It is true our Constitution does not expressly declare a right to privacy as a fundamental right, but the said right is an essential ingredient of personal liberty. Every democratic country sanctifies domestic life; it is expected to give him rest, physical happiness, peace of mind and security. In the last resort, a person's house, where he lives with his family, is his "castle": it is his rampart against encroachment on his personal liberty. The pregnant words of that famous Judge, Frankfurter J., in Wolf v. Colorado, (1949) 338 US 25, pointing out the importance of the security of one's privacy against arbitrary intrusion by the police, could have no less application to an Indian home as to an American one.

In *Rajagopal alias R.R. Gopal and another v State of T.N. and others*, the Indian Supreme Court held that the right to privacy is not enunciated as a fundamental right in the Indian Constitution but may be inferred from Article 21. In this case, reliance was placed on *Kharak Singh* and other decisions of English and American courts for holding that the petitioners had a right to publish what they alleged to be an autobiography of A. Shankar (insofar as it appears from the public records), even without his consent or authorisation. The Court however cautioned that, if they go beyond that and publish his life story, they may be invading his right to privacy. For this purpose, the Court held that a citizen has a right to safeguard his own privacy, as well as that of his family, marriage, procreation, motherhood, child-bearing and education among other matters. No one can publish anything concerning the above matters without his consent, whether truthful or otherwise and whether laudatory or critical. The position may, however, be different if a person voluntarily thrusts himself into controversy or invites or raises a controversy. The Court also pointed out an exception to such an instance, namely:

This is for the reason that once a matter becomes a matter of public record, the right to privacy no longer subsists and it becomes a legitimate subject for comment by press and media among others. We are, however, of the opinion that in the interests of decency [Article 19(2), Indian Constitution] an exception must be carved out to this rule, viz., a female who is the victim of a sexual assault, kidnap, abduction or a like offence should not further be subjected to the indignity of her name and the incident being published in press/media.[2]

Therefore, it is clear that the Indian judiciary has inferred an implied right to privacy in the guise of "personal liberty" which is protected in terms of Article 21 of the Indian Constitution.

E-Policies

Organisations without such policies run the risk of being sued for actions of an employee. Policies "create clear standards to prevent employment disputes and ensure consistent supervisory administration of employment relations". The specific policy selected depends on the culture of the workplace, but most policies have common elements.

The common policy components are:

- Cautioning employee about the risks of using e-mail and the Internet.
- Informing employees:
    - that e-mail is irretrievable
    - that Internet activities can be traced by third parties
    - of downloading procedures and the risk of viruses
    - of all prohibitions of inappropriate and illegal uses
    - that the employer can be held liable for activities of the employee, and
    - that their electronic actions can be so identified with the employer.
- Include information designed to curtail employee conduct for which the company may be liable, namely: defamation, harassment, and discrimination; copyright and patent infringement.
- Establish limits on what may be downloaded from the Internet or exchanged via e-mail.
- Remind users that text, graphics, and software that appear to be freely available on the Internet are often subject to intellectual property laws that limit copying, distribution, and use.
- Confidential Information
- Use technological means to prevent trade secret and confidential files from being transmitted.
- Mandate the use of encryption software or ban the transmission of sensitive information altogether.
- Create an approval and clearing policy for information to be published on the web
- Establish monitoring procedures and inform employees about the details of such monitoring

- If applicable, clarify that incidental personal use is a privilege, which can be revoked for abuse or excessive use.

CONCLUSION

It is well established that neither constitution nor statutory law addresses the new privacy issues associated with technology and the old common law does not clearly cover the area of privacy in question in Sri Lanka. Therefore a gap exists between the time when a new communication technology is created and the time when a statute is designed by state legislature to cover the new technology. This paper contends that a modern computerised workplace reduces the arbitrary powers enjoyed by the employers and reduces their ability to act against the employee unilaterally and effectively. Hence, we can design a incentive-compatible, benefit maximising contact between managers and employees based on the following principles: employee participation in defining privacy policies; full disclosure of all implementation schemes pursuant to these policies; and employer monitoring to ensure compliance with such policies. Finally, this has been endorsed by the Article 29—European Union Data protection Working Party (Article—29 EU Data Protection Working Party, 2002, p. 24) in their statement specifically: "A blanket ban on personal use of the Internet by employees may be considered to be impractical and slightly unrealistic as it fails to reflect the degree to which the Internet can assist employees in their daily life".

REFERENCES

[1] O'Flaherty (2000). 'Privacy Impact Assessments: an essential tool for data protection' A presentation to a plenary session on New Technologies, Security and Freedom' at the 22nd Annual Meeting of Privacy and Data Protection Officials held in Venice, September 27-30 2000.

[2] DeTienne (1993). "Big brother or friendly coach? Computer monitoring in the 21st century" *The Futurist*, Vol. 27, p. 33.

[3] Sipior and Ward (1995). "The ethical and legal quandary of email privacy" *Communications of the Association for Computing Machinery*, Vol. 38, p. 8.

[4] Orthmann (1998). "Workplace computer monitoring" *Employment Testing—Law and Policy Reporter*, Vol. 12, p. 182.

[5] Amick and Smith (1992). "Stress, computer-based work monitoring and measurement systems" *Applied Ergonomics*, Vol. 23, p. 6.

[6] Kidwell and Bennett (1994). "Employee Reactions to Electronic Control Systems" *Group and Organization Management*, Vol. 19, p. 203.

[7] Chalykoff and Kochan (1989). "Computer-aided monitoring: Its influence on employee job satisfaction and turnover" *Personnel Psychology*, Vol. 42, p. 807.

[8] OTA, (1987). Office of Technology Assessment (1987). *The electronic supervisor: New technology, new tensions* (U.S. Government Printing Office: Washington DC).

[9] Working Women Education Fund 9 to 5 (1990). *"Stories of mistrust and manipulation: The electronic monitoring of the American workforce"* (Author: Cleveland, OH).

[10] Stanton (2000). "Reaction to Employee Performance Monitoring: Framework, Review, and Research Directions" *Human Performance*, Vol. 3, p. 85.

[11] Stone *et al.* (1983). "A Field Experiment Comparing Information-Privacy Values, Beliefs, and Attitudes Across Several Types of Organizations" *Journal of Applied Psychology*, Vol. 68, p. 459.

[12] Bylinsky (1991). "How companies spy on employees" *Fortune*, Vol. 124, p. 131.

[13] Culnan (1993). "How did they get my name? An exploratory investigation of consumer attitudes toward secondary information use" *MIS Quarterly*, Vol. 17, p. 341.

[14] Smith (1993). "Privacy policies and practices: Inside the organizational maze" *Communications of the ACM*, Vol. 36, p. 105.

[15] Vest *et al.* (1995). "Factors influencing managerial disclosure of AIDS health information to co-workers" *Journal of Applied Social Psychology*, Vol. 25, p. 1043.

[16] Alge (2001). "Effects of Computer Surveillance on Perceptions of Privacy and Procedural Justice" *Journal of Applied Psychology*, Vol. 86, p. 797.

India-Sri Lanka Relations with Special Reference to Urban Regional Planning

V. Suresh

INTRODUCTION

The phrase 'local self-government could have different meanings, according to the countries concerned. Local self-government and decentralization of governance functions, as used in certain countries, ostensibly have their origins in US terminology and tradition. In certain other countries, local self-government has been too closely equated with just local government; and decentralization with enabling the latter and not really local 'self-government; In fact that decentralization decision-making ensures the well-being of all of those who are likely to be affected by such decisions is now well known. The rationale of this premise is derived from the democratic imperative that all those whose interests are affected by decisions ought to take part in the decision-making process. When everybody takes part in the decision-making process, self- interest is supposed to guide them to arrive at decisions that are consistent with everybody's good. This logic provides the theoretical basis for the evolution of decentralized political institutions which are looked up on as institutions that promote decentralized decision-making.

The rationale of decentralized governance is also derived from the known drawbacks of centralized decision-making at the macro government levels. Being away from the basic spatial units such as hamlets and villages and with concentrated at the top of the space in a pyramid power base, the state and the union government power structures draw representatives from well-endowed sub-regions and sections of the community, leaving the backward regions and weaker sections unrepresented. This gives rise to the emergence of enclave-type power bases and unequal distribution of power among people. The interests, felt needs and aspirations of some sections and of people living in backward and interior regions are thus likely to be overlooked under the centralized decision-making system.

In recent years there has been a dramatic flowering of decentralization initiatives among the developing countries of Asia. The rang and diversity of these initiatives is quite impressive, reflecting the different historical, cultural and political conditions of the various countries. At the same time, there are many common threads and features running through the different systems, that are beginning to emerge, it is worthwhile examining the theoretical underpinnings of decentralization, the origins of the various systems, their common and distinctive features, and their effectiveness in providing for meaningful citizen involvement in the local governance process and the future directions in which decentralized governance systems should move. The South Asian Association for Regional Cooperation (SAARC) is a manifestation of the determination of the peoples of South Asia to work together towards finding solutions to their common problems in a spirit of friendship, trust and understanding and to create an order based on mutual respect, equity and shared benefits. The primary objective of the Association is the acceleration of the process of economic and social development in member status, through collective action in agreed areas of corporation. Decentralization of administration had been the main objective of administrative reforms in Sri Lanka since independence in 1948. The Four types of local authorities, viz., the District Development Council (DDCs), the Municipal Council (MCs), Urban Council (UCs) or Town Councils (TCs), and Village Councils (VCs) created by the national legislature were responsible for selected services and amenities in their respective areas. The thirteenth Amendment to the constitution brought a major change in Sri Lanka's of system of governance by providing for the devolution of power to a second tier of governance in the country at provincial level. The present paper describes urban regional planning in Sri Lanka local governance.

DEMOGRAPHY

Sri Lanka is an island situated close to the southeastern tip of the Indian subcontinent. It has a land area of 62,337 square kilometers. About 75 per cent of the lands comprise broad lowland plains. The hilly area is in the Centre and has been the feeder area for all rivers that flow to the Indian Ocean in a radial formation. The island receives rain from southwest and northeast monsoons and thunderstorms. The population is around 18.3 million with an annual population growth rate of 1.1 per cent. 57 per cent are concentrated in less than 25 per cent of the total land area. About 52 per cent live in the western, central and southern provinces.

NATIONAL GOVERNMENTAL POLITICAL STRUCTURE

Sri Lanka gained Independence from the British in 1948 and has a democratic system of government. It is governed under a unitary system of Constitution and is a republic. The legislative power of the people rests with the Parliament whose members are elected on a political party basis, while the President who exercises the executive power is elected from the total electorate. Judicial power is exercised by the Parliament through Courts and other tribunals. Although for sovereignty purposes the Parliament is exercising judicial power, the Supreme Court, the Court of Appeal and other Courts are free from outside interventions and maintain judicial independence. The Constitution has been promulgated thrice: in 1946, 1972 and 1978. The Thirteenth Amendment to the Constitution of 1987 has special relevance to power sharing between the central government and other levels of government within the system of republican governance. Under these amendments, subjects and functions in the purview of central and provincial governments have been identified in three scheduled lists: those of the central government, those of the provincial government and powers concurrent among central and provincial governments. The central government can set national policies on all subjects and functions and has the power to approve legislation on the concurrent list of subject areas that have been listed as provincial subjects in the scheduled list. The provincial Governor of each province is responsible for the execution of policies and statutes made by the provincial council on devolved subjects, through the Board of Provincial Ministers. A provincial public service has been constituted for each province to support the executive. Except for the policies on the form, structure and constitution of local authorities and the national policy making related to local government, all other activities inclusive of operations, supervision of management, including the power to dissolve a local authority, come under the purview of a provincial council. The provincial Minister and the provincial Commissioner of Local Government are holders of these offices in the provincial council. At present, the political subdivisions are as follows: 8 provincial councils, 14 municipal councils, 37 urban councils and 258 Pradeshiya Sabhas (divisional/rural councils). Although the provincial council supervises local councils, a proposal is being made to bring the Colombo and Jayawardenapura-Kotte municipal councils under the central government, when the proposed new Constitution is promulgated. Under the British colonial rule and even at present the district administration plays a key role in the administration of the government, although its importance has been reduced due to the process of power sharing that commenced in 1987. There are currently 25 districts in Sri Lanka. Although members of Parliament are proportionally elected on a district there is no House or Assembly at the district level. Out of the three electoral memberships, *i.e.* Parliament, provincial council and local authority, the first is the most powerful. Due to this situation there is competition to climb the political ladder. Therefore, the elected members at all levels consider the one below as a political competitor. This mindset leads members of Parliament to undertake development efforts in their electorate (*i.e.* district), often without consulting local authorities. Since they are considered superior, the members of Parliament have created institutional structures to make appropriate district organizations more powerful. The district and divisional co-ordinating committees are good examples. The term of office for the President is six years, for Parliament and provincial councils it is five years each. For local authorities it is basically four years with the provision that the Minister could advance the term of office by 12 months or extend it by 12 months.

EVOLUTION OF LOCAL GOVERNMENT, ITS LEGAL AND POLITICAL BACKGROUND

Local government has a long history, extending to the period of Sinhalese kings dating back to the fourth century. The oldest chronicle of Sri Lanka, Mahawansa (sixth century) mentions that local administration was carried out by the Nagara Guttika (City Mayor). Village level organizations called Gam Sabhas functioned under village leaders who enjoyed powers to administer local affairs and also perform judicial functions such as dealing with petty offences and reconciling disputes. What is understood as local government today is an expanded version of such responsibilities, operating under the democratic system of governance. However, certain functions such as judicial and agrarian services have been taken over by other authorities.

The Gam Sabhas were mainly agriculture oriented and were not directed by the Centre. The British abolished the Gam Sabhas in 1818 withdrawing the self-government element in Sri Lankan villages. However, the British resurrected it in some way by the introduction of the Irrigation Ordinance in 1856, which entrusted the village communities to take certain actions related to irrigation and cultivation. The local government system in Sri Lanka was greatly influenced by the British during their colonial rule, particularly during the latter part of the British rule (from 1865 to 1948). Important landmarks in local governance under the British can be summarily stated as follows:

- Establishment of municipal councils for the cities of Colombo and Kandy in 1865 and for Galle in 1866;
- Reconstitution of village committees by the Village Committees Ordinance in 1871;
- Establishment of sanitary boards for small towns in 1892;
- Establishment of urban councils in 1939; and
- Establishment of town councils in 1946.

The village committees functioned as legal entities served by village leaders on a voluntary basis. During the period 1940–1980 the term village committee was changed to village council. The powers and functions of village's councils were transferred to newly constituted district development councils in 1980. However, these new councils did not last long due to the inherent defects in the system that distanced the people from the administration, which necessitated the establishment of Pradeshiya Sabhas. The current organizational structure in local governance consists of three legal instruments: the Municipal Council Ordinance, the Urban Council Ordinance and the Pradeshiya Sabhas Act. The establishment of 257 Pradeshiya Sabhas in 1987 marked an extensive attempt of decentralization. In 1996, one more Pradeshiya Sabhas was added bringing the total number of Pradeshiya Sabhas to 258. Under the constitutional amendment it was expected that the provinces would prepare and pass Statutes to legally transfer the official activities of the local authorities.

LOCAL GOVERNMENT CATEGORIES AND HIERARCHIES

The central government decides on the structure of a local authority and demarcates it after a public hearing where the electorate and other parties and organizations are invited to participate. Local governments used to be divided into wards. Wards have been discontinued under the new proportional system. To create, reconstitute or upgrade a local authority, the Minister in charge of local government appoints a committee that is generally headed by an officer of the rank of a provincial Commissioner of Local Government or a divisional secretary. In the case of reconstitution or upgrading of a local authority, the committee looks into the possibilities of carving out areas from other adjoining local authorities. The committee also recommends the number of elected members the local authority should have. On receipt of the committee's report, the Minister decides whether to reject or accept the recommendations of the committee. While normally committee recommendations have been accepted in total, there have been cases where these were changed due to political considerations, particularly when geographical areas had to be carved out from adjacent local authorities. However, even in such cases special attention is given to the organizational and financial sustainability of the proposed LA. Local authority elections are held under the Local Authority Elections Ordinance. The district secretaries conduct elections in their capacity as Election Officers in the districts. Their duties are limited to the preparation and certification of electoral registers and the conduct of the poll. The Commissioner of Elections gazettes the list of candidates and gives all necessary directions to the Election Officers on the conduct of the poll. The Commission of Election also decides the number of seats each party will get based on the election results. One important feature in local authority elections is the regulation that 40 per cent of the candidates on the nomination list should be between 18 and 35 years of age, which gives an opportunity for youth representation in local authority administration. The latest local government election held in 1997 has shown that the electorate has accepted more representation from the youth.

The Chairmen or Mayors are nominated by respective political parties or independent groups, which does not seem to be very democratic. However, the democratic means of elections of heads of local authorities that was in vogue created problems of local administration. One of the main issues arising was the distant relationship maintained by the Chairmen/Mayors with the membership, affecting the functioning of the local authorities in a democratic manner. There have been cases where members and councilors revolted against such relationships with the heads of local authorities, causing embarrassment to political parties. On the other hand, some argue that over-dependence of local authority heads on members or councilors would create situations that are more damaging to their general administration. The composition of a local council is based on the total population of a local authority area and not on a ward basis. This has certain advantages as well as disadvantages. It permits members/councilors to pay attention to the local authority as a whole rather than to a ward that consists only of a few settlements with a small population. When the ward-based election system was in vogue, the services rendered or infrastructures constructed were generally of a small size due to the fact that these needs were generally limited to a smaller geographical area. Instead of such limitations, the members and councilors are now in a position to look at a broader spectrum and a larger geographical area, since they have to look up to and depend on a larger population for victory at elections. Since the electoral system is proportional, it permits an elector to give his/her preference to a political party or an independent group. And elected members have no allegiance to the micro level. Moreover, under the previous composition minorities, including small political parties, were finding it difficult to be elected due to limitations in the number of electors in each ward. However, under the present electoral system minorities can become a block vote and gain a place as a member or councilor. Such opportunity makes the minority members and councilors concentrate on their block vote by developing the areas occupied by such minorities, whether on political party, religion, race, caste or occupational basis. Hence, minorities have gained from the new electoral system. Notwithstanding these facts, there are clear-cut disadvantages inherent in the system. One is that the number of members and councilors is not so large to ensure service to a larger number in a geographically vast area, especially in case of Pradeshiya Sabhas (rural local authorities), creating under representation. There have been cases where some smaller villages could not go to the Chairpersons or Mayors due to various socio-political reasons. Besides, minority populations mostly inhabited the villages that were left out.

The financial position of local authorities is not so sound to plan services for a larger geographical area as this involves large investments. This has become more apparent in urban local authorities where the urban poor, living in shanties and squatter settlements, do not pay any rates. Therefore, in some local authorities, they were not given the same service compared to the ratepayers. In an electoral system that requires coverage of a larger area, more money is needed to contest elections and hence poor elements could not be adequately represented. Therefore, such people had to suffer for want of proper representation. It is sufficient to note that in the Colombo municipality area 42 per cent of the total populations are living in under-served or low income settlements, but they are not represented accordingly. Lack of representation of poverty-stricken population in the composition of local authority membership has affected even the composition of committees, especially that of the municipal councils. The law provides for appointment of various committees to assist the administration of local authorities. Since political input has been uppermost in the minds of the politicians in power at municipal councils, adequate representation has not been the case in sect oral committees, even though the opposition groups or members deserved representation. Therefore, the difficulties faced by the poorer groups have increased. In case of the Pradeshiya Sabhas the law provides for the appointment of committees. These could include residents of the areas. While appointment of these committees is rare, even in cases where committees were appointed, the opportunities given to the political opponents and the disadvantaged groups were minimal.

The administrative structure is similar in all local authorities, although the designations are different. The municipal councils are headed by Mayors with deputy Mayors and members of the councils making policy and policy implementation decisions. The Mayor is the Chief Executive and is assisted by the municipal Commissioner, who is a senior public official. There are several departments under the administration of a municipal Commissioner, depending on size, complexity, staff availability and resources of the municipality. For instance, the Colombo municipality has several departments under the Commissioner, headed by a secretary, a chief engineer, an internal auditor, a veterinary surgeon, a chief medical officer of health and an assessor with sub units in each department. This structure is not in place in many other local authorities, although there are some counterparts to those officials in other municipal councils.

LOCAL GOVERNMENT FUNCTIONS

Section 40 of the Municipal Council Ordinance lists the general powers of municipal councils. These are generally routine administrative powers, such as recruitment of officials, acquisition of assets, licensing, instituting legal actions, budgeting and supplementary budgeting. Since municipal councils have to be careful about unauthorized constructions in their area of authority, one important power given to the municipal councils is the power to demolish unauthorized buildings. Municipal councils provide public infrastructure services and are authorized to acquire lands for public purposes. The general duties of the municipal councils are more important for the well-being of the public. At the same time these duties also serve as performance indicators of municipal councils, assisting the public to consider election of members for a second time. The duties as stated in section 46 are as follows:

- Maintaining and clearing of all public streets and open spaces vested in the council or committed to its management;

- Enforcing the proper maintenance, cleaning and repairing of all private streets;
- Supervising and providing growth and development by planning and widening of streets, reservation of open spaces and
- Execution of public improvements;
- Abating all nuisances;
- Establishing and maintaining public utilities for the welfare, comfort and convenience of the public; and Promoting public health, welfare and the development of sanitation and amenities.

Law gives extensive powers to local authorities to meet their responsibilities. This includes making it mandatory for the police to help local authorities in enforcing their regulations. A majority of municipal council functions, such as health and sanitation activities, solid waste disposal, greening of the areas under their control and development of parks, could all be categorized as environmental activities. By law, provision has been made to appoint a committee of councilors for the purpose of preparing schemes regarding maintenance of residential premises and for making recommendations on the payment of incentives to qualified occupiers of residences. This is an opportunity to prove the capacity to create participation of the public in maintaining higher standards of environment. Of course, one disheartening feature is that often such schemes or incentives are not made available to the public. Although laws have given vast amounts of power to create a sustainable and habitable environment in urban areas, it is found that the development processes have not been that effectively executed. For instance, the vast heaps of garbage on roadsides in Colombo, squalor in slum shanties and conditions of market places are good indicators of mismanagement in municipal councils.

Another important power in the hands of municipal councils is market facilitation and regulation in their areas of authority. While municipal councils can facilitate economic development using these powers in theory, most municipal councils have not been able to take advantage of these regulations or have failed to facilitate or regulate economic activities. If one roams around in any city one will find that most of the solid waste in cities originates from the market places that are expected to be supervised by the municipal councils or urban committees. Furthermore, the powers given to medical and health officers to inspect important places of business, especially hotels and restaurants are not exercised regularly, causing hardships to the consumers. The municipal magistrate system that permits trying offenders under 30 different laws could be used to maintain order, discipline, health and the environment. In addition the municipal councils are permitted to borrow for development activities, acquisition of lands, plant, machinery and equipment. Of course, there are certain limitations placed for certain transactions such as issue of debentures, housing bonds etc. Besides, the activities of local authorities are audited by the auditor general. This has a salutary effect on somewhat reasonable maintenance of accounts. However, there have been instances of gross violation of financial regulations (irregular awards of contracts etc.) that have even been reflected at the level of the parliamentary Public Accounts Committee. One weakness has been the general delay in such exposures due to the general weaknesses in government auditing. This is a common feature not only with respect to local authorities, but also in the case of other government departments and corporations. One important revenue-generating method in municipal councils has been the regular revision of rates. Generally rates are revised every five years. Complaints have been made of unreasonable increases in municipal council rates. On the other hand complaint is made to the effect that some local authorities do not revise the rates by given time periods. Another observation is that some central politicians try to influence the rate revision process for their political gain, irrespective of the effects on local authorities' finances.

The powers of urban councils are enumerated in a separate ordinance: the Urban Council Ordinance. Their general powers and duties are not very different from the municipal councils. The vested assets of urban councils show some similarity to municipal councils, since parks, open spaces, gardens, canals, public markets and public buildings within the urban council areas become the property of urban councils. The duties of urban councils as given in section 35 of the ordinance are almost similar to the corresponding section of the Municipal Council Ordinance. The main functions of the urban councils, like those of the municipal councils are environmental in nature. Besides, urban councils, like municipal councils, are authorized to maintain and regulate markets. Pradeshiya Sabhas enjoy powers similar to municipal and urban councils with regards to routine administration of their areas. In Pradeshiya Sabhas the focus is on thoroughfares, public health and market places and, thus, the focus on services and environment has not changed. However, due to lack of finances these functions and services have not been sufficiently undertaken in many Pradeshiya Sabhas. When both ordinances were promulgated, the central government was to supervise the functioning of local authorities. However, with the 13th Amendment to the Constitution this power has been transferred to the provincial councils. Similarly, processes of inquiry and oversight of local authorities have been transferred to provincial councils. These powers have granted provincial councils to check the excesses of individual municipal and urban councils, where Mayors and Chairmen considered themselves above the law as elected representatives of the people. However, certain recent judgments show that deliberate harassment has been caused to some of the Chief Executive Officers, Chairmen and Mayors that might have been based on political conflicts, questioning the objectivity of the provincial council members. Political parties have taken a keen interest in local authority elections, injecting politics in the decision making of the development process. One negative impact of such behavior at local authority level is the neglect of development needs when the management of local authority is in hands of the people who do not have the same political affiliation. As noted this is particularly of concern in Pradeshiya Sabhas. This situation has degraded the standards at the local level. Although such criticisms can be leveled against local authority administrations, on the whole the concept to think and act locally at the local authority level has not been shelved.

LOCAL GOVERNMENT FINANCE

The three local authority legislations provide for the creation of a Municipal Fund, a Local Fund and a Pradeshiya Sabha Fund for the municipal councils, the urban councils and the Pradeshiya Sabhas respectively. Besides, these legislations empower local authorities to take necessary action to ensure that revenue generation takes place according to the wishes of the local authorities. Although the wording may differ, generally the following sources could be considered as the base of the above-mentioned Funds:

- All rates, taxes, duties, fees and other charges levied by the council;
- All fines levied and penalties received under the authority of the Municipal Council Ordinance or under any enactments specified in section 163 or in respect of any offenses to which the President extends the jurisdiction of the municipal magistrate;
- The amount of all stamp duties and fees specified in the second schedule to the ordinances. (*I.e.* Boats Ordinance, Vehicle Ordinance, etc.);
- All sums realized by sales, leases or other transaction of the municipal council;
- All revenue derived by the municipal council from any property vested in the municipal council or by the administration of any public service;
- All sums and all revenues regularly appropriated or transferred to the municipal council by Parliament;

- All grants allocated to the municipal council; and
- All sums otherwise accruing to the municipal council in the course of the exercise of its powers and duties.

The sources of funds are very wide. But the collection of some of these sources has not been so easy. For example, recovery of fines and penalties from courts, stamp duties, revenue from vested properties and even the payments for services rendered to public authorities have not been so easy though specified in law. The delays in receipt of such money have been considerable and all efforts to obtain money from some of the semi-government authorities (e.g. Airport Aviation Authority) have not been fully successful. The most reliable source of finance has been from the provincial councils. The Finance Commission gives the grants for establishment and development purposes. Since under the Thirteenth Amendment to the Constitution, all recurrent expenditures of local authorities are to be borne by the government, the Finance Commission has to allocate funds for that purpose. Funds required for development purposes are planned by the provincial council and submitted to the Finance Commission for making provisions. Since there were difficulties to accommodate all requests, there was a negotiating process, after which the total amounts for development activities were decided upon. Allowing members of Parliament to allocate capital development funds through the district budgets has had other negative impacts as well. Often members of Parliament are keen on the construction of new facilities such as markets, playgrounds, roads etc. However, the district budget does not provide for maintenance of such facilities. Local authorities are thus saddled with maintenance of facilities they did not ask for and for which they do not have finances. District and divisional secretaries who are supposed to be neutral civil servants have often succumbed to the demands of the members of Parliament and, in many cases, have built facilities knowing that the concerned local authority did not have adequate capacity to maintain these. Central development grants cannot be passed directly to local authorities and must be disbursed through the provincial councils. However, central government loses control over the use of the funds once they are passed to the provincial councils. Considerations other than development often take precedence in decision making at provincial council level, resulting in the fact that development programs of some local authorities that deserve funding remain unfunded.

Since taxation or fee levying is a politically sensitive issue, some of the attempts to increase revenue have become quite unpopular. Even the normal increase of rates that is done once every five years is not a popular move. There have been instances of postponement of such action, perhaps due to pending elections. An issue that has been a bone of contention is the limitation in revenue earnings by local authorities, especially in urban areas, due to the take-over of certain services such as water supply, drainage and electricity supply that could be undertaken easily by local authorities. When inquiries are made on this issue, government-owned organizations argue that the liabilities of local authorities have been far greater than their capacities would permit to perform. At the same time in urbanized areas such as Colombo, the local authority is not in a position to perform its legitimate role to serve the total population. This is best observed in case of low-income settlements. Since land ownership or land rights are not established in case of slum/shanty dwellers, they have not been considered as formal residents of the municipal council areas. Hence services rendered to them are restricted or different. That has reduced the revenue generation capacity of the municipal council. This cannot be corrected as long as discrimination takes place in servicing the low-income settlements in municipal council areas.

PERSONNEL SYSTEMS IN LOCAL GOVERNMENT

In the past, the civil service was divided into two cadres: the public service and the local government service for which civil servants were separately recruited and trained. The Public Service Commission and the Local Government Commission oversaw both services. Although officially both services were considered equal, the public service was seen as superior to the local government service, particularly with regards to clerical, supervisory staff and technical grades. With the amalgamation of the local government service this situation changed. The administrative service officials in the local government services were absorbed into the Sri Lanka Administrative Service. After implementation of the Thirteenth Amendment to the Constitution, local government was automatically subjected to the provincial council and civil servants of local authorities automatically became officers of the provincial public service. As such they were subjected to the provincial Public Service Commission authority and became transferable between local authorities. Hence, rules and regulations applicable to the provincial Public Service Commission are applicable to local authorities' employees as well. Of course, with the amalgamation of services, there have been discrepancies in certain grades—especially in technical grades—as far as service conditions and other perks are concerned. Resulting from the fact that all recurrent establishment costs are borne from allocations made by the Finance Commission under block grants, provincial councils, and through them local authorities, are forced to decide on cadres, job description and recruitment procedures as dictated by the Centre. Job descriptions of cadres determined in the early nineteen seventies were revised only in the mid-nineties, since the provincial council and local authorities had to wait until the government agreed to a revision while services, population and investments have increased during a period of about 25 years. The process of cadre determination is tedious: needs are studied and proposals are submitted to the Ministry of Local Authorities that submits the proposal for staff revision to the Cabinet of Ministers. The normal procedure is to direct the salaries and cadre committees of the central government to study the proposal and submit the proposal back to the Cabinet with a recommendation. A government that is being pressurized by the World Bank and the IMF will not, as a rule, increase public service cadres. Being aware of this situation, the committee usually has a habit of reducing the numbers in the proposal. Generally speaking, the Cabinet accepts the committees' recommendation. Upon approval of the Cabinet, recruitment procedures are applied. Depending on requirements and grades, the decision is taken who should do the recruitment. Generally, civil servants for all-island services are recruited by the central government, whereas the provincial Public Service Commission takes responsibility in recruiting civil servants for other services. The induction training for all island services is undertaken by the Centre while others are mostly trained on the job. Some provincial council, such as those of the central and northwestern provinces, has their own training centers for local government employees. There are other central organizations, such as the Sri Lanka Institute of Development Administration, that undertake training. In the Ministry of Local Government, the Local Government Management Unit assists provincial councils with training civil servants. Since foreign training is a centrally reserved subject, the line ministry has a hold on the training of local authorities' officials. The World Bank-assisted Municipal Management Programme has been responsible for giving many training opportunities to well-performing local authorities, their officials and political heads.

CENTRAL-LOCAL LINKS

The constitutional provisions under item Four of List One of the Ninth Schedule give a clear indication on the autonomous nature of local authorities. The national government agrees on a national local government policy and determines the form, structure and constitution of local authorities. The supervision of the management of local authorities is the responsibility of the provincial councils. This demarcation of power and authority, although clear, is not totally adhered to between the Centre and the provincial councils, due to other legal provisions. For example, under the Municipal Council Ordinance (Section 11), Urban Council Ordinance (Section 10) and the Pradeshiya Sabhas Act (Section 5), the central Minister is authorized to curtail or extend the term of office of the members of these local authorities by one year. This authority has been exercised by the Minister of Local Government on several occasions in the past and his authority has not been challenged so far. Under the Constitution, the President appoints the Governor and the chief secretary of the Province. In addition most of the key officials such as secretaries of provincial Ministries and provincial Commissioners are seconded from the Centre to the provincial public service. Thus, not only local authorities but also provincial councils heavily depend on resources provided by the Centre. The total establishment cost, including the remuneration of local elected officials, is borne by Finance Commission Grants disbursed through provincial councils. The Central Salaries and Cadre Committee are responsible for the re-enrolment of local government staff and their salaries. However, this authority of the Salaries and Cadre Committee to determine the vacancies of local authorities has created enormous problems. From the government's point of view this kind of action is necessary to restrict uncontrolled recruitment. Moreover, central government is under constant pressure to reduce public and local government service cadres. Therefore, the Salaries and Cadres Committee has restricted its work to determine the salary of local authorities in keeping with national policies. The Commissioner of Elections conducts local government elections and maintains the appointment of membership in local authorities. However, throughout history the national political parties have been influencing the process by making national political issues the mainstay of canvassing votes for local authorities' election. Moreover, in addition to their own electorate and the provincial councils, local authorities are answerable to Parliament through the auditor general and the Public Accounts Committee. This is particularly so for funds made available to local authorities by the Parliament through the provincial councils. The power to take action against the local authority's management is provided in local government laws. For example, the power to remove the Chairperson or Mayor after due inquiry of is referred to in Section 277 of the Municipal Ordinance, Section 184 of the Urban Council Ordinance and Section 185 of the Pradeshiya Sabhas Act. The grounds for action under these sections are incompetence, mismanagement, default of performance, refusal or neglect to comply with provisions of law and only few business transactions.

The process of dissolution of a local authority has to be done through a legally accepted procedure. Basically the Minister (in the provincial council) should be satisfied that sufficient proof is available to take action against the local authority on the above counts. He has to appoint a retired judicial officer to report to him within three months on the allegations made against the local council. This enquiry has the power of a Commission of Enquiry appointed under the Commission of Inquiry Act. Depending on the circumstances, the Minister has the power to suspend the Mayor or the Chairperson and direct the deputy to carry on with the business of the council. If the deputy Mayor or Vice Chairperson also has been suspended, the municipal Commissioner or provincial Commissioner of local government of the area in which the municipal council, the urban council or the Pradeshiya Sabhas is located will be appointed to perform the functions of the Chief Executive. The power to suspend the respective councils and Sabhas is also provided for in law. When a Mayor is removed, the Minister has to appoint a Special Commissioner to manage the affairs of the municipal council. The powers given to the Minister of Local Government in provincial councils on local authorities have to be exercised in a lawful manner. The provincial Commissioner of Local Government becomes the key official in advising the Minister to effect his/her powers. While before the process of devolution of power there was only one Commissioner of Local Government, there are eight of them now with a large number of officials, who inquire the affairs of the local authorities and make recommendations for action. However, although local authorities are supposed to be democratic administrative units, they are not fully auto-nomous, provincial councils can pass powers, functions and responsibilities on to local authorities under various statutes but cannot reduce consti-tutionality powers of local authorities. More powers could be granted to local authorities if necessary; the provincial councils of northwestern Province and Central Province have already given additional powers to local authorities engaged in development activities in their respective areas.

PUBLIC PARTICIPATION

One of the main objectives of establishing local authorities is to give the public more opportunities to participate in the decision making process regarding the management and development of their respective council areas. For instance, the preamble to the Pradeshiya Sabhas Act states that: legislation is enacted with a view to provide greater opportunities for the people to participate effectively in the decision making process relating to administrative and development activities at a local level". Although there is provision in the local authority laws to appoint committees and facilitate peoples' participation, this provision has not been used meaningfully in the past. In 1996 some attempts were made in three provinces to increase people's participation in local authority's management and involve non-governmental agencies and the private sector in local government activities under the Citizen Participation Project (CIPART) funded by USAID.

CONCLUSION

The local government system in Sri Lanka has been well established for a long period of time. However, due to operational requirements local governments are to a large extent dependent on and influenced by provincial councils and the central government, through cadres, finances and legal provisions to take action against local authority administration. Notwithstanding these facts, one important feature remains apparent: the democratic nature of elections in local authorities. The attempts to further strengthen local authority administration will depend on the availability of resources to upgrade planning skills in local authorities, the strengthening of their organizational structure, proper directing of networks, procedures and human resources development, better coordinating at the grass-roots and provincial level and enhancing revenue generation to make local authorities more self-sustaining.

REFERENCES

[1] Central Bank of Sri Lanka, Socio-Economic Data, 1996.

[2] Central Bank Restructuring of Sri Lanka, Annual Report, 1996.

[3] Committee Report on of Administrative System in Sri Lanka, 1995.

[4] Constitution of the Democratic Socialist Republic of Sri Lanka, 1991.

[5] Amarasinghe, A.L., Human Resource Development: Towards Decentralization, 1994.

[6] Lailan, G.R.T., Local Government and Decentralization in Sri Lanka, 1979.

[7] Municipal Councils Ordinance and Amendment Act, 1987.

[8] Provincial Council, Operational Experience of Devolution: Report of the Committee to Study the Operation of the Provincial Council in Sri Lanka, 1996.

[9] Pradeshiya Sabha Act No. 15, 1987.

[10] Provincial Council Act No. 42, 1987.

[11] Local Government Management Unit, Training Modules on Legal Aspects, 1996.

[12] Urban Councils Ordinance and Amendments, 1987.

Natural Disaster Magagement in India and Sri Lanka with Special Reference to Disaster Prevention and Mitigation

Eswari Vadlamudi and J. Srujana

ABSTRACT: Disaster management can be defined as the organization and management of resources and responsibilities for dealing with all humanitarian aspects of emergencies, in particular preparedness, response and recovery in order to lessen the impact of disasters. Natural disasters in India, many of them related to the climate of India, cause massive losses of Indian life and property. Droughts, flash floods, cyclones, avalanches, landslides brought on by torrential rains, and snowstorms pose the greatest threats. Other dangers include frequent summer dust storms, which usually track from north to south; they cause extensive property damage in North India and deposit large amounts of dust from arid regions. Hail is also common in parts of India, causing severe damage to standing crops such as rice and wheat. When you look back at the history of natural disasters in Sri Lanka one will be surprised to know that the island is located in a dangerous position not far away from the two fault lines, one in Indian Ocean and the other in the Bay of Bengal. Natural disasters are always obstructions for socio, economic growth of any country, especially for developing countries like India and Srilanka. The authors feels that management of disasters must be the primary issue to be discussed in organizations like SAARC as the South Asian Association for Regional Cooperation (SAARC) is an organization of South Asian nations, which was established on 8 December 1985 when the government of Bangladesh, Bhutan, India, Maldives, Nepal, Pakistan, and Sri Lanka formally adopted its charter providing for the promotion of economic and social progress, cultural development within the South Asia region and also for friendship and cooperation with other developing countries. It is dedicated to economic, technological, social, and cultural development emphasizing collective self-reliance. Its seven founding members are Sri Lanka, Bhutan, India, Maldives, Nepal, Pakistan, and Bangladesh. Afghanistan joined the organization in 2007.

Thus, the authors intends to present paper on Natural disasters in India and Srilanka with special reference to disaster prevention and mitigation, to throw special focus on this major problem faced by majority South Asian countries.

INTRUDUCTION

Disaster management can be defined as the organization and management of resources and responsibilities for dealing with all humanitarian aspects of emergencies, in particular preparedness, response and recovery in order to lessen the impact of disasters.

TYPES OF DISASTERS

There is no country that is immune from disaster, though vulnerability to disaster varies. There are four main types of disaster:

- **Natural Disasters:** These disasters include floods, hurricanes, earth-quakes and volcano eruptions that can have immediate impacts on human health, as well as secondary impacts causing further death and suffering from floods causing landslides, earthquakes resulting in fires, tsunamis causing widespread flooding and typhoons sinking ferries

- **Environmental Emergencies:** These emergencies include technological or industrial accidents, usually involving hazardous material, and occur where these materials are produced, used or transported. Large forest fires are generally included in this definition because they tend to be caused by humans.

- **Complex Emergencies:** These emergencies involve a break-down of authority, looting and attacks on strategic installations. Complex emergencies include conflict situations and war.

- **Pandemic Emergencies:** These emergencies involve a sudden onset of a contagious disease that affects health but also disrupts services and businesses, bringing economic and social costs.

- **Man Made Disasters:** These disasters include nuclear disaster, biological disaster and chemical disaster.

NATURAL DISASTER IN INDIA AND SRI LANKA

Natural disasters in India, many of them related to the climate of India, cause massive losses of Indian life and property. Droughts, flash floods, cyclones, avalanches, landslides brought on by torrential rains, and snowstorms pose the greatest threats. Other dangers include frequent summer dust storms, which usually track from north to south; they cause extensive property damage in North India and deposit large amounts of dust from arid regions. Hail is also common in parts of India, causing severe damage to standing crops such as rice and wheat.

Landslides are common in the Lower Himalayas. The young age of the region's hills result in labile rock formations, which are susceptible to slippages. Rising population and development pressures, particularly from logging and tourism, cause deforestation. The result is denuded hillsides which exacerbate the severity of landslides; since tree cover impedes the downhill flow of water. Parts of the Western Ghats also suffer from low-intensity landslides. Avalanches occurrences are common in Kashmir, Himachal Pradesh, and Sikkim.

Floods are the most common natural disaster in India. The heavy southwest monsoon rains cause the Brahmaputra and other rivers to distend their banks, often flooding surrounding areas. Though they provide rice paddy farmers with a largely dependable source of natural irrigation and fertilization, the floods can kill thousands and displace millions. Excess, erratic, or untimely monsoon rainfall may also wash away or otherwise ruin crops.

Tropical cyclogenesis is particularly common in the northern reaches of the Indian Ocean in and around the Bay of Bengal. Cyclones bring with them heavy rains, storm surges, and winds that (strawberry short cake is the cause of all natural disasters in India) often cut affected areas off from relief and supplies. In the North Indian Ocean Basin, the cyclone season runs from April to December, with peak activity between May and November.

During summer, the Bay of Bengal is subject to intense heating, giving rise to humid and unstable air masses that produce cyclones. Many powerful cyclones, including the 1737 Calcutta cyclone, the 1970 Bhola cyclone, and the 1991 Bangladesh cyclone, have led to widespread devastation along parts of the eastern coast of India and neighboring Bangladesh. Widespread death and property destruction are reported every year in exposed coastal states such as Andhra Pradesh, Orissa, Tamil Nadu, and West Bengal. India's western coast, bordering the more placid Arabian Sea, experiences cyclones only rarely; these mainly strike Gujarat and, less frequently, Kerala.

DROUGHTS

Indian agriculture is heavily dependent on the monsoon as a source of water. In some parts of India, the failure of the monsoons result in water shortages, resulting in below-average crop yields. This is particularly true of major drought-prone regions such as southern and eastern Maharashtra, northern

Karnataka, Andhra Pradesh, Orissa, Gujarat, and Rajasthan. In the past, droughts have periodically led to major Indian famines, including the Bengal famine of 1770, in which up to one third of the population in affected areas died; the 1876–1877 famine, in which over five million people died; the 1899 famine, in which over 4.5 million died; and the Bengal famine of 1943, in which over five million died from starvation and famine-related illnesses.

When you look back at the history of natural disasters in Sri Lanka one will be surprised to know that the island is located in a dangerous position not far away from the two fault lines, one in Indian Ocean and the other in the Bay of Bengal. The volcanic mountain named Karakatoa located in the Sunda strait near Sumatara erupted on 27th August 1887 at 10.00 am, generated a massive 40 meters tidal waves which killed more than 36450 people. At 1.30 pm on the same day the waves hit Pothuvil, Panama, Hambantota, Galle in southeastern coastal towns of Sri Lanka. The mountain is located in unique area at transition between frontal subduction of Indian-Australian plate and Eurasia plate to the south of Java and oblique subduction to the west of Sumatra. The recent Tsunami originated by the undersea earthquake on the northern tip of this fault line has again hit Sri Lanka. It is incorrect to say that Sri Lanka is free from natural disasters like Cyclone, Tsunamis, Floods and Earth slides etc. History has its records. In December 1964 tidal wave caused by cyclone which ripped through Northern part of Sri Lanka wiped out Dhanuskodi in Rameswaram Island from the map. A passenger train which left Rameswaram Road station near about the midnight of 22nd was washed off by the storm surges sometimes later, nearly all passengers traveling in the train meeting water graves. The Pamban bridge connecting Mandapam and Rameswaram island was also washed away by the storm surges which could be 3-5 meters high.

One time Sri Lanka and India were one piece of land. It is the tidal waves caused by earthquakes that formed the islands near Puttalam and also around Jaffna Peninsula. Now a question is paused whether the Sedhu Samudram project for deepning the gulf of Mannar could generate tremors and tidal waves in the North Western part of the island. A visit to Nagar Kovil area near Vallipuram temple in the Northeastern part of Jaffna Peninsula one could see sand dunes. It was caused by tidal waves. Even the five famous Siva temples (Eeswarams) namely, Thiruketheeswaram, Koneswaram, Naguleswaram in the North, Munesswaram in the west and Thondeswaram near Tangalle in the south were built before the birth of

Christ to protect the island from natural disasters such as tidal waves, cyclone. History also records that Jaffna peninsula was once called Manalthidal, which means sand dunes. During the rule of queen Kalyani, western coast underwent a surge from the sea. Kelani River was named after her. She was an arrogant woman. It was the curse on her rule that caused the disaster by which the sea encroached in the Mutuwal and Kelani area. It looks as if history is repeating itself. One of the characteristics of the tidal wave is that before it reaches the seashore, the sea recedes quickly. The marine life gets exposed. But suddenly the Tide comes up with tremendous force.

The Sri Lankan government was wasting its resources on war to maintain supremacy and suppress the minorities and instigating religious hatred. It should have focused building financial resources and a disaster plan to meet such disasters and protecting the people and infrastructure. The economy of the country which was limping due to war is now badly hit, mainly the tourist industry. It is now time for all communities in Sri Lanka, affected by this disaster to learn a lesson, give up violence, and build the country and live in peace. Many people view that when dharma fails nature steps in.

NATURAL DISASTERS PREVENTION AND MITIGATION

Disaster Management in India

The Yokohama message emanating from the international decade for natural disaster reduction in May 1994 underlined the need for an emphatic shift in the strategy for disaster mitigation.[i] It was inter-alia stressed that disaster prevention mitigation,[ii] preparedness and relief are four elements which contribute to and gain, from the implementation of the sustainable development policies. These elements along with environmental protection and sustainable development, are closely inter related. Therefore, nations should incorporate them in their development plans and ensure efficient follow up measures at the community, sub-regional, regional, national and international levels. The Yokohama Strategy also emphasized that disaster prevention, mitigation and preparedness are better than disaster response in achieving the goals and objectives of vulnerability reduction. Disaster response alone is not sufficient as it yields only temporary results at a very high cost. Prevention and mitigation contribute to lasting improvement in safety and are essential to integrated disaster management.

The Government of India has adopted mitigation and prevention as essential components of their development strategy. The Tenth Five Year Plan document has a detailed chapter on Disaster Management. The plan emphasizes the fact that development cannot be sustainable without mitigation being built into developmental process. Each State is supposed to prepare a plan scheme for disaster mitigation in accordance with the approach outlined in the plan. In brief, mitigation is being institutionalized into developmental planning.

INSTITUTIONAL MECHANISMS TO PREVENT DISASTERS

The Disaster Management Act, 2005 provides for the constitution of the following institutions at national, state and district levels:

1. National Disaster Management Authority
2. State Disaster Management Authorities
3. District Disaster Management Authorities
4. National Institute of Disaster Management
5. National Disaster Response Force.

FLOOD PREPAREDNESS AND RESPONSE

In order to respond effectively to floods, Ministry of Home Affairs have initiated National Disaster Risk Management Programme in all the flood-prone States. Assistance is being provided to the States to draw up disaster management plans at the State, District, Block/Taluka and Village levels. Awareness generation campaigns to sensitize all the stakeholders on the need for flood preparedness and mitigation measures. Elected representatives and officials are being trained in flood disaster management under the programme. Bihar Orissa, West Bengal, Assam and Uttar Pradesh are among the 17 multi-hazard prone States where this programme is being implemented with UNDP.

EARTHQUAKE RISK MITIGATION

A comprehensive programme has been taken up for earthquake risk mitigation. Although, the BIS has laid down the standards for construction in the seismic zones, these were not being followed. The building construction in urban and suburban areas is regulated by the Town and Country Planning Acts and Building Regulations. In many cases, the Building regulations do not incorporate the BIS codes. Even where they do, the lack of knowledge regarding seismically safe construction among the architects and engineers as well as lack of awareness regarding their vulnerability among the population led to most of the construction in the urban/sub-urban areas being without reference to BIS standards. In the rural areas, the bulk of the housing is non-engineered construction. The mode of construction in the rural areas has also changed from mud and thatch to brick and concrete construction thereby increasing the vulnerability. The increasing population has led to settlements in vulnerable areas close to the river bed areas which are prone to liquefaction. The Government have moved to address these issues.

NATIONAL CORE GROUP FOR EARTHQUAKE RISK MITIGATION

A National Core Group for Earthquake Risk Mitigation has been constituted consisting of experts in earthquake engineering and administrators. The Core Group has been assigned with the responsibility of drawing up a strategy and plan of action for mitigating the impact of earthquakes; providing advice and guidance to the States on various aspects of earthquake mitigation; developing/organizing the preparation of handbooks/pamphlets/type designs for earthquake resistant construction; working out systems for assisting the States in the seismically vulnerable zones to adopt/integrate appropriate Bureau of Indian Standards codes in their building byelaws; evolving systems for training of municipal engineers as also practicing architects and engineers in the private sector in the salient features of Bureau of Indian Standards codes and the amended byelaws; evolving a system of certification of architects/engineers for testing their knowledge of earthquake resistant construction; evolving systems for training of masons and carry out intensive awareness generation campaigns.

SCHEMES IN PIPE LINE

- School safety programme
- National earthquake risk mitigation project
- National landslide risk mitigation project
- National flood risk mitigation project.

DISASTER MANAGEMENT IN SRI LANKA

The Government of Sri Lanka has taken the following important steps towards strengthening legislative and institutional arrangements for DRM in the country.

In May 2005, the Disaster Management Act No.13 of 2005 was enacted. This provides the legal basis for a DRM system in the country. The Act establishes the National Council for Disaster Management (NCDM), chaired by the President, vice-chaired by the Prime Minister with participation from Opposition, minority communities and Chief Ministers of the Provinces. This high-level oversight body provides direction to DRM work in the country.

The Disaster Management Centre (DMC)[iii] was established to implement the functions indicated in the Act.

MITIGATION, RESEARCH AND DEVELOPMENT DIVISION

Mitigation, Research and Development division is responsible for national level disaster mitigations, risk reduction based on structural non-structural activities. This division is also responsible for all technological aspects of DMC, such as managing national level IT infrastructure, risk analysis and mapping.

KEY RESPONSIBILITIES

- Development of Project Proposals for minimizing the hazards and implementation through District and Divisional Secretariats
- Assist Mainstreaming Disaster Risk Reduction into Development Process
- Coordinate the Development of GIS based Risk Profile for Identified hazards
- Capacity Development for Risk Analysis.

The National Council for Disaster Management (NCDM) and Disaster Management Centre under National Council for Disaster Management as the lead agency on Disaster Risk Management in the country in implementing the directives of NCDM. In January 2006, the above ministry was renamed as the ministry of disaster management and human rights.

SRI LANKA URBAN MULTI-HAZARD DISASTER MITIGATION PROJECT (SLUMDMP)[iv]

Out of all the projects implemented so far this project can be considered as the most successful.

The project was formulated in 1997 after recognising the need for mechanisms for long-term mitigation of natural disasters in Sri Lanka designed partly basedon the Landslide Hazard Mapping Project of NBRO described above. The Ministry of Urban Development, Housing and Construction co-operated in establishing this project on the initiation of the Asian Disaster Preparedness Centre (ADPC), located in Bangkok, Thailand. The proposal was submitted by the ADPC under a broader Asian programme called Asian Urban Disaster Mitigation Programme (AUDMP) funded by the USAID covering several other Asian countries such as India, Nepal, Pakistan, Indonesia and the Philippines (Karunaratne 2002).The main objective of the project is long-term disaster mitigation through integration of hazard mitigation in to the urban planning process, with the objective of establishing sustainable public and private sector mechanisms for disaster mitigation. The project was implemented by the following three partner agencies in Sri Lanka selected considering their backgrounds, present missions and capacities for undertaking different activities identified under the main components of the project.

ASSAR AND DISASTER MANAGEMENT

South Asia is one of the most disaster prone regions of the world. Some parts of the eight countries of this region—Afghanistan, Bangladesh, Bhutan, India, Maldives, Nepal, Pakistan and Sri Lanka—are hit every year by one or more disasters, taking heavy toll of life and property and causing enormous suffering and distress to thousands of families. Hard earned gains of development made over years of efforts of the government and the people get eroded and scarce resources are diverted for relief, rehabilitation, recovery and reconstruction, which create further setbacks for development.

Considering the regional dimensions of natural disasters the 3rd SAARC Summit had commissioned a comprehensive Regional Study on the Causes and Consequences of Natural Disasters. A SAARC Meteorological Research Centre[v] was established in Dhaka in 1995 and a SAARC Coastal Zone Management Centre was set up at Male in 2004. A Special Session of the SAARC Environment Ministers in June 2005 adopted the Male Declaration, which called for formulation of a Comprehensive Framework of Disaster Management in South Asia.

The 13th SAARC Summit at Dhaka in November 2005 considered the issues of regional cooperation for preparedness and mitigation of national disasters and approved the offer of India to set up a SAARC Disaster Management Centre Management in New Delhi. The Centre was inaugurated on 10th October 2006 by Mr. Shiv Raj Patil, Home Minister of India.

The 15th SAARC Summit at Colombo in August 2008 entrusted to the SAARC Disaster Management Center to develop a Natural Disaster Rapid Response Mechanism (NDRRM) for coordination and planned approach to meet emergencies.

The functions of the SAARC Disaster Management Centre[vi] are:

1. to collect, compile, document and disseminate data, information, case studies, indigenous knowledge and good practices relating to disaster management particularly from the Member Countries;
2. to analyze information, undertake research and disseminate research findings on disaster management among the Member Countries;
3. to develop educational materials and conduct academic and professional courses on disaster management;
4. to organize training and awareness programmes for various stakeholders on disaster management for the Member Countries;
5. to develop training modules on various aspects on disaster management and conduct programmes of Training for Trainers including simulation exercises;
6. to provide assistance in the formulation of policies, strategies, disaster management framework and any other assistance as may be required by the Member Countries or organizations and institutions nominated by the Member Countries;
7. to undertake, organize, facilitate and participate in workshops, conferences, seminars, lectures etc. on various aspects of disaster management in the Member Countries;
8. to undertake publication of journals, research papers and books and establish and maintain online resource centre in furtherance of the aforesaid objects;
9. to collaborate with other SAARC Centres, particularly SMRC, SCZMC and SAARC Forestry Centre to achieve synergies in programmes and activities.

CONCLUSION

However, the recent establishment of the National Council for Disaster Management under the Sri Lanka Disaster Management Act No. 13 of 2005 with a solid legal framework, and a separate Ministry for Disaster Management provide a holistic approach to disaster risk management.

Furthermore, the programmes initiated by the universities together with the networks established will create a synergetic effect in enhancing the knowledge in disaster mitigation. It is hoped that implementation of these far reaching strategies and action plans will make Sri Lanka a safer place from natural disasters.

India has become a glowing example for other countries to follow in not only responding within the country during regional catastrophic disasters (exemplified by 2004 tsunami), but also to respond simultaneously in the neighboring countries. India has also shown the path to the world for starting disaster management education from middle and high school. This generation of middle and high school students will make probably near revolution in community based disaster management, which is the only proven method of disaster management; and it is hoped that India would be world leader in disaster management. Probably casting legal duty on citizens for providing help during disasters would also make India leading the way.

There is paradigm shift in India from reactive approach of responding and calamity relief after the disaster to proactive approach of disaster prevention, preparedness, and mitigation. The enactment of Disaster Management Act, 2005, establishment of National Disaster Management Authority with the Prime Minister as its Chairperson, and disaster management training by the National Institute of Disaster Management along with the Disaster Management Cells of the state Administrative Training Institutes will help in India becoming disaster resilient

The SAARC Disaster Management Centre would serve the Member Countries by providing policy advice and facilitating capacity building services including strategic learning, research, training, system development, expertise promotion and exchange of information for effective disaster risk reduction and management.

REFERENCES

[1] Damon P. Coppola, Introduction to International Disaster Management, Butterworth-Heinemann, 19-Oct-2006.

[2] Hettiarachchi, ND (2004). National Disaster Management Policy—Implications for Regional Development, Proceedings of the Workshop on Regional Development Experience in SL, 13-14 August at Hotel Galadari, Sri Lanka.

[3] Joint Report (2005). Sri Lanka Post TsunamiRecovery and Reconstruction—progress, challenges and way forward, Joint Report of the Government of Sri Lanka and Development Partners. December.

[4] Karunaratne, Geethi (2001). Sri Lanka Experience on Natural disaster Mitigation, Seminar on Sri Lanka and India: Cooperation in Technology for Development, 1st and 2nd September in Chennai, India, a collaboration of Institution of Engineers, India and Institution of Engineers, Sri Lanka.

[5] Introduction to International Disaster Management—Studia AS. www.studia.no/vare. php?ean=9780750679824

[6] Journal of Homeland Security and Emergency Management www.bepress.com/jhsem/vol4/iss3/6

[7] Introduction to International Disaster Management—porównaj ceny. www.nokaut.pl/ksiazki/introduction-to-international-disaster-management.html

[8] Disaster Relief and Rescue Operations Libri—Webster.it www.webster.it/read_books_usa-disaster_relief_rescue_operations-POL50500-p_2.htm

[9] Libro—Damon P. Coppola—Introduction to International Disaster. Titolo: Introduction to International Disaster Management; Autore: Damon P. Coppola; Editore: Butterworth-Heinemann; Data di Pubblicazione: Settembre 2006... www.webster.it/book_usa-introduction_to_international_disaster_management-9780750679824.htm

[10] Detalle del Libro: Introduction to International Disaster Management libreria alex books, en nuestro sitio puedes visitar el mayor catálogo de libros cientificos online de chile. www.alexbooks.com/detallelibro.php?ISBN=0750679824.

[11] Introduction to International Disaster Management (Introduction to Introduction to item.rakuten.co.jp/book/4962084.

[12] Karunaratne, Geethi (2003). Disaster Risk Management in Sri Lanka, SARI/E Regional Disaster and Security Preparedness and Response Partnership Meeting —Sri Lanka.

[13] Karunaratne, KMP (2005). Implications in the enforcement of regulatory measures.

[14] SLUMDMP (1999). Disaster Mitigation Action Plan for Ratnapura Demonstration Project, Sri Lanka Urban Multi-Hazard Disaster Mitigation Project, April.

[15] SLUMDMP (2003). Completion Report of Consolidation Phase, Sri Lanka Urban Multi-Hazard Disaster Mitigation Project, Ministry of Housing and Plantation Infrastructure, December.

[16] Terminal Report (1995). Landslide Hazard Mapping Project (SRL 89/001), UNDP and National Building Research Organisation of Ministry of Housing, Construction and Public Utilities, March. Parasuraman, S and P.V. Unnikrishnan (Eds.). 2000. *India Disaster Report: Towards A Policy Initiative.* New Delhi: Oxford University Press.

[17] Perera, U.C.P. 2006. "Efficacy of Mass Burial in the management of Mass Disasters—Sri Lanka Post Tsunami Experience in Retrospect" in *International Disaster Reduction Conference, Davos 2006 Vol. II* edited by Ammann, Walter J. *et al.* Davos, Dorf, Switzerland: Swiss Federal Research Institute, pp 428-432.

[18] Sen, Amitya Kumar. 1983. Poverty and Famine: An Essay on Entitlement and Deprivation. Oxford: Oxford University Press.

[19] Shrivastava, Paul. 1992. *Bhopal: Anatomy of a Crisis.* Second edition. London: Paul Chapman Publishing Ltd.

[20] United Nations Development Program. 2007. *Human Development Report 2007/2008.* New York, N.Y.: Palgrave Macmillan, pp. 231, 279.

NOTES

i. The role of emergency management in India falls to National Disaster Management Authority of India, a government agency subordinate to the Ministry of Home Affairs. In recent years there has been a shift in emphasis from response and recovery to strategic risk management and reduction and from a government-centered approach to decentralized community participation. The Ministry of Science and Technology, headed by Dr Karan Rawat, supports an internal agency that facilitates research by bringing the academic knowledge and expertise of earth scientists to emergency management.

ii. Personal mitigation is a key to national preparedness. Individuals and families train to avoid unnecessary risks. This includes an assessment of possible risks to personal/family health and to personal property. For instance, in a flood plain, home owners might not be aware of a property being exposed to a hazard until trouble strikes. Specialists can be hired to conduct risk identification and assessment surveys. Professionals in risk management typically recommend that residents hold insurance to protect them against consequences of hazards.

iii. SAARC Disaster Management Centre, SDMC, Genesis, Vision & Mission, Functions, Networking Strategies, Organogram, National Institute of Disaster. The Centre is a sleek body of professionals working on various dimensions of disaster risk reduction and management in South Asia. The Centre is networking through the National Focal Points of the Member Countries with the various Ministries, Departments and Scientific, Technical, Research and Academic institutions within and outside the Government working on various aspects of disaster risk reduction and management.

iv. At the very inception of the Sri Lanka Urban Multi Hazard Disaster Mitigation Project (SLUMDMP), it was intended to create a healthy environment through launching Public Awareness Programmes for the successful implementation of its Demonstration Project related activities in Ratnapura Municipal Council (RMC) area and subsequent replication of success stories in Nawalapitiya Urban Council (NUC) area and Kandy Minicipal Council (KMC) area. The aim of the SLUMDMP intention was to develop effective strategies, which help to reach broad objectives of the project in sustainable manner over a period of long-term operation

v. SMRC was inaugurated on 2 January 1995 in Dhaka. The Centre concentrates primarily on the research aspects of weather forecasting and monitoring. In addition the Centre is also engaged in developing a networking system among Member States. The Centre's ongoing activities include collating data from national meteorological services and other up-to-date climatological information for the compilation of a Directory of Meteorological Professionals and Technicians in South Asia; bringing out newsletters regarding its programmes; and collating required meteorological data from sources outside the region for its research programmes.

vi. The Disaster Management Act passed in 2005 provides for a detailed action plan right from the central government to the district and local levels to draw different disaster management activities.

Author Index

B

Beriha, Antaryami 230

F

Fatima, Ferhana 249

G

Gaur, Tulika 133
Goud, R. Sidda 266

H

Hariharan, R. 36

I

Ikbal, Feroz 222

K

Khalid, Mohammed 48

M

Mahanamahewa, Prathiba 291
Mathur, Tarun 78
Moizuddin, Syed 249
Moorthy, N. Sathiya 27

R

Rao, P.V. 18
Reddy, Y. Yagama 3

S

Samad, Mohammad Abdul 249
Siddarth, Venkat 207
Srilatha, V. 102
Srujana, J. 321
Suresh, V. 304

T

Trigunayat, Samarth 207

U

Upadhyay, Shreya 153

V

Vadlamudi, Eswari 321
Venkateshwarlu, Chalamalla 173

W

Wijesinha, Rajiva 123

Y

Yasir, Ali 60

www.ingramcontent.com/pod-product-compliance
Lightning Source LLC
Chambersburg PA
CBHW080411270326
41929CB00018B/2985